YOU'RE A BRICK, ANGELA!

The Girls' Story
1839 - 1985

by

Mary Cadogan
and
Patricia Craig

Girls Gone By Publishers

Published by

Girls Gone By Publishers
4 Rock Terrace
Coleford
Bath
Somerset
BA3 5NF

First published by Victor Gollancz Ltd 1976
Published in Gollancz Paperbacks 1986
This edition published by Girls Gone By Publishers 2003

Text © Mary Cadogan and Patricia Craig 1976, 1986, 2003
Design and Layout © Girls Gone By Publishers 2003

Typeset in England by AJF
Printed in England by Antony Rowe Ltd.

ISBN 1-904417-12-4

Schoolgirl fun for Schoolgirl readers.

Contents

Illustrations

"We must follow her."
(*from* The New House at Springdale)

INTRODUCTION

A SEPARATE, comprehensive body of girls' fiction did not come into
being until the end of the last century: it was then a progressive sign,
since it marked a recognition of the particular nature and interests of
young girls. There is an intricate relation between a society and the
kinds of expression it gives rise to, however, and girls' books quickly
became a medium for the reinforcement of social prohibitions and
expectations. Girls' fiction has had a complex, fluctuating history; at
times its predominant mode of expression has seemed retrogressive,
at others less so. It has been marked by paradox, spontaneity, inhibition.
Throughout the middle years of the present century the papers most
closely involved with presenting and refining basic images of
adolescent girls – those of the Amalgamated Press – were produced
almost exclusively by men. This is in spite of the fact that competent
women journalists and "popular" writers had increased significantly
in number since the Edwardian years, when, in fact, they had been
directly responsible for a greater proportion of this type of fiction. At
the present time girls' fiction appears almost redundant as a genre: the
most interesting work which is being produced is capable of
appreciation by anyone. Classification along rigid sexually-determined
lines is, or should be, no longer valid.

This is a trend for the future, however. A vast body of literature
already exists, much of it admirable; its effects can scarcely be
overestimated. Many of the most powerful images which fascinate
and obsess the adult are derived from childhood reading – and
everyone in this society is exposed in childhood to fiction of one
type or another. Even before they can read, children listen to the
rhymes and stories which adults tell them. Sex-differentiated popular
fiction begins here, and persists, in some cases, through teenage
picture-strip weeklies to adult books and magazines.

Before girls are old enough to go to school they are familiar
with Polly Flinders, who is whipped for spoiling her nice, new,
feminine clothes, and with the other Polly who's encouraged

endlessly to put the kettle on and take it off again; they learn that Miss Muffet has an irrational fear of spiders, and see how the little girls who are kissed and reduced to tears by offensive Georgie-Porgie lack the courage to chase him off, and have to wait until the "boys" come out to rescue them. Popular fiction over the last hundred years has drawn heavily on images which are extensions from these, representing girls essentially as passive, domesticated, brainless and decorative. Fortunately it has often been thrown off course by authors whose own experience, integrity, or sheer literary ability, has supervened.

We have tried here to relate each book discussed to the context of its own time, and also to indicate how it is regarded now. This has involved the suggestion of certain criteria on which girls' fiction may be assessed. On the whole, we have applied more stringent standards of criticism to books which, like *Pollyanna*, have been set up as near "classics": there is nearly always something flaccid and sentimental about stories which have been described as "much-loved". Certain types of fiction, on the other hand, like the girls' papers in the '30s and '40s, had a limited objective which was fulfilled competently, without fuss. Often it is difficult to see beyond the stories' unintentional humour: this becomes more apparent as their literary quality declines. It is almost a built-in hazard for the children's writer – or any writer who deals in simplifications and straightforward effects. This is one reason why authors like E. Nesbit and Richmal Crompton, who managed to circumvent it completely, are still read with appreciation on their own terms. Certain writers, like Angela Brazil and Dorita Fairlie Bruce, are unintentionally funny but nonetheless good; others, like L. T. Meade, are not.

This is basically a study of *girls'* fiction, but we have included a number of books not written specifically for girls. The William stories from the start appealed equally to children of both sexes, and this is true also of the "adventure" stories discussed in chapter 18. At the time when these were most popular – the late '40s and early '50s – it became almost a rule that boys' stories should have no girls in them; books which featured both sexes were more likely to be read by girls. On the other hand, the middle section of this survey covers a wide range of actual, unmistakable schoolgirls' stories. As far as American books are concerned, we have considered only two basic types: those which attracted a large readership in this country, and those which provide parallels or prototypes for certain kinds of fiction which became popular here. Of course we have had to be selective in the choice of books to analyse in depth; but we have found that certain writers – not necessarily those who are best known – stand out from their contemporaries, for reasons which we hope we have made clear. Some are just remarkably good or bad, some are completely original, others exemplify, more or less consciously, the predominant attitudes of their own time. In the last chapter we have tried to indicate the lines along which children's fiction is developing, and to take a critical look at some of the books produced over the last fifteen years.

Details of publications have been deliberately omitted from the text when these are included later in the Select Bibliography and the list of Works Discussed. We should like to thank The American Camp Fire Association and The Girl Guides Association of Great Britain for their co-operation. We are especially grateful to Mr L. E. Ransome and the late Mr John Wheway for information about the Amalgamated Press papers; to Peter Day, the editor; and to our families and friends for advice and criticism, particularly Alex and Teresa Cadogan, Nora T. Craig, Jeffrey Morgan, Val Warner and Ray Hopkins.

Mary Cadogan
Patricia Craig
London, 1976

PREFACE TO THIS NEW EDITION

IT IS NOW more than twenty-five years since *You're A Brick, Angela!* first appeared in England. It came out at a time (the mid-1970s) when interest in children's books – and in particular, in girls' fiction – appeared to be dormant. However, the reception of this study, in the media and elsewhere, took us, its authors, by surprise, and indicated that an enormous fund of enthusiasm for the subject lay waiting to be tapped. It seemed that we had latched on to something already in the air (albeit unconsciously): a wish to rediscover, and reappraise, whole tracts of significant childhood reading.

Before that time, mainstream surveys of children's literature were few and more or less staid, according to the expectations of the day. It's true that enterprising critics such as E. S. Turner had shown a way forward – however, the title of his particular contribution to the still rudimentary genre – *Boys Will Be Boys* (1949) – indicated plainly where the emphasis fell. It fell on the exploits of one gender only, whether ragamuffins or public schoolboys. The other half of humanity was short-changed in the significance attached to its juvenile reading, as in much else. At that time, the 1970s, women and girls were rebelling against all kinds of anti-feminist preconceptions, and here, it seemed to us, was another instance of side-lining, positively crying out to be addressed. We, as tyro authors[1] considered ourselves well placed to tackle the subject of girls' literature and its ramifications, for a number of reasons. First, we'd been "inhalers" of fiction (to borrow Elizabeth Bowen's pungent expression) from the word go. Each of us had read voraciously, right from the instant when words on a page began to make sense, and unfold into a story. At that moment, for both of us, at separate times and in different countries, a lifelong addiction was initiated. And moving on from children's books, as we inevitably did, didn't mean leaving them behind. They'd had far too powerful an effect on us to be discarded completely, and if returning to them as

[1] *You're a Brick, Angela!* was not only our first joint undertaking, but the first book either of us had ever written.

11

adults (whether as collectors or critics) entailed casting a wry adult eye over material we'd once lapped up – well, we'd try to bear in mind the sheer enjoyment disseminated by a story with a title like "The Girl Helper of the Hooded Four" too. It is hard to keep out an element of levity when one is writing about schoolgirls' stories (or, for that matter, boys' stories, or sexually undifferentiated children's stories) – but it was always our intention to temper the impulse towards mockery with a concomitant benevolence. It's true that our book was conceived as a work of criticism, and indeed we found much to criticize, at a social, literary or psychoanalytical level. Nevertheless, as far as we were concerned, *You're A Brick, Angela!* added up to a kind of homage to certain icons of our childhoods.

In fact only a fairly small part of *You're A Brick, Angela!* was devoted to school stories. Perhaps we should here add a special note about our comments on and feelings for the stories of Angela Brazil, Elsie Jeanette Oxenham, Dorita Fairlie Bruce and Elinor Brent-Dyer. It would have been easy enough to let nostalgic affection for their work overcome the critical standards which we applied here, as well as to all the other books which came under our scrutiny. We were anxious, however, to ensure that their work was accorded the same dignity and received no less serious literary assessment than we gave to recognized classics such as the books of Edith Nesbit or Arthur Ransome. (Yes – in retrospect we might have been slightly tough on, or frivolous about, certain aspects of the school stories; but I believe that, at the very least, we succeeded in presenting these, for future mainstream literary critics and social historians, as a suitable and worthy subject for treatment – M.)

Of course, we – both of us – were fonder of some works of fiction than we were of others. But one of the things we found endlessly fascinating, in the course of our researches, was to gauge the extent to which this or that story upheld or subverted the prevailing ideology – the prevailing ideology, that is, in connection with the supposed limitations of female capacities. It was encouraging, in this respect, to uncover an enormous amount of subversion, as heroine after heroine ducked out of the straitjacket of "ladylike" behaviour. At the same time, certain assumptions of popular literature at various periods before the

1970s made our hair stand on end, and reinforced our conviction that serious attention needed to be paid to the content, history and general assessment of this especially heady and rewarding genre, the girls' story.

Under that heading, just to underscore a point, we included some works of fiction held in equal affection by girls *and* boys: Richmal Crompton's "William" stories, for example, and Enid Blyton's "Mystery" series. Girls have always read "boys" books; there's a sense in which you could claim the boys' story is the girls' story too. (We didn't; for reasons of space, no less than semantic confusion.) That the opposite isn't true, or true to the same extent, is itself an implicit comment on the manner in which an insidious anti-feminism had worked its way through the whole spectrum of writing for children, from the nursery rhyme on. This, and similar perceptions, were coming to a head around the time we began work on *You're a Brick, Angela!*; and we, of course, were no less susceptible than anyone else to the mood of the time. But it wasn't only an ephemeral attitude that engendered the book; we both held strongly, and still hold, to a firm belief in an egalitarian ideal.

Rereading the book, in connection with the current reissue, what do we find? Well, perhaps we came down a bit too heavily on Enid Blyton (to take that example), in view of all the stupendous entertainment she's provided for at least three generations of juvenile readers (though I still think *The Six Bad Boys* is a terrible book – P.). And we mightn't have been hard enough on repellent pursuits of the mid-twentieth century, such as fox-hunting (though we didn't approve of blood sports any more then than we do now – M. and P.). On that note – though it fell outside our remit, being aimed at six- or seven-year-olds – an anti-cruelty picture book like Roald Dahl's *The Magic Finger* of 1966 showed the way the wind was blowing with regard to the slaughterer's gun: disablingly. Then, it would have been good to accord consideration to such excellent school stories as Elsie Jeanette Oxenham's *Dorothy's Dilemma* or *Deb of Sea House* – which hadn't come our way at the time. (Along with a great mass of children's books – still, the nature of such an undertaking is to be selective.) Neither, of course, had those books published towards the end of the century, whether in the Lively/

Gardam tradition (subtle and illuminating), forthrightly up-to-date, or breaking new ground altogether – we are thinking here of the Rowling/Pullman phenomenon; and certainly, had Harry Potter or *His Dark Materials* been around at the time, we'd have counted them among the glories of children's literature available to girls, no less than boys.

Whatever we omitted, deliberately or otherwise, is likely to have been tackled elsewhere in the intervening quarter-century. Since 1976, vast numbers of critical studies, theses, newspaper articles, scholarly papers and so forth, have taken girls' literature as their theme, and extended, ratified or questioned our rationale, and the arguments put forward by us, at the start of the drive to upgrade the whole enticing genre. Nowadays, it is taken seriously – sometimes *too* seriously! It's important to remain alive to the merriment of the genre, as well as its various sociological implications. And, although we might wish to revise the odd opinion, adjust an emphasis or change a detail here and there – and who wouldn't, after such a lapse of time? – we would have to stand by the spirit in which the project was originally undertaken, along with the majority of its conclusions.

We would like to thank Girls Gone By Publishers for this new edition of *You're A Brick, Angela!*

Mary Cadogan, London
Patricia Craig, Antrim
2002

I

Counting Their Blessings

> " ... In country cottages or the drawing-rooms of
> ancestral mansions, the tide of time has left high and
> dry the pathetic collections of crochet mats, anti-
> macassars, and elaborate 'bedsides' which represented
> the endless empty days of long-dead women."
>
> (Vera Brittain, *Lady Into Woman*)

IF CHARLOTTE M. YONGE were alive today she would be an arch-
opponent of the Women's Liberation movement, but nevertheless
the history of girls' fiction begins with this passionate believer in
self-denial and woman's subservience. She was one of the first
English writers to realize that girls too old for nursery tales yearned
to identify with heroines who embodied recognizable aspects of
themselves. Her reputation as a Sunday School instructress over
several decades no doubt helped to promote the sale of her books
for girls, most of which contained characters of irreproachable
humility and piousness. Miss Yonge's stories, as far as entertainment
is concerned, may seem somewhat inadequate to the modern reader
and their popularity is explicable only when they are seen in the
context of their own time.

By the middle of the nineteenth century, after the transient
licentiousness of its early years, England had settled down firmly to
an epoch of respectability. Fashions reflected the emphasis on
propriety, and revealing, flimsy dresses had been abandoned in
favour of dark silk skirts, which expanded as the century progressed.
The crinoline almost succeeded in turning women, in actuality, into
the kind of female that Queen Victoria represented: a figurehead,
stationary and statuesque. Tightly corseted, almost crippled by

From one of the earliest popular books for children, Holiday
House, *by Catherine Sinclair, 1839*

proliferating underskirts and more covered up than at any time in history, woman expressed in her appearance the image tenaciously projected by male-dominated society of what femininity ought to be.

Despite the challenge and social upheavals of growing industrialization, in middle- and upper-class life the cult of the "idle lady" was fashionable. (Though it was accepted without question that working class females, young and old, could slave for a pittance in the mills: until Lord Shaftesbury's Act of 1842 they also crawled hot, half-naked and filthy, with chains between their legs, dragging heavy trucks through coal-mines.) For the more favoured woman, to be idle was a mark of status, and a compliment to the husband or father who maintained and "protected" her. Early Victorian men, convinced that they alone were made in the image of God, had become the unchallenged Lords of Creation. Their wives were legally equated with mental defectives and criminals, considered incapable of controlling money, property, children or their own destinies. Man's high-sounding but often hollow marriage promise to his bride – "With all my worldly goods I thee endow" – in those days actually meant that he was taking over everything she possessed, and every penny she might earn in the future. The British Empire had officially freed its slaves in 1833, but liberation for women at home was not to come for many decades.

Romantic images of female uselessness had been established by the popularity of Sir Walter Scott's novels and Byron's poetry. Wordsworth too had done his bit for male supremacy by glorifying

A perfect woman nobly planned
To warn, to comfort and command.

Scott's pseudo-mediaeval chivalry, Byron's assessment of women as odalisques and Wordsworth's "phantom of delight" had conveniently encouraged passive femininity and domestic subordination in the girls who devoured their writings.

In the seclusion of their drawing-rooms, these "genteel" creatures with no career prospects apart from becoming sadly underpaid governesses or dressmakers, saw marriage as their only fulfilment; therefore they diligently practised those accomplishments intended to endear them to the male. Not surprisingly, female education, whether from untrained governesses at home or at "refined" boarding schools, consisted mainly of recitation, music, scripture and endless varieties of needlecraft, while the crinoline effectively prevented participation in any sport more vigorous than croquet. Laced-up little girls, like their mothers, cultivated the delicate look, and an "interesting pallor" was even occasionally accentuated by drinking vinegar. Hair was worn in elaborate ringlets, achieved by the nightly agony of rag binding, and frilly pantaloons beneath flounced dresses in muslin, silk, gingham or tartan completed the picture of prim little maiden offspring, those models of covered-up meekness, so beloved by Victorian parents.

These were the girl readers for whom Charlotte Yonge was to produce "uplifting" fiction, encouraging their view of themselves as eventual wives and mothers, counting their blessings, doing their duty and maintaining the established structure of society.

The docility of Miss Yonge's heroines was echoed in her own life, which like that of so many Victorians embodied the patriarchal, moralistic and class-ridden spirit of the age. She was born at Otterbourne near Winchester in 1823, the daughter of a retired army officer who had fought at the Battle of Waterloo. Military discipline, as well as uncompromising Christian ideals, may well have influenced her upbringing, which was spartan even according to the standards of the day. Asking the child-like question, "Am I pretty?"[1], weaker characters than little Charlotte might have been daunted by her mother's rejoinder: "All young animals, even pigs, are pretty." Miss Yonge had to rise above this, as well as reproofs at table for "even a sidelong glance" to see what pudding would be served, as this was considered an indication of greed. Charlotte's literary diet too was rationed and censored by her parents. "She was never permitted to read a ghost story, and fairy stories were discountenanced, if not actually forbidden." Maria Edgworth's tales, and such books as *Polite Little Children* and *The Faithful Little Girl*

[1] *Girl's Realm Magazine*, 1899.

were permitted, and Charlotte's love for Scott's poetry began in childhood and continued throughout her life.

Instead of reacting, as a normal twentieth-century child would have done, against her excessively religious upbringing, Charlotte Yonge took it very much to heart. Her piety was intensified by contact with John Keble, one of the originators of the Oxford Movement who came to Otterbourne in 1835, and her proselytizing instincts soon found an outlet in teaching and writing. She began helping to teach at church schools when she was only a child, and in her teens she was writing features for a Sunday School journal, *Magazine For The Young*: in 1843 when Charlotte was just twenty a publisher accepted her first novel, *Abbey Church, or Self-Control And Self-Conceit*. Charlotte's submissiveness to her father, the hero whom she tried to please in all things, was then clearly shown. He "gravely put it to her that there were three reasons which might induce anyone to publish – love of vanity, or of gain, or the wish to do good". Apparently so impressed was she by this "high-minded admonition" that for several years Miss Yonge wrote anonymously, "so that there should be no temptation to personal vanity, and she counted it a point of honour, and even duty, not to expend a fraction of her literary earnings upon herself".

In spite of this humility, Charlotte Yonge's constant desire to point a moral indicates a belief in her own religious superiority, and she held the prevalent view that "the poor" existed for the spiritual benefit of the middle and upper classes to which she and most of her readers belonged. Early Victorian writers of girls' fiction set their stories in the affluent backgrounds of their own experience: artisan children rarely played leading rôles, but were often introduced as "horror" elements to throw into sharp relief the joys and privileges of upper-class childhood. In fiction, as in fact, the "lower orders" – as well as the "inferior sex" – kept to their "proper" place in society. Few real-life working-class children then had the time or capacity to read much fiction. Many still worked long hours in factories, and bickering amongst opposing religious groups held back the establishment of State elementary schools, and the growth of literacy, until the 1870s.

The atmosphere of many mid-nineteenth-century English homes was accurately conveyed in Miss Yonge's successful novel for girls, *The Daisy Chain, or Aspirations,* which was published in 1856. This unfolds in 662 closely printed pages the saga of Dr Dick May's Daisy Chain – the name by which he patronizingly refers to his numerous children, whom he sees not apparently as individuals, but collectively. The opening chapters describe them: Richard, the eldest brother, away from home; Margaret – "a fine, tall blooming girl of eighteen"; Flora, "a pretty fair girl" –

A typical blessing-counting picture from Aunt Judy's Magazine, Vol. 1, 1866

seventeen; and Etheldred at fifteen, "thin, lank, angular and sallow". We learn that Norman is sixteen, Harry twelve and Mary ten: then there is Blanche, "a pretty little maid of five", and "a solemn looking boy of three". Youngest of all is Daisy (Gertrude Margaret), not quite six weeks old.

At this point in the narrative the modern reader may well be appalled at the thought of Victorian women worn out with constant child-bearing, and so often dying before their time. But – incredibly – "Here entered with a baby in her arms a lady with a beautiful countenance of calm sweetness, looking almost too young to be the mother of tall Margaret ...". (To say nothing of all the others!) Possibly Charlotte Yonge's idealized picture of motherhood was enhanced by the fact that she herself remained unmarried, never knowing the actualities of Victorian sex, pregnancy and childbirth. However, Mrs May does not have to sustain her maternal serenity for long, because early in the story she is killed when her carriage overturns. This dramatic death in the midst of such abundant life underlines Mrs May's earlier admonition to eldest daughter Margaret (and Miss Yonge's sincere belief): " 'Depend upon it, the only security is not to think about ourselves at all, and not to fix our minds on any affection on earth. The least share of the Love above is the fulness of all blessing, and if we seek that first, all these things will be added unto us …'."

Girl readers of *The Daisy Chain* immediately responded to its teenage heroine, Etheldred (Ethel May), who was awkward, plain, untidy and short-sighted, but kind-hearted, with a great dedication to religion. Early in the book we are told that Ethel is trying to keep pace in her studies with brother Norman, eleven months her senior: *he* has the advantage of a tutor, while *she* has to struggle on her own, a fact which seemed totally natural to both author and readers when the story was written. Ethel, over-eager and clumsy, dreams of writing historical romance and poetry to make money for building a church on the wild, godless moorland area nearby. With her hair pins always flying out, and "her muddy ankles and petticoats … not fit to be seen", she shows the zeal of reformer and educationalist. Elder sister Margaret encourages these ideas so long as Ethel starts with "little things" – like making clothes for the needy. (Miss Yonge, in common with many Victorian writers, never missed an opportunity of urging her girl readers back to the needle or the kitchen.) Margaret is fearful of Ethel's ambitions, in case these should take her too much outside the home and beyond the pale of respectable society. " 'Dear, dear Ethel, how noble and high she is! … If those high purposes should grow out into eccentricities and unfeminineness, what a grievous pity it would be.' "

Ethel's reforming instincts must have appealed to Miss Yonge's readers as strongly as Florence Nightingale's achievements in the Crimea in indicating aspects of "worthwhile" feminine behaviour less restrictive than the tedium of drawing-room gossip and embroidery. Florence Nightingale's example in fact sounded the death knell of the "idle lady" – but she took a very long time to die! – and in the 1850s popular fantasies about The Lady with the Lamp had little relevance to reality. The upper-class women and girls who persisted in regarding Miss Nightingale as an inspiration – do-gooders to be found in insanitary cottages resolutely ministering to the sick – became a commonplace of Victorian society and fiction. "The poor", however, were expected to be worthy and to count their blessings gratefully, while aspiring social reformers usually lacked understanding of the stark realities of life for those who were on the receiving end of their offerings.

In spite of the firm hold which religious ideals had taken on popular imagination, there was no sympathy or help for women and girls who had been forced into prostitution. This had grown with mass migration from close-knit country communities to overcrowded city slums, as a result of the industrial revolution, and the desperate poverty of female workers in "sweated industries" at home after the old cottage industries had declined. Double standards of Victorian morality – which cast a girl who had been made pregnant outside society's protection though it happily accepted the male seducer – added to the number for whom there was no alternative method of survival but prostitution. The same hypocrisy permitted child prostitution: the "age of consent" in Britain was twelve until 1875, when it was raised only to thirteen, and brothel traffic in young girls, though exposed by various individuals and organizations, was allowed to continue throughout the nineteenth century. Females in more favoured circumstances felt the need to safeguard at all costs their chief assets – respectability, chastity, humility – and therefore viciously attacked "adulteresses" (but not adulterers), unmarried mothers and their pitiful, illegitimate children. Those who yearned to "do good" saw no dichotomy in forcing their pregnant maid-servants without notice into the streets or workhouse.

In fiction, George Eliot's Hetty Sorrel illustrates the impossible plight of the seduced girl. Hetty (in *Adam Bede*), having lost the right to be regarded as "respectable", wanders demented through the countryside. She gives birth prematurely and succumbs to the overwhelming temptation of what seems an easy way out: she murders the child. When she is condemned to death, a misogynic but not unsympathetically presented schoolmaster sums up society's justification: " ' ... The sooner such women are put out o' the world the better; ... What good will you do by keeping such vermin alive? eating the victual that 'ud feed rational beings.' " Incidentally, it was partly George Eliot's own unorthodox social position that forced her to write under a pen-name. If it had been known that the author of *Adam Bede* lived with a man to whom she was not married, "every newspaper critic would have written against it"[1] – in spite of the book's impeccable moral standpoint. As it was, the publication of her *Scenes From Clerical Life* was followed by a prolonged controversy: was the book written by a clergyman or was it not? Only the astute Dickens wondered if the author of the *Scenes* might conceivably have been a woman. An added incentive for Marian Evans to conceal her identity was of course the fact that female writers were taken less seriously: the Brontë sisters had originally written under masculine pen-names and "when *Jane Eyre* was finally known to be a woman's book the tone noticeably changed".[2] Fiction which society had considered acceptable, when thought to originate from a man's mind, suddenly became dubious after its feminine authorship was discovered.

Charlotte Yonge came into her own when in 1851 she was asked to become the editor of a new magazine, *The Monthly Packet.* In the pages of this periodical she was for the next 40 years to admonish, educate and amuse her girl readers. It was a journal of "Evening Readings for Younger Members of the English Church", published by John and Charles Mozley at 8d [4p] a copy, containing 112 pocket-sized pages, solid with small print absolutely unbroken by illustrations. Naturally many of its articles were religious in nature, and some of their titles – "Conversations on the Catechism" and "Sketches of the Offices of Baptism and Extreme Unction" – suggest that these were heavy going, even for conscientious Victorian teenagers. However it had lighter touches which they most certainly enjoyed, and Miss Yonge's historical romance *The Little Duke,* still

[1] Gordon Haight, *George Eliot*, OUP, London, 1968
[2] Ibid

in print today, was the first serial to adorn its opening numbers.

A periodical which tried to enliven fiction for children was *Aunt Judy's Magazine,* which began in 1866 under the editorship of Mrs Margaret Gatty. Unlike Miss Yonge, Mrs Gatty was married and had produced ten children including Juliana, whose later fame as Mrs Ewing soon eclipsed her mother's. Mrs Gatty was born in 1809, and her father, like Charlotte's, had played his part in the defence of the nation in the Napoleonic wars: as chaplain to Lord Nelson he had been on board H.M.S. *Victory* during the Battle of Trafalgar. *Aunt Judy's Magazine* was intended for a younger age group than *The Monthly Packet*, and had occasional whole-page illustrations. It attracted many distinguished children's writers during the nineteen years of its existence, including Lewis Carroll, Mrs Molesworth and Hans Christian Andersen.

Although both *The Monthly Packet* and *Aunt Judy's Magazine* went in for social comment as well as "elevating" fiction, their girl readers were encouraged only to support reforms which allowed them to remain on the tightrope of respectability. Contributors and readers were more concerned with counting their blessings than with changing the *status quo.* An article appearing in an 1861 issue of *The Monthly Packet* typifies middle-class attitudes towards working girls of the day. Long hours of hard, uncreative work are taken for granted as their lot, and describing daily routine in a home for factory girls the anonymous author laments rather testily "… the great difficulty we had to overcome on Sunday was their tendency to lie down and go to sleep. It was more habit than anything else, and a listless idleness. … The habit is a most exhausting one, for it is not sleep they require, nor rest of that description. A walk a few miles out into the country would do far more to recruit a weary frame." It doesn't occur to the writer that toiling ten hours a day, six days a week for little financial return (and no hope of ever changing one's circumstances) inevitably deadens both mind and body. Many of *The Monthly Packet's* readers, growing up in comfortable homes which still fostered the "idle lady" image – even though its edges were now becoming tarnished – secretly envied factory girls their "independence", having no insight into the sordid drudgery of their lives.

In the same issue, Mrs Ewing's first published story, "A Bit of Green", also exasperatingly illustrates the understanding gap between the upper classes and "the poor". With heavy pathos she describes a young man dying in a filthy slum room: he has the double affliction of being a cripple *and* a consumptive, but consoles himself with the prospect of being able to sell his shabby, pathetic sticks of furniture to pay for his funeral. He finds happiness in the contemplation of a pot of musk, his "Bit of Green". "What more," he wonders, "can a man want?" The author sanctimoniously echoes "What indeed? Unsatisfied heart make answer!" and goes on to tell her readers of the "Greatest of all Blessings – the Presence of the Lord". Satisfaction with one's lot, of course, was a convenient doctrine for an age when pressure for social reform was being applied from increasingly lower strata of the community. Religion – and sentimentality – were restraining influences in the potential hotbeds of unrest spreading across over-populated disease-ridden, jerry-built industrial city slums.

Mrs Ewing produced another maudlin deathbed scene in her last book, *The Story Of A Short Life*, published by the Society for the Propagation of Christian Knowledge in 1885, the year of her own death. In this she gives a colourful picture of the army life with which she became familiar after her marriage in 1867 to Major Alexander Ewing of the Pay Corps. Set against all this military vigour is beautiful velvet-and-lace-clad-little-Leonard, who becomes tragically crippled when trampled by horses at the Military Field Day. The six-year-old boy soon accepts pain, disability and early death with incredible resignation. " 'I shall die pretty soon, I believe. I meant to die young, but more grown-up than this, and in battle.' " The family motto, *Laetus Sorte Mea* (Happy with my Fate) sustains Leonard, and might well have been the maxim for many nineteenth-century children.

The deathbed ritual, merely by dint of repetition, must have become farcical even in its own time.[1] The most famous is that of Dickens's *Little Nell* and perhaps the funniest that of William in

[1] "No man of feeling can read the death of Little Nell without laughing." OSCAR WILDE

Mrs Henry Wood's *East Lynne*. Like all good, dying, Victorian, Christian children in fiction, William remembers to call on Jesus to come and fetch him at the appropriate moment, but his deathbed is better remembered for Lady Isabel's melodramatic line, " 'Dead – and never called me mother!' " (This did not occur in the original novel, but was introduced in its stage version.)

Early nineteenth-century writers found it almost impossible to resist this urge to wallow over youthful deathbeds. Catherine Sinclair, whose *Holiday House* (written as early as 1839) got off to a light-hearted and promising start, nevertheless finally succumbed. Dying Frank has been so well instructed in religious principles that he refuses to be dosed with laudanum – " 'I can bear pain ... but I cannot willingly enter the presence of my Creator in a state little short of intoxication' ". Catherine Sinclair wrote about two realistic and mischievous children, Laura and Harry, but her sympathy with their lively aspirations was soon overlaid by current repressive attitudes. " 'Punishment is as sure to do us good when we are naughty, as physic when we are ill.' " Laura and Harry are up against the unyielding determination of their nurse, Mrs Crabtree, to make them virtuous, "though she were to flay them alive first". Laura must have endeared herself to many girl readers by cutting off her hated and torturing ringlets, which inspired one of the earliest claims to sexual equality in juvenile fiction – " 'I was quite as naughty as Harry ... I was cutting off my hair with Mrs Crabtree's scissors all the time he was setting the nursery on fire' ". However in spite of her robust action, Laura demonstrated the feminine feebleness expected by readers when she and Harry were confronted by a mad bull. "Laura's knees tottered under her, and she instantly dropped on the ground with terror, feeling as if she would die the next minute of fright. Harry felt quite differently, for he was a bold boy ..."

An early and horrific fictional illustration of a father going to any lengths to discipline his children was contained in Mrs Sherwood's *The Fairchild Family* (1830). Mr Fairchild takes his offspring to study a corpse which has been hanging for four years on the gallows, to show what happens to children who are deceitful. Even in affluent and affectionate real-life families, Victorian girls were not over-indulged. Lady Emily Lutyens, daughter of the first Earl of Lytton, recalls her childhood in *A Blessed Girl*.

> My mother had a great idea that we were not to be brought up in luxury, and three dresses – bad, better, best – for winter and summer was my allowance in clothes. In winter I can remember a horror in the shape of a dress of red, and another, of yellow plush, while for summer I had two cotton frocks and a white one made like a sailor suit … when the yellow plush was almost new, I had the misfortune to spill some ink down the front, and thereafter I was made to go on wearing it, with its ink stains, until it was worn out.

The sympathetic *Aunt Judy's Magazine* too contained its share of dire warnings to those who failed to count their blessings. One instance is *The Princess Discontent*, a serial anonymously appearing in its pages in 1867. A little princess, possessing all earthly delights, cries bitterly for the moon and stars to play with. This "young and presumptuous mortal" persuades her fairy godmother to change her into a fairy, but she soon tires of her winged and lonely journeys through the skies, and longs to regain human shape. Worse is to come: "Her wings fell off suddenly! She fell right through the air and fainted in the fall-down to earth: and when she awoke, horror of horrors, she was transformed into a TOAD, a horrid loathsome toad, down in a cave … ".

Aunt Judy's Magazine regularly published verses, fiction and articles by the Gatty family story-teller, Juliana, who had been nick-named "Aunt Judy" from childhood. Being a member of a large family she was well qualified to write about relationships between brothers and sisters; her spirited story, *A Great Emergency* (serialized in *Aunt Judy* in 1874 and reprinted in Gollancz Revivals 1967) bears little resemblance to her dreary deathbed tales. This describes the enterprises of two brothers and their sister, who hopefully train themselves to cope with any emergency that might overtake them. Rupert at twelve is "head of the family", as their father has been long dead; next comes Henrietta, followed by nine-year-old Charlie. Henrietta was a "tomboy" – who sometimes wrote her name as "Henry" and "parted her hair on the boy's side", which annoyed Rupert: he also resented (ostensibly because it was unladylike) the fact that she could play cricket as well as he, and that she was prepared to argue various issues with him. Rupert " … said that even if she were in the right, that had nothing to do with it, for girls oughtn't to dispute or discuss. And then Henrietta argued that point too … ".

Of course boys from middle- and upper-class families, who took for granted the benefits of secondary or public-school education and organized games, felt a strong sense of superiority over their "vapid", stay-at-home sisters, to whom these facilities were still denied. Increasingly too, as they realized the disproportionate rights of husbands over their wives, boys became aware that mothers and sisters were expected to take second place to the male members of their families.

Charlie, being younger than Rupert, had less resentment against his sister's embryonic Women's Liberationist activities. Planning to avenge himself in a fight against a bigger boy at school, he even used her as his sparring partner, for wrestling and boxing. "She was always willing to do anything tomboyish … and her biceps were as hard as mine for I pinched them to see." Their mother was easily upset and spent a lot of time lying uselessly on the sofa. Her spineless behaviour supported Rupert's low view of feminine capabilities: when their home was burning down she was overtaken by fainting fits, and had to be quietly removed by servants from the scene. But Henrietta, realizing that Baby Cecil had been trapped in the house, ran back inside, followed by Rupert, and together, half suffocated by smoke, they rescued their little brother. Gratifyingly Rupert was then full of admiration for Henrietta's pluck: let us hope he recanted his earlier dismissive words to her " ' … women are not expected to do things when there is danger' ", and developed a lasting respect for his sister.

Charlotte Yonge too was very eloquent on the brother/sister theme, with earnest and touching belief in "a gentle, conscientious girl's power to bring chivalry into the life of a brother. … No time of her own should be grudged that is devoted to his service, the only thing she should never do to please him is what she knows to be wrong." In some families, one of the things girls did to please the boys (though it hardly seemed conducive to the male chivalry mentioned by Miss Yonge) was to wear their brothers' boots until these had been broken in. Female self-sacrifice again, and therefore acceptable to the revered author who, unlike Mrs Ewing, had stern words to say to "the sport or tomboy ... the jolly girl and no end of fun. ... She can never be quite a boy and as she grows older she had better not try to be one. ... Men may laugh but do not respect – no, not even the brothers, who are strict judges of what is becoming to the opposite sex and do not like to see their sisters lower themselves." Throughout her long literary career Miss Yonge never tired of impressing upon her girl readers the virtues of "maidenliness" and amiable acceptance of subordination.

In 1883 one of her short stories, "A Patchwork Fever" (adapted from *Bessy's Troubles At Home,* by Mrs Gaskell), clearly punched the moral of sisterly duties. Although written over 90 years ago this demonstrates the essential dilemma still relevant to many twentieth-century girls – the conflicting claims of domesticity and other creative fulfilments.

Frances, the central character in "A Patchwork Fever", was only thirteen, and entrusted with managing the household for her father, two brothers and small sister whilst her mother was away for a few days. As well as shopping, cooking, laundering, mending and cleaning, Frances was expected especially to amuse her twelve-year-old brother, so that he would stay at home, away from the dubious company of other village lads. Without the benefits of modern labour-saving equipment Frances would indeed have had her hands full, and (almost sinfully, according to Miss Yonge) she became determined to complete a beautiful patchwork table-cloth as a birthday gift in time for her mother's return.

Alas, the "fever" to complete the patchwork led to some neglect of her domestic duties, resulting in little Clara's catching cold and father being forced to suffer occasionally undercooked meals. Most traumatic of all, brother Gilbert got into real trouble for hoydenish activities with his rough little mates. These included bawling around the village, using bad language, waylaying girls out at night and letting off squibs under the squire's horse. As a result he lost his employment at the squire's stable, was temporarily dismissed from the church choir and whipped by his father. Twentieth-century girls reading this story might consider that he got what he deserved, but Miss Yonge attributed everything to Frances's neglect. As her mother later explained to the vicar " '... she didn't take heed to amuse her brother in the evenings. Menfolk take such a lot of attention" '. Gilbert too uncharitably upbraids his sister for driving him out of the house with her "fads and fancies". It is significant that none of the family expected Gilbert, though nearly as old as Frances and a member of the "superior" sex, to have any sense of personal responsibility, and his sister was supposed to be his conscience and his keeper.

Victorian England must have been full of real-life girls like Frances – conscientious, eager to help others but yearning for outlets other than domesticity. In our own age they are represented by women trying to write or paint on the edge of their kitchen work units, in between cooking meals or tossing garments into the voracious family washing machine. Happily though, today's society harvests a smaller crop of males like Gilbert than in Miss Yonge's time, who demand as their right the self-sacrifice of mothers, sisters and wives.

We cannot move away from counters of blessings without mentioning the slaughtering sincerity of Mrs Octavius Frank Walton, who conducted her own personal crusade to save young girls from entering the arena of the devil (i.e. a theatrical career), and to bring them to Christian Salvation. The Religious Tract Society published her novel, *A Peep Behind The Scenes,* in 1877 and surprisingly, in view of its now extremely outdated picture of what-happens-to-girls-who-go-on-the-stage, it has since been frequently reprinted, appearing as recently as 1972 in a new paperback edition.

Rosalie, the twelve-year-old heroine, lives in a caravan with her frail mother and coarse father, and they are all members of a travelling theatre company. Rosalie acts in " ... a foolish play" which apparently includes "a strong mixture of very objectionable language; yet it was highly appreciated by the audience" and "there were many young girls there – some of them servants in respectable families. They looked up at little Rosalie with eyes of admiration and envy! They thought her life was much happier than theirs, and that her lot was greatly to be desired. … But they knew nothing of the life behind the scenes. …".

Mrs Walton, of course, was determined to enlighten them, and the book's 264 pages leave no details of travelling backstage life – or the joys of Christian Salvation brought about

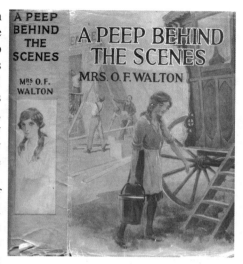

The dustjacket of Mrs. O. F. Walton's frequently reprinted A Peep Behind the Scenes

by illustrated tracts – to the imagination. Like other writers of the period Mrs Walton warned girls of the folly of leaving secure and loving families for careers outside their homes, likely to result in the downward path of deprivation, degradation and early death. In the story each loose end is firmly tied so that every character is either utterly Saved or totally Damned. Religion, for Mrs Walton, implied no half measures.

Let us return to Charlotte M. Yonge, the literary giant whose tenuous influence no English woman entirely escapes, to sum up the spirit of girls' fiction in its early days: "Remember, maidens, that you are the hope of England, and her joy: and this you can only be, if you are modest, gentle, brave, truthful and Godly, alike as girls and as women."

II

Pilgrims and Pioneers

"…the nations must remember
That Uncle Sam is not a fool,
For the people do the voting
And the children go to school…"
(Hutchinson, "Uncle Sam's Farm")

ACROSS THE ATLANTIC in the middle of the nineteenth century the
independent spirit of America's pioneers still flourished. Neither
prosperity nor the bitter divisions of the Civil War subdued its energy,
which spilled over into many aspects of life, including fiction and
popular song. "Uncle Sam's Farm" was written by the Hutchinson
family singers in the 1840s. It reflected the pride felt by many
Americans in the land and opportunity which had been won by their
fathers and consolidated through later technical achievements.
However the lyric substituted enthusiasm for accuracy. Suffrage was
still denied to a large proportion of the community, including all
white women and of course negro slaves of both sexes. Also
educational facilities for children were fragmented and far from
universal.

As they entertained, the Hutchinson family campaigned for
women's suffrage, temperance and the abolition of slavery, three
causes which were often interrelated, and for which support was
increasing, especially in the northern states. Traditions of feminine
inferiority had been meaningless in pioneer life: freer attitudes
developed among early immigrants who had escaped from religious
and political oppression in Europe. (The Quakers, for instance,
accepted the equality of men and women, and had made education
available to girls as well as boys since the seventeenth century.

Quaker women did not promise to obey their husbands and were encouraged to speak in public at religious meetings.) Men and women facing hardship and danger together had wrested farmlands and homes from the wild country. Even when pioneering days were over, self-reliance, rather than over-sentimentalized femininity, remained the quintessence of many American women. They were becoming real partners in marriage, no longer dominated, pampered or hoisted on to pedestals.

Yet women's legal position remained as anachronistic and degrading as in early Victorian England. In 1849 the Tennessee Legislature solemnly decreed that women should not be given the right to own property as they had no souls. This was bigotry at its most ludicrous, but legal and economic control remained entirely in the hands of men, and double standards of sexual morality persisted. In 1848 the first Women's Rights Convention took place. This was organized at Seneca Falls by Mrs Lucretia Mott and Mrs Elizabeth Cady Stanton, two Americans who had met in 1840 at an Anti-Slavery Convention in London. Ironically, because of their sex, Mrs Mott and Mrs Cady Stanton were debarred from taking part in this conference as many of the male delegates, though sufficiently progressive to seek the abolition of slavery, still held entrenched prejudices against women. The Seneca Falls meeting demanded suffrage and equality for women, and marked the beginning of an organized American feminist movement.[1] Its leaders were colourful and determined, and in 1849 *The Lily* appeared. This was a monthly journal devoted to women's interests, which became increasingly outspoken and challenging. Its editor was Mrs Amelia Bloomer, who is more famous for the bifurcated garment which bears her name than for her literary achievement.

American girls and women were as handicapped by their restrictive clothes as their English counterparts. Multiple underskirts were reinforced with horsehair and straw, while waists and midriffs were tortured by steel and whalebone corsets. *The Lily* came out strongly against stupidities of dress, and drew attention to the

[1] The struggles of the early American feminists are well drawn in Charles Neilson Gatty's *The Bloomer Girls*.

disproportionate amount of time spent by many women on the drudgery of making over-decorated clothes and household linen. In the spirit of vegetarians advocating that all meat eaters should themselves kill the animals for their table, Mrs Cady Stanton suggested that everyone, men and boys included, should be made to do their own sewing and that clothes should be kept functional. The Bloomer was one result in 1851 of women's efforts to produce a sensible item of clothing. Contemporary illustrations of these ankle-length Turkish pantaloons, worn under a skirt reaching below the knee, suggest impeccable propriety. However bloomers produced apoplectic resentment among conservative factions of society when they were adopted for three or four years as the battle uniform of leading feminists. The Bloomer had great publicity value, and became synonymous with the demand for physical and psychological emancipation.

Although girls who were growing up in the challenging atmosphere of nineteenth-century America demanded a more expansive literature than their English contemporaries, one of their first and longest surviving fictional heroines embodied the most conservative values. Elsie Dinsmore was a moralistic little girl created in 1867 by Martha Finley (Farquharson), a school teacher from Chillicothe, Ohio. Elsie's roots are in the didactic tales of early Victorian England, and throughout the 28 volumes of her saga we find a sermon on almost every page. In the first book Elsie is still in the schoolroom, and though there are signs that her character is based upon "the ornament of a meek and quiet spirit", she is "not yet perfect and often had a fierce contest with her naturally quick temper". (It should be remembered that Elsie Dinsmore is only eight years old at this time.) Emphasis on the "golden brown curls and pure complexion" and little Elsie's reflection that "it was dear ole mammy who first told ... how He suffered and died on the cross for us" remind modern readers that this is the south, where the devastation of the Civil War had taken place only a very short while before *Elsie Dinsmore* was published. Former slaves, according to Miss Finley, in spite of emancipation remained loyal and servile to their white masters. In a later book, *Elsie's Widowhood*, an old coloured nurse, Aunt Chloë, assures Elsie's children when they ask for news of their dying father, " 'Yo' old mammy'd die to keep massa here for yo' sake. But de Lord's will mus' be done, an' He neber makes no mistakes.' " Twenty years after the publication of the first *Elsie* book, negroes in children's fiction were still rather surprisingly yearning for the " 'Libely times we all use to hab down t'dat old plantation.' " In 1887 the juvenile monthly magazine *St Nicholas* featured two stories by Jessie C. Glasier which unconvincingly extolled the excellent relations between coloured and white families. The complete text of "Ole Mammy Prissy" is

A typical illustration from the American journal St Nicholas: "Ole Mammy Prissy", 1887

delivered in first-person pidgin English by the devoted mother-substitute-servant herself: her five-page-long eulogy contains phrases like " 'dat little yeller head ... dem curls shinin' like gol' ' ": this refers to the child whom she had nursed in the good old secure and happy days of slavery, and with whom she has just been reunited. Besotted subservience to her white employers makes her rebuke members of her own race – those " 'no 'count Black critters' " who cannot understand the difference between " 'a common eb'ryday free niggah, an' an ole fam'ly suvvant w'at had al'ays lived right 'mong'st de bery top sort!' " "The very top sort" in the assessment of nineteenth-century children's fiction writers were more likely to be white than black. In spite of her sympathy with the exploited negro, Harriet Beecher Stowe had established this literary tradition in 1852 with *Uncle Tom's Cabin.* There is a pointed contrast here between white Eva, the "bright angel", "christ-like" child, and "shrewd, cunning, goblin-like" black Topsy.

Unrealistic pictures of cheerfully docile coloured people found an antidote in the impressive person of ex-slave Sojourner Truth, who had spoken passionately and effectively at the 1853 Women's Rights Convention in New York. This 82-year-old woman had had a lifetime of hard work in the fields, had borne many whippings and seen most of her thirteen children sold into slavery. Not unnaturally Sojourner Truth voiced contempt for the hypocrisy of society which sanctified Christian family life and female modesty (and implied that women's suffrage would undermine these), yet condoned the sexual degradation of negro women, and the disintegration of their families as members were sold to separate owners.

No hint of the vigour of Sojourner Truth was ever injected into Martha Finley's *Elsie* stories, or those featuring her other exemplary character, Mildred, whose exploits were extended to fill seven volumes. From childhood until she became a grandmother Elsie insists on rigid adherence to the established codes of society and religion. She joyfully invites suffering for herself and her family: typical of her frequent homilies to her nearest and dearest is " 'Ah, we could never choose for our precious children exemption from such trials and afflictions as He may see necessary to fit them for an eternity of joy and bliss at His right hand!' "

Elsie's endurance is stretched somewhat when her husband is smitten with an unnamed disease of agonizing ferocity. Readers however have the consolation of a whole chapter lovingly devoted to a description of his death bed, and Elsie remains a model of decorum and domesticity.

Fortunately many real-life American girls and women did not reflect Elsie's meekness. During the middle years of the nineteenth

Frontispiece from Elsie Dinsmore *by Martha Finley,*
1867

century, anti-feminine prejudice from members of the clergy was backed by biblical quotations which were frequently hurled against the Bloomer brigade. In *The Lily* and from the platform at public meetings these were ably countered by feminists, especially their greatest advocate, Susan Brownell Anthony. Miss Anthony, the exact contemporary of Florence Nightingale, was a teacher from a Quaker family who had become active in the women's suffrage campaign after her earlier work with Abolition and Temperance movements. Forty years later, when the misogynist utterances of St Paul and the supposed perfidy of Eve against God and the weak-willed Adam were still being used as anti-feminist arguments, Mrs Cady Stanton and a committee of women produced the controversial *Women's Bible.* This was a serious attempt to translate ancient texts with greater accuracy, and included Mrs Stanton's radical comments on passages previously emphasizing the "inferiority" of women and the "maleness" of God.

Josephine March, perhaps the most celebrated "tomboy" in the whole of girls' fiction, was brought to life by Louisa M. Alcott in the same year as the first *Elsie* book was published. *Little Women,* though sentimental by modern standards, provided humour and a degree of verisimilitude that were lacking in Miss Finley's turgid stories. The adventures of Meg, Jo, Beth and Amy were based on Louisa Alcott's own family life, and the book was first serialized in a magazine called *Merry's Museum* in 1867 before its publication a year later. Sales quickly reached a million, and *Little Women's* popularity has remained constant for over a hundred years. Readers demanded further stories of the March sisters, which followed in *Good Wives* (1869), *Little Men* (1871) and *Jo's Boys* (1886). Before she died in 1888 Miss Alcott wrote several other novels for girls. She had become a breadwinner early in her life, as her philosophical father Amos Bronson Alcott gave his family affection and idealism but few material advantages. In her middle teens Louisa worked in domestic service and teaching, but her ambition was always to become a writer.

Even before the Civil War of 1861-65, girls living in northern states were encouraged to be more independent than those in the

Two illustrations by Margaret Tulloch for a 1930s reprint of Louisa Alcott's Little Women: *Marmee, Meg, Jo, Beth and Amy (above) and Jo's Hair Cut Short (below).*

south, where society was based on conservative, patriarchal land-owning traditions. The rôle of southern women was largely domestic, although their help in administering family estates sometimes brought about involvement in public service, without the recognition of public office. Girls were dependent on the status of their fathers or husbands, as it was not considered proper for them to earn their livelihoods. The position of women in the south, both white and coloured, is underlined in *Uncle Tom's Cabin,* when Mrs Shelby of Kentucky frets about the separation of two of her married slaves, Tom and Chloe. Tom has been sold to another owner and, in spite of good intentions, Mr Shelby cannot afford to buy him back again. Mrs Shelby confides to her husband that as she has taught her slaves " 'their marriages are as sacred as ours' " she is planning to give music lessons to earn sufficient money to buy Tom and reunite him with Chloe. Mr Shelby's response typifies the nineteenth-century southern husband and slave-owner: " 'You wouldn't degrade yourself that way Emily? I never could consent to it.' "

In the north young women from poorer homes went into factories, and those who were better educated frequently worked outside their homes as teachers and governesses. The March sisters echo their author's determination to become financially self-supporting. They also have no doubts that it is possible for a woman to find fulfilment without a man, and understand their mother "Marmee's" advice – " 'better be happy old maids than unhappy wives.' " (Amelia Bloomer's definition of an "old maid" was stronger " ... a lady who has attained the age of twenty-five without having married a fool, a gambler, a knave or a drunkard.") [1]

Louisa Alcott never married but in deference to readers' wishes she provides Jo, a fictional representation of herself, with a husband. Jo rejects Laurie, her childhood friend and first suitor: " 'I don't believe I shall ever marry. I'm happy as I am, and love my liberty too well to be in any hurry to give it up for any mortal man.' " In spite of Miss Alcott's arguments about Jo and Laurie's strong wills and quick tempers making the match impossible, readers have never forgiven her for separating the enchanters, and allowing lively Jo

[1] Charles Neilson Gatty, op. cit.

eventually to settle for prosaic, middle-aged Professor Bhaer. The Bhaers establish a residential school for their own children and other people's unwanted or problem offspring, but Jo's transition from tomboy to great-earth-mother is disappointing and unconvincing. In common with many later writers of girls' fiction, Miss Alcott was less able to create attractive adult characters than juveniles. Jo is best remembered as a coltish teenager with literary ambitions and a contempt for affectation, and she epitomizes the desire of many girls for participation in intellectual life. Louisa Alcott manages to make the March sisters seem natural, even in mawkish situations. Jo is always wholehearted, whether burning the skin off her nose by excessive boating in the sunshine, reading till her eyes give out, or selling her abundant chestnut hair to provide money for "Marmee" to visit her husband when he is in hospital, badly wounded in the Civil War. Luxury-starved Meg's preoccupation with fripperies, and spoiled Amy's vanity arouse readers' sympathy and amusement, while thousands of young girls have suffered with uncomplaining Beth as "... on the bosom where she had drawn her first breath, she quietly drew her last, with no farewell but one loving look, one little sigh." Apart from "Marmee", Beth is the character who has dated most but her gentleness is a perfect foil for Jo's vitality:

"It's bad enough to be a girl, anyway, when I like boys' games, and work, and manners. I can't get over my disappointment in not being a boy, and it's worse than ever now for I'm dying to go and fight with papa, and I can only stay at home and knit like a poky old woman," and Jo shook the blue army-sock till the needles rattled like castanets, and her ball bounded across the room.

Five years before *Little Women* was published Louisa Alcott, the real-life Jo, had played her part in the Civil War as a military nurse. There had at first been a resistance to women nurses, but Miss Dorothea Dix successfully organized women in this service. Her work provided the basis for improved hospitals and a strong profession for many women after the war ended in 1865. By 1864 women doctors were coming to be accepted, and 300 had graduated from medical schools. In both north and south war conditions had made it necessary for more women to work in factories. They had also learned to manage farms and businesses in the absence of husbands and sons, as well as occupying more jobs in teaching. After the war there were further opportunities for women in reconstruction, charity and social work. Old patterns of life had been destroyed for ever, especially in the south, where the aftermath of war was poverty and humiliation for the men who returned weak with typhoid, dysentery and other illnesses, to their disillusioned women. The feminist movement in America would have advanced more rapidly if it had received as much support in the south as in the north, but for many years southern women had to devote their main energies to rebuilding their homes and society, before they could overcome their bitterness towards the northern states.

Women had further reasons for anger: suffrage had been awarded to all male negroes when slavery was abolished, but was still denied to women of every class. Abolitionists who had benefited from the support of feminist groups now did nothing to further their cause. In addition the growth of venereal disease during the war had strengthened women's determination to end double standards of morality and to discourage prostitution: in this connection the need for improvements in wages and labour conditions for women and girls was urgently stressed. Women's clubs, which began to proliferate in the 1860s, became educational pressure groups as well as organizations for social service. (At first they were criticized for attempting to destroy family life by creating radical attitudes and encouraging women to take part in activities outside the home.)

Young girls who demanded vitality from their fictional heroines enjoyed the *Katy* books by Susan Coolidge (Sara Chancey Woolsey) from Cleveland, Ohio. *What Katy Did* appeared in 1872: Katy Carr, a tall, rangy, self-willed tomboy lives with her widowed doctor father, sisters Clover, Elsie and Joanna, and brothers Dorrie and Phil. "Katy tore her dress every day, hated sewing and didn't care a button about being called good." But her hoydenish nature cannot be allowed to go unpunished: as the result of disobedience, Katy has an accident which prevents her from walking again for several painful years — "Just for the want of the small 'horse-shoe nail' of obedience". In spite of the author's inability to resist pointing the occasional moral, the atmosphere of the stories is generally liberal and sympathetic with juvenile high-spiritedness. American girl readers must have identified with Clover who, like Laura in the English book, *Holiday House*, resents having her hair wetted and screwed tightly into curl papers. At least in the Carr household this is not a nightly misery but a weekly prettification in honour of the Sabbath. The irritated boredom engendered in nineteenth-century children by enforced Sunday Observance is well conveyed. "Sunday always began with a Bible story, followed by a breakfast of baked beans, which two things were much tangled up in Philly's mind." The rest of the day is filled with morning church, then Sunday School, afternoon readings, and evenings of hymns being repeated aloud by the children to their father and aunt.

Sixteen-year-old Katy, with younger sister Clover, is sent to boarding school in the second book of the series, *What Katy Did At School* (1873). After the Civil War more schools and colleges had been opened to girls so that they could receive training for careers, and economic independence. However the school attended by Katy and Clover seems more concerned with "finishing" young ladies than educating them. Many of the girls are narrow-minded snobs or vacuous flirts. Katy, Clover and a lively senator's daughter, Rosamond Redding (Rose Red) soon create a more wholesome atmosphere in the school; but Katy's popularity is resented by Miss Jane, a waspish teacher soured through her long and unfulfilling engagement to a missionary. She unjustly disgraces and punishes the Carr sisters. Even when the incident is forgotten by most of the school, there remains "a sore spot in Katy's heart, and one page in Rose Red's album, upon which … were written these words, headed by an appalling skull and crossbones in pen-and-ink: 'N.B. PAY MISS JANE OFF'."

It would be difficult to imagine a young girl in one of Charlotte Yonge's stories of the same period being allowed to debunk a pompous adult in a position of authority, but Rose Red gets away

Picture by K. Lucas for What Katy Did at School *by Susan Coolidge 1874*

with it. Her memory is long: months later on 14 February Miss Jane receives a curious Valentine, which is hardly in the best of taste. It is in verse and purports to come from a cannibal who has just eaten Mr Hardhack (Miss Jane's missionary fiancé). The Valentine contains a supposed lock of his hair, together with the recipe by which the tribe cooked him; also a testimonial to the effect that they found him "very nice" and that "he turned out quite tender". Rose Red's enterprise typifies the confidence and independence of the American girl.

What Katy Did Next was published in 1886 and Rose Red, exuberant as ever, is by then married and the mother of a baby girl. Katy does the grand trip to Europe where she meets a young US naval lieutenant to whom she becomes engaged. Further books about the Carr family were *Clover* (1888) and *In The High Valley* (1891). Like *Little Women* and its sequels, these stories are still popular today.

The reading horizons of American children were widened by an attractively illustrated 90-page monthly journal, *St Nicholas*, which was started by Mary Mapes Dodge in 1873, and edited by her until she died in 1905. Mrs Dodge, who was an excellent editor, had written a best-selling book for children in 1865, *Hans Brinker: Or The Silver Skates*. *St Nicholas* ran for over 70 years and as well as fiction it contains factual articles which give a vivid picture of customs and attitudes peculiar to various parts of America. National pride is much in evidence, and a feature in 1901 about the USA's patent laws begins: "While there are in other countries, perhaps in all other countries, people as clever as any in the United States, no other country has so many clever people as our own. ... It has been the good fortune of the United States to have had for at least two hundred years a population more intelligent and better educated than that of any other country."

But a few years earlier in 1887 *St Nicholas* had dwelt upon harsher realities of American life. General Adam Badeau contributed six accounts of Civil War battles, stirringly written to appeal to the imagination of youth, which produced vigorous controversy in the magazine's correspondence pages. The war had been over for twenty years but memories were still raw for many parents of the children who read *St Nicholas*: although published by the Century Co. in New York, it was presumably distributed all over the United States, including the still smarting south. General Badeau's articles praise the courage of Union generals Grant, Sherman and Sheridan, and the legendary Robert E. Lee and Stonewall Jackson from the Confederate states: Sherman's famous march through Georgia is glorified, in spite of the devastation which it inflicted on homes and farms in the south. A bitter letter in the August 1887 issue points out that these articles are unedifying reading for children in any of the American states, and quotes instances of pillaging by Union soldiers which resulted in starvation and death for people in the south. The grim note struck by this letter is in marked contrast with the mood of 24 other letters published in the same correspondence pages, most of which were in unadulterated praise of Frances Hodgson Burnett's recently ended *St Nicholas* serial, *Little Lord Fauntleroy*.

St Nicholas catered for a wide age range and many of its stories for older children probably appealed more to boys than girls. Wild West and Red Indian adventures appear regularly, and there are animal stories by the English-born Ernest Thompson Seton, who emigrated to Canada in childhood with his family. Some years later his nature lore was to inspire the founders of the American Camp Fire Girls' Movement. (See chapter 10.) Some of the girls' stories contained copybook maxims: "All that glisters is not gold", and stressed at the same time that "homely virtues" should not be underrated. But independence is far and away the most popular theme, even at practical levels, as fourteen-year-old girls are encouraged to master all the problems of maintaining their own wardrobes. Girls as well as boys are urged to be adventurous in their careers, and unlike Mrs Walton and *The Girl's Own Paper* in England at the same time, *St Nicholas* is full of respect and admiration for girl performers in the theatre. Women and girls driving plunging horses in circus chariot races come in for their share of praise, and Ardressi, a male trapeze artist, explains how he has made acrobats of his wife and daughter, and "… that any ordinary woman may become a good trapeze performer in a few months if she has the right instruction." Shorts by Louisa Alcott describe girls earning their living through artistic and musical careers, and there are features on the work of competent young women stenographers. The invention of the typewriter in the1870s had added a new and more rewarding woman's occupation to those already available in factories, shops and domestic service.

Greater economic independence for women increased their demand for political rights, but the new desperation which had entered the battle for women's suffrage after the Civil War produced only limited results. Wyoming in 1869 became the first territory to give women the vote, as well as jurors' rights and improved legislation concerning their ownership of property. But many other states were slow to follow this example. As its readers looked forward to the start of the twentieth century, *St Nicholas* published two stories illustrating the strength of the American girl. The first, "Tom Junior —Tomboy" by Izola L. Forrester conveys the tang of the plains and the pioneers; the second, "Miss Arrogance" by Marguerite Stabler, deals with that intriguing phenomenon, the American college girl.

Tom Junior is a teenage girl whose father has deserted the family ranch to take up a political career. The ranch is failing and Tom, with the light of battle in her eyes, goes to Washington and interrupts her senator father at an important political conference. Like a "whiff of the mountain breezes" she sweeps him along with her in "all the cow-boy gossip that lay at her tongue's end" and the senator feels "the old restless longing … to be free, to be king in his own domain … to be in the saddle again … on one of those glorious, helter-skelter whirls in God's free country, with the grandeur of plain and hill around…". The resourceful Tom soon has her father back on the ranch and she, like other heroines in American fiction, is shown as an instigator and not simply a supporter of male-initiated ventures.

Miss Arrogance is a college-girl, Constance Barrowes; this archetypal heroine is classified by superlatives: "richest", "most beautiful" and so on. The real "point" of the story, however, is focused not on a human being but on a white graduation dress. It is a college custom that each dress should be laid out for inspection a week before the graduation ceremony, when it can be admired by "wide-eyed" groups of juniors, "sophs", "freshies" and "preps". Miss Arrogance's dress, of course, "a filmy heap of lace and frills" puts everything else in the shade, and calls forth from each inspection party "a little scream of ecstasy". But Constance Barrowes's friend, Lucy Cobb, possesses only a common muslin, with simple hems and few trimmings, which is the best that her poor but loving family can provide. Constance comes out with a few trite words of consolation: a simple dress made with love, she says, means more than anything that money can buy. This story provides an addition to the Victorian "Count your Blessings" genre, but it does have one moment of poignancy which is almost convincing. Miss Arrogance appears at the graduation ceremony wearing instead of the elaborate dress which would have "distinguished the class of '99 for ever … a plain white muslin gown, as nearly like Lucy Cobb's as she had been able to find … ".

Possibly no one except the American college girl can fully appreciate the symbolical import of her white graduation dress. It is a device which frequently recurs in American fiction, where it seems almost as important as the bridal gown – perhaps because it is a token of a step towards independence, that condition eagerly sought by girls in the USA since the time of *Little Women*.

III

Alice and After

"Knowledge is now no more a Fountain seal'd ...
... lift your natures up!
Embrace our aims: work out your freedom, girls!"
(Alfred Lord Tennyson, "The Princess")

Alice's Adventures in Wonderland, published in England in 1865, began to lead children's stories away from sermonizing into more enjoyable areas. Candid and extroverted, Alice was a new type of heroine whose adventures were motivated by curiosity – a quality which most mid-nineteenth-century parents did not encourage in their children. With surprising insight the Reverend Charles Lutwidge Dodgson (Lewis Carroll) – shy, stammering and unmarried – created this sturdy small girl who was to become one of the most popular personalities in fiction. She has been appreciated not only by children but adults, from Queen Victoria to Virginia Woolf, and from historians to hippies. *Alice's Adventures in Wonderland* did not only entertain: in parodies of prevalent nursery poems Lewis Carroll questioned didactic attitudes, and Alice occasionally found herself bewildered in a world of intolerant grown-up characters. In sending Alice down the rabbit-hole her author demanded the recognition of childhood as an adventure to be enjoyed, and not merely a grim training ground for adult life. Early Victorian magazines had demonstrated the solemnity which had been demanded of children, and the morbid concepts with which they were expected to grapple. Lewis Carroll influenced not only his readers but other writers, and a more lively spirit began to infuse girls' fiction. This owed something, however, to increasing educational opportunities.

In the first half of the nineteenth century, stories for girls in

An illustration by Harry Furniss of Alice's Adventures in Wonderland *for Arthur Mee's re-telling in* Children's Encyclopaedia

England were usually concerned with home and family life. They fluctuated between nursery-tale simplicity and the heavy sentimentality of women's novels. By the last two decades of the century, stories of school life and robust adventure in outposts of empire were taking over from hearth and home.

The middle years of the nineteenth century marked many changing attitudes: in the 1850s Charles Darwin's controversial *Origin Of Species* was published. Florence Nightingale in the face of official opposition showed what one determined woman could achieve, when she organized an efficient nursing service in the appalling conditions of the Crimean war; and in the 1860s women at home began their long struggle for the vote. Compassion was increasing for the misfits and outcasts of society – the orphans, cripples and mentally retarded, who earlier had been objects of grotesque derision.

In 1846 improvements were made in elementary education, which had previously been designed to keep the "labouring classes" fit for drudgery in the guise of providing education technically suited to their needs. (Many schools in the early years of the century had taught working-class children to read, but not to write. Reading was useful, as obedience to society's codes could be instilled through instructive moral tales, but writing was considered an inflammatory art for members of the poor.) The fragmentary reforms of 1846 were consolidated by the 1870 Education Act, which gradually expanded the isolated islands of elementary schooling into a national network. To the newly literate, knowledge brought hopes that their circumstances could be transformed. There was soon an avid demand for all kinds of reading material, from "bloods" and romantic novelettes to religious tracts and political manifestoes.

For younger readers from well-to-do families came the monthly magazine *Little Folks,* first published by Cassell in 1871. Invitingly illustrated with line drawings and occasional pages in full colour, it catered, like the American periodical *St Nicholas*, for a wide age-range and for both boys and girls. Pages were set aside for Very Little Folk, with stories carefully and clearly written, like "Ka-tie's Kit-ten" and "Char-ley's Puss-ies"; for those a little older there were fairy stories, "A King Who Couldn't Laugh", "Olga And Rupert In Gnome-Land" etc., and gory adventures for boy readers about Wild West frontier life with threatened death at the hands of "Redskins". Girl heroines, though not yet participating in these hazardous exploits, were beginning to discover learning and comradeship in the new world of school. But many girls who read *Little Folks* in the 1870s were probably still receiving their education from governesses at home, for in spite of the establishment of more girls' schools, society retained its fears of these engendering radical attitudes and immodest behaviour. As long as their daughters stayed at home, parents could supervise their work, play and reading. Domestic skills were stressed and plenty of time was allowed for training in music, dancing and deportment; girls still used backboards to induce uprightness in sitting, standing and walking. In countless well-ordered nurseries little girls were encouraged to play with a variety of dolls – wax, china and stuffed, or wooden Dutch dolls which could be bought for a farthing each. As well as being playthings, dolls strengthened girls' images of themselves as mothers, and making dolls' clothes provided an incentive for more accomplished needlework. Other acceptable pastimes for girls were making scrap albums and collections of pressed leaves and flowers, or playing board-games, marbles, cats-cradle and noughts and crosses. Of course there were also lively nursery games but these could be prevented by mothers or nannies from becoming too hoydenish.

Pity for the suffering was a strong thread running through *Little Folks* from the 1870s until it ceased publication in 1933. From the magazine's early days its readers supported schemes to help poor and sick children. (Later they were to raise thousands of pounds to maintain Little Folks' Home, the Bexhill Branch of Queen's Hospital for Children, Hackney.) Illustrations show a marked contrast between the "Little Lord Fauntleroy" outfits and sailor suits of privileged boys and girls – usually accompanied by well-starched nurses or maid-servants – and the soggy-looking clothes of artisan children. There are cheerfully grimy working boys wearing clothes which call to mind "chimney boys" like Tom in Kingsley's *The Water Babies.* These characters are shabby but irreproachably industrious, and their female counterparts are small flower-girls, wearing broken boots, curiously bunchy dresses and ragged shawls. In a sentimental, illustrated poem a flower-girl is talking with a barefoot urchin, who carries a broom: he asks if he might smell a bunch of her violets, sadly explaining that he cannot possibly consider buying because

> Mother's ill, and trade is bad
> (Only twopence earned today);
> Folks forget the sweeper lad
> When the streets grow warm and gay . ....

Some of the real-life abandoned orphans who provided the

inspiration for many stock characters in Victorian fiction eked out a livelihood by sweeping roads and pavements, and begging pennies from passers-by for their services. In *Little Folks,* street arabs are portrayed as honest little citizens, who know their place and are grateful for the meagre patronage they receive from their "betters": Dickens provided a more accurate picture of these hungry, desperate children, often driven to theft and violence, and of the slums which created them. Charles Kingsley's *The Water Babies* (1863) also aroused public protest against the exploitation of boy chimney sweeps who were forced to climb narrow and dangerous flues, to clean out the soot. Earlier preventive legislation had not been implemented, but this was made more effective in Acts passed in 1864 and 1875, largely as a result of Kingsley's book. Increasing awareness of the plight of deprived children brought about the formation of the Society for the Prevention of Cruelty to Children in 1884.

Little Folks did its best to foster sympathy in its readers not only for abused and over-worked children but for animals. It published numerous stories which movingly described the rapport between man and his faithful dog, a theme still guaranteed to appeal to most children. These animal stories might have been inspired by Anna Sewell's *Black Beauty*, first published in 1877, in which compassion is the guiding spirit. Anna was born at Yarmouth of a Quaker family, and became painfully crippled as the result of a fall in childhood. This made her especially sympathetic with horses whose spirits – to say nothing of their backs – were often broken by brutal treatment. *Black Beauty* contains an early and rare example of an outcry against blood-sports. Beauty and his mother witness a hunt where the hare is torn and bleeding after being savaged by hounds, and one of the riders is thrown and killed. " 'And serve him right, too,' " declares one of the colts, while even the older, more conformist mother of Black Beauty is provoked into saying: " '… though I am an old horse, and have seen and heard a great deal, I never yet could make out why men are so fond of this sport. They often hurt themselves, spoil good horses, and tear up the field: and all this for a hare, a fox or a stag that they could get more easily some other way. But we are only horses, and don't understand.' "

Anna Sewell's invalidism progressed and she died soon after the publication of *Black Beauty*. Even at her funeral the horses drawing the hearse were held in check by the hated bearing reins, until Anna's mother ordered their removal. *Black Beauty* for nearly a hundred years has furthered the cause of animal protection and is still widely read throughout the world. It was the forerunner of the horse and pony story which has reached its peak in girls' books and periodicals of recent years.

As well as indicting cruelty to animals, Anna Sewell touched on other squalid aspects of Victorian life which cried out for reform. Better conditions for many workers were created during the 1860s and '70s because of Britain's trading prosperity and the growth of the Co-operative and Trades Union movements. Wages, however, were still extremely inadequate and there was no social security. Black Beauty becomes a cab horse and his master tackles another driver, "Seedy Sam", about the way he overworks his horse. The man replies that because fares are low he has no alternative: if the horse works less his family will starve. Already he and his children often go hungry though he works fourteen or sixteen hours a day, seven days a week. " '… tis mockery to tell a man that he must not overwork his horse. … You must put your wife and children before the horse. … There's wrong lying somewhere – never a day's rest, never a quiet hour with the wife and children. I often feel like an old man, though I'm only forty-five… .' " A few days later poor "Seedy Sam" is dead, after raving and moaning his last words: " 'I never had a Sunday's rest.' " Premature death and ill-health were commonplace in the back-to-back houses and damp basements into which many families were still crowded.

In 1891 two *Little Folks* serials appeared which had a special appeal for girl readers. These were *A Pair Of Pickles* by Evelyn Everett Green, a popular writer of girls' books from the 1880s to the early 1930s, and *Four On An Island* by L. T. Meade. (This author published almost 250 novels and with her interest in college life anticipated the girls' school story genre. It is noteworthy that Angela Brazil, who became the chronicler *par excellence* of schoolgirls' adventures a generation later, mentions in her autobiography how much she enjoyed *Little Folks* and especially L. T. Meade's stories.)

Evelyn Everett Green in *A Pair Of Pickles* writes about two orphan boys, one rich and the other poor, who through adoption live together as brothers in the care of an elderly lady. But like most children's fiction this story emphasizes that it takes a man to manage boys: Lionel and Benjie soon become spoiled, so a tutor is suggested. Both boys resist this innovation until Lionel is persuaded by Violet, a small girl acquaintance, that the tutor will prepare him for those masculine sports he will one day pursue at Eton. But when Lionel tells Benjie " '... Violet is older than me – she knows best' ", the younger boy's response typifies nineteenth-century male prejudice:

> "No, she doesn't – 'cause she's a girl – girls are no good, and boys didn't ought to do what they tell them. Women are to obey men. Men don't have to obey women – everybody knows that."
>
> "Well, Benjie, the Queen is a lady; and men obey her, I suppose."

Though possibly gratifying to boy readers, this was rather hard on Evelyn Everett Green's audience of girls, especially as arrogant little Benjie's belief in male supremacy remains unshaken by this reference to the authority of their monarch. " 'Well, the Queen has to obey Parliament – and Parliament is men. If I go to ... Parliament with you some day, Li, the Queen will have to obey *me*.' " The more moderate Lionel is slightly shocked and lamely defends the Queen by saying that ever since she was a little girl she has tried hard to be good, and that those who rule "ought to be very good indeed".

Queen Victoria deserved Benjie's dismissal: during her reign when feminist pioneers were campaigning energetically she remained aloof, regarding their efforts as vulgar displays in support of a passing and unworthy fad. Instead of helping to improve the status of women in Britain, their Queen and Empress preferred to prolong the *hausfrau* tradition, even suggesting that one well-known suffragette deserved a good whipping.

Evelyn Everett Green was versatile, and as well as writing girls' stories had studied at the Royal Academy of Music and later followed a nursing career. It is a far cry from her *Pair of Pickles* in velvet suits, sashes and lace collars to her historical adventures, where death and torture are not neglected. She wrote for many years and added to the tomboy traditions of girls' fiction with *A Difficult Daughter* (1930). Vivian, the only daughter of Lord and Lady Lyon, unexpectedly shatters the peace of her conventional aunt's home one day:

> Pacing at her side was a noble blood-hound as large as a calf, and held by a leash in her hand was a strange creature. [This turns out to be a cheetah.]
>
> "O Aunt Etty!" cried a clear young voice, full of audacious laughter, " I hope you don't mind – but I've run away! I just couldn't stand it any longer – all the lectures I was getting. I just cut and ran, and here I am …".

To many nineteenth-century authors, tomboyishness in their heroines was acceptable as long as it was outgrown once adulthood was reached. For L. T. Meade it was tied up with the qualities of resourcefulness and independence, as she shows in *Four On An Island*. This *Little Folks* serial describes the adventures of a group of children between the ages of nine and fourteen who go adrift in the darkness on a shark-infested sea. With considerable courage and improvisation the older boy and girl manage to bring their battered little boat and crew to safety on the shores of a rocky coast. Here they learn how to cope with hostile creatures and the elements. Isobel, the elder girl of the party, finds that her athletic tendencies stand her in good stead. " 'What a good thing that I was always as much boy as girl!' said Bell with a quiet smile. 'Oh dear! My mistress at the old school in England used to prophesy all kinds of bad things of me because I would climb trees…'."

L. T. Meade's main concern is with these "old schools in England": in fact they were not so old, because her books were reflecting the awakening pride felt by contemporary girls in schools and colleges only recently available to them. Between the 1840s and the 1870s, colleges for women were started in London, Cheltenham, Cambridge and Oxford. Maria Grey and her sister founded the Girls' Public Day School Trust in 1872, and by 1891 it had established 36 schools. Just as working men struggling for literacy equated the growth of education with a kind of freedom, girls and women of the middle and upper classes were finding that secondary school and college life suggested new ideas of fulfilment to them in the shape of career possibilities. John Stuart Mill's *The Subjection Of Women,* published in 1869, had resulted in increased support from both men and women for the feminist movement, and its early successes were in the field of education rather than politics. The 1867 Reform Act had extended parliamentary franchise to include many working men, but suffrage and participation in government were still denied to all British women. In spite of its distrust of intelligent women, Victorian society had produced an abundant crop of them. Elizabeth Garrett Anderson made history by being the first woman doctor to practise in England; Annie Besant, feminist, radical and birth-control crusader, provided a somewhat alarming, disruptive image for women's revolt against convention. And of course there were the nineteenth-century women writers: the highly-charged Brontë sisters, the socially conscious Mrs Gaskell and the masterly George Eliot. These had very little practical effect on writers like L. T. Meade: she pronounces *Jane Eyre* unsuitable for the young girls at her fictional Lavender House, a school which she created in *A World Of Girls* (1886). At Lavender House "sounds of laughter and merriment filled the air: the garden was all alive with gay young figures running here and there. Girls stood in groups under the horse-chestnut tree – girls walked two and two up the shady walk at the end of the garden – little ones gambolled and rolled on the grass – a tennis match was going on vigorously, and the croquet ground was occupied by girls of the middle school."

At this sentimentalized school, girls who misbehave are tamed by their intolerably worthy headmistress, a Mrs Willis, who sings to her pupils, reads them stories and kisses them good-night for their Sunday treat: this "mother-kiss and a murmured blessing" sets the girls up for the coming week full of good and worthwhile resolutions.

Illustration to A World of Girls *by L. T. Meade, 1886*

No doubt the author hoped that this kind of smothering dialogue would have the effect of encouraging readers to "respect", even to "love", the adults set in authority over them. This is the type of mawkishness which was swept out of girls' school stories by Angela Brazil and writers who followed her. L.T. Meade's girls, however, did play games (see above), though always decorously. By the end of the century, in fact, far more emphasis was being placed on sport at girls' schools and colleges. The crinoline had been replaced by less hampering skirts which permitted, as well as the staid croquet, energetic games like tennis: at some schools hockey, lacrosse and netball were taught and early versions of the gym tunic were introduced with skirts shorter than those used for normal wear. In childhood and adolescence girls' bodies still tended to be well hidden from men by woollen underwear and plenty of petticoats, but married women were beginning to leave off their corsets, when at home, and to wear unrestrictive tea gowns. The tremendous popularity of bicycling prompted the resurrection of the Bloomer in the late 1880s, but it was too radical a fashion to be widely adopted.

L.T. Meade's *A Sweet Girl Graduate,* however (also published in 1886 by Cassell) did have her own ideas of independence. Nineteen-year-old Priscilla Peel goes to St Benet's College for Women to train as a teacher, and eventually to provide for herself and her younger sister. (Not surprisingly they are orphaned and impoverished.) Her aunt encourages this ambition, though she "doesn't hold with the present craze about women's education". (There are many indications in contemporary stories and articles that higher education for women and girls was considered to be nothing more than a temporary aberration preceding a general drift back to domesticity.) Priscilla is befriended at college by Maggie Oliphant, a brilliant, unstable girl, who also is an orphan, but very rich. Maggie is one of those hot-blooded heroines for whom L. T. Meade has a great predilection. They appear in several of her books as a foil for more sober girls, by whose virtuousness they are moulded into acquiescent personalities. This was all part of the tomboy-taming process accepted by writers and readers of nineteenth-century girls' fiction: if the wild ones were not subdued by the influence of their friends or family, religious conversion or falling in love could be relied upon to bring about the inevitable character transformation.

L. T. Meade's own ideas of progressiveness were limited: it is clear that she considered herself enlightened in allowing her fictional students to hold cocoa parties in one another's bedrooms, wear white silk dresses, velvets and sables, and even meet up with male students. Passion, however, is largely confined to friendships between the girls – who exchange photographs, kiss, and behave generally towards one another with unnatural intensity. It is in the author's attitude to these friendships that the fusty tone of the books is crystallized. She has tried to redress this by stressing the students' ambitions, and joy in learning, underlined in their dramatic presentation of Tennyson's poem, "The Princess".

Tennyson's rather surprising outburst in support of feminism also provides the theme of a literary competition in the *Girl's Realm* magazine during 1899. It is headed "The women question in poetry fifty years ago", and the editor explains that "The Princess" was written in 1847 when " ... the air was full of the revolutionary spirit though some earnest pioneers of the woman's movement object that it is not sufficiently serious". Readers are invited to submit essays on the poet's vision of a college where women learn to live "for and by themselves": the editor stresses that although the princess and her maidens failed in their efforts to become independent of men – "because of the love of the man for the maid ..." – they nevertheless failed "tenderly, beautifully and nobly". According to the *Girl's Realm* Tennyson managed to vindicate both old and new ideals by establishing "... love, based upon a true intellectual, or rather spiritual, equality between woman and man".

Feminists in the 1890s wanted more than poetic expressions of spiritual equality between the sexes, which were meaningless as long as disproportionate educational, economic and political opportunities continued. Since the publication of "The Princess" some progress had been made in the provision of education for girls. Also in 1870 and 1882 Parliament had passed the Married Women's Property Acts which at last recognized that a wife had the right to own property: more women from both the middle and working classes were looking for careers outside their homes and some measure of economic independence. But in spite of nearly 40 years of constitutional agitation women were still completely denied political rights, and beginning to demand the last resort of militant action to achieve their aims.

Although the *Girl's Realm* encouraged its readers to discuss the new rôle of women in society, it was never radical enough to affront their parents. To give girls a sense of participation the magazine arranged frequent competitions which encouraged them to write on a wide range of subjects. L. T. Meade had headed an authors' popularity poll organized by the *Girl's Realm* in 1898 and Evelyn Everett Green stood high on the list, together with Charlotte M. Yonge, Rosa Nouchette Carey, Mrs Molesworth and Frances Hodgson Burnett. The paper awarded a prize of a £20 Lady's "Swift" bicycle to the reader "who named the six writers found by the general vote of the competitors to be the most popular". The bicycle was a happy choice for this prize, suggesting modernity and liberating athleticism to girls on the threshold of the new century. The editor proudly announced that contributions from all these writers would appear shortly in the paper, and as well as some of their stories, the *Girl's Realm* featured articles about their girlhood, with facsimiles of manuscripts and portraits. More than one of these authors had been subjected in childhood to a parental embargo on writing, and denied supplies of paper. In the middle of the nineteenth century, writing – like the stage – had not been considered a suitably modest profession for girls.

The *Girl's Realm* has no fears that women authors might be subversive. "In the novels by the six ladies you have crowned there are the presentation of some of the sweetest, bravest and noblest types of girlhood." One of these chosen writers was of course Mrs Molesworth, and the magazine quotes her as saying that it is healthier for children to read fairy stories than tales of ordinary life, which might lead them to compare themselves with fictional heroes and heroines. There could surely be little in Mrs Molesworth's own gentle stories to disturb the young. She was born in 1839 and lived until 1921, writing in the region of a hundred books, some of which are

Girls allowed to share adventures with boys in L. T. Meade's "Four on an Island", Little Folks, *1891*

still in print today. Although best known for her stories about young children, Mrs Molesworth wrote for older girls as well. *Imogen or Only Eighteen* (1892) describes the mental agonies of a young woman who is the victim of a hoax. Imogen Wentworth and her vacuous mother go to stay with wealthy friends at Grey Fells Hall. It is a "coming out" for Imogen, who has just left school. She meets a Major Winchester, who takes up a friendly, protective attitude towards her. Imogen is tricked by two jealous girls into thinking that the major has proposed to her by letter. When the truth is later discovered, she undergoes severe depression and illness, caused by shame at becoming involved in such an indelicate situation. It is difficult for modern readers to understand what all the fuss is about: Imogen's problem is that she is more worried about society's artificially erected standards than her own genuine feelings. But Mrs Molesworth, like many of her contemporaries, is particularly concerned with "correct" behaviour and gives tremendous importance to "good breeding" in both children and adults. Morals are sedulously pointed. In *The Carved Lions* nine-year-old Geraldine Haddon runs away from her lonely and bewildering life at boarding school. In spite of her distress and haste, Geraldine is so well-schooled in practical behaviour that she takes the trouble first to dress "... as sensibly as if she had been a grown-up person..." choosing "... thickest boots and warm jacket, and arming [herself] with ... waterproof cape and umbrella". Readers of *The Carved Lions* would not be surprised at Geraldine's thoroughness: in middle-class Victorian families no self-respecting small girl would go out without remembering to put on her bonnet, gloves, boots and – according to the appropriate season – shawl or parasol. Mrs Molesworth's heroines, if driven hard enough by circumstances, might take destiny into their own hands and run away. However they are seeking not adventure, but domestic security. In *My New Home* Helena is another young girl who takes this drastic step because she feels neglected, and is afraid of being sent away to boarding school. Her flight is an attempt to recapture the happiness of her former home, where she and her grandmother-guardian had been devoted to each other.

Mrs Molesworth did not share the growing feeling in girls' fiction that school was exciting and liberating. Home seemed to her the only domain for girls and women of all ages, and her heroines were permitted no more than the merest hint of rebellion against the established order. In *Greyling Towers* the girls of the family are discussing their routine at home which seems so much less rewarding than that of their brother who looks forward to going away to school:

> "It isn't only about today being rainy that I mind," the elder little sister went on, "It's all our life! I do think it is dull. One day after another much the same. Breakfast, dinner and tea – history, jography, French, writing, sums; going to bed and getting up, and then all beginning again just the same."
>
> "There's dancing twice a week," said Viva, rather timidly … "and there's holidays sometimes."

Bessie Marchant, whose first stories were published in the 1890s, specialized in depicting girls who were not the slaves of destiny. Her intrepid teenagers saw the old century out with a flourish, dashing off in search of adventure to all corners of the globe. Bessie Marchant's "winds of change" braced girls' fiction for the impact of the Edwardian new woman, who was soon to follow. Marchant has been called "the girls' Henty" and her vigorous stories contain some of the excitement of that author's books for boys. But since her books *were* written for girls, whose place in late Victorian society was perilously ambivalent, she was been unable to break with tradition in too revolutionary a manner. She continued writing until just before her death in the 1940s and produced some 150 books. Her stories take place in India, Canada, Borneo, Persia, South America, Russia and other exotic locations.

The Half Moon Girl or The Rajah's Daughter (1898) recounts the adventures of two teenage girls from widely differing backgrounds, each of whom is in pursuit of her own kind of freedom, and whose paths eventually cross. The orphaned Song, daughter of a rajah in Borneo, is sold by her guardian to a ruthless Chinese skin

One of Bessie Marchant's less fortunate heroines (from The Half Moon Girl, *1898)*

trader: in a desperate effort to escape, she goes into the jungle disguised in the skin of an orang-outang. In England Hester Dayrell determines to join an expedition setting out for Borneo to find a specimen of orang-outang "as the missing link in the Darwinian theory". (Science was becoming a respectable study, even for girls, at the end of the century.) Friends protest against Hester's undertaking "... the toil and terror of journeying among savages like the Borneans ... though had she been a boy they would not have demurred". Hester observes, " 'Everything is wrong ... when one has the misfortune to be a girl ... ' ", but by tact and clever management she achieves her objective. In Borneo amongst malarial swamps and head-hunting tribes Hester encounters what she at first takes to be an orang-outang: as it is walking upright and holding a stick she is convinced that it is indeed the missing link needed to complete the evolutionary chain. But of course it turns out to be Song, who is at the end of her endurance and glad to find a compassionate female friend. By contrasting the hopeless position of the outcast Eastern girl with the young English woman's determination to widen her own experience, Bessie Marchant emphasizes her conviction that – at least in Europe – girls could look forward to considerable advancement of their status in the new century.

One of her heroines seeks education instead of adventure as a method of liberation. In *A Princess Of Servia* (1912) Mary arrives in Servia after living in Canada, where she has been to college and studied French, Latin and Greek. She soon learns that in Servia a woman's situation is very different, and that the greatest opponents of freedom for girls are often to be found amongst older members of their own sex. Mary's aunt forbids her to continue her studies, considering that this would set a dangerous precedent for other young women in the community: "'You can never be sure what they will do in these days of compulsory education: when every child, however poor, is compelled to learn how to read and write, there is endless temptation to idleness …'." Mary manages to overcome these reactionary objections but her studies are soon curtailed when she has to impersonate the princess to save her from being kidnapped. She is plunged into action and murderous intrigue to which the decorous heroines of girls' fiction only a few decades earlier would never have been subjected. Bessie Marchant's stories contain many inconsistencies but she is able to sustain a sense of atmosphere: readers can almost hear the swords jangling and horses snorting in frantic chases across the snow by heroes and villains in Cossack hats, swirling moustaches, long coats and high boots. Typifying the new status which girls were demanding at the beginning of the twentieth century, Mary meets every challenge with courage and intelligence. "… with a dauntless air and flashing eyes …" she faces abductors, drunken soldiers and killer bandits, and rides for her life and freedom across the bleak terrain of Servia. She is eventually flung into the arms of Paul, the man she has learned to love, and they start their new life together in Canada, which Bessie Marchant sees as the Land of Promise.

England provides a less bizarre background to some of her stories, but even here Bessie Marchant's heroines are sure to meet with adventure. Paradoxically war, which essentially opposes so many of women's basic interests, has led more than once to increased career opportunities; girls' fiction writers have been quick to exploit these. *A Girl Munition Worker* (1916) introduces readers to Deborah Lynch, who with "… fiery zeal and red-hot patriotism" not only "walks with death" in the dangerous cordite factory, but uncovers espionage. With a wounded sentry's rifle she takes a pot shot at a light from a window, which is obviously a signal to an approaching zeppelin. The light is extinguished and later one of the factory guards finding "… the tip of a finger that had been literally torn from the hand [of the spy] and that was still warm and bleeding" says grudgingly " 'that … was a fair shot – for a girl!' "

Inspired by the example of Bessie Marchant's heroines, girls were beginning to question the truth of Charles Kingsley's "… Men Must Work and Women Must Weep …": no longer content to be simply backers-up of male empire builders, girls were seeking new worlds of their own to conquer.

IV

Rags to Riches and Riches to Rags

"Magic is always pushing and drawing and making things out of nothing."
(Frances Hodgson Burnett, *The Secret Garden*)

Girl's Realm readers had voted Frances Hodgson Burnett one of their favourite authors, and in 1898 the magazine invited her to describe the special challenges which the approaching new century might offer to girls. Bessie Marchant – although rather less "serious" – would possibly have been a more appropriate choice for this assignment. Her stories at least attempted to express positive attitudes towards the social changes demanded by contemporary women and girls. However in 1898 Frances Hodgson Burnett had been an established and acclaimed author for over twenty years while Bessie Marchant's work had not yet achieved respectable recognition. In spite of its occasional lapses into sentimentality, Mrs Burnett's writing was on the whole robust enough to bridge the gap between Victorian contentment with the *status quo* and the more independent spirit of the twentieth century.

In "The Makers Of The Twentieth Century" *(Girl's Realm,* 1898) she considers pioneers of past generations as well as future leaders. Impressed by the democratic atmosphere of the USA – to which she emigrated from Manchester at the age of sixteen – Frances Hodgson Burnett reflects that every child in the eighth grade of any ordinary American school will either make or mar the new century. With characteristic and dramatic rhetoric she urges her girl readers to shoulder their particular responsibilities in working for a better world: "… if you refuse to do the work Life gave you to do, it is *your* fault, not Life's, not Nature's, not Fortune's. Yours! Yours! Yours!" This is stirring stuff but, as Mrs Burnett neglected to define these exciting duties, readers probably interpreted them as being domestic rather than political or radical. This writer's strong sense of drama erupts frequently, and the article mentions her attraction to a youthful benefactor of mankind who has been cut off suddenly from life at the age of fifteen. Leland Stanford, the son of an American multi-millionaire, had expressed a wish that less fortunate young people could share his own educational opportunities: after his death Leland's parents had built Stanford, "… one of the noblest colleges in America" where "… any boy can go … and make of himself the best there is in him". (But only boys: although more and more American girls were seeking higher education most of them were still waiting vainly for the chance to bring out "the best" that was locked inside them.)

Frances Hodgson Burnett praises Michelangelo for bringing beauty to the world, Dr Edward Jenner, the discoverer of vaccination against smallpox, and Dr Simpson of Edinburgh, who introduced the use of chloroform as an anaesthetic. "The man who adds happiness to life is a king: the man who removes anguish is a god." Gods and magic are recurring and closely related preoccupations with Mrs Burnett, though in her stories these are skilfully grafted on to prosaic and believable backgrounds. Ironically, in this article addressed to girls, the author does not single out any women in history for special mention. Possibly in the eyes of her readers she repairs this omission by choosing Queen Victoria to represent girl builders of the future "… not only because she is Queen of England" but because of the "dedicated manner" in which she accepted the "almost awful" responsibility thrust upon her during girlhood.

Mrs Burnett not only admired Queen Victoria but had a soft spot for most princesses, whether real or fictional. This was matched by her interest in Cinderellas and transformations, themes which are almost as popular in girls' fiction today as in early Victorian novels about abandoned street waifs eventually finding shelter and affection. She is adept at bringing about reversals of circumstance and character; her heroines sometimes are taken from riches to rags and back again in the same story. Cinderella situations occur in her best-known books, *Little Lord Fauntleroy, A Little Princess* and *The Secret Garden.* Mrs Burnett continues in this mood even when writing about dolls *(Racketty Packetty House*, 1907). In a small girl's nursery the inhabitants of an old, neglected "Racketty Packetty" dolls' house are in rags whilst those who live in the new Tidy Castle are glossy and aristocratic. Always under the threat of destruction, the Racketty Packettys are saved by the intervention of a young princess. She is delighted with the old-fashioned house and Dutch dolls, as they remind her of a similar establishment treasured by her grandmamma (Queen Victoria again!) and the Racketty Packettys go to live with the princess in her palace.

The Cinderella quality existed too in Mrs Burnett's own life: after a period of poverty in childhood she earned money by her literary efforts. Frances Hodgson was born in Manchester in 1849, and after her father died leaving a widow with five children to bring up, the family was badly off for many years. When she was young, Frances enjoyed making up stories and like Sara Crewe, her Little Princess, she related these to

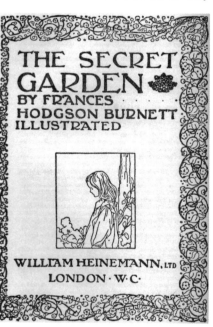

Title Page by Charles Robinson, 1911

friends who could not get enough of them. In nineteenth-century Manchester's stark industrial atmosphere Frances developed her flair for discovering magic in ordinary life. According to the *Girl's Realm* she was denied writing paper because her mother feared that

*Mary, Colin and Dickon when the Secret Garden begins to flower again
(illustration by Charles Robinson)*

Frances's "scribbling" would interfere with her studies, but this veto did not act as a deterrent, for she resorted to writing on the margins of discarded tradesmen's order books (this story may be apocryphal, a polite version of the old masterpiece-written-on-lavatory-paper notion). After going to live in America in 1865 she continued to write stories set in Manchester, which were published in *Godey's Magazine* and other journals. The labouring classes of her native city inspired her first and extremely successful novel, *That Lass O' Lowrie's,* which came out in 1876. This almost certainly owed its derivation also to the first novel of an earlier woman writer, Mrs Gaskell, who like Frances Hodgson Burnett wrote from personal knowledge of the privations of working-class families in Manchester. The action of *Mary Barton* takes place in the "Hungry Forties" against a background of starvation wages, strikes and rioting: Mrs Gaskell dramatically portrays the fight for survival which the cotton operatives have to wage against the mill-owners at a time when it was not uncommon for whole families to "clem" (starve) to death. As the wife of a compassionate Unitarian minister, Mrs Gaskell had seen decent working men driven to violence and drunkenness as a result of degradation – "the miserable home and the desolate future" – forced on them by a dehumanized society. "Many a penny that would have gone little way enough in oatmeal or potatoes bought opium to still the hungry little ones, and make them forget their uneasiness in heavy troubled sleep." Although sympathetic with the workers' independence and determination not to be ground down, in common with many of her liberal middle-class contemporaries, Mrs Gaskell had strong reservations about trade unionism. "Combination is an awful power. It is like the equally mighty agency of steam; capable of almost unlimited good or evil. But to obtain a blessing on its labours, it must work under the direction of a high and intelligent will; incapable of being misled by passion or excitement. The will of the operatives had not been guided to the calmness of wisdom." It was hardly realistic to expect such equilibrium in the chronically undernourished, inadequately clothed, squalidly housed and desperate workmen of the 1840s. In *That Lass O' Lowrie's* Mrs Hodgson Burnett leaves the initiation of reform in the hands of one of the more humane and progressively minded "masters", thus avoiding any controversial discourse on the power of trades unions. Although the Riggan coal-miners are aware that inadequate safety precautions are likely to result in pit explosions, they work on stolidly with "a knowledge of their own helplessness against their fate". Mrs Burnett is mainly concerned with the transformation of Joan Lowrie from coarse pit-girl to "womanly" paragon, fit to become the wife of one of the "masters"; the story's industrial background exists to provide dramatic incident rather than, as in Mrs Gaskell's *Mary Barton* and her later *North And South,* a demand for social reform.

Like Mary Barton, Joan Lowrie is a working-class heroine, who had to be made appealing to the girls from affluent backgrounds who were likely to read the novels of Mrs Gaskell and Mrs Burnett. Both characters were created by middle-class writers, for in spite of the poverty of Frances Hodgson's childhood her father's early prosperity had given her an outlook which was fundamentally different from that of contemporary industrial workers. To be acceptable as heroines with whom middle- and upper-class readers could easily identify, Mary and Joan had to stand apart from the communities which bred them. Mary Barton did so by her unconvincing and unnatural refinement, and Joan Lowrie by her remarkable physical and psychological strength. *Mary Barton* is a more distinctive first novel than *That Lass 0' Lowrie's* but Joan Lowrie emerges as a working-class character of greater cogency than Mary. Mrs Gaskell strikes a false note by a sentimental inflation of Mary's delicate beauty – the "soft deep grey eyes" and "the rich treasure of her golden hair" in whose "warm beams the motes kept dancing up and down". Also Mary is allowed to speak upper-class English whilst her family and associates use rough Lancashire dialects and, to emphasize her more refined nature, Mary becomes a dressmaker's apprentice rather than a factory-girl. Joan Lowrie speaks as broadly as the rest of her work-mates and Mrs Hodgson Burnett has no reservations in making her labour at the pit-head. Joan even goes underground with the otherwise all-male rescue party after a colliery disaster – " 'Let her go lads! She's worth two o' the best on you! Nowt fears her!' " Usually Mrs Burnett resists the temptation of flowery panegyrics on her heroine's virtues, preferring to give her a rather bleak personality. Occasionally, however, an overblown tone does creep in: "Here is a creature with the majesty of a Juno" ... "so superb, so statuesque, and yet so womanly a figure that a thrill shot through the heart of the man watching her". (The model for Joan was a sturdy-looking girl whom Mrs Burnett saw once in a Manchester square, resisting violent threats from her drunken father by looking "... him full in the face without flinching and, going on with her knitting" walking quietly away.)

Perhaps because she was closer to them, Frances Hodgson Burnett's descriptions of contemporary factory and pit-girls are tougher than Mrs Gaskell's. In *Mary Barton* "somewhat loud-talking girls, whose ages might range from twelve to twenty, came by with a buoyant step" and though "not remarkable for beauty" they are redeemed by "an acuteness of intelligence of countenance, which has often been noticed in a manufacturing population...". However the "stunted, overworked girls" in *That Lass 0' Lowrie's* "did not look like women...", they "wore a dress more than half masculine ... talked loudly and discordantly .... had faces as hard and brutal as the hardest of their collier brothers and sweethearts...".

Mary Barton is a virtuous but rather shallow girl who achieves maturity in melodramatic circumstances. The man she loves is falsely accused of murdering the factory-owner's son who also has been attracted to Mary. It is in fact her father John Barton, a "Chartist, Communist, all that is commonly called wild and visionary" who has committed the murder as a gesture of revenge on behalf of the oppressed mill-workers who are striking vainly for a living wage. John Barton, enquiring, intelligent and disillusioned with the hypocrisy of a nominally Christian but exploiting society, is the most rewarding character in Mrs Gaskell's book. Unfortunately his ruggedness is reduced to banality by a deathbed scene which crystallizes Victorian sentimentality at its most crudely unbelievable. In spite of his earlier rejection of religion, Barton has gone back to the Bible for consolation in his last days: Carson, father of the murdered young man, at first meets Barton's plea for forgiveness with hatred and implacable resistance. But the mill-owner undergoes a change of heart, inspired – incredibly – by the sugary and forgiving behaviour of a pretty little girl towards a "rough, rude errand-boy" who has pushed her over in the street. Almost as John Barton draws his last breath Carson rushes to his bedside proclaiming pardon, and sharing the guilt of Barton's crime. "He raised up the powerless frame, and the departing soul looked out of the eyes with gratitude." A little earlier in the story Mrs Gaskell writes: "Rich and poor, masters and men, were then brothers in the deep suffering of the heart!" She returns with more understanding to the theme of interdependence between employers and operatives in her later book, *North And South* (1855). The relationship between John Thornton, a tough but fair-minded mill-owner, and Nicholas Higgins, an independent workman, is described realistically and without sentimentality. Mrs Gaskell is able too to write more authoritatively about the middle-class heroine Margaret Hale in *North And South* than the refined but artisan Mary Barton.

Frances Hodgson Burnett spares her readers the embarrassment of an out-of-character deathbed repentance by Joan's brutal father. Dan Lowrie's plot to maim or murder Joan's admirer, Fergus Derrick, goes awry and rebounds on himself. During his slow and painful death he curses and abuses his daughter as vigorously as he has always done.

That Lass 0' Lowrie's includes one of the most dreary stock ingredients of nineteenth-century fiction – the gullible working girl who is seduced, and of course later abandoned, by a well-to-do lover. " 'Dom such loike chaps, say I. What would they think if working men 'ud coom meddlin' wi' thear lasses.' " Seventeen-year-old Elizabeth Barnes (Liz) features in Mrs Burnett's narrative not so much to point the obvious moral (which could never be hammered home too strongly) but rather to throw into sharp relief Joan's strength of character as Liz's protector, and to illustrate the hypocrisy of the society which rejects the seduced girl. Abused by almost everyone except Joan, Liz goes away for a second time with her unsatisfactory lover, is again abandoned and returns to die melodramatically on Joan's doorstep. Her stupidity seems to endorse an assertion made by Samuel Craddock, an outspoken anti-feminist in the story: " 'Th' female intylect is na strong at th' best.' " Mrs Burnett fortunately disproves this theory in the person of Anice Barholm, the rector's daughter, who organizes "neet skoo" (night school) for the local working women and is far more intelligent than her sententious, bigoted father. Anice's capabilities excite reluctant appreciation from Samuel Craddock who admits that she's " '… a wonderfu' little lass – *fur* a lass, I mun admit. Seems a pity to ha' wasted so much good lad metal on a slip o' a wench, doesna' it?' " This view was commonly held in 1876 when the book was published, even though there was growing acceptance of the fact that girls had minds as well as bodies. Intellectual, artistic and organizational achievements by a woman were still likely to produce surprise that the initiator was female rather than to provoke impartial, critical assessment. Although more at home when creating fairy-tale situations than discussing the status of women, Mrs Burnett in *That Lass O' Lowrie's* shows herself capable of irony. "Young ladies who go out of the ordinary groove are not apt to be attractive to the average English mind. There are conventional societies in which they may indulge – there are Sunday-schools, and rheumatic old women and flannel night-caps and Dorcas societies …". And anything more radical than that was likely to savour of "strong-mindedness and 'reform' – perhaps even politics, and a tendency to advance irregular notions concerning the ballot box …".

To counter-balance Anice Barholm's progressiveness, Mrs Burnett softens Joan's Amazonian tendencies — " 'hoo allus wur a queer-loike, high-handed wench' ". The good old mellowing stand-bys of Victorian writers – religious conversion, romantic love and maternal longing – work their transformation on Joan: this process begins as "… with Liz's sleeping child on her bosom", and an increasing sexual awareness of the upstanding young engineer, Fergus Derrick, Joan confronts a picture of "Christ in the last agony" which "seized on some deep, reluctant emotion" in her.

After the success of *That Lass O' Lowrie's* Mrs Hodgson Burnett produced some 40 novels. Far removed from her monolithic and dour Joan Lowrie were the studies of sweet and amiable diminutiveness which followed. Mrs Burnett contributed several stories to *St Nicholas,* which in 1885 serialized her *Little Lord Fauntleroy,* to the joy of its young readers. It appeared as a book in the following year, when it quickly became a best-seller, and eulogy after eulogy was heaped upon it. Today it is still in print (published in England by Dent Dutton) but to most modern children the words "Little Lord Fauntleroy" are synonymous with "sissy" and equally insulting if used epithetically. This response is rooted in modern distaste for the fussy golden curls and lace-collared velvet suits worn by American-born Cedric Errol, who at seven years of age becomes Lord Fauntleroy. It may owe something also to the fact that in dramatized versions the young aristocrat was represented by a girl (Vera Berringer in the1888 stage version and Mary Pickford in the film of 1922). Freddie Bartholomew, who played the part in Hollywood's 1936 production, did not add sufficient robustness to Cedric's image to make him acceptable. Cedric was inspired by one of the sons of Frances Hodgson's marriage to Dr Swan Burnett, and the story reflects Mrs Burnett's admiration of the more egalitarian structure of American society. Transported from back street poverty in New York to fairy-tale splendour in an English castle – " 'I never saw such a beautiful place. It's prettier even than Central Park' " – Cedric remains unspoiled, republican to the core and rather ashamed of his newly discovered aristocratic background. Most of the Americans in the story are irritatingly honest and lovable in spite of the contempt in which they are held by Cedric's crusty old grandfather, the Earl of Dorincourt, and some of his servants: " 'Wot can he iggspect from a child brought up in pore circumstances in that there low Hamerica?' " Although besotted with Cedric's sweetness, Mrs Burnett cannot resist a demon-king threat to his happiness by introducing rival claimants for his title and estates, but like all Cinderella stories *Little Lord Fauntleroy* ends with the triumph of innocence over evil.

In 1887 *St Nicholas* serialized another of this author's stories of incredibly self-contained children. *Sara Crewe: Or What Happened At Miss Minchin's* attained the same degree of popularity as *Little Lord Fauntleroy*, and in 1902 Mrs Burnett wrote a more dramatic version for a stage production. In 1905 she decided to re-write Sara's adventures for publication, this time based on the play and using its title, *A Little Princess*. Mrs Burnett's passion for princesses and angelic children was at odds with her respect for individuality and democracy. It is obvious that some people from all walks of life possess magnetically attractive qualities which inspire devotion in others, but acceptance of one girl as a "princess" tends to relegate the other members of her school or family community to the inferior status of admirers, imitators and "courtiers". Sara's rather contrived and sometimes implausible princess-like behaviour makes her appeal less lasting and profound than that of Mary and Colin, the plain, occasionally unsympathetic but realistic children in *The Secret Garden*. Sara Crewe's almost magical popularity at Miss Minchin's school – where she is the richest and most indulged pupil – arouses jealousy in some of the meaner girls who abusively dub her the "Little Princess". The title sticks, through good fortune and bad, even when Sara is suddenly reduced to the rôle of scullery maid, errand girl and drudge after her elaborate eleventh birthday party when the school learns of her father's death and bankruptcy. Earlier, as a parlour-boarder, complete with a personal French maid, pony-carriage and a lavish wardrobe, Sara has befriended Becky, an undersized fourteen-year-old orphan who is Miss Minchin's bullied maid of all work. Becky did not appear in the original *Sara Crewe,* but she typifies the loyal, acquiescent, blindly adoring working-class child who knows her "place" and is satisfied to stay there. When she and Sara are "skivvies" on terms of equality in their desolate rat-ridden attic rooms, Sara says

"Oh, Becky ... I told you we were just the same — only two little girls. ... You see how true it is. There's no difference now. I'm not a princess any more."

Sobbing with love and pain [Becky cries] "Yes, miss, you are. ...Whats'ever 'appens to you – whats'ever – you'd be a princess all the same – an' nothin' couldn't make you nothin' different."

Cedric, as Little Lord Fauntleroy
(illustration by Reginald B. Birch, 1886)

Sara defiantly challenges Miss Minchin
(illustration by Reginald B. Birch from Sara Crewe
by Frances Hodgson Burnett, 1888)

Sara's fortunes are astoundingly reversed yet again, when her father's wealthy friend at last finds and adopts her, restoring to Sara all the "princess" trappings of fine clothes, carriages and opportunities to dispense charity to underprivileged children, for whom she now has even more sympathy than before. Significantly, however, Becky, though an equal partner with Sara in the days of drudgery and semi-starvation at Miss Minchin's, does not become a "sister" to the Little Princess, but her "delighted attendant" – in other words, her maid.

In spite of its unlikely situations *A Little Princess* has remained attractive to several generations of readers, because of Mrs Burnett's moments of insight into the minds of her girl characters. In *The Secret Garden,* which was first published in 1911, she shows even deeper perception of childhood. Her heroine is very different from the appealing diminutive lord and "princess" of the earlier books. Mary is sour and self-absorbed, and her inner state is reflected by an unattractive physical appearance of limp hair and yellow skin. At the beginning of the story she is ten years old, and suddenly orphaned as cholera sweeps off both her parents in India, as well as her nurse and almost the whole household of servants. (Frances Hodgson Burnett makes a thorough job of orphaning her characters and establishing completely new environments for them.) Mary goes to live with her uncle, Archibald Craven, in a large house on the edge of the Yorkshire moors, where she is left largely to her own devices as her uncle is withdrawn and often away from home. Some years earlier his wife had died after an accident in the beautiful, walled garden she had made, since when Mr Craven had kept the garden shut up and untended. "Ordinary" children without aspirations to become fairies, angels, gods or princesses must have found it possible to identify with Mary and her cousin Colin, who like themselves knew loneliness, fear, boredom and bad temper. Mr Craven's son Colin is an invalid with a morbid fear of death and of growing a hump-back if he tries to walk about and lead a normal life. Mrs Burnett convincingly portrays the claustrophobic atmosphere of Colin's invalidism and the companionship which grows between him and Mary. Together the two unloved and unlovely children begin to take their destinies into their own hands, and to transform themselves, almost unknowingly, into lively, purposeful people. This is achieved undramatically, through their increasing self-knowledge. They are helped by the secret garden, which they discover and bring back to life, and by Dickon, the young brother of Mary's down-to-earth Yorkshire maidservant. Dickon, though an artisan character, is unlike Joan Lowrie or Becky. He is a bastardized juvenile version of St Francis and Henry David Thoreau, a "nature boy" who whistles and talks to plants to make them grow, and whose animal companions include a fox cub, a squirrel, a crow, a lamb and a white rabbit. Dickon is the least believable component of the story, but acceptable as part of the magical superstructure which Mrs Burnett is able to sustain against commonplace backgrounds.

She competently controls the flowery imagery of the secret garden's transforming influence from getting out of hand, as "... the seeds Dickon and Mary had planted grew as if fairies had tended them", and in Colin and Mary health and vigour begin to flourish. By the end of the book, they are laughing, scuffling, naturalistic children playing together: " 'Aren't you glad, Father? ... I'm going to live for ever and ever and ever!' " The story *is* sentimental but it is skilfully told, and the characters experience the satisfaction of transformation by their own efforts rather than by outside agencies. When – departing from fiction – Mrs Burnett tried to encourage the *Girl's Realm* readers to behave in a similar way, her language became inflated and less convincing: "Then let the young Makers of the Century to come stand upon the threshold of their palace with reverent, glowing souls, clear eyes, strong hands and warm generous hearts."

V

The New Woman and the New Girl

"When love is no more bought or sold, when it is not
a means of making bread, when each woman's life is
filled with earnest, independent labour, then love will
come to her … not sought, but found."

(Olive Schreiner, *The Story Of An African Farm*)

THE *Girl's Own Paper* – like so many things intended for females –
started as an offshoot of Adam's Rib. The Religious Tract Society
was very busy during the last 30 years of the nineteenth century
producing reading matter demanded by the growth of literacy. They
created the *Boy's Own Paper* ("B.O.P.") in 1879 and their brain-
child became a giant which straggled across six reigns, survived
two major wars and inculcated into several generations a belief in
the value of wholesome adventure, cold baths and Christianity. It
achieved immediate success, quickly reaching a circulation of
160,000. This prompted the ever-energetic Religious Tract Society
to bring out a fourteen-page penny weekly for young ladies, the
ambivalently slanted *Girl's Own Paper* ("G.O.P."). From its
beginning in January 1880 until its collapse (in the name of *Heiress)*
in 1956 the creators of "G.O.P." could never quite decide whether
they were writing for girls or for women. There was an exception
for fifteen years from 1931 to 1945 when someone at the Religious
Tract Society had the sense to make the distinction by bringing out
two separate journals: their *Woman's Magazine* then catered for adult
readers whose main interests were considered to be home, family
and fashion; and the "G.O.P.", at a time when schoolgirl fiction was
in its heyday, for a short period lived up to its name.

The magazine's early ambivalence underlined society's attitude to girls in Victorian England. Although it was commonly accepted not only that boys would be boys, but that men often remained boys if given the opportunity, girls were expected to become women early in their lives: not for them the fantasies and freedom of childhood, but rather conditioning as embryonic little mothers and homemakers.

The difference between the atmosphere of "B.O.P." and "G.O.P." is shown by the popularity of G. A. Henty's epic adventures in the former – a typical episode including pictures of a "black" undergoing a whipping by Arabs: "... they flogged him several times till he fainted"; at the time the "G.O.P." was offering its readers domestic fiction, rather drab school stories and gentle anecdotes about the childhood of Queen Victoria.

Whatever their divergencies, one thing both these early boys' and girls' papers shared was their uncompromising attitude to readers who applied to them for personal advice. Any sign of youthful presumption was relentlessly put down, and misspelt, poorly written letters from enquirers seemed, in the eyes of the editors, almost as deserving of condemnation as the frequently discussed "sinful habits" (masturbation) for which hard work, cold baths, rigorous exercise and prayer were recommended under the encouraging heading "Nil Desperandum". Of course some of the questions answered by the "B.O.P." were of a different nature from those received at the "G.O.P." office. Boy readers, if we can judge from their paper's frequent injunctions not to capture wild animals and deprive them of liberty, were constantly seeking information about how to identify, tame and skeletonize beetles, mice and birds. Girls were more interested in obtaining advice on cooking, poetry and music, as well as contemporary manners and moral codes. Superfluous hair, poor complexions and excessive perspiration preoccupied many readers and it seems that nineteenth-century remedies were more drastic than those available today: "You must take a cold bath every morning using Sanitas soap to the armpits, and now and then a solution of borax. Live as well as you can but do not eat too much meat...".

In its early days the "G.O.P." addressed itself to both mistresses and servants. It was not unusual in the same issue to read an article headed "How I Keep House On £350 A Year", and a feature describing the advantages for domestic servants of emigration to remote parts of the empire. "Ten shillings a week is what an ignorant, untaught girl commands [in New Zealand] and any servant ... with a character and experience, will earn £35 to £40 [per annum] as easily as she does £16 to £18 at home." Also "... however plain of feature a lass may be, when in service at a sheep farmer's homestead she is certain of receiving several offers of marriage from steady men, whose wages, including their food, begin at £50 per annum...".

For girls of the "lower orders" domestic service was the employment most encouraged by the "G.O.P." in the 1880s. (As late as 1911 there were in Britain 2,100,000 women in service, far more than in any other work.) For uneducated girls there were few respectable alternatives, and this periodical felt that young women were safer employed in private homes than in shops or factories. The "G.O.P." followed Mrs Octavius Frank Walton's example, imploring girls about to be seduced into theatrical careers to consider the attendant "awful dangers to which they [would be] subjected, body and soul". In 1884 a dramatic article about the work of London theatrical missions elaborates on "the poverty, blighted lives and unnatural excitement of the 21,000 actors and actresses" in "this great wilderness of London... full of pitfalls for the young and ignorant". The theatre missions, we are told, with their appropriate motto, "All Is Not Gold That Glitters", try to bring Christianity into the lives of dancers and actresses, and whenever possible to wean them from their doubtful profession into "respectable trades". Apparently this crusade met with only small success, and sadly: "Once on the stage, those wishing to leave it and to live religious lives found much prejudice from prospective employers." Throughout its long history the magazine returned frequently to the horrors of stage life for girls.

The Religious Tract Society had grudgingly recognized that girls could cope with articles which were mentally stimulating, and a few of these appeared in conjunction with fashion and domestic advice. Considering the period of social ferment which followed its inception, however, the paper's approach was hardly enlightened. Charles Peters

Frontispiece by H. R. Millar, for E. Nesbit's
The Story of the Amulet, *1906*

(who had previously been with Cassells) was the first editor of the "G.O.P." from 1880 until he died in 1907. He soon achieved a greater circulation than the "B.O.P." but as long as he was at the helm the magazine was steered through fairly safe waters, and the challenge of its fiction and features remained acceptable both to the conservative mothers of its younger readers and to the husbands of older ones. (Men as well as women read the "G.O.P." and John Ruskin expressed his admiration of it.)

At the beginning of the twentieth century, Hutchinson's *Girl's Realm,* a "middle-class" magazine aimed at a younger age group than the "G.O.P.", was more progressive. It encouraged readers to become as well educated as possible and to train themselves for careers. As early as 1899 it had published "The Strike Of The Sisters" by Isabel Orman, in which teenage Agatha and Amelia refuse to continue to act as "lady slaves" to their three inconsiderate brothers. "A woman's soul yearns after something higher than the life of eternal drudgery to which she is expected to submit." The girls present their brothers with a bill of feminine rights: this demands that the boys' discarded garments must not be dropped all over the home for the girls to clear up, that shaving apparatus should be put away after use, and that the boys arrive punctually for meals and refrain from scattering cigarette ash over all the furniture. As there is no response to this appeal, the strike lasts for five days but Grannie, who is in charge of the household, eventually blacklegs: " '... it is woman's province to do these little things ... the boys must be made comfortable ... Remember man is woman's superior in every way, and any lowering of their position must of necessity be also a lowering of ours.' " The *Girl's Realm* obviously felt unable to challenge too deeply the strangely suspended life that it was expected most girls would follow once schooldays were over and they waited hopefully for marriage. If they came from sufficiently affluent backgrounds there was often resistance to their going out to work, so intelligent girls stayed at home and felt trapped by meaningless domestic routines.

The sisters in this story consider that sport is one area in which they can express their frustrated energies. Amelia is a first-class bat, Agatha excels at billiards, they both scull and "Agatha can cycle all down Ladbroke Grove and home through Cambridge Gardens without once putting her hands on the handlebars". The *Girl's Realm* was a great believer in the beneficial effects of athletics for girls. Alice Corkran (whose allegorical book *Down The Snow Stairs* had been praised by Charlotte Yonge and other critics) was one of its regular contributors. She sees the contemporary girl as a "sports-loving Amazon .... I often think when I see her scudding along on her bicycle or brandishing racquets, tossing balls aloft, and hitting them as if her life depended upon it, what a deal of fun the girls lost who were not born during the latter half of the nineteenth century."

Unfortunately – apart from a few dedicated pioneers and educationalists – many people still regarded the games and schooling which were becoming more fashionable for girls as occupational therapy or the means of acquiring extra accomplishments to add to their marriageability. Girls wanting serious education often found parents uncooperative. In her autobiographical book, *Testament Of Youth* (1933) Vera Brittain describes her frustrations in 1913 when, having left school, she wants to go to college. She finds life in provincial Buxton a "purposeless-pottering" in a "bridge and dance-dominated atmosphere", where girls' marriage prospects were assessed on "the basis of their popularity as dancing partners". And marriage was the only goal. Vera Brittain's demand for university education was considered "ridiculous ... strong-minded ... and eccentric". " 'How can you send your daughter to college, Mrs Brittain? Don't you want her ever to get married?' "

Vera Brittain was experiencing in real life the difficulties met by H. G. Wells's fictional *Ann Veronica* (1909). She too was an intelligent, bicycling, sporty heroine – who, after leaving school, quickly exhausted the attractions that Edwardian suburban society offered to its middle-class girls. There was "nothing for her to do, except a functionless existence varied by calls, tennis, selected novels, walks and dusting in her father's house". The "valiant fight for Newnham or Somerville" was lost because "her father had met and argued with a Somerville girl at a friend's dinner table, and he thought that sort of thing unsexed a girl". Ann Veronica, however, refuses to accept her brother's summing-up of prevalent attitudes: " 'The world isn't ready for girls to start out on their own yet; that's the plain fact of the case. Babies and females have got to keep hold of somebody or go under – at least for the next few generations.' " Ann Veroinica has the courage to leave the protection of home and achieve some measure of economic and spiritual freedom, although her difficulties in doing this underline the period's resentment of women who were seeking independence. Ann Veronica's search for a rational means of self-assertion, however, has an unintended result: she ends up living with a man to whom she is not married. This was so shocking to the conventions of 1909 that although H. G. Wells's book is a plea for more liberal atittudes, it may have achieved the reverse effect.

The *Girl's Realm* published regular interviews with "Girls Who Excel At Sports", and as early as 1899 it included forward-looking features on gymnastics. These were illustrated by photographs of young women doing "press-ups" – "a capital exercise for girls" – and performing the exercises recommended by Mr Eugen Sandow, "the Strong Man who has fought with and conquered a lion". At his school of physical culture dumb-bells, barbells and other intriguing apparatus are used. A photograph of one of his special exercises for obesity and indigestion shows a girl perilously hanging upside down from chains and pulleys. The article ends with a picture of the paternalistic Strong Man himself resplendent in waxed moustaches and a dark, formal suit. For the benefit of his girl readers he is quoted as saying rather smugly " '… in the old days a warrior did not enter the inner circles of heroes until he had beaten the Amazons' ". The next issue produced further pictures of girls engaged in Indian Club exercises, rope-climbing, vaulting over wooden horses, fencing, performing on parallel bars and throwing themselves through the air on swinging ropes or a trapeze. Disproportionate and bizarre interest in physical culture was part of the desire for modernity. It prompted frequent articles in the national press suggesting that sport was damaging to girls (and particularly to their capacity for producing babies). However many girls' schools continued to accept the advice given by Dr Elizabeth Garrett Anderson in the 1880s and included regular gymnastics in their time-tables.

Although a heavy pleated gym tunic was worn for the purpose in

The Gymnasium of the North London Collegiate School for Girls
(Girl's Own Paper *1882)*

some schools, athletic activities were still generally performed by girls in their everyday restrictive clothing. Vera Brittain deplores Edwardian conventions which "wrapped up my comely adolescent body in woollen combinations, black cashmere stockings, 'liberty' bodice, dark stockinette knickers, flannel petticoat and often, in addition, a long-sleeved, high necked woollen spencer ...". On top of all this, of course, high-collared, tightly cuffed long-sleeved blouses and long skirts were worn.

As well as parading its enthusiasm for sport, the *Girl's Realm* extolled the breezy camaraderie of college life, and the satisfaction for girls of pursuing careers. Its liberality was sometimes offset by its weakness for ideas of:

> A noble type of good
> Heroic womanhood...

of which Florence Nightingale seemed the embodiment. (The *Girl's*

Realm could not leave "The Lady with the Lamp" – or Louisa Alcott and Queen Victoria – alone.) Through the seventeen years of its existence, the magazine featured episodes of Florence Nightingale's life from childhood to old age, when she began to "shed the lustre of her name upon a new century". *Not* quoted in the *Girl's Realm,* though relevant to some of its readers, was Florence Nightingale's remark: "Some forsake marriage, because they sacrifice all other life if they accept that." Married women were still debarred from many careers, and also the frequently claustrophobic atmosphere of Victorian and Edwardian marriages militated against wives working outside their homes except in cases of absolute economic necessity.

By 1914, just before its end, the *Girl's Realm* (at that time published by Cassell) had become more conformist, possibly in a desperate endeavour to increase flagging circulation. Its September 1914 issue contains a degrading example of the type of story sometimes served up to girls. "A Serious Woman", by Eva Bretherton, archly describes its heroine – who is not even given the individuality of a name – as "just twenty-three ... A little woman, plump and round and delightfully, comfortably soft, with tiny dimpled hands and feet like a baby's". Everything else about her is equally and nauseatingly infantile, especially her intellect. She is a pseudo-serious and actually incredibly stupid woman who is meant to typify the author's assessment of those who have embraced the cause of women's suffrage. The hero of the story is the all-tolerant and all-knowing husband. The "little woman" joins the militant Suffragettes and, hurling a hammer through a shop window, injures her husband, who happens to be coming out at that precise moment after buying her an extravagant birthday present. It goes without saying that she is not even adept at window-breaking – " ... hands like a baby's are not the very best kind for effectually wielding a hammer". All this banality gives the husband an opportunity to demonstrate his wisdom and forbearance, and eventually enables the "serious woman" to whisper repentantly as together they coo over their "charming baby's" cot " 'the only things that matter to a woman are close at hand and have nothing to do with votes' ".

After this the *Girl's Realm* deserved to fail. The *Girl's Own Paper* in contrast became increasingly liberal when Flora Klickmann succeeded Charles Peters as editor in 1908. She had already worked on other periodicals after abandoning the musical career she had originally planned. This editor tried to bring a rather fey kind of charm to the "G.O.P.", as well as a wider and more imaginative range of illustrations. These often ran riot across pages of text quite unrelated to them, so that, for instance, an interview with Thomas Edison in 1914 is illustrated by photographs of frolicking kittens.

Flora Klickmann was obsessed with nature and the simplicities of village life: whenever possible she retreated to the whimsically named "Flowerpatch", the home which she shared with her husband in the hills of the Wye Valley. She began to look upon the *Girl's Own Paper* as her metaphorical Flowerpatch, sometimes to the paper's detriment, and continued as editor until her retirement in 1931, after which she enjoyed over twenty years of happy retirement in her Wye Valley home.

Under Flora Klickmann's early editorship, however, the "G.O.P." developed a slightly more forward-looking policy, reflecting the changing structure of Edwardian society. Increasing competition in world markets, the Boer War, demands for better wages and working conditions at home, and the growth of socialism were factors contributing to the shake-up of values in the early years of the twentieth century. In 1903, after 50 frustrating years of constitutional agitation which had got them nowhere, the Suffragettes began their period of militancy. By 1906, in spite of contemptuous comment from many newspapers and periodicals, the campaign led by Emmeline Pankhurst had become too big to be ignored. Although it was predominantly a middle-class movement, newly articulate artisan women were inspired by the example of Annie Kenney, the mill-girl who had thrown in her lot with the Pankhursts. Annie, of course, was referred to as a modern St Joan, the usual epithet for a woman who is "dedicated to a cause".

George Bernard Shaw's *St Joan* (first produced in New York in 1923) actually owes more to a contemporary image of one kind of womanhood – selfless and militant – than to the usual idea of the fifteenth-century peasant girl. Joan, who "refused to accept the specific woman's lot, and dressed and fought and lived as men did" *could* be made out to have affinities with the Edwardian new woman, the sport or tomboy who would rather play a vigorous round of golf with a man than go to bed with him. Shaw in his preface to the play suggests that Joan was burned essentially "for what we call unwomanly and insufferable presumption" and that her heresy was a basic refusal to accept society's conventions, as much as a matter of religious conviction.

By 1910 violence had become an essential element in women's struggle for the vote, as they drew attention to their demands by window smashing, letter-box burning and chaining themselves to railings. The establishment responded in kind by denying imprisoned Suffragettes the rights normally given to common criminals: they had no daily exercise period, and were subjected to the restraints of leather jackets and handcuffs, and the brutality of forcible feeding. The climax of violence came in 1913 when Emily Davison, just released from six months in prison for setting fire to a letter-box, went to the Derby and threw herself under the King's horse, to die a few days later.

The Suffragettes were a gift to humorous writers of their day, and the conservative mainstream of children's fiction suggests that their rating was then much the same as that of witches and vampires. Charles Hamilton, famous as the begetter of Billy Bunter, used to portray them as hefty insensitive harridans, whose comic antics must have been enjoyed by boy readers of the phenomenally popular *Magnet* and *Gem.*

Another children's author who opposed the campaign was Edith Nesbit. She feared that the vote would be obtained only for educated women of the affluent classes who would probably support the Conservative Party and thus delay the fulfilment of socialism. (At that time suffrage was still denied to some of the poorest male members of the community.) In 1884 she and her husband Hubert Bland had become original members of the Fabian Society, which attracted people of the calibre of George Bernard Shaw (with whom Nesbit was once supposed to have been in love), Annie Besant, H. G. Wells and Beatrice and Sydney Webb. The young and attractive Mrs Bland was much admired in Fabian circles, and she revelled in the prospect of a new, expansive socialist-inspired age.

Edith Nesbit was born in 1858, and the quality of her often lonely childhood is described in a series of autobiographical articles which she wrote at the request of the *Girl's Own Paper,* who published them in 1886 and 1897 as *My Schooldays* (reprinted in 1966 under the title *Long Ago When I Was Young).* This delving into personal memory, prompted by the "G.O.P.", seems to have sparked the flame of E. Nesbit's creativity: her first stories about the Bastable children followed soon afterwards in the *Illustrated London News, Pall Mall* and *Windsor* magazines, and she had suddenly at the age of 40 found her true level as a writer. The sentimental poems and articles of Edith Nesbit's earlier years were totally eclipsed by her series of brilliant children's stories.

She was a pioneer in the field of children's literature, just as she was a pioneer in other respects (in cutting her hair short, smoking in public and in the abolition of restrictive clothing, for instance). *The Treasure Seekers* came out at a time when children's fiction was still produced largely by writers whose creative impulse was directed towards the pointing of a moral in the most sanctimonious way. Edith Nesbit was the only children's writer of genius to emerge in the last quarter of the nineteenth century and the only one capable of extending and disciplining the dream-sequence effect of the Alice books. Her fantasies are less allegorical and less rarified, though no less humorous, than Lewis Carroll's, and for this reason her books are better appreciated by the children for whom they were intended. However extraordinary and far-fetched the adventures which befall her fictional children, their lives still remain firmly – and prosaically – rooted in the Lewisham Road or in Camden Town.

Edith Nesbit's own childhood experiences left her with a craving for emotional security. After her marriage, in spite of a veneer of almost flamboyant independence, she clung to Hubert but again this security was denied her. Her husband considered himself "an experimentalist in illicit love" and two of the five children in the Bland household were not Edith's, but Hubert's offspring by Alice Hoatson, the friend and companion who shared their *ménage à trois* for almost 30 years. Another tragic circumstance in Edith's life was the death of her fifteen-year-old son, Fabian, after the administration of an anaesthetic before a minor operation was to take place.

From this somewhat unconventional background E. Nesbit projected in her children's stories the cosiness and security of Edwardian middle-class nursery life. However, readers who enjoy the exploits of the Bastables and her other naturalistic children may occasionally be surprised at the anti-feminist tone which sometimes comes into her books. Her most sympathetic characters are usually boys, whose frequently expressed contempt for their rather insipid sisters is rarely redressed in Nesbit's narratives. "Noel had turned quite pale. He is disgustingly like a girl in some ways." "You may treat girls as well as you like ... but there is something unmanly about the best of girls. They go silly, like milk goes sour, without any warning." *(The Treasure Seekers,* 1899.) It is unlikely that Edith Nesbit herself accepted these assessments of feminine stupidity but she was expressing attitudes which she must have felt would conform with her readers' opinions.

Nevertheless she created one "strong-minded" woman in the person of the Queen of Ancient Babylon in *The Amulet,* which was published in 1906. Cyril, Robert, Anthea and Jane, brothers and sisters in search of an amulet, have visited past cultures, including Babylon, where they have established excellent relations with its Queen. She later arrives in London, in ancient Babylonian dress, causing a sensation in Fitzroy Square. When the Queen demands to be shown the city, the children are embarrassed by her "startling splendours", and to keep these out of the public eye they go to the lengths of spending their limited funds on a hired cab. It is typical of paradoxical Nesbit that through this imperial tyrant she decides to give expression both to her socialist conscience and her doubts about universal suffrage as a panacea for society's ailments. The Queen gives some attention to London's famous buildings but is more interested in its human element.

> "But how badly you keep your slaves. How wretched and poor and neglected they seem," she said, as the cab rattled along the Mile End Road.

"They aren't slaves; they're working people," said Jane.

"Of course they're working. That's what slaves are. ... Do you suppose I don't know a slave's face when I see it? Why don't their masters see that they're better fed and better clothed? Tell me in three words."

Stunned by this challenge, Cyril explains that these modern "slaves" are reasonably satisfied with their lot and unlikely to revolt, as the Queen has suggested, because " 'they have votes' ".

"What is this vote?" asked the Queen. "Is it a charm? What do they do with it?"

"I don't know," said the harassed Cyril: "It's just a vote, that's all! They don't do anything particular with it."

"I see," said the Queen, "a sort of plaything."

Another popular Edwardian writer, Mrs George de Horne Vaizey, born two years after Edith Nesbit in 1860, frequently championed the cause of the working girl, and sent a string of spirited heroines to school or college in search of independence. Her stories gave vigour to the *Girl's Own Paper,* although she disapproved of both socialism and women's suffrage and considered that men should manage the country and the business world. *The Independence Of Claire,* serialized in the "G.O.P." in 1914, tells the story of a nineteen-year-old high school teacher struggling against prejudice and poverty: like most of Mrs de Horne Vaizey's characters Claire finds her independence evaporating at the end of the story as "... from the shelter of her lover's arms her heart went out in a wave of tenderness towards ... the countless hordes of women workers for whom life was a monotonous round of grey-hued days, shadowed by the prospect of age and want". Claire's story – like Ann Veronica's – highlighted the fact that she lived in "a man's world", and in a society ridden with class-distinction and mistrust of the career-girl.

Mrs Vaizey wrote some 40 novels, most of them dealing with "... the essence of femininity in the springtide of life". Her best-known heroine was Pixie O'Shaugnessy, and the first Pixie book,

A lively moment from Mrs de Horne Vaizey's Pixie O'Shaugnessy,
illustrated by W. H. C. Groome

originally serialized in the *Girl's Own Paper* in 1900, is largely a school story. "Pixie O'Shaugnessy was at once the joy and terror of the school. It had been a quiet, well-conducted seminary before her time, or it seemed so, at least, looking back after the arrival of the wild Irish tornado, before whose pranks the mild mischief of the Englishers was as water unto wine." Pixie was one of the earliest irrepressible Irish schoolgirl heroines in popular fiction. As the century progressed they became stock figures of the genre, presumably re-hashed for successive generations of Irish girl readers who had settled in England.

Mrs de Horne Vaizey seems to admire the bohemianism of the O'Shaugnessy family who live in rapidly decaying splendour at Castle Knock in Ireland. The turn in the tide of the family finances is eventually brought about when the second daughter Joan (Esmeralda) marries a rich Englishman: Joan is dark-haired, attaining such heights of loveliness that strangers gasp with delight when first meeting her. Bridget, the eldest O'Shaugnessy sister, is a gentle, blonde beauty and there are also three extraordinarily handsome brothers, Jack, Miles and Patrick. In contrast Pixie is extremely plain, though in spite of this she becomes the darling of the whole family, with more than sufficient character to make up for her lack of good looks. Her fortunes are followed into womanhood in two further books, *More About Pixie* and *The Love Affairs Of Pixie* (both published by the Religious Tract Society). Like many sequels to schoolgirls' stories these were insipid compared with the original – mainly because on reaching maturity girls were expected to abandon exuberance in favour of acquiescent domesticity. The *Pixie O'Shaugnessy* and *Peggy Saville* books *(About Peggy Saville*, 1900, and *More About Peggy Saville,* 1901) were Mrs de Horne Vaizey's best-sellers. The author preferred *The Salt Of Life* (1915) which was based on the experiences of her family and friends. This is a perceptive and often amusing story about two families of girls on the threshold of adult life and romance.

Mrs George de Horne Vaizey was one of seven children, and in family sagas of lively friendships and shared adventures between girls and boys she described the better aspects of late Victorian and

Edwardian childhood. She was born in Liverpool, the daughter of an insurance broker, and began to write very early though she did not publish until her first marriage (as Jessie Mansergh). Her second marriage took place in 1899. She had a daughter by her first marriage, and by her second a son, George. Like his mother, Mr de Horne Vaizey has written several successful novels, and he remembers her as "a woman of great courage … Shortly after my birth she contracted typhoid/rheumatoid arthritis. Yet in pain, and having to be wheeled about in a bath-chair, she still contrived to write happy books." Mrs Vaizey died in 1916.

As late as 1915, although encouraging activities outside the home – "Vital interest in work is a splendid tonic for the nerves" – the *Girl's Own Paper* remained cautious about what it called "the free and militant woman". It saw girls as supporters of male-inspired ventures, and not innovators. (A serious study of one prominent woman educationalist, Dr Maria Montessori, was carefully prefaced by a statement that the "G.O.P." in no way endorsed the whole of her theories.) The contributor of "The Cry For Newness In Modern

An inept 'Suffragette', pictured by A. Gilbert for Eva Bretherton's Girl's Realm *story, 'A Serious Woman', 1914*

Life" expressed the fear that "the new independence of woman" would give the selfish man an excuse for lowering his standards of social behaviour. "Courtesy in public places is distinctly deteriorating and we don't like it." The most vigorous point made in an article under the promising heading of "The Business Girl Of Today" was that women telephonists wore such unsuitable clothes that they might soon be forced into uniform. Generally speaking the magazine seemed more at home with articles like "Ennobling The Menial Tasks" than its slightly discouraging features on "The Intellectual Life".

During the early years of the first world war popular fiction for boys urged them to become heroes in defence of their country, while girls' magazines offered their readers mainly the vicarious thrill of knitting for the boys in the trenches. (At first even nursing in foreign parts was viewed with suspicion, and girls were recommended instead to give their energies to comforting the bereaved families of fallen soldiers, through their church communities.) At times the *Girl's Own Paper* was even doubtful about its readers' capacities in the knitting direction. Under a heading "Women And War", it endorsed "sound advice from the Duchess of Albany": "Please let me plead that only those who are used to the work shall knit socks. It is very important that a soldier should not get sore feet, and unless you are accustomed to knit, and your socks are worn with pleasure ... do not try to make them, but give your money to buy good socks."

Fortunately women of all ages were not deterred by this admonition and the image it evoked of an army crippled by orgies of inept knitting from wives and sweethearts. They not only knitted, but became nurses and ambulance drivers, munition workers and coal heavers, till their war efforts eventually wrested the reward of partial female suffrage from an exhausted establishment in 1918.

VI

Orphans and Golden Girls

"And Kingdoms, like the Orchard
Flit Russetly away"
(Emily Dickinson)

ENGLISH FICTIONAL CHILDREN at the beginning of the century tended
to have their moral shortcomings ironed out in the course of a story;
in America the process was inverted, with hardened adults gradually
being humanized by contact with impossibly well-adjusted and
sunny-dispositioned children, whose own characters needed very
little modification. The first of these catalytic small girls was *Rebecca
of Sunnybrook Farm* by Kate Douglas Wiggin (1903); the most
expertly realized was *Anne of Green Gables* by L. M. Montgomery
(1908); and the most idiotic was *Pollyanna* by Eleanor H. Porter
(1913). This group of stories was augmented with Gene Stratton
Porter's emotionally deprived *A Girl of the Limberlost* (1909) and
Jean Webster's soap opera orphan, Jerusha (Judy) Abbott (*Daddy-
Long-Legs*, 1912).

Rebecca is set in the New England village of Riverboro in the
1870s, though the book was not published until 30 years later. This
may account for Kate Douglas Wiggin's tone: sentimental regret
suffuses every page; and the attempt to present Rebecca more or
less realistically and fairly – "she was a very faulty and passionately
human child" – soon gives way to flowery adulation: "there was a
hint of everything in the girl's face – of sensitiveness and delicacy
... the sweetness of the mayflower and the strength of the young
oak". When the author herself is not discoursing on Rebecca's
wonderfulness, she is reporting someone else's corroboration of the

narrative view. Rebecca "was described by Adam Ladd as the most remarkable and winning child he ever saw"; Uncle Jerry Cobb "thought wistfully ... of the sweet reasonableness of her mind ... of her quick decision when she had once seen the path of duty"; and so on.

Rebecca's character has to bear the whole weight of the book, which, structurally, is nothing more than a series of anecdotes devised to illustrate it. She appears ready-formed at the beginning; indeed, there is little scope for development in a child who was already "plucky at two and dauntless at five". It's her pluck which enables her to make the best of the brick house, where she comes to live with her aunts Miranda and Jane Sawyer, of whom, in the tradition of elderly virginal ladies, one is cantankerous and the other ineffectual. Rebecca Rowena Randall is "a little half-orphan from a mortgaged farm up Temperance way"; the aunts have charitably undertaken to pay for her education in order to relieve her widowed mother of the burden of bringing up at least one child. Rebecca, like Wordsworth's charmingly obstinate rustic girl, is one of seven, though in her case only one of the younger children dies; a gratuitous death which neither affects the plot nor has any appreciable effect on Rebecca. Its only possible purpose is to provide another little "gravestun" to complement the one remembered so zealously by Mr and Mrs Cobb, a simple old couple with a deep and inarticulate appreciation of the finer things in life – among them Rebecca. Mr Cobb, for whom only the most basic emotions have any meaning, thinks that Miss Miranda Sawyer "would be a heap better woman if she had a little gravestun to remember"; but Miranda Sawyer not only has had to do without her – in one of the lurid phrases of which Kate Douglas Wiggin is fond – "woman's crown of blessedness", she has never even approached it. Her sister Jane, on the other hand, has; *her* inner life is centred on a personal sorrow, a Confederate sweetheart who died in her arms; this circumstance enables her to respond openly, if uncomprehendingly, to Rebecca's instinctive sympathy. Jane, the author tells us, is not intelligent enough to appreciate Rebecca's finer points, though she is prepared to behave affectionately towards the little half-orphan. The only prominent character in the book who fails to make a fuss of Rebecca is her Aunt Miranda – though in her too the mellowing influence is seen to have been all along surreptitiously at work. After her death she is found to have willed the brick house to her niece: Rebecca's industrious efforts to like this aunt, whom she could not love, have paid off; though characteristically she indulges in a reverie of remorse (for imagined ingratitude) and sentimental optimism: "God bless Aunt Miranda! God bless the brick house that was! God bless the brick house that is to be!"

"Uncle" Jerry Cobb, driver of the stage coach which runs between Maplewood and Riverboro, is the first person to be impressed by Rebecca. The undersized but voluble child confides to him, among other facts, that the dearest thing in life to her is a pink parasol, the gift of a Miss Ross, "a lady that paints"; at this point the slow-witted Mr Cobb begins to get the message that "the bird perched by his side was a bird of a very different feather from those to which he was accustomed in his daily drives". The reader has had the message five pages earlier, "his one unnoteworthy little passenger" plainly implying the opposite to what it states. The wisp of a child, in over-starched calico and cotton gloves, is presented straight away as resolute and vulnerable; two qualities which for the American public signified childhood – at least those aspects of it which it wished to see perpetuated. Mary Pickford in innumerable rôles – among them that of Rebecca – provided a screen embodiment of such winsome toughness: the good, smart little mock-termagant who is not afraid to speak up in defence of anyone slighted or victimized. Such a child always has her priorities right – and priorities were very clearly defined, with charity, well-meaningness and Christian forbearance coming near the top of the list. A liking for babies and a sense of local patriotism were also included; a touch of vanity was permissible as long as it remained innocent and didn't lead to self-absorption.

As far as appearance is concerned, Rebecca's most notable feature is her eyes – and here even the romantic novelist's hyperbole gets out of hand. Inhibited by verisimilitude, if not artistic restraint, from creating a heroine who is radiantly beautiful, the author compensates Rebecca by endowing her with "a pair of eyes carrying such

One of Kate Douglas Wiggins' Rebecca stories.
Dustjacket illustration by J. M. Hartley

messages, such suggestions, such hints of sleeping power and insight, that one never tired of looking into their shining depths ...". Conventional good looks, since they are temporarily denied to Rebecca (the implication is always there that she will "blossom" at the right moment) are disparaged whenever they occur in someone else. Huldah Meserve, with delicate skin and abundant auburn hair, is vulgar and sexually precocious; Rebecca's friend Emma Jane, like Diana in *Anne of Green Gables,* is pretty but insipid, amiable but uninspired. For all the synthetic sweetness of her tone, the author can be unkind enough when it's a question of highlighting her heroine's attractions: by contrast, poor Emma Jane's blue eyes "say nothing"; her "neat nose" has no character; she has "red lips, from between which no word worth listening to had ever issued".

However, Emma Jane's prosaicness is entirely plausible: the terms in which she is characterized are far more effective than the meaningless, pseudo-poetic outpourings which Kate Douglas Wiggin has considered suitable to convey an impression of Rebecca. Where Emma Jane "could have seen the libraries of the world sinking into ocean depths and have eaten her dinner cheerfully the while" Rebecca is a child "sensitive to beauty and harmony": "as 'dove that to its window flies' her spirit soared towards a great light"; and again – in case the reader may have missed the point: "the young soul is ever wingèd; a breath stirs it to an upward flight". The effect on a truly sensitive young reader may be to prejudice her against beauty and harmony: but fortunately it turns out that Rebecca's idea of those is bound up with a commonplace phrase suggestive of both a Sunday School sermon and the cheaper kind of women's magazine: " 'The Rose of Joy'. Listen, girls! Isn't that lovely? 'The Rose of Joy'. It looks beautiful, and it sounds beautiful. What does it mean, I wonder?"

What it means in practical terms is that Rebecca wins 50 dollars in a literary competition by taking it as the title for her essay. The emotion for which it is intended to be a metaphor is not at first precisely stated; but Rebecca interprets it to her own satisfaction as "love". By this stage in the book the spirited, sometimes perceptive child has become a dreary adolescent with "a passionate longing for the music, the beauty, the poetry of existence". The twelve-year-old could occasionally rise to wit:

> "Oh, Rebecca, don't let's say that!" interposed Emma Jane hysterically. "It makes me feel like a fool."
> "It takes so little to make you feel like a fool, Emma Jane," rebuked Rebecca, "that sometimes I think that you must *be* one."

But the strain in her which predominates is the sentimental one. Even as a child, when she is supposed to be imaginative she often appears silly: asked in school to repeat the subjunctive mood, past perfect tense of the verb to know, " 'Oh, it is the saddest tense!' sighed Rebecca, with a little break in her voice; 'nothing but *ifs, ifs, ifs*!' " The village schoolmistress who encourages Rebecca in such flights of fancy is conceded even by the author to be a poor teacher: confronted with an essay of Rebecca's, Miss Dearborn asks, " 'Why did you put in anything so common as picking up chips?' " and her final word of criticism is " 'I don't like a cow in a composition' ". But Miss Maxwell, "niece of one of Maine's ex-governors and daughter of one of Bowdoin's professors", teacher at the Wareham Female Seminary where Rebecca becomes a pupil, is equally besotted with the "gifted child". In a scene in which the last remains of probability are sacrificed to a further endorsement of Rebecca's rarity and pricelessness, Miss Maxwell and Adam Ladd, one of the institute's trustees, quarrel good-humouredly over the question of who has "discovered" the "prodigy" – whom one regards as "a rare pearl ... of satin skin and beautiful lustre", the other as a "clover blossom ... sweet and fragrant and wholesome".

Adam Ladd, on whom the youthful Rebecca has imposed the embarrassing nickname of "Mr Aladdin", would have liked to impose eternal childhood on Rebecca: " '... He doesn't like grown-up young ladies in long trains and wonderful fine clothes ... they frighten and bore him' " (he states himself, in unconsciously case-book terms). In another context his motives for cultivating Rebecca's friendship might have been more rigorously analysed; as it is, the emotional background is sketched in – "an innocent, pink-and-white daisy" of a mother, who died "for lack of love and care, nursing and cherishing" – without the least psychological significance being attached to it. (In real life Lewis Carroll, who also was fond of small girls, was not so fortunate: his proclivities have been subjected continuously to a sexual interpretation.) In the prettified world of Wareham and Riverboro, the most obviously suspect emotions are taken at their face value. And, with psychological inconsistency, Adam Ladd veers from lamenting Rebecca's passing childishness to actually anticipating its conclusion: he is left "waiting at thirty-five for a girl to 'grow up' a little more simply because he could not find one already grown who suited his somewhat fastidious and exacting tastes".

The book preaches the desirability of contentment with the *status quo* – though it was left to *Pollyanna* to reduce the doctrine of making the best of things to the level of complete absurdity – in language which increasingly savours of the pulpit. When Kate Douglas Wiggin begins to preach about the narrow way, being upborne by the sense of right doing, and the joy of self-denial, she takes away from Rebecca any cogency as a flesh-and-blood character which she might have had. The tendency to moralize goes hand in hand with the most facile imagery: "the clouds blew over, the sun shone again, a rainbow stretched across the sky, while 'hope clad in April green' smiled into her upturned face and beckoned her on", so that the reader is left with the feeling of having wallowed in something extremely soggy. " 'You're soft, Jane,' " Rebecca's Aunt Miranda remarked once, " 'you allers was soft, and you allers will be. If't wa'n't for me keeping you stiffened up, I b'lieve you'd leak out o' the house into the dooryard.' " Unfortunately there has been no one to perform a similar function for the book.

Rebecca, "the nicest child in American literature" was succeeded by Anne, "the sweetest creation of child life yet written". The terms in which they were described are not the only point of similarity between the two: L. M. Montgomery has openly appropriated, or modified only slightly, a great many qualities for her heroine from the earlier book, though she makes of Anne a more valid creation than the endlessly overpraised Rebecca. Both children are quaintly original, both are imaginative and highly-strung; both are compulsive talkers; both make their homes with elderly people, one of whom – to begin with at least – is difficult to get on with. Both have placid, agreeable "best friends" whose function is to throw the heroines' uncommon attractiveness into relief; both do well at school; each triumphs over the disabilities of her background. Each, to begin with, is represented as infinitely pathetic – "funny little", "small pink", "odd", "scrawny little", and so on, implying a diminutiveness which cannot fail to arouse the protective instincts of the reader.

But Anne's predicament at the beginning of the book is far more dire than Rebecca's, and her achievements correspondingly more effective. The celebrated starting-off point for *Anne of Green Gables* was an entry in L. M. Montgomery's journal: "Elderly couple apply to orphan asylum for a boy. By mistake a girl is sent them." Out of that note she evolved the entire fabric of the book, superimposing her idea of the effects of that mistake upon remembered aspects of her own childhood on Prince Edward Island.

Anne of Green Gables

Her skill as a story-teller is evident right away. In the scene where Anne is driven to Green Gables, the tension produced by the reader's awareness that a mistake has been made, the child's happy ignorance, and Matthew's acute mental discomfort, ensure that interest in the story will be sustained. Of course the outcome is not *really* problematic – but, up until chapter six, when Marilla capitulates and agrees to keep the little orphan even though she is "not a boy", it is allowed to appear so.

Anne's effect on Matthew is instantaneous, but his somewhat unbending sister Marilla is less susceptible to the charm of the little girl's volatile chattering. However, after only three weeks, even Marilla is "perfectly willing to own up that I'm glad I consented to keep the child, and that I'm getting fond of her ...". Anne, who is twice described as "a freckled witch" proceeds to enchant the inhabitants of Avonlea; and the idyllic childhood which she enjoys is all the more to be relished since she so nearly missed it altogether. Systematically, she sets about filling her life with the elements which it had lacked:

"Marilla," she demanded presently, "do you think that I shall ever have a bosom friend in Avonlea?"

"A – a what kind of a friend?"

She finds one in Diana Barry, "a very pretty little girl", but by accident causes Diana to become drunk on currant wine; after which Mrs Barry decides that Anne is not "a fit little girl for Diana to associate with" (" 'Diana and I had such an affecting farewell down by the spring. It will be sacred in my memory forever.' "). Mrs Barry relents, however, when Anne saves the life of her younger daughter, Minnie May, who conveniently has an attack of croup, and the friendship, with its emotional embellishments, is resumed.

Unselfconscious emotionalism is the keynote of Anne's nature: "the pleasures and pains of life came to her with trebled intensity." She is presented constantly as imaginative; but the quality of her imaginings isn't exactly original or enlightened. " 'Lovers' Lane,' "she enthuses, " 'is a very pretty name. So romantic!' " And " '… maples are such sociable trees … they're always rustling and whispering to you.' " When her observations are not banal, they are often nauseating: " 'Do you think amethysts can be the souls of good violets?' " Such excesses of whimsy cry out for suppression – but for the author and her audience, they seemed the authentic expressions of a heightened sensibility.

Anne's romanticism is most palatable when it's treated as parody – and even here the author relies for her effects on the most obvious juxtaposition: pompous phrases in conjunction with a red-haired mite.

"… My life is a perfect graveyard of buried hopes. That's a sentence I read in a book once, and I say it over to comfort myself whenever I'm disappointed in anything."

"I don't see where the comforting comes in myself," said Marilla.

"Why, because it sounds so nice and romantic, just as if I were a heroine in a book, you know. I am so fond of romantic things. …"

But inevitably the parody and the author's view of the child's real nature coalesce. The echoes from one kind of cheap fiction which L. M. Montgomery consciously evoked, merge in another which is less conscious. All the way through there are indications of the essential viscidity at the core of *Anne*, but there's a point from which the book noticeably deteriorates. When Marilla comments, "'You don't chatter half as much as you used to, Anne, nor use half as many big words. What has come over you?'" Anne's reply shows her up for the droopy fifteen-year-old she has become: "'It's nicer to think dear, pretty thoughts and keep them in one's heart, like treasures.'" Those dear, pretty thoughts form the substance of the rest of *Anne of Green Gables* and its seven sequels; and by the end of the first book the homely, flower-patch moralizing quality which so marred *Rebecca* has also crept in: "... if the path set before her feet was to be narrow, she knew that flowers of quiet happiness would bloom along it."

The problem of a character who grows up in the course of a story is one which few children's writers have managed to deal with successfully. (An exception is the school-story series in which the heroine moves from one form to another up the school – but these do not take her into adulthood, only to its brink; and the school setting tends to provide a formal framework within which continuing childishness, even at eighteen, is believable.) For the kind of sugary innocence which Anne, and others, embodied, a child is the only valid symbol; transferred to an adult, or semi-adult, it can only ring false. Of all biological phases, adolescence surely is the one in which bodily experiences are of paramount importance; yet for reasons of convention, squeamishness, and the idea that their audience was in need of moral guidance at every level, children's authors until recently have been prohibited from mentioning many of its most fundamental aspects. For want of a more comprehensive formula, it came to be designated by a state of "dreaminess", irrespective of the character of the child in question. Since fictional girls like Anne and Rebecca were totally asexual, their "spirituality" had to be emphasized; and in this respect Kate Douglas Wiggin and L. M. Montgomery acquiesced completely in the Victorian idea that part of a woman's duty was to provide a spiritual haven for a world-weary man. Both were successful authors, both had worked in competitive situations, yet both preserved an unrealistic belief in "the intuitive and spiritual qualities of women, their faith and imagination". L. M. Montgomery sidetracked the issue of feminism by taking refuge in meaningless flippancies: "I have no desire to be equal to man. I prefer to maintain my superiority."

In view of this, it's not surprising that Anne expresses her "femininity" by stating that she would "rather be pretty than clever" – the corollary being that it's only an "unfeminine" girl who would not. Of course Anne turns out to be both – it would be an unusual story-book heroine who did not – but the career which she might have had is abandoned unregretfully several books later when she becomes a wife:

> "Some people might think that a Redmond B.A. ... was 'wasted' as the wife of a struggling country doctor in the rural community of Four Winds."
> "Gilbert!"
> "If you had married Roy Gardner, now," continued Gilbert mercilessly, "*you* could have been 'a leader in social and intellectual circles ...'."
> "Gilbert *Blythe*!"

Anne's tempestuous first meeting with curly-haired Gilbert Blythe in the Avonlea schoolroom – when she cracks a slate over his head because he has called her "carrots" – in the popular novelist's terms can have only one outcome; but here L. M. Montgomery, in her desire to prolong the uncertainty of the situation, almost overbalances into unromantic honesty. Anne's "unpraiseworthy tenacity for holding grudges" leads her to reject Gilbert's good-tempered overtures of friendship on more than one occasion; but of course the combined clichés of the stormy petrel who is really dying to be subdued, and the familiar childhood sweetheart, morally irreproachable, whose persistent devotion finally pays off, have too strong a pull to be resisted.

L. M. Montgomery modestly thought that the book might appeal to girls in their teens; its success appears to have taken her by surprise. Logically, after the first half of *Anne of Green Gables*, it can, or should, please no one: the child reader cannot identify with a heroine for whom growing up has meant that the zest is taken out of her; the adult is irritated by the falsity of the sentiment. Possibly its greatest appeal has been to grown-up people who wish to remember only the least disturbing elements of their own childhood – and it is certain that, like Mark Twain's, part of the author's plan was "pleasantly to remind adults of what they were … and what queer enterprises they sometimes engaged in". But unlike Mark Twain, in L. M. Montgomery the pleasantness has taken over, lightening and diminishing everything.

Pollyanna, the most puerile of the little rays of moonshine, is also the most intellectually debilitating – particularly if the book is read on its own terms, not for its inadvertent funniness. It *is* funny, in the way that a great many silent films now seem funny (however they may have struck audiences at the time of their release): for its bathos, antiquatedness, and the number of memorable lines which it contains. (" 'And you knew my mother, really, when she was just a little earth angel and not a Heaven one?' "; " 'I just love people' "; " 'I'd *like* a home – jest a common one, ye know, with a mother in it, instead of a Matron.' ") But it wasn't due to its humour, conscious or otherwise, that *Pollyanna* became a best-seller: its author has simply pandered to the lowest level of her readers' emotions. *Pollyanna* makes no demands on the reader's ability to think; response to its images is nothing if not automatic. Out of the sentimental rag-bag comes every cliché in the business: lost kittens, stray dogs, dirty but proud orphan boys, crippled children, stern men softened by "a child's presence", faithful old retainers, unhappy love affairs, rich aunts. The film director, D. W. Griffith, who was not notably averse to themes which now seem horrifyingly sentimental, considered *Pollyanna* "the most immoral story ever produced on the screen". [1] He went on to refer to its "fake philosophy

[1] Frederick James Smith, "The Moral and Immoral Photoplay" *Shadowland* VI Vol VIII No 1, Sept 1920

of gilded bunkum". But *Pollyanna* is widely regarded as a classic children's book and has never been out of print (it was issued as a Puffin Book in 1969). Not only that, the character of Pollyanna was taken over by other writers (at least four of them) after the original author's death in 1920, Pollyanna having so endeared herself to her readers that she couldn't, without loss of happiness – and money – be relinquished. But sentimentality is always with us, even if its manifestations change. (This is not to say that it cannot be used effectively: in E. Nesbit, for instance, overtly sentimental ideas are contained within an arrangement which exploits and enhances them.)

Pollyanna's imbecile cheerfulness – her "glad" philosophy – is derived from an incident which she relates with relish:

> "You see, I'd wanted a doll ... but when the barrel came the lady wrote that there hadn't any dolls come in, but the little crutches had ...".
>
> "Well, I must say I can't see any game about that, about that," declared Nancy, almost irritably.
>
> "Oh yes; the game was just to find something about everything to be glad about – no matter what 'twas. ... And we began right then – on the crutches."
>
> ... "Well, then, suppose *you* tell *me*," almost snapped Nancy.
>
> " ... Why, just be glad because you *don't – need – 'em*!" exulted Pollyanna triumphantly.

Pollyanna is stupid. She is tactless and infuriating. She comforts a sick woman by telling her: " 'I thought – how glad you could be – that other folks weren't like you – all sick in bed like this, you know.' " Her inability to apprehend reality indicates a serious mental imbalance: of her aunt, who dislikes her (to begin with) she says: " 'My Aunt Polly is the nicest lady in the world, now that my mother's gone to be a Heaven angel.' " She is the same age as Rebecca and Anne when they first appear – eleven – yet her vocabulary is that of a four-year-old. (" 'What is being pro-fi-ta-ble?' " she lisps.) Her exploits are unoriginal, to say the least: she restores her aunt to the bosom of her long-estranged lover and provides a "child's presence" for an elderly gentleman who feels the need of one. He has offered to adopt Pollyanna herself (" 'And, oh, little girl, little girl, I want you so!' ") but " 'Oh, Mr Pendleton, I couldn't leave Aunt Polly – now!' " He is persuaded to settle for a male orphan named Jimmy Bean (" 'I have seen Jimmy Bean and … he's going to be my boy hereafter.' "). In the midst of these little acts of kindness Pollyanna is run over by a car and severely injured – but survives: the early twentieth-century equivalent of the Victorian dying child is the child who has a near-fatal accident, suffers with fortitude, and makes an unbelievable recovery. Pollyanna, however, needs those little crutches after all – damage to her spine leaves her temporarily paralysed. (" 'You never know how perfectly lovely legs are till you haven't got them – that go, I mean.' ")

Pollyanna, like Anne and the others, grows up. The book in which she does so contains another male orphan, whimsical but crippled (Mrs Porter's recurrent symbol for the triumph over adversity is crutches); a shopgirl whom Pollyanna innocently saves from the usual fate of pretty working girls in Boston; a rich lady, who, like Mr Pendleton, is pining for a child's presence – which Pollyanna again supplies. She does these things at twelve, then reappears eight years later. Pollyanna at twenty is not an ambitious girl: " 'Oh, I want to cook and keep house,' smiled Pollyanna, with a pensive sigh. 'I just love to beat eggs and sugar, and hear the soda gurgle its little tune in the cup of sour milk.' " But Jimmy Bean – now Pendleton – is relieved to find that her mental development has not been totally arrested: " 'Even you were worried, it seems,' Pollyanna laughs, 'lest I should be at twenty just what I was at ten!' " In fact there is no discernible difference in her behaviour or outlook, though we have the inevitable romantic preoccupation grafted on to the juvenile personality. (" 'You don't mean to say there's anything *serious* between you and – Jimmy Bean.' ") The plot of *Pollyanna Grows Up*, such as it is, involves the sorting out of several couples – one member of each believes that the person whom he or she loves, is in love with someone else. It is a common theme, but rarely has it been handled so grossly; but the combination of artless contrivance and arch dialogue is congruous with the light-hearted pathos and

SNAP HERE → | IF YO

irect when
rance...

off contents,
f when you buy online.

e from 20.06.12 to 01.10.12. Up to 50% discount
to any add-ons purchased. Minimum premiums apply.)

line.com

direct line

soft-centred banalities which it's Mrs Porter's literary mission to express. It's surprising that even a cup of milk is allowed to be sour; of course in Pollyanna's hands it is bound to end up sweet.

A Girl of the Limberlost is presented within a slightly more "serious" context; but if the book is on the whole a more solid piece of work than *Pollyanna,* its style is more lurid and intense. It is still in print, though hopelessly out of date. It is full of archaisms, the most obvious of which are the chapter headings. "Wherein" savours of both the tome and the tombstone; "Wherein Elnora goes to high school and learns many lessons not found in her books" manages to sound at once heavily arch and lightly philosophical, and in this way sets the tone for the whole book.

The book follows the career of a Limberlost girl from adolescence to marriage. Its romantic theme functions on two levels: underlying the obvious inflation of the girl's sterling character and emotional difficulties is Gene Stratton Porter's glorification of Nature (" 'We Limberlost people must not be selfish with the wonders God has given us. We must share with those poor cooped-up city people the best we can' "); and the "richness" of the countryside is expressed in practical terms when her heroine, Elnora Comstock, pays her way through high school by selling moths and other insects which she has gathered from the swamp.

Elnora suffers horribly from an intermittently demented mother, who sometimes goes out at night to implore the swamp to give her back her dead husband – for whose death she most unreasonably blames her daughter. He had drowned in the swamp while she – on the point of giving birth – was unable to help him; since this unfortunate incident she has subjected Elnora to the most blatant kind of mental cruelty. On page one she is jeering " 'You are so plum daffy you are forgetting your dinner' "; before the end of the chapter, having refused to give Elnora a penny to pay for the books which she needs, and having gone out of her way to ensure that the girl makes a fool of herself on her first day at high school, she blusters, " 'Of course I knew you would come home blubbering! But you don't get a penny! ... Have your own way if you are determined, but I think you will find the road pretty rocky.' "

The culmination of the cruelty comes when Mrs Comstock, having undertaken to provide a graduation dress for Elnora, gives her at the last minute an old white dress which she's simply washed and ironed. The emotional build-up for this seemingly unimportant event is morbidly fostered, with the author thrumming for all she is worth on the exposed nerve-ends of Elnora, who ends up reliving the episode where her father was drowned, in a dream. " 'I saw it last night just as he went down. And, oh, Aunt Margaret! I saw what she did, and I heard his cries. No matter what she does, I don't believe I can ever be angry with her again,' " she declares; but Mrs Comstock goes too far in the affair of the dress, and when, shortly afterwards, she wantonly destroys a rare moth which Elnora needs to complete a collection worth $300, her daughter's alienation seems assured.

But, "one of the Almighty's most delicate and beautiful creations was sacrificed without fulfilling the law, yet none of its species ever served so glorious a cause, for at last Mrs Comstock's inner vision had cleared". The clearing process is helped on by a nifty piece of amateur psychotherapy on the part of a neighbour, who stands up to Mrs Comstock and tells her the truth about the man whom she has idolized for twenty years.

" 'I had an idea that it would kill you to know, but I guess you are tough enough to stand anything. Kill or cure, you get it now!' " The brutal truth is simply that Mr Comstock had been coming from another woman when he was drowned. The immediate effect of this revelation is highly melodramatic:

> Mrs Comstock gripped the hoe tighter, and turning she went down the walk and started across the woods to the home of Elvira Carney.
>
> "Mercy!" gasped weak little Elvira Carney. "Have mercy! … If you knew what I've suffered. … All the neighbours have suspected and been down on me. I ain't had a friend. I've always felt guilty of his death. I've seen him go down a thousand times plain as ever you did. Many's the night I've stood on the other bank of that pool and listened to you, and

A Girl of the Limberlost, *drawn by Pearl Falconer*
(frontispiece to Brockhampton edition)

I tried throw myself in to keep from hearing you, but I didn't dare. I knew God would send me to burn for ever, but I'd better done it; for now He has set the burning on my body, and every hour it is slowly eating the life out of me. The doctor says it's a cancer—"

The moral message is plain by this point, but Gene Stratton Porter cannot relinquish the hell-fire attitude which she has struck: " 'Instead of doing a woman's work in life you chose the smile of invitation and the dress of unearned cloth. Now you tell me you are marked to burn to death with the unquenchable fire. And him! It was shorter with him, but let me tell you he got his share ... '." Every last drop of retribution is extracted by Mrs Comstock from this sadistic confrontation; and then Elnora's delightful mother, with a complete change of face, returns home to lavish affection on the daughter whom she has persecuted and resented: "the girl was almost suffocated with tempestuous caresses and generous offerings".

At this point the second phase of the novel begins. Having had one intolerable emotional relationship smoothed over, Elnora is ripe for another: fatalistically, she falls in love with a man who is engaged to someone else. Of course he soon decides that he prefers Elnora – but both, with pigheadedness and inflexibility masquerading as chivalrousness, consider his engagement binding.

"Elnora," he whispered, "will you kiss me goodbye?"
Elnora drew back and stared at him with wide eyes. "I'd strike you sooner!" she said.

It can only be the repressive society in which such a nonsensical attitude is credible, even creditable, which is responsible for the misdirected sexuality with which the book seethes. Two images in particular stand out, and are at once ludicrous and horrifying. Two women racked with guilt and frustration (one suffering agonies for having, as she sees it, lured a man to his death, the other for having failed to save him) making fools of themselves in the dark at opposite sides of a pond, is one; the other is a night marauder, who, surreptitiously and salaciously, watches Elnora prepare for bed.

Three steps out on the big limb the man shuddered. He was within a few feet of the girl.

He could see the throb of her breast under its thin covering and smell the fragrance of the tossing hair ... nothing was worth a glance save the perfect face and form within reach by one spring through the rotten mosquito bar. He gripped the limb above that on which he stood, licked his lips and breathed through his throat to be sure he was making no sound.

This is the language of the shilling shocker: Mrs Porter's overwrought imagination veers, characteristically, from biblical ranting to erotic titillation, though no doubt she would have repudiated the latter. "Purity", here, is as much to be glorified as "Nature" – indeed the two are in some way implied to be interchangeable, however biologically paradoxical that may seem. Mrs Porter's high-minded young couple are impelled only by the purest of motives, and inhibited at every turn by airy-fairy scruples. Elnora gets her man, since the "children's book" context demands a happy ending; but not until both have indulged in a great deal of emotional masochism. To make the ending even more palatable to unrealists, a transformation is wrought in the empty-headed ex-fiancée, principally by contact with the ennobling Elnora.

Gene Stratton Porter's chief – indeed, her only – literary merit is an ability to convey to the reader her acute sense of place. The Limberlost, with its gnarled tree trunks, Indian relics and profuse vegetation, is as far removed from a clean New England village, or the pretty island where Anne grows up, as Elnora is unlike Rebecca and Anne. She is the least whimsical of heroines, and, in company with her creator, the most humourless. Mrs Porter's feeling for the swamp has determined the quality of her prose: both are lush, oppressive, unhealthy, and productive of noxious fumes.

With *Daddy-Long-Legs* we are back in musical-comedy land. Of 97 orphans in the John Grier Asylum, one is chosen by a mysterious trustee to be educated at college. For a reason which is never made clear, he childishly keeps his identity a secret; his protégé is forced to refer to him as "Daddy-Long-Legs" (she has caught a glimpse of his long legs as he dashes through the orphanage hall). This twee nickname, reminiscent of Rebecca's "Mr Aladdin", gains in appropriateness when she begins to regard him as a father figure (he pays for her education).

After the first chapter the book consists of a series of letters (a literary form which better writers than Jean Webster have found cumbersome) from the fortunate orphan, Judy Abbott, to her benefactor – who has directed that they should be addressed to John Smith. The tone of the letters is alternately playful and prickly – but the foundling's not unnatural resentment is kept to a minimum. If Judy's childhood deprivations continue to rankle ("Whatever faults I may have, no one can ever accuse me of having been spoiled by my family!"; "You can't know how I dreaded appearing in school in those miserable poor-box dresses") they are outweighed by her present advantages. "Six dresses, all new and beautiful and bought for me," she writes. "... You gave them to me and I am very, very, *very* much obliged." One would have expected the weight of that obligation to prove intolerable – indeed it is impossible to imagine a more "difficult" relationship than the one-sided one which Jean Webster has devised for her heroine. But in the light-hearted – and headed – romance, blitheness is all. (The feeling all the way through that Judy is about to burst into song was finally realized in 1953, when a musical version of *Daddy-Long-Legs* was produced on the London stage.)

With its waif-to-wife theme, its sweetly exuberant heroine and its undemanding literary style, *Daddy-Long-Legs* was bound to be a best-seller. Unfortunately, it has remained one: within the fairy-tale context, Judy's coy and submissive behaviour is hardly less believable today than it was in 1912. The few observations which *do* date the book – "Don't you think I'd make an admirable voter if I had my rights? I was twenty-one last week. This is an awfully wasteful country to throw away such an honest, educated, conscientious, intelligent citizen as I would be"; "Are women citizens? I suppose not" – also provide its only point of general interest, although one's impression here is that they are thrown in merely to delineate the student. No student, especially one as intelligent as Judy is supposed to be, could have failed to be aware of current social trends – or, ultimately, less concerned with their outcome. (Judy's most spectacular achievement is also what must constitute the ultimate power-fantasy of any orphan: she ends up owning the orphanage.)

Jarvis Pendleton, who, we are told early in the book, "does not care for girls" can have had only one motive for undertaking to pay for Judy's education. Having failed, like Adam Ladd, to find a girl who suits his "somewhat fastidious and exacting tastes" he has determined to fashion one for himself, by a process of fairly remote control. Orphans are notoriously malleable – one thinks of Thomas Day, a disciple of Rousseau, whose search for the "perfect wife" led him to adopt two orphan girls whom he reared by hand, instilling moral courage into them by pouring boiling wax on their arms. Judy, however, obligingly falls in love with Jarvis Pendleton without knowing that he is her benefactor – so no one can accuse him of having unfairly exploited his advantage.

These books were all written between 1902 and 1915, when women were just beginning to emerge from the Victorian cocoon of sentiment and insentience, yet not one reflects a positive attitude to social change. This of course may account largely for their popularity, since they appealed to the conservative element in their readers – which was fostered by institutions such as the Church and certain educational bodies. "If ladies enter our colleges and compete in the long course, with the other sex, they must do it by sacrificing the female accomplishments – the piano, cultivated singing, and attractive dress," the Rev. John Todd, TT, announced in 1871. That this view had not been ridiculed to death by 1912 is indicated in one of Judy Abbott's more pointed asides (it is interesting that it should occur in so trivially girlish a book as *Daddy-Long-Legs*): "It doesn't matter what part of the United States or Canada they come from, or what denomination they are, we always get the same sermon. Why on earth don't they go to men's colleges and urge the students not to allow their manly natures to be crushed out by too much mental application?" Grover Cleveland was predicting in 1905 that increasing agitation for "women's rights" would prove ruinous to "the integrity of our homes" *(Ladies' Home*

Journal, May 1905). And even where the achievement of "women's rights" was considered to be a desirable goal, it was often seen within strictly defined limits. Catherine Beecher, a campaigner for better education for women, still believed that "Heaven has appointed to one sex the superior, and to the other the subordinate station, and this without reference to the character or conduct of either". Women's supposed moral superiority was stressed by certain feminists, such as Elizabeth Cady Stanton and Frances Willard, who concerned themselves not only with the integrity of their homes but also with the integrity of the nation.

One significant advance in the early twentieth century was the number of women in full-time employment. Professional and business women more than doubled their numbers between 1910 and 1930; saleswomen and clerks increased by 93.3 per cent. By 1927, typing, stenography, filing and secretarial work were regarded as "women's trades". And opposition from people who had feared that women were incapable of sustained effort gave way to a more subtle attempt to keep them in their biological place. By overreacting to ordinary proficiency when it occurred in women, they drew attention to its unexpectedness. If women could not be dismissed as subhuman, they had to be represented mockingly as superhuman. The man who enthuses about "the goddess of the typewriter, the fairy of the newspaper office, the grace of the telephone" is *really* saying that women are dear, strange creatures who have to be indulged. Marie Dressler's 1910 hit, "Heaven Will Protect the Working Girl" tended slightly to misrepresent the situation. She – especially if she was pretty – had plenty of other would-be protectors.

Efforts to achieve prettiness came in for their share of condemnation. The Rev. John Todd, TT, who had feared that educated women would lose the ability to sing in tune and dress becomingly, was followed by a Brooklyn priest whose bugbear with regard to women, educated or not, went in the opposite direction. His picturesque indictment – "We are living today in a pandemonium of powder, a riot of rouge, and moral anarchy of dress" – is remarkable now chiefly for its innocence; but it shows plainly how responsibility for the nation's moral tone was supposed to devolve on women.

In an era of industrial development, nostalgia was rife for a rural past. The America of good housekeeping, patchwork quilts, pumpkin pie, potted geraniums, straw brooms, bottled fruit, wheat loaves, apple cakes, starched calico, red and white checked gingham, horse-drawn buggies, came to stand for a good deal that was felt to be missing from urban American life. In the five books discussed above, traditional virtues predominate. With the exception of Pollyanna, each heroine is educated to an advanced level, yet the future of each is clearly marked out along the conventional path. Each sees herself ultimately as a nest-maker and breeder. Rebecca's sole gesture of rebellion is over and done with in the first few pages: " 'Boys always do the nice splendid things, and girls can only do the nasty dull ones that get left over,' " she remarks unbotheredly, and goes off to ginger up the nasty dull things – rescuing babies and selling soap – as far as possible. Anne happily swops independence for a "house of dreams" – which soon, as L. M. Montgomery archly puts it, is visited by a stork. By attempting to represent adult experiences in terms comprehensible to (and suitable for) children, these authors created a hybrid literature, wholly regressive in effect and execution. In England, at a slightly later date, Elsie Oxenham tackled the same problem by confining her characters within a social environment which is less flexible (in which symbols are invested with more meaning) – but failed equally to find an adequate formula to convey emotions which she could not state. (It is only in the last ten years that fictional girls – and boys – have begun to grow up convincingly.)

There are two kinds of well-known fiction: books which represent the lowest common denominator of popular taste, and those which have received a great deal of *critical* acclaim (the most obvious example here is *Alice's Adventures in Wonderland*). All the above books come into the first category: no doubt better children's books were being written in America at the same time, but these, because of their widespread impact, are the ones which have survived and which are known outside the continent. These, together with *Uncle Tom's Cabin*, *Little Women* and *What Katy Did*, are the standard American girls' books.

VII

Jolly Schoolgirls and Bosom Friends

"The school platform meant much to Lesbia. It was the centre of her little world, and to have taken her place upon it tonight was the fulfilment of a long-cherished ambition."

(Angela Brazil, *Loyal to the School*)

ANGELA BRAZIL'S FIRST school story struck at once an optimistic note; *The Fortunes of Philippa* (1906) could hardly fail to be popular, when so many Victorian heroines had been characterized solely by their misfortunes. Though she was not the first to write about girls' schools as such, Angela Brazil's early stories indicated the way in which the genre was to develop. The schools created by her predecessors were apt to be cheerless places, savouring less of school than of Sunday School; the books themselves were oppressive – with their gilt-edged paper and finely-etched chapter headings, they seemed to be approximating as closely as possible to the prayer book. The matt paper on which Angela Brazil's books were printed may not have been responsible for their success; but it does have the effect, now, of making even the early versions appear readable – as opposed to being merely decorative.

By 1906, the Sunday-School syndrome had become less dominant in children's fiction, but the association of goodness with religious belief persisted (as, indeed, it has up to the present time). However much children's writers aimed at entertaining, their underlying purpose was to edify – and an unquestioned assumption was that social virtues were inseparable from a belief in God. This ceased to be stated overtly from about 1900 onwards, when a person's religion began to be regarded as a private matter to which it was considered tactless to allude, but it remained a latent force in juvenile fiction. Angela Brazil's own Christianity was moderately unorthodox: a compound of pantheism, nostalgia for a Druidic past, and the peculiarly English notion of "honour". Though she insists, in her autobiography, *My Own Schooldays,* that she wasn't an irreligious child ("I was well taught, and I said my little prayers") she did not enjoy going to church, not, at least, in the absence of "stained-glass windows and ivy-mantled walls" – rather obvious accessories which her "artistic temperament" craved. Unfortunately, from her point of view, her Celtic ancestry endowed her with no particular psychic abilities; she did see one fairy in her youth, but it "had a plum-pudding for a head, and almonds for eyes, nose and mouth" – this, in spite of the fact that "I was no glutton – I was not even very fond of plum-pudding". In a sentence which provides immediate insight for the reader into her character, she adds wistfully "I would so infinitely have preferred the bluebell variety of sprite".

The Fortunes of Philippa, which appeared at a period of transition, harked back to a certain extent to the Victorian era. At The Hollies "we played cricket, hockey and all modern games, but we used backboards and were made to walk around the schoolroom balancing books on our heads". The tone of the book is occasionally stilted, unsure, almost ponderous; the author may have been trying out certain effects of style before deciding which to discard. (Apart from her autobiography she never wrote another book in the first person.) A certain school, mentioned in *The Fortunes of Philippa,* where the girls are noticeably unladylike ("they behave so badly, sitting on the edges of the drawing-room tables, and bolting their cake, and talking the most atrocious slang") might have been taken as the model for future schools which she was to create. At *Miss Kaye's* (1908) Sylvia is "much happier here than I expected. This morning I fell into a tub full of mud and spoilt all my clothes" – an escapade which presaged many others, though not all Angela Brazil's girls are so ingenuously careless of their appearances. " 'Don't be piggish,' said Mollie. 'One has no need to cultivate a tough skin, just because one's fond of cricket and hockey. I hate to see girls with hard red cheeks and freckles.' "

Girls, of course, come in all shapes and sizes (" 'We know a young damsel named Pat/She's big, and she's floppy and fat' ") but two unmistakable types are the hoyden and the "young madam".

"It's a grizzly nuisance having to change one's frock!" groused Betty Moore. " … I hate the bother."
"Do you?" exclaimed Irene Andrews. "Now I like it. I think it would be perfectly piggy to wear the same serge dress from breakfast to bedtime."

The schools which followed Miss Kaye's were, on the whole, progressive. (" 'If there's any jolly thing that it's possible to do Miss Drummond thinks of it.' ") No educational experiment went untried: callisthenics, self-expression, various guilds and leagues, different systems of regimentation, all form the background to one story or another. A French mistress, watching her pupils sliding in the snow, finds it "strange to see what is permitted to your English Mees". The twentieth century was still enough of a novelty for any mention of it to induce an instant sense of up-to-dateness, a quality which was held at a premium. The era of the young lady had at last come to an end; and, as they burst through one restriction after another (and out of their gym-tunics) schoolgirls appeared to proliferate: "Girls! Girls everywhere"; "… tall girls, short girls, fat girls, slim girls …" "everywhere, girls!" Girls – Angela Brazil's girls at least – had become "a rosy, racy, healthy, hearty, well-grown set of twentieth-century schoolgirls". The thimble and the backboard had been replaced by, among other things, "a pile of new books, a chest-expander and a hockey stick".

The chest-expander may be more bizarre, but the last item is the significant one. Angela Brazil's own schooldays had been marred by a lack of facilities for sport: hence the emphasis in her books on organized games. (" 'I think most of us like Miss Latimer best, the games mistress. She's very popular with everybody. You see, we have such fun at gymnastics, and of course we love hockey and cricket.' ") She missed out on hockey-playing by having been born as early as 1868; an event which she describes somewhat archly: "Amy [her

Waiting for the results. Stanley Davis illustrates
The Girls of St Cyprians

older sister], it seems, before my advent, had added to her prayers such urgent and importunate demands for a baby sister, that perhaps in the never-never land I heard the call, and drifted to earth to supply the want." The Peter Pan overtones, the tendency to gush, which are more or less kept under control in Angela Brazil's books, are allowed to run riot in her autobiography. (True, we find dear little villages and pink bundles of babies and cosy wee sitting-rooms in the books, but they're interspersed with enough running about and candid behaviour to make their presence fairly inoffensive.) "Friendships", it begins, "are the flowers on life's pathway" – an observation equalled in triteness in the last 70 years only by the verse of Patience Strong. Angela Brazil succeeds in representing herself as an obnoxious child, skipping pertly about in a little fairy dress ("frolicking" as she puts it " 'neath the pansies"). A donkey is described more sympathetically: they hired it "at Sunderland Point, to draw my grandmother about in a Bath chair. It was a most intelligent little beast and knew Sunday as well as a Christian." Little Angela learned to read at quite an early age, but her critical faculty seems not to have been at all highly developed, either at the time or later. "Dear books!" she enthuses. "They were full of such fascinating stories." Criticism is reserved for an illustrated edition of Foxe's *Book of Martyrs*, whose lurid pictures "exercised a dreadful fascination". But by then she was an adolescent, troubled, she writes obliquely, "by questions which had troubled me not at all before" – a subject she does not enlarge on. Growing up, for little Angela, was simply a process of transferring her "sneaking weakness for dolls" to "a neighbour's babies" – curiosity about the facts of life, one feels, would not have been consistent with "the family ideal, a line of high living that had its rootsprings in the eternal".

Her glorified family included two brothers, who "were heroes in my eyes. I could not do much for them but I used sometimes to polish the spokes of their bicycles on Saturday mornings ... " – thereby, no doubt, reinforcing distinctions which the age persisted in making between boys and girls. Her attitude of hero-worship was not so much outgrown as transferred to other objects – some of them female, which possibly did something to redress the balance. Still, it is something that a person whose father *would* refer to girls as dear little silly-billies, could write sympathetically of girls who intended to earn a living – though Angela Brazil's attitude to this is tinged faintly with regret for "the old, easy, sheltered days of reliance for support on fathers and brothers [which] have passed away for' all but a favoured few. The majority must shoulder their share of the world's work, and trust to their own hands and brains."

Angela Brazil's value as a social commentator is negligible, as far as her autobiography is concerned. She is far too busy creating an atmosphere of sweetness and light to bother about recording mundane customs and events; only occasionally does a recognizable or evocative image stand out from the welter of prettifications: her grandmother in the Bath chair; herself "in a little tweed coat with many pockets, which I fancied greatly, and a hat of the same cloth, edged with scarlet satin, and a gilt quill stuck in the side, and a leather satchel full of books"; "a tiny wooden box" which cost a penny – "containing a snake made of a curled shaving of thin horn. It had a head, bead eyes, and a red flannel tongue." One "marvellous sight", the burning of the Liverpool landing stage, is ruined by the inclusion of "My Lady Moon riding tranquilly overhead" – which reduces it at once to the level of a greetings card.

The inadequacies of her early schooling are glossed over: "possibly it was as well for our brains not to be overstimulated and may have prevented 'nerves' later on". Manchester High School, which followed "dear old Miss A's" was "a most jolly experience". Here, on one occasion, during a lull in class, a prophetic voice piped up from the back of the room, "Let Angela Brazil tell us a story". It was perhaps Angela Brazil's overstimulated emotional faculty which led her to transmute Ellerslie College, where she became head girl, into "a beautiful educational flower [which] bloomed, faded and made way for something else": as a metaphor this is singularly inapt.

Directly she went to school, she tells us, she "became plunged in friendships with girls". If the past participle suggests abandon, it is not, in context, excessive; her friendships *were* inclined to be unrestrained. ("Lellia was a perfect dear. If human beings have auras hers and mine must instantly have mixed.") The theme of "bosom friends" is one which she used, in her books, over and over again –

but fortunately Angela Brazil's fictional characters were nearly always more believable than her factual ones. One of her best books is *A Fourth Form Friendship* (1912), in which the subsidiary theme of character-moulding (also a recurrent feature, though no one's character is moulded quite so drastically as that of Mary in Mrs Hodgson Burnett's *The Secret Garden*) provides a unity which many of her later books lack. The friendship in question is between the self-willed Aldred Laurence, a new girl, and the exclusive Mabel Farringdon, whose aloofness, surprisingly enough, is accepted by her classmates: " 'Everybody likes Mabel, but somehow she is a little different from other people. You see, her grandfather is Bishop of Holcombe and her uncle is Lord Ribchester.' " But, we are assured, "Mabel's popularity at the Grange was thoroughly well deserved, for it rested more on her personality than her social standing". Personality in fact is a characteristic which Mabel totally lacks, but since the book is about Aldred and her overburdened conscience, this does not matter. Mabel's admiration for Aldred is based on the mistaken belief that she once rescued a child from a burning house; an act which Aldred is unable either to deny – since this would cost her Mabel's friendship – or to confirm, since she has done nothing of the sort. The ending is neat, if unsubtle: Aldred expiates her tacit deception by saving Mabel from being burnt to death – and is finally able to get the whole thing off her chest.

Mabel is one of those tedious girls whose "straightness" borders on the sanctimonious. Aldred, on the other hand, is one of Angela Brazil's purposely unidealized heroines, "a girl who, like most other girls, had her pleasant and her disagreeable moods, her high aspirations and good intentions, and her occasional bursts of bad temper". By insisting on the averageness of her principal characters, she ensured their appeal; few children can identify with a paragon or an out-and-out rotter. When she has to moralize, which happens quite often, Angela Brazil does so in the character of a kind relative, an older sister or an aunt, thereby emphasizing the reasonableness of what she has to say: "Gwen was tired out … and hungry, and very miserable, or I think she would not have talked in so lawless and foolish a strain." Headmistressy aphorisms occur from time to time: "Very few people can realize their ideals, so it is something to be able to idealize our real." Though she stated that her aim was always to write stories from the schoolgirl's point of view (one reason why she never forced herself "into a scholastic mould" or became a headmistress) she cannot consistently be successful in this. She has to draw on her own experience – and her experience goes beyond the schoolgirl's, and has coloured her attitude to the part of it which is relevant. This is a problem which all writers for children have to face; in a fundamental sense they are in a false position. However effectively they express the simplified outlook of childhood, all sorts of things are involved behind the scenes – memory, revaluation, a propensity for dissimulation. Perhaps Angela Brazil kept herself up to the mark in this respect by continuing to write "at a little desk which was made for me when I was nine years old" – but not infrequently an incident described from a headmistress's viewpoint creeps in. Headmistresses, after all, have their problems like everyone else: " 'A suitable head girl makes all the difference to a school and if we happen to choose the wrong one it may completely spoil the tone.' " Bearing in mind that "schoolgirls are thoughtless creatures, very often heartless" Angela Brazil lost no opportunity to put in, in her own character, a good word for the afflicted. On page 241 of *For The School Colours* she mentions a society called "The Poor Brave Things"; and shortly afterwards becomes so carried away that she has the girls organize – with more enthusiasm than tact – a "Romp Day" for crippled children.

Girlishness comes across overwhelmingly in the many passages of dialogue – when schoolgirls weren't prancing about wildly on the hockey field or exchanging emotional confidences by a cabbage patch, they were vying with one another to express their personalities through the use of current expressions.

"Oh, isn't it piggy and nasty!" exclaimed Annie.
"What a chubby place!"
"Oh, hold me up! This child's knocked over entirely!"
"Did you have jolly hols?"
"Absolutely ripping, thanks."
"Miss Jones is a stunt, as jinky as you like."

The ability to speak up for oneself was appreciated (" 'I put it to the meeting – are you willing to sit down and be tyrannized over by the Sixth?' ") though unorthodoxy was not: " 'Only seniors may wear their sailors on the backs of their heads. It's a strict point of school etiquette. You may jam on your hockey cap as you like, but not your sailor.' " Schoolgirls are usually conservative, needing approval to stabilize their fluctuating sense of personal worth, liking to belong to a clique – hence the emphasis on tradition, which is to be found in all large schools, real or fictional.

"Did you hear?" she remarked. "They actually want to join the Dramatic!"

"Cheek," murmured Consie, and the others giggled.

"And why shouldn't we join?" flamed Gladys Wilkes.

"Why? Because you're day-girls, and the Dramatic's only for boarders. That's the reason."

An experiment in comprehensive education is described in *For The School Colours* (1919). Two schools are amalgamated, to the dismay of the posher one: " 'The Hawthorns! Those girls whom we never spoke to, wouldn't have touched with a pair of tongs!' gasped Irma." Schoolgirls are nothing if not outspoken (" 'She's the plainest girl in the school – that's my opinion of her!' ") and their resistance to change sometimes turns them into downright bullies: for example, this occurs in a scene at the beginning of *The School By The Sea* (1914). A new girl, Gerda Thorwaldson (" 'Our ducky, chummy little room to be invaded by a third – a stranger!' ") is forced to perform in the dormitory:

"You either dance this very instant, or you stand on that table and sing a song – in English, mind, not German!"

… "This is easy enough," volunteered Annie Pridwell, by way of encouragement. "Now, come along, and do as I do."

"Fly, little birdie, fly," mocked Betty Scott.

"She's too stupid!"

"She's going to blub!"

Angela Brazil's A Fortunate Term

A dramatic moment from Ruth at St Ronan's.
Drawn by Frank Oldham

"Leave her alone!"
"No, make her dance!"
"Don't let her sneak out of it!"

The persecution of Gerda derives its impetus from the fact that
the girls believe her to be German (" 'You may call it British prejudice
but I can't stand foreigners,' Dulcie remarked with a gusty sigh") –
though she turns out to be as English as anyone, and not a spy. This
was Angela Brazil's first war book; five or six followed, to form a
peculiar series which stands out from the bulk of her work. Like
other children's writers of the time she tried to represent the war as
an opportunity for heroism, and created an unreal situation in which
everyone is "simply longing" to dash off to the front, to behave
pluckily and with a great deal of resource in order to show the "Huns"
what being British is all about. ("She was burning to do something
to help – to nurse the wounded, drive a transport wagon, act as
secretary to a staff-officer, or even be telephone operator over in
France.") Angela Brazil quite shamelessly exploited the reinforced
sense of nationality which is endemic in times of international crisis
– this was the time when her popularity was at its peak. To be English
had suddenly become an obligation, as well as a privilege; and there
is a great deal of talk about one's "duty" to this and that. Duty was
sometimes seen in terms of its immediate effect:

> "It is the duty of every British girl to make every possible
> sacrifice to keep those unspeakable Huns out of our islands. I
> appeal to you all to use the utmost economy and abstinence,
> and voluntarily to give up some of the things that you like … ".
> "It'll mean knocking off buns, I suppose," sighed Sylvia
> mournfully.

Angela Brazil was not fond of foreigners at the best of times – apart
from Americans, whose carefree spirit of independence she admired
– but during the war they became positively villainous. Among others,
we find a nasty Mr Hockheimer who opportunely if euphemistically
"went to settle his great account. He and his car were found in the

river at Chadwick this morning", and a charming Russian adventuress who is bowled out by two perceptive girls. The plot of *The Luckiest Girl in the School* (1916) has an interesting twist (noticeable in an author who tended to rely rather too heavily on the usual children's book stand-bys: missing wills, long-lost relatives, the "rough diamond" from the backwoods who turns out to have aristocratic connections). Winona Woodward arrives proudly at Seaton High School, having been awarded a scholarship – to which, unknown to her, she is not entitled: there has been a mix-up in the examination papers. Of course, all turns out well in the end; she is allowed to stay, and makes good on her own account, becoming Games Captain and a valuable member of the Sixth. Not enough is made of this adjunct, however; like most of Angela Brazil's stories, the elements of this plot are far too diffuse, without underlying unity.

A great deal of the usual "patriotic knitting" goes on in the background: when Winona's rather feckless brother joins up, she "began a pair of socks for him at once". Predictably, the army is the making of him. " 'It's wonderful what serving their country has done for some of our fellows; in their case the war has been a blessing in disguise.' "

If the complacency of that is infuriating, there is a scene in *A Patriotic Schoolgirl* (1918) which goes beyond superficiality into pure farce:

> The walls had been decorated for the occasion with flags and evergreens and patriotic mottoes. In a large tub in the centre stood the Christmas tree, ornamented with coloured glass balls and tiny flags. Some of the parcels, tied up with scarlet ribbon, were hanging from the branches.
>
> Marjorie ... had never been inside a hospital of any kind, and a military one particularly appealed to her. ...
>
> "This is Peters; he keeps us all alive in this ward. He's lost his right leg but he's going on very well and takes it sporting, don't you, Peters?"
>
> ... "Jackson has lost his right leg too," said Elaine.
>
> "The only thing that troubles me," remarked Jackson, "is

that I'd paid a quid out in Egypt to have my leg tatooed by one of those black fellows. He'd put a camel on it, and a bird and a monkey, and my initials and a heart. It was something to look at was that leg. And I've left it over in France!"

For a time, the war permeated and glamorized everything. Whatever was done, was done for a worthwhile purpose. Yet at the same time an undercurrent of excitement was generated, which made previously unquestioned routines seem tedious. The impatience of girls to be off, careering recklessly through the enemy's lines in a truck, may have been exaggerated in Angela Brazil, but the spirit of enthusiasm which she travestied was none the less a real one. It may have had more to do with changing attitudes to women than with vapid patriotism, however; never before had there been a national campaign in which women were actively involved. The principal difference between real war girls and Angela Brazil's characters is in the latters' total ignorance of what they might be letting themselves in for. The only severed limbs which get into her books are decorated ones – and those have to be bolstered up with Christmas parcels and their owners' British stamina.

If war, in the main, was an abstraction, its effect on some girls was expressed in precise enough terms: " 'There used to be riding lessons before the War,' sighed Irene. 'Now the riding master has gone to the front. I wonder if things will ever be the same again? If I don't learn to ride properly while I'm young, I'll never have a decent seat afterwards, I suppose.' " Thoroughly British Marjorie – the *Patriotic Schoolgirl* – is one of Angela Brazil's least sympathetically treated heroines; she is allowed to make a fool of herself all along the line, to the extent of planning (unwittingly) to help a German prisoner of war to escape. She founds the Secret Society of Patriots (SSOP); in an access of zeal she writes a letter to an unknown British "Tommie", who responds by offering to "keep company" with her when he gets back to "blighty". Marjorie, taken aback, had "had a vague idea the army consisted mostly of public-school boys. To find that her protégé was an uneducated working man, who had entirely misconstrued the nature of her interest in

'We must rush before they open the door.'
Three Terms at Uplands; *illustration by D. L. Mays*

him … made poor Marjorie turn hot and cold." His letter falls into the hands of Mrs Morrison, the headmistress, who expels Marjorie; she is reinstated when the innocence of her motive for writing to the "Tommie" is established.

Less satisfactorily resolved is the episode of her friendship with Chrissie Lang ("Chrissie is the most adorable girl … we do everything together now"). This is almost the only occasion when Angela Brazil indulges in irony: when Marjorie thinks "Probably [Chrissie's brother] is a shirker or a conscientious objector … and to such a patriotic girl as Chrissie it must be a dreadful trial" she doesn't for a moment suspect that patriotic Chrissie (unlike the unfortunate Gerda in *The School by the Sea*) is a genuine German spy. When she is finally brought face to face with the truth, she asks the headmistress: " 'Is it right to forgive the enemies of our country?' " Mrs Morrison replies bleakly and melodramatically, " 'When they are dead' " – a brief exchange which can hardly have done much to foster a spirit of tolerance among Angela Brazil's readers.

Tolerance, of course, was not fashionable – and schoolgirls were dreadfully prone to fads and fashions. "Miss Dunkworth was immensely popular with the girls. It was the fashion to admire her. 'I think the shape of her nose is just perfect!' declared Francie Shepherd." Girls were always falling madly in love with one another, and occasionally with older women; innumerable friendships "flamed to red heat". The headmistress in *A Patriotic Schoolgirl* is forced to cough warningly from the audience when love-making during a charade threatens to become too passionate – but with her usual disregard for the implications of any situation which she sets up, Angela Brazil keeps all this firmly on a sentimental plane; there is no suggestion of the physical. Her own attitude to emotional behaviour was less straightforward: she veered from frowning, with the most starchy of her headmistresses, on "the sentimental", to condoning the more idiotic of its manifestations: "The friendship, which had begun conventionally with the orthodox 'Miss Lindsay', now expressed itself by 'Margaret', 'Peggy', or such pet terms as 'Carina' and 'Love-angel.' " In terms of real life behaviour, the girls were at an age when they had to fall in love with someone; to pick on members of their own sex may have been just a matter of expediency.

The few boys – brothers, cousins and so on – in Angela Brazil's books treat girls with usual good-humoured condescension, being moderately surprised when a girl shows herself to be resourceful or physically active, always ready to make allowances for girls' weaker mentalities. " 'Well, you don't want girls to swat as hard as boys,' said Piers ' ... spoils their complexions. They're put in the world to do the ornamental.' " A doctor's son, in *The Youngest Girl in the Fifth*, remarks: " 'There's some quite decent stuff in the dispensary, and sometimes the bottles are coloured pink, especially if they're for girls.' " Angela Brazil's first heroine, Peggy, in *A Terrible Tomboy* (not a school story) *did* distinguish herself by fighting, and overcoming, a boy who'd been bullying her brother; future tomboys on the whole were rather less terrible. Girls, in Angela Brazil as elsewhere, were always seeking boys' approval (those bicycle spokes must have imprinted themselves on her subconscious). The assertion "a girl is as good as a boy any day" (that commonplace of children's literature) would never have been necessary if it hadn't been for the universal assumption that she was *not*.

One of those ubiquitous school societies was The Rainbow League (in *A Popular Schoolgirl*, 1920) – "a society for schoolgirls who wish to help in the great work of reconstruction after the War" – which held, among other things, that "woman's greatest and strongest weapons are love and sweetness". Evidently, it was time for the munition workers and transport drivers to get back to the home – and Angela Brazil, receptive as ever to public opinion, was helping (probably subconsciously) to reconcile them to this. Forthrightness was definitely her forte: when she departed from it she inevitably became silly or banal. One of her most fundamental misconceptions was her idea of herself as a sensitive flower: what she's constantly putting across is a prosaic person's concept of the poetic. So, "Celtic glamour" for her is inextricably bound up with "piskies" and Cornish wishing-wells; and a Hertfordshire village inspires in her no more profound response than the feeling that she was "in an Elizabethan dream".

140

For a writer whose name has come to stand for the idea of jolly English girls' public schools, the schools themselves – the actual buildings, the classrooms and corridors and assembly halls and outhouses – play very little part in Angela Brazil's stories. Surprisingly, she succeeds best in evoking the character of a particular setting when she writes about rain – which she disliked; characteristically, she preferred sunny weather. "The overflowing gutter-pipe emptied veritable rivulets into a temporary pond on the front drive; the lawn appeared fast turning into a morass; and even indoors the atmosphere was so soaked with damp that a dewy film covered bannisters, furniture and woodwork, and the wallpaper on the stairs distinctly changed its hue. In VB classroom the girls hung about disconsolately." It's almost as though her more admirable qualities as a writer were arrived at in spite of herself. In her autobiography – which, admittedly, siphoned off a great deal of the dross in her literary repertoire – she remarks: "Schoolgirls – dear things! – are the same the world over"; a truism which her fictional schoolgirls – many of whom were less sentimental than she was – would have been the first to repudiate.

VIII

Millgirls, Madcaps and Mothers Superior

"... A woman of that class looks a worn out drudge of
fifty a year after she's married."
                    (George Bernard Shaw, *Pygmalion*)

IN THE FIRST decade of the century, when middle-class adolescent
girls were devouring Angela Brazil's school stories and the edifying
offerings of the *Girl's Own Paper* and the *Girl's Realm*, a different
type of popular fiction was arising to satisfy the tastes of artisan
girls. In spite of social reforms and the increasing influence of the
Trades Union movement, which doubled its membership between
1901 and 1913, poorer families in urban areas lived and worked in
deplorable conditions: trade unions had done little to improve the
position of girl employees in factories and shops, fearing that
women's work would undercut and reduce men's wages. Marriage
– her only escape from factory life – resulted for the working girl
merely in a change from one background of unremitting drudgery
to another. It often meant producing and bringing up many children
with the whole family living in one room, and several houses sharing
one water tap.

Although the "feminine illness" of menstruation was used by
men as an excuse to keep women out of well-paid executive
positions, it was not considered a bar to their performance of arduous
tasks in ill-equipped homes, nursing or domestic service, dirty
factories and sweat shops. In 1906 there were still girls carding hooks
and eyes at home and earning only five shillings [25p] weekly for
an eighteen-hour day. Almost two million girls were in service, many
of them employed as hard-pressed maids of all work in lower-middle-

class homes. In London a female's average factory wage was between seven [35p] and sixteen shillings [80p] a week, though a little better for higher skilled millgirls in the northern cloth industries. Like the below-stairs household skivvies, factory girls were the sub-stratum of a society which maintained the superstructure of "Edwardian elegance". In factories and sewing rooms, for a bare subsistence wage, they made the elaborate corsets, huge flowery hats and flowing dresses, with the extravagant frills and furbelows which were considered essential for the adornment of upper-class women.

The millgirls' clogs and shawls, and the crumpled, coarse looking clothes of working men waiting in lines for grossly underpaid casual labour, contrasted savagely with the gracious aura surrounding the more affluent Edwardians. They, in common with their Victorian forebears, offered temperance, limited education and free hand-outs of food, but still saw leisure as destructive for the poorer classes. Children who danced to barrel organs in the streets – their only playground – often suffered from rickets and were neglected by mothers forced to work long hours outside the home. Although methylated spirits, beer and gin were cheap, for many families the consolation of drink simply increased and brutalized their poverty.

There was however a growing resilience in the working classes which demanded more from life than gruelling work followed by the sleep of exhaustion. Like the militant Suffragettes and the Irish who campaigned for Home Rule, the Labour movement was challenging the paternalistic attitude towards the underprivileged which had existed for decades. Hard work, gratitude and subservience had brought the poor little more than bread and dripping, while the better-off members of the community consumed gargantuan meals which ought to have precipitated many more Edwardian heart attacks than have been recorded. Plenty of working-class people must have agreed with dustman Alfred Doolittle, in Shaw's *Pygmalion*, that as they were "up agen middle" (and upper) "class morality all the time" they might as well enjoy being the *un*deserving poor for a change, and see where that got them. By 1908 the Education Acts had been in operation long enough for members of even the most poverty-stricken families to be able to read for pleasure, and sixpenny [2½p] and one shilling [5p] novels were widely available. Echoing the claim for participation rather than patronage, non-servile working-class heroes and heroines began to emerge in popular fiction, giving the modern reader interesting insight into Edwardian society from the viewpoint of the skivvies, shop-girls and factory hands: these were not always as loyal and loving to the "toffs" who employed them as the more idealistic fiction of the period suggests.

Unlike some of the intellectual Fabian writers, Alfred Harmsworth, who in 1905 became Lord Northcliffe, was very much in touch with "the common man" and the lively reading matter his increasing literacy demanded. Launching the *Daily Mail* in 1896 and the *Daily Mirror* in 1903, Northcliffe rapidly built up an empire of popular journalism founded on his frequently sensational presentation of news. The culture and entertainment that were liberally thrown in for good measure were to offshoot into another proliferating branch of his publishing enterprises. Always imbued with a crusading sense of responsibility for the moral and social values of his readers, Northcliffe realized the efficacy of fiction as a means of influencing young minds, and produced an enormous range of inexpensive, attractive, and long running juvenile magazines and "pulp" papers.

His penny weekly, the *Girls' Friend* (1899–1931), and its sister papers, the *Girls' Reader* (1908–1915) and the *Girls' Home* (1910–1915), were an amazing amalgam of millgirls, madcaps and mothers superior, catering largely for working-girl readers in late teens and early twenties. Titles taken at random when the *Girls' Friend* was in its heyday around 1908 indicate the range of the stories and serials, and the type of readership: *The Shame Of The School*, "Only A Barmaid", *Slave Of The Shop*, *A Wedded Schoolgirl*, "Madge O' The Mill", "Only A Laundry Girl", *Bride's Veil Or Nun's* and *A Mormon's Wooing*.

Mormons and Quakers were minority groups held in great suspicion by the *Girls' Friend*, but much of its fiction was obviously intended to appeal to another religious minority – the Roman Catholic Irish-girl immigrants working in English factories (and

144

likely to buy the paper). Described as "The flower of the convent" and "The sweetest woman in the world", Mary Latimer, nun, was frequently serialized in this trio of girls' journals. In fact she was rather more than a nun: incredibly, although only about nineteen years old, Mary had already risen to the heights of Mother Superior at St Agatha's convent. She gave sanctuary to the oppressed, hope to the despairing and affection to all who crossed her path. Particularly Mary Latimer was the helper of lovers, believing that "... women are meant to love and to be loved..." and that "... the

A George Gatcombe illustration for the 1907 Girls' Friend *serial.*
Convent Bells, or Cloistered Life *by Mrs De Winter Baker*

best fortune of all is a good man's love, unless one has a vocation". Concerning vocations, the sweetness of Mary Latimer and her religious sisters is often dwelt upon but little emphasis is placed on the rigours and disciplines of the contemplative life. Lord Northcliffe never forgot that with popular fiction it paid off to entertain rather than to instruct. The young Mother Superior remains serene in the face of all dilemmas, fortified, we gather, by religion in the present and romance in her past. Occasionally she whispers of "Desmond my love", – Desmond having been her "ideal soul mate" before the distressing day when "… 'ere the wedding band of gold could make them one, the hand of death claimed him for its own". Although convent life can hardly have had a practical appeal for many millgirls and housemaids, "bride's veil or nun's" was a persistent theme in the *Girls' Friend.* Mary Latimer, who appeared so regularly, was never credited to any author's name – perhaps the anonymity of her creation was supposed to enhance her other-worldly qualities.

Less other-worldly, but probably more popular with Irish girl readers feeling nostalgic for the country they had left behind, was Glory O'Shea. Glory was as cliché-ridden, storybook Irish as they come; with fresh complexion and roguish twinkling eyes, she continually spread warmth, cheer and her broad brogue all around, becoming the darling of her schoolmates and most of the holy sisters. She managed to achieve a great deal of freedom during her convent schooldays, and her adventures included trips to Paris, abduction by unwanted lovers, encounters with gipsies and skirmishes with sour, tyrannical and love-crossed nuns. Glory's exploits were brought to a triumphant close when she was at last married off: the indefatigable author, Mrs de Winter Baker, then at once demonstrated her versatility by producing a dramatic serial called *Convict Chains.* But that obviously never got off the ground like the "convent-bells" theme, and sure enough Mrs de Winter Baker was soon back again on safe and familiar paths with long-running epics about Glory O'Shea's daughter, who was cast in the same irrepressible convent-cheer-leader mould as her madcap Irish mother.

Although these papers were designed for working girls whose education had begun and ended at elementary schools, many colleges and "educational establishments of some pretension" were featured in their pages. However it is significant that hardly a paragraph is written about classroom activities, and with few exceptions these college girls are vacuous, man-catching madcaps, who hold in contempt all well-educated women, especially their teachers. These are represented as ugly, muddleheaded, old-fashioned frumps, summed up in the following rhyme concocted by a typical *Girls' Friend* college heroine:

> There was an old party named Simms
> Who was full of strange fancies and whims
> Her figure and face
> Were a perfect disgrace
> And they frightened away all the hims.

The large, tinted pages of these magazines contained some of the most attractive illustrations of all Northcliffe's Amalgamated Press story papers. George Gatcombe, their artist *par excellence,* created page after page of girls who looked good enough to eat, wearing boaters, crisp blouses, large ties and long skirts, with their luxuriant tresses waving impeccably down beautiful backs. However he drew the older female characters (teachers and employers) as desiccated freaks, with hatchet faces and skimpy hair scragged back into fussy little Victorian bonnets. The middle- and upper-class Suffragettes – who sought reforms for working-class girls but didn't welcome them into their movement – were similarly resented in the pages of the *Girls' Friend,* in spite of the fact that one of Northcliffe's popular authors was Cecily (Max) Hamilton, who wrote the rousing words of the Suffragettes' anthem, "The March Of Women", to Dame Ethel Smyth's music.

This dichotomy between "us" and "them" in the minds of the *Girls' Friend* readers is easily understandable. There were no well-paid or satisfying careers for poorly educated women. "Going on the halls" or into the chorus was an alternative which was open only to a handful. Most of the girls in factories, shops or domestic service could expect little glamour or escape from their hard-working routine except through romantic fantasies. Class divisions in Edwardian England were rigid, and few people married outside their place in society. According to the *Girls' Friend,* the best way for a working girl to enter into an honest and respectable relationship with a son of the more favoured classes was to get herself run over by his bicycle or motor car. He would then carry her insensible but lovely form to the nearest cottage and, in relief at her revival from the point of death, fall inescapably in love with her. Of course there still remained the up-hill task of demolishing prejudices held by members of the young man's upper-crust family, but love could be expected to find the way.

Usually, however, the *Girls' Friend* specialized in fiction with whose down-to-earth settings its readers could identify. Girls who yearned to get away from it all through the wildest extravagances of romantic fiction were better satisfied with contemporary authors other than those who wrote for these Northcliffe papers. Marie Corelli's quasi-mystical interpretation of "nature", Elinor Glyn's torrid passion and Florence Barclay's religious sentimentality all basically perpetuated the Victorian tradition of the passive, flower-like female, worshipping at the altar of romantic love – her true and only fulfilment, glorification, crown, halo, etc. It must have been difficult for most Edwardian working girls to equate these escapist visions of the feminine rôle with the toughness their own lives demanded: the *Girls' Friend,* the *Girls' Reader* and the *Girls' Home,* whatever their literary shortcomings, at least endeavoured to make their stories believable as well as entertaining.

One of their most popular and prolific writers was Mabel St John. "Mabel" was actually Henry St John Cooper, the half-brother of Gladys Cooper, who was to enjoy fame on the London stage and in the cinema for over half a century. As well as churning out thousands of words of girls' fiction every week, he wrote regularly as Henry St John for several of Lord Northcliffe's boys' papers, including *Boys' Friend, Boys' Realm, Pluck, Marvel* and the *Union Jack.* (He also found time to be a successful breeder of bulldogs!) In her autobiography *(Gladys Cooper,* Hutchinson, London, 1931), Gladys Cooper mentions that her brother "… often wrote 10,000 words at a

Above: A typical teacher-debunking episode in Girls' Friend, *drawn by George Gatcombe*
Below: Coosha takes charge (from Mabel St. John's Pollie Green at Cambridge, Girls' Friend, *1908*

'sitting', and on one occasion when he was asked if he would do a 'rush' story for a Christmas Annual of 32,000 words in 24 hours, he did it in a little more than half that time ...".

"Mabel" St John was unequivocally on the side of the underdog, and "her" melodramatic 1909 serial describing the dreary background of the single-handed maidservant bullied by her boss must have endeared this author to many readers, who felt themselves similarly exploited. *Plain Jane* is a young, orphaned "slavey" in the dingy home of brutal Mrs Bagshaw, who beats, kicks and humiliates her. "Mrs Bagshaw had thrashed her – hundreds of times – and when you've little food in your body, and have to work unceasingly from morn till night, powers of retaliation are apt to be weak ...". (Mabel St John believed in spelling things out.) "From the small scullery came the sickening smell of boiling linen and soap. The kitchen was half filled with steam. With her cheek tingling from the blow, the girl went into the scullery and bent over the wash tub ... for an hour she worked. 'Ain't you nearly through yet, you lazy hussey?' the woman asked presently. 'Have you rinsed them things in the blue water? ... 'Urry yourself will you?' " (Before the advent of the washing machine, the burden of the weekly wash must have proved intolerable to stronger characters than Plain Jane, in fact as well as in fiction.)

Henry St John's rather theatrical stories owed more to the raucous good humour of the music hall than the serious drama in which his actress sister excelled. During the first decade of this century the music hall, with gallery seats at a few pennies a time, provided excitement and temporary escape for the poorer members of the community. It was popular all over England, a spontaneous theatre growing out of public house sing-songs, and rooted in the industrial working classes. With its sentimental songs, comedians, conjurors and contortionists, the music hall made no claims to gentility or refinement, and many of St John's underprivileged characters echoed this robustness and refusal to be patronized. Em Hammond, for instance, the working-class heroine of *The Shame Of The School,* when sneered at by her upper-class college mates, simply ups and walks out of Ida House, to join a panorama show. (Where despite her much vaunted "yellow hair" she plays the part of an Arab girl on stage, and somewhat surprisingly has to whistle through her yashmak "The Man Who Broke the Bank at Monte Carlo".) When the snobbish teacher Miss Cronk succeeds in finding Em, she comes up against the showman, Mr Cobb, who proves to be one of the strong-minded and articulate examples of the British working man crossing swords with his superiors whom Mabel St John so much enjoyed creating. " 'Don't apologize, for goodness sake, in case you crack your lips,' " quips Mr Cobb. Miss Cronk replies by calling him "insolent scum", at which Mr Cobb summons his wife to the fray. " 'Hi, missus, here's a saucy puss a-trying to make love to yours truly.' " " 'I'll love 'er!' " says Mrs Cobb, who then proceeds in the strongest possible terms to tell the staid 60-year-old teacher what she thinks of women who lust after other people's husbands. Another typical St John character is the school cook, a jovial, motherly woman who sings music-hall songs whilst at work in the kitchen, and slaps her knees violently, rolling around on the floor in silent mirth whenever she encounters anything mildly amusing.

The resistance to theatrical careers, to which better-class magazines like the *Girl's Own Paper* tenaciously clung for decades, was not shared by the Northcliffe "millgirl" papers. These were less inhibited by overtones of religious respectability and nothing was taboo that made a good story: they recognized that their audience expected its fiction to be on a par with the entertainment provided for them in the music halls at the time.

Henry St John furthered this tradition with his happiest brain-child, Pollie Green, who first danced through the pages of the *Girls' Friend* in 1908. [1] So popular was she that her adventures were quickly repeated in the *Girls' Reader* and the *Girls' Home*, and soon reprinted yet again in the monthly *Girls' Friend Library*. It is true to say that these Northcliffe papers are collected today mainly for the appeal of Pollie Green, whose saga began with schooldays, and joyously chronicled her subsequent escapades until the time of her marriage. The *Girls' Friend* blazed euphoric banner headlines proclaiming

[1] The Pollie Green serials, in chronological order, were: *Pollie Green, Pollie Green and Coosha, Pollie Green at Cambridge, Pollie Green in Society, Pollie Green Engaged* and *Pollie Green at Twenty-One.*

Pollie's attractions: "She's as fair as the heather is Pollie Green", "Get to know the sweetest girl in the world – Pollie Green", "The girl of our heart is Pollie Green", "Always our favourite is Pollie Green", "The pride of the country is Pollie Green", "The queen of our heart is Pollie Green".

Pollie's charms, vividly illustrated by George Gatcombe, resulted in the widespread issue of paper patterns for Pollie Green blouses and, as well as being a fashion originator, Pollie must have influenced the thinking of the *Girls' Friend* readership on various social issues. She was another heroine in the irrepressible madcap tradition of the papers, but she had sufficient intelligence to approach new situations without prejudice: she was also in advance of her time by about 40 years in her unsentimental friendship with a coloured girl named Coosha. This was as different from the turgid Eva/Topsy *Uncle Tom's Cabin* relationship as Margaret Drabble is from Ethel M. Dell. Friendship on equal terms between Africans and Europeans had, as early as 1901 with Jack, Sam and Pete, proved a popular theme in one of Northcliffe's boys' papers, *The Marvel.* S. Clarke Hook's stories featuring this strangely assorted trio of Oxford undergraduate, American trapper and Zanzibar negro remained in great demand until the early 1920s, and a film was made about these characters in 1919. Pollie, though less rebellious against society's established values than another, more intellectual, contemporary heroine – H. G. Wells's Ann Veronica – nevertheless symbolized tolerance and liberality to the working-class girls who followed her fortunes.

At the beginning of the series Marguerite (to give Pollie her proper name) is seventeen. With happy contempt for convention she wears a rough fisherman's jersey, an ancient faded shirt and boys' hobnailed boots. But (to use only a selection from Mabel St John's plentiful epithets) she is tall and slender, "… with a dainty impudent and entirely charming face". And she is crowned by "… a tumbled mane of hair … neither golden nor brown nor red, but which was either – or all three – just as the sun and the shadows ordained". (From which we can see that Pollie is indeed a force to be reckoned with, and that new ideas are considered acceptable in a pretty girl, though not in older women and "Blue stockings".) Mabel St John describes her as "the wittiest, prettiest and sauciest girl at Nunthorpe School, who dismays by her audacity and disarms by her charm". When Coosha, the Zulu chieftain's volatile daughter, erupts into the school and is dragged screaming into the classroom, Pollie alone realizes that she is frightened and tries to understand her. In common with many other writers, St John overdraws the African girl. He attributes to her pidgin English of the "coon" variety and an unutterably wild-eyed and woolly-haired physical appearance. " 'You de ugliest ole woman I neber did see ... you ole monkey-face woman – I get a big knife and cut off yo' head!' " "Coosha was something of a jackdaw when it came to personal attire, wearing a collection of odds and ends of beads, buttons, feathers, ribbons and even stones, sea-shells and drawer-handles." She soon settles down at school and becomes more believable, though she remains irreverent and completely unpatronizable.

Pollie and Coosha move on to Mead House College, Cambridge, mainly so that Pollie can demonstrate her impatience with cheap flirtations – indicating that her mind is on other, though not noticeably higher, things. " 'You know it's awfully bad form now to be early Victorian' " – to girls who can't play cricket; and, to snobbish schoolmates, " 'Go away, you mean spirited, catty creatures! ... I'll mix up your face bloom and your nose whiting and your eyelash blacking, and put it with your golden hair wash, and stand over you and make you drink the lot ...'." Pollie inspires adulation from several male college students, but though appreciative of their attentions insists on putting each relationship on to a platonic basis. Her upright undergraduate admirers have to settle for this – or nothing. Cads and bounders too are inflamed to passion by Pollie Green: to them she offers only furious expressions of contempt which, needless to say, add fuel to their ardour. Later Pollie is to have London society at her feet, and social pressures result in her becoming engaged to the Duke of Hammersford, a condescending and ruthless member of the ruling class whom Pollie soon has the sense to throw over. He then promptly not only commits suicide but obligingly leaves Pollie his fortune, thus smoothing the way to her eventual happy marriage with the besotted but poor Bruce Hardaker who has always loved her. (Mabel St John championing the underdog again.)

Back at Cambridge, Coosha has been victimized by Miss Trumpinshaw, an officious, typically "us and them" teacher, on whom the coloured girl avenges herself when helping to organize a charity fête. Miss Trumpinshaw is a grim-faced lady whose pince-nez and mannish trilby emphasize her astringent features. The cut of her ancient black coat and skirt is formidable, and Coosha neatly appends to Miss Trumpinshaw's stalwart rear a prominent notice advertising: "One Kis – 3 Pens" [pence]. Expectedly trade is not brisk but Miss Trumpinshaw has to ward off one unattractive and over-enthusiastic military gentleman. Coosha is always quick to visit terrible retribution on anyone who treats her as an inferior.

Although sympathetic with Coosha, Mabel St John shows less respect for another type of foreigner. Germans – Northcliffe's perpetual *bête noire* and threat to British supremacy – are parodied mercilessly. Coosha, who becomes infatuated with an inept, golden-haired young German gentleman rejoicing in the name of Hans Schmitzenhausen is, though declaring herself "in lub", forced to admit of her beloved " 'Him bery beautiful but don't tink him particler cleber' ". Germans were expected to display arrogance and stupidity in Northcliffe's publications for young people, but similar qualities in Britishers were deplored. Coosha's guardian, General Burgum, returns to England after four years in India during which time he has serenely disregarded his Zulu ward. On his return, acting under a strict sense of duty, he feels the time has come to knock the independent Coosha into respectable shape. " 'I know how to deal with these niggers, male and female ... When they see they've got a man to deal with who ain't taking nonsense from them they soon come to their knees.' " Coosha happily does not, and soon outwits and humiliates the blimpish general.

The *Girls' Friend* candid-coloured-girl and daredevil-Irish-colleen characters were to become stock ingredients over the next four decades for gingering up a great deal of girls' fiction set against the sedate background of English boarding-school life.

In 1908 Northcliffe's juvenile papers reflected Edwardian

England's uneasy balance between openness to new ideas and fear of drastic change. Society's existing structure was beset by the challenge of revolutionary new worlds of science, technology, occultism, free love and socialism. The *Girls' Friend's* attitude to racial and ideological "aliens" in their midst was to absorb them wherever possible, and thus reduce their potential revolutionary impact. The challenge of Suffragettes and the "new woman" was taken lightly as something which could be laughed off: Irish immigrants, however, were here to stay so they were well treated in girls' fiction. Missionary fervour amongst religious groups, together with the Boer War and contemporary pride in Britain's far flung empire, had drawn attention to African and Indian communities. (Sentimental imperialism was just as popular in the songs of the music hall as in the writings of Kipling.) The England of the early 1900s never dreamed it would ever open its doors to large groups of coloured immigrants, so society had nothing to lose by racial tolerance – at least in fiction.

The menace of other strong European nations and Britain's unpreparedness for war were themes constantly reiterated by late Victorian and Edwardian writers. They soon settled on Germany, who was rebuilding her navy, as the real enemy: even one of Mrs Molesworth's mild stories *(Imogen,* 1892), describing a London lodging house swathed in fog, declares "… you feel a certain thrill of not unpleasant excitement: the end of the world, or a German invasion". With *The War Of The Worlds* in 1898 and *The War In The Air* in 1908, H.G. Wells had heightened expectations of the old and established order breaking down completely. Northcliffe campaigned vigorously and specifically for stronger defence, when in 1906 Germany "invaded" England through the pages of his *Daily Mail*,[1] as well as frequently through the Amalgamated Press boys' fiction papers. Sexton Blake, popular detective-hero of the weekly *Union Jack* – who seemed to enjoy a love-hate relationship with Kaiser Wilhelm – brought about Britain's salvation by unearthing Germany's invasion plans: other "Britain invaded" series appeared

[1] "The Invasion of 1910" by William Le Queux, in which Lord Roberts is supposed to have co-operated by planning the fictional miliatry tactics.

in the *Boys' Friend, Marvel* and *Boys' Herald*. The editor-in-chief of this group of magazines was Hamilton Edwards, who also edited the *Girls' Friend*. Anti-German feelings in the girls' papers were not so clearly defined, possibly because girls were not expected to concern themselves with matters like national defence.

The general tone of the *Girls' Friend* and its sister papers was carefree and non-repressive, but Hamilton Edwards seemed anxious that his female readers should not depart too drastically from the duties which society expected of them. Chatting up his audience in "Among My Girls" and "Your Editor Advises His Friends", he describes "the popular girl": "She is sweetly self-effacing" with "the happy knack of listening – that greatest of all gifts" and she "does what every man delights in – seems to be solely interested in him". Further intimations that the "strong-minded woman" appeared *persona non grata,* and sex appeal was the paramount virtue, came in the *Girls' Friend* advertisements. Many drawings depicted incredibly proliferating tresses brought about by use of hair tonics, and the equally amazing figures of wasp-waisted Edwardian women who exhorted readers, "Don't be fat when Phatolene tablets will cure you absolutely" (without starvation or aperients). Special and unrepeatable offers of ladies' underclothing were lovingly illustrated: in 1909 "5 articles for 8/11d, [1] Post Free", included nightdress, camisole, petticoat, chemise and knickers – all luxuriant with lace insertions, tucks and threaded ribbons.

In 1922, when many of the original readers of Pollie Green were married with adolescent daughters of their own, Northcliffe's Amalgamated Press brought out an up-dated, teenage fiction paper, the *Girls' Favourite*. This was intended as much for thirteen-year-olds, dreaming of becoming eighteen, as for those who were already there. Like Northcliffe's more successful "schoolgirl" papers of the 1920s and '30s, it was edited, written and illustrated by an almost entirely male team. It discussed burning issues of the day: "Should girls play football?", "Bobbed hair or long?", "Etiquette for schoolgirls" and "Artificial silk stockings versus wool". The fictional heroines were typists rather than millgirls, easily – in the more democratic post-war

[1] [45p]

Revenge on Miss Trumpinshaw,
from Pollie Green at Cambridge

era – "getting off" with their bosses' sons, who were breezy, blazered and utterly British to the backbone. The *Girls' Favourite* carried its heroines – and readers – to the rapturous peak of becoming engaged, but rarely across the threshold of married life with its attendant and more mundane responsibilities. The paper lasted for five years but Northcliffe's male authors were not yet so competent as they became in the 1930s, when teenage girls' papers were at their best.

Other publishers brought out their own versions of factory-and-shop-girl papers [1] and took over some of the Northcliffe stock characters, as their story titles suggest: *I'm Only A Shop-Girl*, *Winnie The Workhouse Brat*, "He's Gone And Married A Mill-Girl" etc. In D. C. Thomson's *Girls' Weekly* the harassed, household Cinderella was portrayed in the seemingly endless and awful adventures of *Outcast Effie or They Made Their Blind Cousin Their Drudge*. Bunty Brown, an exuberant college girl, was the *Girls' Weekly's* answer to Pollie Green, but she lacked Pollie's liberality and was indiscriminately flirtatious, unlike her prototype. The same magazine in 1913 featured an ex-workhouse child called Jemima, "the hard-

[1] e.g. *Girls' Weekly*, 1912–1922; *Peg's Paper*, 1919–1940.

working, sunny-hearted maid of all work at Mrs Beddoe's boarding-house" whose "smiling face did everyone good". She scattered and picked up aspirates as liberally as her good cheer – " 'I ought to be on at the Hempire by rights.' "

As the years advanced, these "working-girl" papers began to cater for a more adult readership, and inevitably the joys of "romance" and domesticity were stressed. The papers seemed less sympathetic with their readers' position. By 1921, in the last months of the *Girls' Weekly*, film-star John Barrymore was tetchily griping in its columns about typists taking long tea-breaks and lunch-hours.

Newnes and Pearson's *Peg's Paper*, before ceasing publication in 1940, returned to the escapist, aphrodisiac qualities of the desert which E. M. Hull had exploited in *The Sheikh* as long ago as 1919. In *A Sin To Marry*, Nancy's "… cheeks flamed in the darkness. She was remembering those kisses which Sheikh Kazan Mohammed had poured on her face, eyes and lips, and the desperate thrill which had surged through her in response to them … .How could there be anything between an English girl and an Arab Sheikh? … If only he had been a man of her own race, instead of an Arab!" He *is*, of course: like E. M. Hull's lurid original, the *Peg's Paper* sheikh turned out to be a European after all. He was Colonel Allan Le Fevrine of the French Special Service, so all was well, and no one's racist traditions were affronted.

The same issue jolts its readers back from desert-fevered romance to the austerity of war-time England with a prominent advertisement for Pearson's two shillings and sixpenny [12½p] publication, *Home Pickling*. "Lord Woolton wants every woman to 'Go to it and pickle surplus garden produce. Here is the book which tells you all about it.'" With its (almost) dying breath, *Peg's Paper* by this incongruous juxtaposition of sheikh-and-pickle symbologies had summed up the entire range of feminine interests, as seen by the editors of women's "romance" weeklies in the 1920s and '30s. It was up to the writers of juvenile books and papers of the same period to do a better job for their girl readers.

IX

Stretchers, Staves and Sphagnum Moss

"The first Guides… just jolly well started out with a copy of *Scouting For Boys* and their own common sense, and learned how to *do* things."
(Catherine Christian, *The Marigolds Make Good*)

SOON AFTER ITS formation in 1908 the Boy Scout movement was gatecrashed by large numbers of girls, to the embarrassment of its founder, General Sir Robert Baden-Powell (later Lord Baden-Powell), who felt that their participation would make scouting seem feeble and unacceptable to boys. Equally he feared that hoydenism might be encouraged in the 6,000 young women who with considerable relish were putting into practice the tracking, tramping, drilling, first-aiding and adventure-seeking indicated by his *Scouting For Boys* (1908).

These unofficial Girl Scouts displayed a pioneering vigour which became somewhat muted when, towards the end of 1909, Baden-Powell was persuaded to draw up a scheme for establishing the Girl "Guides". This emphasized that the training laid down for Boy Scouts should, with girls, "be administered with great discrimination; you do not want to make tomboys of refined girls, yet you want to attract, and thus raise the slum-girl from the gutter". Significantly, Baden-Powell thought that "The main object is to give them *all* the ability to be better mothers and Guides to the next generation". (But not, apparently, to achieve through their own individuality and initiative.) So the rough and ready, improvised patrols of Girl Scouts had to become Girl Guides, to distinguish their movement clearly from that of the boys, and they were to work under the respectable control of "the right kind of ladies" who would see that more attention than before was given to domestic activities, and less to "boyish" pursuits. It is not surprising that some of the original Girl Scouts resented what they considered to be this enervation of scouting. They even had to change their patrol emblems, replacing animal names with flowers – which to Baden-Powell presumably seemed more suggestive of femininity – as Rose Kerr describes in *The Story Of The Girl Guides*: "When Guides first started, we refused to join them, for having been Peewits and Kangaroos, we thought it a great come down to become White Roses and Lilies of the Valley."

The official Girl Guide movement brought into being a specialist branch of girls' fiction, beginning in 1912 with Dorothea Moore's *Terry The Girl Guide* and surviving until a little after the end of the second world war. Many stories were written by women who were themselves Guiding officers, and they undoubtedly intended not only to please enthusiastic Guide readers, but to bring new recruits into the organization. To the non-Guide, however, the heroines of these books must have appeared daunting in their aspirations and energy, and it is doubtful whether Girl Guide fiction was ever read widely except by the converted. That the uninitiated preferred to remain in ignorance is suggested by a popular, playground skipping rhyme of the 1930s, when the movement was at its height:

> I'm a Girl Guide, dressed in blue,
> These are the actions I must do,
> Salute to the King, and bow to the Queen,
> And twist right round to the fairy Queen.

This not entirely accurate assessment of Guiding seems far removed from the robustness of the early Girl Scouts, which had inspired fiction in Lord Northcliffe's juvenile papers of 1909, before the spate of more orthodox Guide stories began. In July of that year the male editor of the *Girls' Reader* blazes the trail for a forthcoming serial which "will treat of a wholly fresh phase of woman's activity, – viz. that of Scout life. ... This force is made up of healthy, open-air, adventure-loving young women, who go about their work of tracking, spying, signalling and what not with a zeal and intelligence that may well set an example to their male confreres."

The Amazonian atmosphere evoked by this introduction to Evelyn Yates's story, *The Girl Scouts,* is negated by the postscript to its first episode: this is headed "A Girl Scout's Puff Bag", and describes how "a dainty bag for a powder-puff which would be of inestimable use to any Girl Scout can be made from two circles of pasteboard and a bone or wooden ring". The editor seemed to be smitten with a sudden fear that without the prettification and "feminizing" influence of powder puff bags his paper's first Girl Scout story might prove too bracing for his readers.

The heroines are nieces of the Bishop of Hawkesbury, who agrees to give the "two sweet darling [motherless] little girls" a home whilst their father's regiment is in India. The bishop's wife unearths treasures of old embroidery and sprigged muslin, preparing pretty rooms and frilled dresses for the "little mites", who soon afterwards make their entrance at one of the bishop's sedate garden parties for colonial Church delegates: of course the nieces, Mollie and Virginia, turn out to be strapping damsels of sixteen and fourteen, swinging towards the horrified bishop " with long steady strides – a couple of straight-backed, eager-looking young girls clad in khaki skirts and soft felt 'cowboy' hats, each carrying a pole … " (There were many variations in the unadopted but enthusiastic patrols which were springing up in different parts of Britain. However, almost without exception they shared a "liberating" uniform, attractive to potential recruits who were tired of trailing around, even for sporting activities, in ground-length skirts and high-collared, tight, long sleeved blouses. All the early Girl Scouts seemed to compete with each other in wearing the broadest brimmed hats and carrying extraordinarily long staves [broom-handles] which could quickly be converted into stretchers with the addition of netting, blankets or any other available pieces of cloth. Skirts reaching only to the calves were businesslike rather than decorative, and their sturdiness was enhanced by the wearing of leather belts and the inevitable "scout" knives.)

In the *Girls' Reader* serial, to illustrate her scouting prowess, Mollie "… rounded up her red lips and sent across the bishop's velvety lawn a long, lusty ear-splitting call, which … must carry to the other end of town". This disruptive noise, which the bishop likened to a steam siren, is the signal of the Curlew patrol. (Mollie and "Virgie" were fortunate enough to start Scouting before birds and beasts had to transform themselves into buttercups and daisies.) Their conservative uncle yearns for his nieces to abandon belts, broom-handles and haversacks in favour of "dainty" attire: nevertheless he has to admit that Scouting gives them a high standard of consideration for others. The well-trained (and much publicized) Scout powers of observation soon come into operation. Mollie points out to her apparently half-blind uncle that the "problem child" at his Church-maintained orphanage is savage only because her hands are frequently tied brutally together by those in charge, until her wrists are bruised. Naturally the grateful charity girl then finds salvation by joining the Curlews, and summoning aid by emitting the clarion patrol call whenever she is being bullied. Mollie and Virginia cheerfully continue to challenge the established order of feminine things by converting all and sundry to the supposed fulfilment of emulating "the hero of Mafeking". Evelyn Yates's story is undistinguished but mildly amusing, and memorable simply because it was one of the first "Guide" stories to appear in the popular press.

Very soon afterwards in an August 1909 issue of Northcliffe's boys' paper, the *Gem,* the Girl Scouts found an ironic advocate in Charles Hamilton. He is writing about St Jim's – a school second in popularity only to his long-lived Greyfriars. In *The Boy Scouts' Rivals* Hamilton describes the reaction of D'Arcy, a junior boy, to the news that his cousin Ethel, hitherto an irreproachably subordinate female, has now become a Girl Scout. Arthur Augustus D'Arcy (Gussy) considers it his duty to wean Ethel away from this new and unwomanly activity. (Gussy's affectations of speech serve as a constant reminder to readers that he comes from an aristocratic background.)

A man bein' so much supewiah to a woman in intellect is bound to look aftah her and give her fwiendly advice. … I shouldn't like Ethel to become a suffwagette. ... I wegard it as necessawy for a woman to wemain in her place. ... It would be absolutely howwid for women to get into Parliament, you know, when you considah what kind of boundahs they would have to mix with there. ...

D'Arcy is in fact stating a view, widely held by men of the period, that women were too noble (or too foolish) to participate in government. He also equates Girl Scouts with Suffragettes, who were very much in the public eye with their militant campaigning. Like the Suffragettes, early Girl Scouts and Guides were anxious to draw attention to themselves, so that they might receive public recognition and increase recruitment, as Rose Kerr's book clearly shows: "Any church parade, club feast, or other procession always found us well in the limelight, and we must have tramped miles at the tail of the 'Oddfellows' "

Charles Hamilton's story shows Ethel very much in command of the situation. With

Cover from The Gem, *1909*

the other members of her patrol she is camping, unchaperoned and unassisted by adults. (All the early Guides longed for camp, with its promise of freedom from many of society's restraints: in contrast, over-protective parents suffered torments at the idea of their virginal and vulnerable offspring going away to live under canvas.) Gussy's lordly attempts to persuade cousin Ethel of the error of her ways are emasculated by the fact that he has had to be ignominiously rescued

ARE YOU A GIRL SCOUT?

☞ TWO MEMBERS OF THE CURLEW PATROL GIRL SCOUTS. ☞

EVELYN YATES' THRILLING AND UNIQUE SERIAL,

"THE GIRL SCOUTS,"

Starts in Saturday's "Girls' Reader," the unique story paper. Price One Penny, of all Newsagents. Read also the Grand Serials—THE SHAME OF THE SCHOOL, THE BRIDE OF DUTTON MARKET, ZOLA LEE, THE GIPSY, AND SLAVE OF THE SHOP.

Trailer for one of the first magazine Guide stories
(Girls' Reader, 1909)

by the Guides from ragging by boys of a rival school. Ethel not only rejects his arguments about the "Gal Scouts", but challenges the St Jim's boys to a scouting contest – in which scouts of both sexes equally share the final honours. It is surprising that the girls were allowed to do so well, as contemporary children's fiction – especially when addressed to boys – usually stressed masculine strength by exaggerating feminine weakness. Illustrations of Edwardian Ethel show her with boater and long dress abandoned, wearing a "wideawake" hat and short skirt, and carrying the inevitable stave which is as tall as herself.

The suspicion and resentment which aristocratic, fictional Gussy felt for the Girl Scouts was expressed rather more forcibly in real-life situations by poorer members of the community. Although many people found the improvised apparel of the early Guides attractive, others were repelled by the sight of girls in uniform. Miss Stockdale from Liverpool – one of the original patrol leaders quoted in Mrs Kerr's history of the Guide movement – recalls that her girls were often mistaken for the Salvation Army, and had "all sorts of filth" thrown at them. Patrols suffered physical assaults from onlookers, and in some of the rougher districts it was unwise for Guides to walk alone in uniform through the streets. Internal disagreements were easier to cope with, as Miss Stockdale explains: "... when the girls got at loggerheads with each other we made them put on boxing gloves and settle their differences in cold blood. This really was very effective and stopped tale bearing, etc ...." It is to be hoped that the techniques of fisticuffs thus acquired were put to good use by Girl Scout pioneers against the jeering louts who were so ready with their rotting fruit and violent abuse. The uniform also created resistance in the mothers of enthusiastic Guides, especially "dark knickers and no petticoats", at a time when a girl's propriety might be gauged by the number of petticoats she wore.

The atmosphere of early Guiding is well conveyed in Dorothea Moore's *Terry The Girl Guide* (1912) which carried a foreword by B.P.'s sister Agnes Baden-Powell, who became the Girl Guides' first president. This praises the "bright, clever" and adventurous girls of all classes who had decided to follow their brothers in the delights of scouting. Agnes Baden-Powell implies that henceforth girls would not only find fulfilment in proving their "prowess in the jungle, tracking Red Indians", but would enjoy the added bonus of sharing a mutual interest with the boys in their families: "... what is there to talk to our brothers about in the evenings? They do not want to hear about our hats, or the new stitch in crochet." Overshadowed by her distinguished brother, Agnes Baden-Powell seemed anxious that Guiding should produce resourceful, but still auxiliary, females.

Although the Guide movement was probably of greater sociological importance for girls from underprivileged homes, Dorothea Moore's story, like a great deal of Guide fiction, is concerned with girls from the middle and upper classes. Terry's adventures – set in an expensive girls' boarding-school – created the pattern for dozens of books which were to follow. Terry is independent, intrepid, but above all an entrenched imperialist, whose every action echoes the sentiments of a fellow Guide's "poem":

> While boys and girls are learning
> To be their Empire's fence,

We needn't really be afraid
Of National decadence.

Terry shows her resourcefulness by forming herself with some school friends into an unadopted patrol and improvising their uniforms. "The Patrol were unanimous in favour of the 'Dolly Dye' and Terry undertook to lock herself into a bathroom with the dye and six white blouses, and turn the Patrol out khaki-coloured at the cost of fourpence halfpenny [2p]." (Original companies sometimes favoured the khaki of their male counterparts, rather than the dark blue which eventually became the recognized Guide uniform colour.) Terry, having thus successfully launched Guiding at her school, then heroically defends several small children from attack by a mad dog. This impressive display endears her to a one-armed Boer War hero, Captain Evelyn VC (who is trailing fictional clouds of B.P.'s South African glory). "With an odd expression in his blue eyes" he modestly offers to take charge of Terry's unofficial patrol, which is in search of an adult leader: " 'I do happen to know something about tests – I was through Mafeking.' " So Terry gets the next best thing to the Chief Scout himself.

Admiration of the personality of "The Founder" was still strong in Guide authors who wrote several decades later than Dorothea Moore, and whose heroines, like Baden-Powell when a Charterhouse boy in his early teens, were endowed with red hair, freckles and "twinkling eyes". Catherine Christian in *The Marigolds Make Good* creates a whole patrol of auburn-haired Girl Guides, from sandy through "the deep shiny copper of an old warming-pan" to violent red. The young teenager's propensity for hero-worship might safely be chanelled towards the Chief Scout, who to many people seemed an indestructible embodiment of honour and patriotism: "You see – one doesn't bleat all the time about the Promise, and the Laws, but they're always there, somehow, in the background, something to measure life up against, a standard to go by."

The imperialism which pervades *Terry The Girl Guide* was an exhortation to its young readers to work together to maintain the British Empire and to protect the weak. However, the author – and the book's

Frontispiece of one of the first hardback Guide stories,
Terry the Girl-Guide, *1912*

heroine – had little sympathy to spare for the lower orders near at hand, who, it seemed, required repression rather than help or protection. Terry takes to task some of the local factory workers who are on strike: "… there were such a lot of rowdy young men employed at the mills", one of whom presumes to criticize the officers of the British army. " 'Them fine dandy officers always 'angs together, sending poor men to the front to be shot instead of them.' " Terry boiled … 'It's people like you that make the national decadence … How dare you talk about soldiers when probably the only kind of fighting you've ever seen is a terrier killing rats.' " As an afterthought – and presumably a concession to the Guide daily "good deed" – Terry patronizingly gives the striker a Bath Bun: "… he looked rather as though he might be hungry now: he certainly looked as though he had smoked a great deal too much when he was a boy."

Against a background of increasing strike action and industrial unrest, there was fear, not only of "national decadence", but of working-class undernourishment that might produce a generation inadequate as "cannon fodder" in future conflicts. Although the first world war was still two years ahead, 1912 held a sense of foreboding that the end of society's present structure was fast approaching. The sinking of the *Titanic* appeared to the superstitious as an omen of world-shattering disasters soon to come. In the same year, the opening of *Hullo Ragtime* on the London stage seemed a further, unwelcome pointer towards change from old forms and patterns. The new music sounded discordant to many English people, who possibly also reacted against its negro inspiration.

Terry's imperialism never falters, and she revels in the preparedness of the Girl Guides: " 'They get ready: they won't have to keep out of the way because they're no use if the big thing comes.' " To the junior who demurs that surely it is the big girls who will nurse soldiers or defend the empire in emergencies, Terry replies, " 'I don't see that size has got anything to do with it …. You're English, whether you're First Form or Sixth.' " At Terry's school the greatest compliments are, "It's British of you …", and "one can trust a Guide": "unmitigated slugs" (bullies etc.) are abused for their "unutterable meanness and *un*imperialism".

Terry's patriotism keeps her going, even when, scorched and almost suffocated, she is removing a small box of gunpowder from a burning room to prevent an explosion. "It was at that moment, when she was groping desperately in thick, hot smoke for a door which seemed to have disappeared, that Terry struck up 'God Save the King'."

Dorothea Moore, who wrote a wide variety of girls' fiction from 1902 to 1939, became a Guide Commissioner. It is surprising and unfortunate that *Terry The Girl Guide* emphasized nationalism, with its implicit separatism, instead of international co-operation and the breaking down of class, creed and colour barriers which were integral aspects of Scouting. Many other authors equally failed to exploit these worthwhile tenets of the movement. Terry's banal adventures were echoed in successive Guide stories, with heroines endlessly receiving medals for spectacular bravery. In fact the early Guides who were standing by with their staves and stretchers often had little opportunity of showing their mettle to a society which refused to take them seriously, and it was even sometimes difficult to find opportunities for the "good deed a day". Adventure was expressed "in leaping over dykes, and crawling about in fields on hands and knees, or even on one's tummy" rather than in administering first-aid to the injured or courageously saving lives. When assistance was required, its application tended to be over-zealous and disproportionate: "Nora Lascelles complained bitterly that when she fell down the last three steps of the Red House staircase her leg was tied up in a splint made out of somebody's old pair of stays, before she had time to explain that she had only knocked off a piece of skin the size of a threepenny bit."

When all else failed the Guides could, as Ethel Talbot indicates in "Luck", always prove their usefulness by collecting sphagnum moss, a natural disinfectant to be found growing abundantly on British moorlands. "Picking sphagnum moss is ripping; quite apart from the jolly feeling that you're really doing something to help things along, there's always the chance of being bogged." Sphagnum-moss collecting provided themes for many writers, and Girl Guides' struggles to win an almost infinite variety of badges was also popular as a fictional subject. For instance in *The Marigolds Make Good*:

> "I'd like to qualify for horsewoman, and rifle-shot and pioneer, and pathfinder, and all the badges nobody ever thinks of getting, wouldn't you? I'm sick of doing things I know how to do—"
>
> Patsy grimaced. "I'm much more sick of failing needle-woman's – I've failed it three times. ... It's holding me up for first-class."

Camping, more than any other activity, encouraged self-reliance and inspired enthusiasm in both readers and authors. A typical example is May Wynne's *The Camping of the Marigolds*: " 'The Camping fever is in my blood. I shall go dotty when I see the lorry arriving.' " Guide authors lavishly illustrated the joys of camping – "There were blackberries, raspberries, the promise of nuts, the jolliest brown rabbits, sunshine and shadow in these magic woods..." – and also songs round the camp-fire, bogs, bulls, pow-wows, the pitching of tents, field kitchens, palliasse beds stuffed with bracken, and recurring crises which could be overcome only by Guide honour, grit and prayer.

Perhaps the most believable account of a Guide camp is given by Mrs A. C. Osborn Hann in *Peg's Patrol*. Dorothy Hann was Captain of the 12th Southwark Guide Company in the 1920s when her series of Peg books was written, and she remained active in the organization for many years. Her books attempted to convey the reality of Guiding, as distinct from the sentimentalized and over-heroic fiction set in "the nice little stories one reads of Guides in schools – 'Young Ladies' Seminaries' ". Mrs Hann lived and worked in one of London's poorer areas, and the leading characters in *Peg's Patrol* are girls from working-class Walworth families, for whom Guiding widened both physical and psychological horizons. The story's authenticity is enhanced by the author's photographs of Peg and the girls in her Daffodil patrol. Camping has special meaning for these city Guides, giving many of them the chance to visit the sea and the countryside for the first time in their lives.

"I'm longing to get to the sea … until today I'd never seen it." … When at last the sea came into full view there was a long-drawn "Oh – oh – oh!"

"Isn't it heavenly?" said Maude.

"I think it's rough and horrible-looking," said Sue.

Sue is a town-bird who doesn't respond to the austere beauty of Lympne's expanses of marshland and sea, but who craves the picture-postcards, band-stands, piers and deck-chairs she has seen in magazine pictures. Before the patrol even get to camp they have to overcome the perennial problem of insufficient funds for equipment, as "lots of the girls' fathers are out of work". Mrs Hann was fictionalizing actual events in the lives of the Guides in her own company during the 1920s, when there was extensive unemployment. They published in *The Guide* an open letter to better-off companies, explaining their difficulties, and the wholehearted response in large and small donations described in *Peg's Patrol* is an account of what really happened. (Guides in fact and fiction seem to develop a genius for raising money, by jam-making and fancy work, mending, weeding, cutting lawns, minding babies and performing an incredible range of errands. In the second world war the 1940 Guide Gift Week realized over £50,000, buying the first two flying ambulances to be used for the RAF, a life-boat which took part in the Dunkirk evacuation, twenty motor ambulances for the Royal Navy and several other pieces of expensive equipment.)

The author allows the Daffodils – Peg, Spud, Sue, Dolly, Rosie and Pollie – to speak in the natural idiom of working-class children of the period.

"Girls, I've got an idea!"

"Don't let it go, Peg. It might hurt!" said Spud, dodging behind Polly.

…

"Peg, I'll murder you!" cried Polly.

…

" … don't we look posh?"

"I think you're all a set of silly fools, if you ask me."
...
"Oh Captain – it ain't 'arf a scream!"

Dorothy Hann's characters were always believable. Like so many fictional Guides Peg resembled Robert Baden-Powell, with "thick, carroty hair and blue eyes making her everywhere conspicuous": at first she resists the "goody-goody" Girl Guides, who used to "swank about in uniforms and short skirts" thinking "they're going to boss the world and show their mothers how to do things". But once converted Peg becomes a "splendid" patrol leader, "quite a mother to the little ones", especially "Dirty Dolly" – the "kid" who never washes. Dolly Dangerfield is the awkward member of the patrol who eventually, through everyone's combined efforts, is made into a "real smart Guide".

Hopeless duffers and "outsiders" were popular ingredients of Guide fiction, redeemable always by the character-building propensities of guiding activities. Ethel Talbot, an energetic writer of Guide, school and adventure stories during the 1920s and '30s, was adept at creating girls whose conception of the Guide Law had sadly miscarried. In *Peggy's Last Term* (1920), eleven-year-old new girl Sylvia Armstrong proves to be a typical specimen of the kackhanded tenderfoot who "doesn't know a Union Jack from a Stars and Stripes, you bet, and I don't suppose she knows a granny from a reef-knot". To help her along the path of reformation, and to bring their patrol up to par with others in the company, "... in a kind of frenzy ... the dormitory turned their eyes Sylvia-wards" taking turns in coaching her in the Guide Law, the Salute, the Union Jack and woodcraft signs. In the end Sylvia scratched the Union Jack with her pen-knife on to her desk lid, so that it was always available for study, and "she drew arrows and crosses with her fingers and toes at every odd hour of the day". Knotting was even more obsessional – the tenderfoot having "a long piece of string secreted under her pillow at nights" for practising the intricacies of reefs, and grannys, sheet bends, clove hitches and bow lines. Perhaps not surprisingly after all these tortuous endeavours Sylvia gets so carried away by competitive enthusiasm for the Patrol Cup that she uproots plants and destroys the gardens of the other patrols. " 'I did it for *you*,' " she pleads to Peggy, her patrol-leader heroine, whose grim rejoinder is, " 'Don't you know when a thing is playing the game and when it isn't? Don't you know how to be sporting, and – clean, and – straight?' " (With Ethel Talbot we are of course once more back in elite boarding-school companies.)

This author enjoyed writing about characters who made a fetish of "blade-straightness to the narrowest edge" – which usually implied unquestioning conformity to the established morality of their group: however, the predicament of individual girls who refused to be regimented was also highlighted by Ethel Talbot, who probably sensed that many of her readers felt incapable of emulating the rigid (and often ruthless) "honour" which seemed to seep out of the very pores of fictional Guide and schoolgirl heroines. *Patricia Prefect* (1925) describes the growing understanding between Veronica, a young "rebel", and the impeccably conformist senior prefect within the tradition-ridden precincts of St Chad's. Helping "temperamental" Veronica Lutyens (plus fiddle) on to a train at the beginning of term, Pat notices immediately "… in that horrid single minute, that the new girl's expression had been tense and strained looking, that she was unChad'sy, very; ungamesy somehow, too, altogether!" Even "jolly comradey games talk" and hockey, – "lots of it" – fail to exorcise Veronica's "loathable" ways, and Patricia suddenly finds herself at the receiving end of Veronica's passionate "schoolgirl crush". At St Chad's, "brief, bracing and business-like in the extreme", the slightest show of emotion is taboo – as well as the remotest attempt to treat "outsiders" imaginatively – so Patricia is in dire trouble. Although Ethel Talbot is too easily side-tracked by the wholesomeness of hockey matches and head-girls' homilies on "straightness", she at least made some attempt to consider the deep emotional problems often attendant on intense relationships between a junior and a senior girl. Most Guiding writers preferred to leave this tricky subject well alone, apart from implying that involvement in the movement would of course redress any emotional imbalance.

Of the many duffers in Guide stories, one of the most predictable

A C. E. Brock illustration for Peggy's Last Term *by Ethel Talbot*

was created by Dorothea Moore, fifteen years after *Terry The Girl Guide.* Her *Brenda Of Beech House* chronicles the transformation of Brenda from bored middle-European princess to bouncing English boarding-school Girl Guide, at first useless but by the end of the book resourceful enough to save the life of the head girl, when her horse bolts during a pageant. Another princess is Elinor Brent-Dyer's Elisaveta (*The Princess Of The Chalet School*, 1927) who is so responsive to the good old Guide training that she faces with equanimity the prospect of descending a precipitous mountain slope in nothing but her royal knickers. She and schoolmate Joey have slit their stockings into strips with a scout knife to make an improvised rope, which alas is not long enough to carry them to safety.

"Our frocks?" suggested Elisaveta.

Joey shook her head. "No, I don't think we'd better do that. People might have fits if we wandered to Briesau in only knickers."

So instead of frocks their cellular vests, at the princess's suggestion, are pressed into action to save the day – and their propriety.

Even more helpful to Guiding than their fictional counterparts were real princesses. Mrs Kerr's book records that when in 1911 Her Royal Highness Princess Louise "graciously consented to become Patroness" the seal of respectability was firmly stamped upon the organization "hitherto looked upon as rather eccentric" (and para-military?) by the cautious British public. In 1920 King George V's daughter, Princess Mary, became Girl Guide President, an office held later by Princess Margaret whose interest in Guiding, like her sister's, began in childhood. The *Girl's Own Paper* of April 1940 pictures Queen Elizabeth II (then Princess Elizabeth) in Guide uniform, outside the Association's London Headquarters, with Brownie Princess Margaret. The magazine quotes a letter from the elder princess – an enthusiastic member of the Buckingham Palace Guide Company – to her captain: "... we have been knitting very hard for the Red Cross, the evacuees, and the soldiers, and sailors and also gathering sphagnum moss. Please would you send me the details of the War Service Badge?"

The first and second world wars presented new challenges which Girl Guides were quick to answer. Between 1914 and 1918, in a changing social climate, people who were forced to accept women doing "men's work" in the services, industry and agriculture, no longer resented women and girls in uniform. Fears of revolutionary "new women" were forgotten as the Guides, with their preparedness, proved to be a well-organized force of auxiliaries in many areas of voluntary work. (" '... somehow Guides are more jolly important in war' " – Ethel Talbot, *Peggy's Last Term.*) Death was constantly glorified in contemporary fiction for adults and children, and sentimentalized consolations offered to the bereaved by the popular press seemed incongruous to the point of insult: "I think Heaven must be a specially lovely place now, so full of young people." (*Little Folks*, 1919.) Wartime opportunities also provided a shot in the arm for patriotic Guide fiction, which abounded with self-sacrifice, spy-catching and heroism. Christine Chaundler, however, who was sub-editor *of Little Folks* and a keen Guiding author, managed to retain a sense of proportion about scouting capacities. "It was rather a guesswork progress, for, although the Blackbirds wouldn't have admitted it for worlds, their ideas upon tracking were primitive." *(Bunty Of The Blackbirds,* 1925.) One of the Blackbirds is characterized as unable to light a camp fire without setting the common alight, ripping her skirt from hem to waist and burning a hole in her knickers. Christine Chaundler's *Little Folks* series, *How We Won The War,* describes the overenthusiastic and inept patriotic efforts of a family of children who are engagingly reminiscent of Edith Nesbit's Bastables. Every one of their carefully calculated schemes grotesquely misfires: " '... when we told mother about our efforts to help our country and how disastrously they had all ended ... she persuaded Dad to let Peter and Timothy belong to the Boy Scouts, and she arranged for me to join a troup of Girl Guides that were working just then up at Waterloo Station. ...' "

By the time the second world war began in 1939 the Guides had become an international organization, accepted and established in many parts of the world – though not in Nazi Germany, where Hitler had outlawed the Scout and Guide movements. This ban was ruthlessly imposed in all the territories which Germany subsequently occupied, but Guiding still managed to survive in most European countries. The bravery and dedication of many "underground" patrols provided an incentive to British Guides to intensify their own endeavours as salvage collectors, ARP and Home Guard messengers, helpers with evacuees and in Red Cross work. In the middle of their exertions came the news of the Chief Scout's death in 1941. His farewell message to the Girl Guides stressed his concept of woman's rôle as "... the chosen servant of God in two ways: first, to carry on the race, to bring children into the world ... secondly, to bring happiness into the world by making happy homes, and by being yourselves good, cheery comrades for your husbands and children". In spite of his exposure to over 30 years of energetic Guiding, Baden-Powell apparently remained as convinced in 1941 as in 1909 that a Guide should take "... an interest in ... [her] husband's work and aspirations" rather than seek to express her own.

The flow of Guide fiction throughout the 1920s and '30s was unabating, though much of it had already become outdated and moribund. Fortunately Catherine Christian, who edited the Association's official journal, *The Guide,* from 1939 to 1945, was more able to respond to change than many writers for girls. She prepared an impressive factual survey of wartime Guiding in *The Big Test* (1947) and successfully translated the spirit of some of these achievements into believable fiction. In *The Kingfishers See It Through* she touches on one of the war's more serious social problems – the integration of evacuees, sometimes from slum districts, into their new communities. An uprooted cockney patrol meet indifference and snobbery instead of the expected Guide hand of friendship from the "posh" local company: " '... stuck up, that's what you are. Guides! Yar! Yer never wanted us, ter begin wiv ...'."
The Seventh Magpie is concerned with an English patrol who become increasingly aware of the sufferings of people in Nazi-invaded countries. Catherine Christian's heroines try to emulate the work of the Guide International Service Committee, which was formed in

1942 to train Guides and raise funds for the immediate rehabilitation of Europe after the end of hostilities.

Dorothea Moore remained singularly unresponsive to altering environments and attitudes. Her 1930s characters – like Terry in 1912 – were usually in danger of drowning in the vacuity of their own pseudo-heroics. The incredible virtue of *Judy Patrol Leader* probably put off hundreds of potential Guide recruits, both in 1930 when the book was first published by Collins, and even more emphatically in the post-war period when, surprisingly, The Children's Press reprinted it. Orphan Judy was the irritatingly resourceful kind of girl who could rustle up at high speed a tasty meal from her landlady's dingy fare of dry crusts, gristly mutton and a few old potatoes and onions: " 'You bet I'll find everything I want – I'm a Guide.' " Next she saves the lives of two girls cut off by the tide: " 'I'll go down and tie the rope … I know about knots; I'm a Guide.' " And it is an easy matter – " 'Right as rain' " – for her, single-handed, to catch a burglar at her new school. By now understandably resistant, her schoolmates remain unconverted to Guiding in spite of Judy's inspiriting pep-talks on "tracking and stalking, and the nearness to the little wild things which Guide woodcraft brings". But difficulties are all in a day's work to Judy. A ramble on the beach throws her into contact with a lame little boy, left in a cottage with his baby sister who is in the throes of dreadful convulsions (soon overcome "by the Guide first aid that she [Judy] had learned with the Ambulance Class"). Subtlety was hardly Dorothea Moore's strong suit, and in the course of the next few paragraphs the cliff falls down on the cottage, and Judy not only saves the children's lives by protecting them from the main weight of the avalanche but, whilst buried alive, prepares them a simple meal of bread and milk, remembering first to wash out the baby's bottle. The reader is not allowed for a moment to forget that only a Guide could perform such miracles: banality surpasses itself when later a frantically digging rescue party realize they are nearing success because they hear Patrol Leader Judy beneath the debris "whistling like a blackbird". Before they can even drag her out, Judy yells: " 'Please tell Billy's father that the baby has come out of her fit. One up for the Child's Nurse Badge!' " Any normal girl reader must surely have loathed this epitome of preparedness, based one hopes on Dorothea Moore's ideal of the Guide movement rather than the reality.

Judy Patrol Leader had a more acceptable namesake in Elinor Brent-Dyer's *Judy The Guide* (1928). Judy and her friends undermine school discipline in a "kiddish" and "underhand" way by wrongful exploitation of their scouting skills. (They communicate with each other in class by tapping out messages on their desks in morse.) But Guiding works both ways, for students *and* staff can belong to the organization: Judy struggles under the handicap of having a teacher who can add to the normal school-mistressy rebuke for wrong-doing, " 'You, of course, realize that you have broken the first, the fourth and the fifth Guide Laws.' " It seems unlikely that Winifred Darch, who was for many years senior English mistress at Loughton County High School as well as a Guide Officer, would take similar mean advantage of her pupils. She was blessed with a sense of humour and able to keep the Girl Guide movement in its true perspective: in *Poppies And Prefects* (1923) one of her characters defects and starts an anti-Guide Society, which is vigorous, though short-lived.

Stories by numerous popular authors on Guide themes were often serialized in the Association's journals before being published in book form. In its early days the organization could not, like the Scouts, afford its own journal, so Pearson's allocated two pages of their weekly woman's paper *Home Notes* for reporting Guide matters. Rose Kerr's book reports that there were objections from upper-class members about this arrangement, where Guide business was rubbing shoulders with advice to the lovelorn and fashion features. "Miss Lawrence, for instance, said it was not at all the sort of paper for the Roedean girls and their like." Roedean standards prevailed, and *Home Notes* was abandoned for space in the *Golden Rule*, a monthly published by Martin Shaw & Co. In 1914 the movement was able to start its own official magazine, the *Girl Guides' Gazette*, later known as the *Guider*. Today three journals are published: the *Guider*, *Today's Guide* and the *Brownie.* Like the organization which they represent they have had to modernize their image to survive in a society which is moving towards class and sex equality. Imperialistic and Edwardian overtones, however attenuated, are unlikely to appeal to contemporary teenage girls for whom freedom can no longer be symbolized by stretchers and staves, or camping and cowboy hats.

X

Camp Fire and Country Dance

"Drink, Mary, drink your fizzy lemonade
And leave the kingcups; take your grey felt hat
Here, where the low side window lends a shade
There, where the key lies underneath the mat,
The rude forefathers of the Hamlet sat."
(John Betjeman, "*An Archaeological Picnic*")

THE CAMP FIRE movement was founded in America in 1911 by a "spiritually enlightened" husband and wife, Dr Luther Halsey Gulick and Mrs Charlotte Vetter Gulick. It never really caught on in this country; English girls who felt the need of regimentation were more likely to opt for the straightforward Girl Guides, whose terse motto, "Be prepared", reflected its no-nonsense outlook. Camp Fire, however, was supposed to appeal to the more introspective type of girl; but while its advocates waffled on about inner vision, harmony and so forth – concepts as nebulous as the Great Outdoors from which its impetus was derived – its real appeal was to a specific childhood impulse: dressing up. On special occasions members wore Indian squaw dresses and headbands, embroidered by themselves with designs "symbolic of their individual activities". Lighting a fire in a wood was described portentously as "a great primal experience"; and inevitably women's rôle as traditional "fire makers" was stressed. The whole movement, in fact, arose out of the Gulicks' concern that "increasing employment of women and girls was destroying adequate opportunities in the home for human relationships" (an ambiguous remark: presumably they didn't mean to imply that working women were too tired to be interested in copulation?). In any case, it was a totally reactionary preoccupation at a time when working women needed all the encouragement they could get, and when a more socially relevant objective might have been the promotion of employment opportunities. The Gulicks conceded the laborious nature of housework but thought they were fostering in their girls an attitude which would enable them to see it in a more attractive light. Proficiency in each aspect of domestic work was rewarded by the presentation of a string of beads on a leather thong: "… as she stands before the campfire and receives these tokens, the things which are everyday drudgery are thereby indicated as romantic and adventuresome."

In other words, girls were to be duped into investing drudgery with romantic overtones, by associating it with flickering firelight, fringed Indian dresses and inflated ceremonial presentations. The organizers' greatest efforts were directed towards the cultivation, in the girls, of that "inner vision [which] is needed to show the real beauty that is back of daily work". Obviously: normal vision certainly would have been insufficient to see anything so amorphous as this "real beauty" – which as a concept is positively dangerous, in that it substitutes a poeticized vagueness for unpalatable facts. Girls who found themselves unable to go about their daily chores in the right frame of mind might have been forced to wonder where they had gone wrong.

However, in spite of the mumbo-jumbo the Camp Fire movement did teach practical skills which would have been useful to anyone. Many of these were considered to be exclusively relevant to girls: the ability to make ten standard soups, for instance, and to recognize three different kinds of baby cry. (Camp Fire Girls were divided into three ranks: wood gatherers, fire makers and torch bearers; more appropriate designations might have been wool gatherers, self-effacers and child-bearers.) Although the Camp Fire Girls of America corresponded closely to Boy Scouts, "there is a fundamental difference, and to copy the Boy Scout movement would be utterly and fundamentally evil, and would probably produce ultimately a moral and psychological involution which is the last thing in the world that we any of us want. We hate manly women and womanly

men, but we all do love a woman who is thoroughly womanly ..."
Thorough womanliness implied passivity; and although girls were
encouraged briefly to be physically active (in an environment which
would put them in touch with "cosmic forces", which might be
expected ultimately to reinforce the passivity), the movement's

A typical 'Camp Fire illustration, c. 1917

association with the image of an Indian squaw – that most submissive
of stereotypes – was not an arbitrary one. The raw material –
adolescent girls in middies and bloomers – was to be developed in
such a way that the end product would approximate as closely as
possible to the traditional idea of womanhood: an objective as

stultifying as it was unrealizable. All the pious clichés which originated as compensatory facets of the myth of feminine inferiority were lovingly reasserted: women as guardians of the hearth, as mothers, as custodians of "beauty", were to be (symbolically) exalted. For all the Camp Fire connotations of the good earth, its members rarely came down to it.

Camp Fire girls quickly became standard characters in American girls' books, although in most cases the movement was almost completely incidental to the plot. Series after series related the impossible adventures of different sets of girls, in which missing heiresses, cruel guardians and jewel thieves featured prominently. One of the best known of the American writers was Jane L. Stewart, who, in *Camp Fire Girls At The Sea Shore* (1914), pushed the idea of self-reliance in a way that can hardly have been flattering to her readers: "... And that's what we want to make of our own Camp Fire Girls – girls who can help themselves if there's need for it, and who don't need to have a man wasting a lot of time doing things for them that he ought to be spending in serious work – things that she can do just as well for herself." The raw material here must have been very raw indeed – and there's an unfortunate implication that the benefits of practical training are of less importance in relation to the girls themselves than for their effects on a man's "serious work". However, Jane L. Stewart's girls *do* prove to be resourceful and quick-witted; adept at life-saving and at foiling plots. Another writer, Harriet Rietz, created a Camp Fire version of Pollyanna (*Mary Lee, the Campfire Girl*; 1917). The orphan Mary Lee predictably brightens up the lives of crippled and underprivileged children and unbending gentlemen, but her behaviour is neither so coy nor so cloying as Pollyanna's. Stella M. Francis brought to Camp Fire fiction some peculiar taboos of her own – " 'Detective is entirely too coarse a term to apply to any of my Camp Fire girls and 1 won't stand for it' " – and a literary style which teeters unhappily between precision and verbosity: " 'There surely are some malicious mischief makers in this vicinity,' Helen Nash observed. 'I suppose the person who did that was the one who threw a stone into our bonfire and hooted our watchword so hideously.' " Stella M. Francis seems at times to be edging towards the splendidly high-flown verbal inaccuracies of the Irish writer Amanda McKittrick Ros; but in the creation of farcical situations she is surpassed by Julianne Devries, whose Camp Fire girls in one story, *Camp Fire Girls at Holly House* (1933), are silly enough to knock themselves unconscious, one after the other, leaving their senseless bodies strewn at intervals along an underground passage.

An English writer who featured the Camp Fire in at least one of her books is Angela Brazil. *For The Sake of the School* (1915) relates the adventures of a girl whose ambition is to be a torch bearer, and the school's Camp Fire league has for its Guardian "a charming young American lady" whose "winsome personality made her a prime favourite at The Woodlands". But the girls' writer in this country whose name is most closely associated with the Camp Fire movement is Elsie Oxenham.

Elsie Jeanette Oxenham was herself a Camp Fire Guardian, and she has brought the organization into many of her books, though only one series (Camp Keema) is built around it. Her other enduring preoccupation was with English country dancing, and she has simply transferred her enthusiasm for both these activities to many of her characters. She is best known for her Abbey girls stories; this series began with *Girls of the Hamlet Club* (1914), which has all the admirable qualities of the later books and rather less of their weaknesses. Its girls are real schoolgirls, not grown-up ones; the girls' friendships are described with restraint; the country-dance motif seems a natural extension of the pastoral setting. It is also an excellent school story; the word "school" in some of the later titles is deceptive, since school hardly plays such a large part again. In the *Hamlet Club*, Elsie Oxenham has localized the traditional conflict between town and country in "Miss Macey's school"; its pupils are divided into two factions, "townies" and "hamlets", who exist side by side in acute disharmony. Cicely Hobart, a newcomer and the central character in this book, forms the "hamlets", the outsiders, into a club of their own. It has to be called the Hamlet Club – which gives it a ready-made motto: "to be or not to be".

Elsie Oxenham's literary impulse involves edifying her readers at every turn; but there is plenty of surface frivolity and light-

Five original members of the Hamlet Club. Drawn by Harold Earnshaw
(Girls of the Hamlet Club *by Elsie J. Oxenham)*

heartedness, as well as a whole built-up ambience in which ritual, rules and symbols play a large part. (This is evolved step by step after the first book, until the permanent heroines are established in or near Abinger Hall, while a succession of transient characters are prominent in turn and then recede.) Within the wider, formalized world of Elsie Oxenham, specific rituals are encompassed: the May Queen tableau, for instance, and the various Camp Fire ceremonies. The former, a feature of the Hamlet Club, is based on an actual ceremony which takes place in Whitelands College in south west London; it was instigated by John Ruskin in 1881 and involves a queen who wears embroidered robes and a floral crown.

This author made much of the character-building function, as she saw it, of both the country dancing and Camp Fire movements. Both these activities put the emphasis on group participation. One can fulfil oneself only through purposeful association with others: this debatable precept is expressed decoratively in each. To these was added the Abbey – bequeathed to Joan Shirley, in the second book of the series, because of her obsession with it: this comes to stand for the mediaeval Christian concepts of sanctuary, charity and humility. The monks to whom it originally belonged " 'do seem to have been decent old chaps' ": " 'All Cistercians had to work. They didn't just pray and meditate.' "

With all these factors working for her below the surface, adding layers of meaning and significance to even her most scrappy or made-up plots, Elsie Oxenham's books appear to have a density which perhaps is not warranted. Where she does excel is in the depiction of a pretty scene – when she's not carried away by her own sense of the picturesque, which results in pretty-prettiness. Particularly in the case of Joan's Abbey she fails to convey its austere, mediaeval quality which undoubtedly she felt; what she makes of it is a charming ruin in a corner of the grounds, overcoloured as a picture postcard of an old English village.

Her Buckinghamshire villages in the *Girls of the Hamlet Club* are less folksy, more subtly evoked. This is Hampden country (John Hampden, whom every schoolgirl must remember for his refusal to give way on a question of principle); his shade is called up to be an inspiration to vacillating girls. Country walks are not invariably sunny ("Carry Carter always grumbles on rambles"); girls who tramp across the fields come up against mud and dead leaves – which the later books conspicuously lack. Here, the folk tradition of which Elsie Oxenham was so conscious is summoned up almost explicitly; it is the only book in which she comes near to conveying the flavour of what T. S. Eliot described as "the weak pipe and the little drum" – the ghostly connotations of certain enduring ritual acts. The idea of continuity is worked out down to Cicely Hobart's Elizabethan name; another hamlet girl, Marguerite Verity, has Huguenot ancestors, which leads on to an exposition of the book's central idea: " '... she belongs to a very old French family. There's really no need for the others to despise us, you know.' "

It's the plague of ill-feeling and snobbery in the school which Cicely sets out to eliminate (" 'It's true, and it's hateful, but I'll alter it before I'm done!' "). She allies herself with the underdogs but emphatically is not of them: there are a country mansion and a couple of upper-class grandparents in the background, waiting to claim her. The girls' reactions to Cicely show them up at once for what they are: the town girls are impressed by her clothes, the country girls by her ideas. Elsie Oxenham also felt the need to speak up for the less privileged, but not to the extent of putting herself, imaginatively, in their place. The point of view is always that of the benefactor, not the recipient of patronage (with one typical variation: the poor girl who is really, unknown to herself, an heiress). The country girls here are not sentimentalized, however: they are neither rustically pure and simple nor – with the exception of Miriam Honor – excessively noble-minded. But an unmistakable implication is that they have absorbed virtue – which is expressed as basic decency – from the woods and fields. This sentimental fallacy of course was not confined to children's books; it found its sickliest expression in Marie Corelli and perhaps its most coherent in Wordsworth and Coleridge. George Eliot, Thomas Hardy and the Powys brothers, among others, subscribed to it to varying degrees, but brought to it their own powers of transmutation. Cicely's achievement in this book is to show up artificial distinctions which urban snobbishness has fostered; she causes the village girls to be accepted on their own merits. Of course it is made clear to the reader that Miriam and the others are not *really* inferior, socially or otherwise, to the town girls; it is simply the latter's abominable insensitivity which has created the division. And Cicely's own circumstances show that it is not necessary to be moderately poor in order to be worthwhile.

It would have been difficult for Elsie Oxenham, herself a product of a particular social stratum (her father was John Oxenham, a prolific minor novelist with a religious bias) to have written unpatronizingly of an out-and-out peasant or slum dweller. The poor working girls in her later books are always genteelly poor; daughters of impoverished clergymen or badly paid journalists, who have to be chided for addressing their wealthy friends as "Miss": " 'Now, never let me hear you say *Miss* Joy again! It will hurt my feelings dreadfully ...' "

"Miss Joy" and her cousin Joan are the original Abbey girls, who appear in the book of that name, *The Abbey Girls* (1920). They have been left more or less unprovided for: Joan has a rather ineffectual mother, who, several books later, is overtaken by premature senility; this, presumably, is to give the girls a free rein. They are acting as caretakers of the Abbey when they are discovered by Cicely Hobart who sends one of them – Joy – to Miss Macey's school, on a Hamlet Club scholarship. The moral point here is that the scholarship has been offered to Joan – who selflessly gives it up for her cousin's sake. The cousins' financial problems, however, are romantically solved with the death of Joy's crotchety old grandfather, Sir Anthony Abinger, who leaves the Hall to one girl and the Abbey to the other; he has been impressed to the point of beneficence by Joan's competence as a guide, and by the sight of the girls, in workaday pinafores, dancing a minuet on the cloister garth.

Joan is the prominent person in this book, but later she fades into the background of the series; she is one of those well-behaved girls whose moral uprightness is boringly unshakeable. Her place is taken by Jen Robins – Jenny-Wren – who is more lively and more dashing, though of an equally sweet disposition. But it is in Joy Shirley – at least in the early books – that Elsie Oxenham comes nearest to making at least one of her heroines believable. Joy, imperative, thoughtless, effortlessly charming, is a more complex character than any of the others; but it is precisely when her complexity threatens to become apparent that Elsie Oxenham pulls herself up sharply, and causes Joy to revert to some kind of typical – for the genre – but unlikely behaviour which will have a moral significance for her readers. Joy, who is well aware of her own shortcomings, takes care to surround herself with people who will keep her morally up to scratch – and occasionally outdoes them in acts of charity. Since charity does not come naturally to Joy, it tends to take a lurid and extreme form. The image of a lady bountiful is never an attractive one, but when it involves fastidious Joy and a group of crippled slum children, to whom she devotes one day a week, it becomes laughable.

Here we have an instance of Elsie Oxenham's inability to write about the lower classes without resorting to the most shameless sentimentality. Rose of Tin Town, who sounds like a prostitute but is in fact the paralysed daughter of an uneducated workman, provides another: yellow-haired, exuberant Jen Robins bursts into the room where Rose is lying, gives an exhibition of morris dancing, and inspires in the invalid hero-worship of an exceedingly servile nature (*Jen of the Abbey School*, 1927). Not content with cheering up one invalid, Jen rushes off at once to turn herself into a fairy on a lawn for the benefit of another; a small sick boy whose heart-rending nickname is Wriggles. Elsie Oxenham was very much a hit-or-miss writer as far as evocative images are concerned. Occasionally memorable (" 'We danced all one winter, on Saturday nights, in a barn lit by lanterns, and had Old English dresses, and nobody knew what we were doing' "), these are more often maudlin; in the above case she seems to have lost her sense of proportion altogether. One sick child is just about acceptable, in the context of the time and in view of the author's concern with her upper-middle-class readers' attitude to sick children; two turn the whole sequence into a farce.

The farce continues, on a more deliberate note. Rose, whose feelings must not be hurt, laboriously knits a jumper for Jen, who is recovering from a serious accident (characters in children's books were an excessively accident-prone lot). The jumper is *frightful,* purple and yellow stripes which make a mockery of Jen's efforts to instil into the village and Tin Town girls ideas of beauty and harmony – beginning, obviously enough, with colour. This worthy objective is derived from a principle of the Camp Fire movement: "… the use of poetic form, beautiful colour, and the use of symbolism to show inner meanings" were elevating devices for which Elsie Oxenham provided a literary application. Camp Fire precepts tend to permeate even those books in which the movement is not mentioned. By the late 1930s, however, Elsie Oxenham's Camp Fire orientation had merged with her sense of custom and tradition to become a general preoccupation with sources of "psychical food" (Dr Gulick's phrase) for modern girls.

Folk song and dance had also ceased to figure quite so prominently, though the Hamlet Club and its queens continued to flourish in the background right until the last Abbey book (1959). In the early '20s the Abbey girls' enthusiasm for country dancing was at its height, and the Hamlet Club's amateurish performances are soon corrected with a little professional help from the English Folk Dance and Song Society. Founded for the purpose of promoting interest in English folk ballads and tunes, this society had been in existence since 1898. In the nineteenth century a curious belief had arisen that folk music had never evolved in England to a noticeable extent; industrious collectors of folk songs – notably Cecil Sharp – were able to knock this fallacy on the head. Cecil Sharp himself, lightly disguised as "the Prophet", appears in *The Abbey Girls Go Back To School* (1922). Nearly all the subsidiary characters in this book, in fact, are identifiable members of the Folk Dance and Song Society, who can hardly have taken kindly to Elsie Oxenham's somewhat effusive presentation of them. Two or three persist for several books; "the Pixie", for instance, who is tiny, indomitable and jocular, and to whom the Abbey girls occasionally take their more serious ethical problems. The "school" here is the society's summer school at Cheltenham, which Joan, Joy, Jen and Cicely attend. They find that their dancing is not up to standard, but, in the proper spirit, are pleased to be corrected: " 'Oh, please keep on at us as much as ever you like! That's what we've come for. Besides,

Jack and Jen were assaulting Joy with pillows.
Elsie Anna Wood illustrates The Abbey Girls Go Back to School

we enjoy it; I do! It's the funniest thing that has happened to me for years. Pull me up for every old thing you can; I really want to get the dances right, and if we've been messing them up I'm sorry...' "

"Madame", their first teacher, becomes a stop-gap love object for Cicely (and to a lesser extent for the others):

> "Coo!" Joy murmured. "Isn't she a treat? She looked jolly before, but in her gymmy she beats herself into fits!"
> "You see so much *more* of her," Jen remarked truthfully. "And when she's as topping as that, the more you see the better!"

But soon a more potentially satisfying relationship is provided for Cicely – who disconcerts her friends by becoming odd and grumpy. Cicely and Joan "grow up" in this book, with as much grace as they can muster; in common with all Elsie Oxenham's heroines, they keep up a pretence of aversion to marriage, until the point when they are about to marry. (" 'But do you really think she likes him?' Jen pleaded excitedly. 'It's awfully difficult to think of the President – well! Think of all the things she's said about getting married!' ") This nervous mannerism, which persists in girl after girl throughout the saga, was evidently considered normal behaviour in a well-brought-up, reticent young lady, whose energies had had plenty of above-board outlets. In real life, obviously it had a great deal to do with face-saving: since most girls' ambitions were centred on the idea of marrying well, the possibility of failing to marry at all had to be nullified in advance by affected indifference. From being negative and defensive, however, this standpoint was modified in girls' fiction into a positive corollary of healthy-mindedness: girls were expected to be uninterested in the *idea* of marrying, but to be in favour of it as soon as it became a practical proposition. In the above instance, Cicely's capitulation to the social pressures of adulthood is couched in the following terms: " 'I *never* thought ... that the next time I saw him I'd be in gym things! I say, Joan, tell me straight! Do I look decent in a tunic?' " Cicely and Joan are married off, and all but disappear. Like all the Abbey girls, the reversal of their attitude to marriage is sudden and overwhelming; there is no gradual leading up to a change of view. In so far as she covers the ground of the romantic novelist, Elsie Oxenham subscribes to the stock romantic idea that only one marriage partner is "right" for each girl, and that he will be instantly recognizable. Only in the case of Jen is an alternative suitor presented, and Jen's relationship with Dicky Jessop (*Queen of the Abbey Girls*, 1926) is rudimentary in the extreme.

The hoydenish girls are transformed too abruptly to be convincing as highly fertile young women, and the adjustment in their own view of themselves is expressed by a deplorable smugness ("Jen tilted her chin defiantly. '... I'm quite married. I've been married for a fortnight. I'm Lady [Ken] Marchwood,' and she curtseyed") which justifies the instinctive resentment felt by those who are left outside:

> "They've made friends. Isn't that awfully nice? But it leaves you two out in the cold. Shall I give you a man to look after, too?" To Joy, with mischievous eyes.
> "No, thanks!" Joy said promptly. "I've got no use for them. I didn't think those two had, either."

But Joy has to grow up too; and her "weaker" character provides the author with several opportunities to express a fundamental attribute of balanced maturity: thoughtfulness for others. Joy's excessively carefree adolescence is brought to a dramatic end when she crashes a motor bike and nearly kills Jen; and in this episode the author demonstrates the effectiveness of guilt as a means for controlling wilfulness or egotism. Girls whose characters are not quite irreproachable are usually brought up to scratch by a sudden shock to the nervous system.

It is absurd that twenty-year-old Joy should be made out to be incapable of understanding adult motivations and tastes; but since childhood had come to be represented in children's books above all as a phase to be enjoyed, it follows naturally enough that it should not be relinquished willingly. Here, before the tensions and responsibilities of maturity start to obtrude, the Abbey girls regress openly and happily: " 'It's the influence of her legs. She's not used to seeing quite so much of them. She always was a bit weak in the head, and the sight of her gym stockings has thrown her off her balance. She's gone back ten years. Even I feel a touch of it coming on, and I'm two years farther off from school than she is…' " Four books later Jen is still clinging, though with increasing uncertainty, to a girlhood which any normal girl must have outgrown:

"… Growing up is fun, you know."
"Is it?" Jen sounded doubtful. "I'm not keen on it, Pixie. I want to go on playing cricket."

In writers like Elsie Oxenham, the tendency to emphasise the joys (the "fun") of childhood was part of a deliberate attempt to counter teenage precocity, noticeably more widespread since the rise of Hollywood. In the 1920s the cinema was still a long way from being accepted by the English middle classes; and its influence was generally deplored as being conducive to shoddiness and vulgarity. Girls who persisted in regarding the behaviour of screen heroines as a sanction for their own more disreputable impulses were decried in fiction as misguided or worse. That these impulses rarely involved anything more questionable than the desire to wear make-up or a taste for magazine fiction, was in fact an evasion of the crucial issue of self-indulgent sexuality. But girls' writers were in the artistically awkward position of having to deny, by implication, the nature of adolescence: they were far more concerned with their effects on readers than with the realities of their theme. This is particularly noticeable in Elsie Oxenham, since she has chosen to chronicle the external consequences to her characters of growing up: marriage, children, and so on. Each girl's attitude to these is the same, the most socially desirable one; just as the girls' misfortunes are always of a socially acceptable kind. Husbands may die, but they never run off with other women; no one's marriage turns out to have been a mistake. No one has disreputable inclinations. No one so much as *smokes*. What Elsie Oxenham has achieved, in fact, is a complete reversal of the pre-Rousseau tendency to depict children as small adults: her adults are no more than large children who put hair-brushes in one another's beds and have never outgrown the child's need for instant emotional satisfaction. If the weakness of this is to some extent circumvented by the fact that they tend to appear in episodes in which childish exuberance is acceptable, on another level it is intensified by the sense that the author's reticence has more to do with propriety than with literary conciseness. Of course her treatment of potentially adult subject-matter was determined by the fact that the books *were* written for twelve- to seventeen-year-olds; no one expects her to have been brutally or boringly explicit. But even the child's-eye-view could have allowed for a suggestion of complexity or incomprehensibility in the adults' behaviour, particularly since the adults continue to play such a large part. (The climax of the anomalous relation between the books and their readers is reached at the point when the principal characters are mothers in their thirties and children under ten.)

Having been forced to "grow up" (in *The Abbey Girls Go Back To School*), Joy does it thoroughly: in the next book (*The New Abbey Girls*, 1922) she lumbers herself with a couple of teenage "daughters", whom she insists on adopting. "Difficult" Maidlin, a half-Italian heiress, and self-possessed Rosamund, whose parents are abroad, come to live at Joy's Hall, and stay there, respectively, for eleven and seven years. Maidlin, with the double handicap of a Latin temperament and an "artistic" one – she is an embryo opera singer – is socialized through her violent attachment to Joy: here the author's view of life as a series of interrelated emotional attachments reaches its culmination. The connection between an intended effect and its antithesis also is apparent here. That Maidlin's relationship with Joy is *not* "healthy" or "normal" (two of Elsie Oxenham's favourite adjectives: two others are "jolly" and "happy") is brought home to the reader in the extraordinary episode which precedes Joy's wedding to Andrew Marchwood (*Queen of the Abbey Girls*). Joy insists on having Maidlin to sleep with her, in spite of Jen's remonstrances:

"Joy!" Jen exploded. ... "You know you never sleep well

when you have her. That really is the limit! It's too bad. And you're being married tomorrow! You ought to have a good night's rest. Joy, I'm sorry for the kid, but you mustn't spoil your wedding to please her. ..."

"Jenny-Wren, it's no use. I'm going to have my way in this. ... Be a dear, and say 'good-night and good luck to you', and leave me and Maidie alone together, Jenny-Wren."

The amount of time which the girls spend in one another's bedrooms is a measure of the degree of intimacy between them. Mary-Dorothy Devine, Joy's secretary and writer of girls' books, instigates a ritual of dispensing cocoa and sympathy, late at night, to girls who feel in need of them. Mary-Dorothy has had to come to terms with her own psychological problems: country dancing has acted as a solvent on the emotional block which caused her to waste time in unproductive fantasizing, and the support and encouragement of the Abbey girls has done the rest. In *The Abbey Girls Again* (1923) dowdy, stick-at-home Mary-Dorothy is ineffectually trying to control her young sister Biddy, who has got in with a lax crowd of cinema enthusiasts; two books later she is installed in her own suite at the Hall and has become a surrogate older sister to everyone. Biddy's re-orientation is easily effected by the atmosphere at the Hall and the friendship of Rosamund and Maidlin: " 'I've an idea it may be very good for your Biddy. I've two very jolly kids at home, just about her age, and absolutely healthy and normal.' "

Jen's reluctance to grow up turns out to have been justifiable. Her initiation into adulthood is brought about by a series of misfortunes: first is her own serious accident; her father dies, then her mother (*The Abbey Girls Win Through*, 1927). Here, the religious sentimentality which Elsie Oxenham had been secreting is released, with cloying effect: " 'I believe in Heaven, of course; but – but it seems so big. Everybody there! How can I be sure they'd ever meet? ... He'll take care of her, won't He?' " Jen returns from her mother's funeral in time to greet Joy, who has been on safari in Africa with her husband. Andrew Marchwood is to follow her, but he never does; he has been murdered by "a handful of very wild natives".

The shock of this news causes Joy to give birth prematurely to twins – an experience which nearly kills her. Jen marries Ken Marchwood, Andrew's brother; but Ken departs for Africa after a week's honeymoon in order to tidy up his brother's affairs. Jen returns to stay with Joy at the Hall (*The Abbey Girls at Home*, 1928); Joy is recovering when Betty McLean, a visitor of Jen's, is involved in an accident at the Abbey gates (due to Maidlin's reluctance to run over a hen); she is carried into the Abbey where she nearly dies. Rosamund is then summoned to her mother who is dying in Switzerland; Joy's aunt, Mrs Shirley, dies; and then Lady Marchwood, the mother-in-law of Joy and Jen. But at the end of all this Jen – after another of those coy and mysterious pregnancies of which no one seems to be aware (sixteen-year-old Maidlin apparently had not realized that Joy was eight months pregnant with *twins*, since their arrival came as a surprise to her) – has a baby boy, which makes up for everything:

> "What's his name, Jenny-Wren?"
> Jen's eyes met Joy's. "Our little Andrew," she said; and Joy knelt and kissed her.

In this book, and the preceding one, it is not only Maidlin who is maudlin. Together, they show how precarious was the author's ability to analyse, or even describe, feeling. Her efforts to define objective "goodness" result invariably in a subjective, sweetened distillate of Church of England morality:

> ". … There's been a Power helping and guiding my life … and I try all the time to put myself in line with that Power, which is God; to carry out His plan, to do what He wishes, to find out His way for me, and to follow it. That's all that has happened, Jenny-Wren."
> "All! Yes, but it's everything," Jen said quietly. "You'll never fail anyone again, you know, Mary, dear."

This is didactic writing at its worst. Lacking the force of overt fanaticism, it comes across merely as flaccid and ultimately meaningless: Mary-Dorothy's philosophy is not applicable to any real situation. Its vagueness protects it from ever being put to the test. The comfortable sense of striving after virtue which it may induce in the characters reacts on the reader to produce irritation. Elsie Oxenham can hardly ever be serious without being sanctimonious; and she gets no nearer to humour than horseplay and teasing.

These are some of her limitations. Others come to the fore as the saga progresses; but the intensity and intermittent liveliness of her style have ensured that the books will be at least mildly addictive. She evolved a system of inter-connecting series of remarkable complexity. Characters in one set of stories are carried over to the next; events which take place in one book have prolonged repercussions in others, not necessarily in the same set. Of course the content often falls short of the overall design; the technique allowed for a great deal of looseness in the presentation of character. Rosamund, for example, is the heroine of several books (beginning with *The Abbey Girls on Trial*, 1930). She is the only Abbey girl to find the sheltered atmosphere constricting (which she ascribes, of course, to a deficiency in herself). If Joy is a study, though never a very deep one, in the suppression of baser instincts, Rosamund seems at first to illustrate the necessity of finding a means of self-expression. Not obviously "gifted" she hankers after a life of buying and selling (" 'I'd love to have piles of boxes, all sizes, and pack things in each' ") and briefly sets up a handicrafts showroom in a converted cottage. The author cannot leave her there, of course; and Rosamund, who would have settled happily for a tea shop and independence, is given a castle: she becomes the Countess of Kentisbury when she marries an ailing earl.

Rosamund's most startling feat is to have twins twice within ten months. By this time (*Robins in the Abbey*, 1947) Elsie Oxenham has been completely carried away by the twin motif. Joy's twins, which started the ball rolling, are followed by Maidlin's, Rosamund's, and finally Jen's. Baby-loving Jen goes one better than the others: she has twin *boys*. The author does not make it clear why it should be better to have boys: it is simply taken for granted that it is. The (grown-up) Abbey girls engage in an unspoken competition to out-breed one another as light-heartedly as schoolgirls might take part in an egg-and-spoon race. The sense of unreality involved in the coy presentation of this aspect of married life reaches its apex in the names which Rosamund chooses for her baby girls: what Elsie Oxenham is unmistakably describing is a child naming dolls (Rosabel, Rosalin, Rosanna, Rosilda), but by a double inversion the reader is asked to equate the actual regression to a nursery idiom with what the archetypal little girl in the nursery is mimicking.

It is in Joy, always a gauge of the author's potential strength and actual weakness, that her later shortcomings are most noticeable. The course of Joy's moral development is never convincing; it's as if the author lacked the courage to follow up her own indications of restlessness and cynicism in Joy's nature. Throughout the series, subtlety is sacrificed to jolliness; Joy is dehumanized in Lady Marchwood, later Lady Quellyn. By the 1940s the whole Abbey environment had become ludicrously outmoded (and the last links with reality are abandoned when the Abbey begins to enjoy perpetual summer); and glossy, romanticized Lady Quellyn is an anachronistic figure as well as being a cardboard one. (Given a little encouragement, Joy might have developed into a version of Daisy Buchanan, the falsely encouraging lady in L. P. Hartley's *The Hireling*, or even Gwendolen Harleth in George Eliot's *Daniel Deronda*. Rosamund could have gone the way of Constance Chatterley; Joan has distinct affinities with Susan in Virginia Woolf's *The Waves*; Maidlin was almost bound to take to drink and become a clinging bore; and Jen might have found herself breaking down in Harrods, like the fecund heroine of Penelope Mortimer's *The Pumpkin Eater*.)

The books show no attempt to take social change into consideration. The Abbey girls remain serenely unaffected by external events, wars or contemporary trends. The first world war had at least rated an acknowledgement (in *The Abbey Girls Go Back To School*), though from a viewpoint as silly as Angela Brazil's. The Pixie, who had taught folk dancing to the troops, brightened up a soldiers' mess by putting flowers on the tables and yellow shades on the lamps: "The old man nearly cried for joy when he saw those lampshades …

A mishap!
Frontispiece by Rene Cloke for The Reformation of Jinty

Said the place made him think of Home and Mother ...." Since the 1939–45 war is rather more difficult to describe in terms of Home and Mother, it is simply not mentioned – this is in contrast to other popular girls' writers (Elinor Brent-Dyer, for example, and Dorita Fairlie Bruce) who welcomed the dramatic material it provided.

The uneasy relationship which had come about between the Abbey books and the society in which they were being written may have led Elsie Oxenham to attempt a re-creation of the earlier, more solidly based Abbey ethos. The seven "retrospective" Abbey books (written between 1938 and 1957), which feature Joan, Joy and Jen as schoolgirls, form a dreary little group of second-rate tales of burglary and buried treasure, as boring in effect as they were escapist in intention. The "timeless" quality which they embody is wholly negative; but it is perhaps because of it that they have remained in print; they are not obviously datable.

Elsie Oxenham's literary nourishment was chiefly derived from three concepts: sense, fancy and spirit. "Sense" is the common sense which enables the girls to behave in the end with equanimity; "fancy" is indulged through the May Queen ritual and country dancing; "spirit" is symbolized by and contained within the Abbey, when it is not equated openly with the Church of England. It is always tempting to trace a decline in the work of any writer whose output was large (Elsie Oxenham wrote over 80 books); but in the later "second generation" Abbey books there are unmistakable signs of tiredness and uninterest. It is perhaps indicative of the author's deterioration that she, who had been so vigorously opposed to affectation (in the "country dancing" books there is an insistence that the dancing should not be cheapened by "dressing up": "There were elementary school children, some, to the amusement of the Rocklands crowd, in fancy costume, with sun-bonnets and milkmaids' frocks, which they no doubt thought peculiarly appropriate for country-dancing"[1]) should dress up the last caretaker of the Abbey, Rachel, in monks' robes. In *Two Queens at the Abbey* (1959) Joy's twin daughters show that they have not developed significantly from babyhood; the story is a variation on *The Abbey Girls* theme, but sadly curtailed.

[1] *Jen of the Abbey School.*

The impeccable morality conveyed by the Abbey books, their gentle delineation of "proper" attitudes, must have appealed to 1920s and '30s parents as much as their romantic view of friendship and the unaggressive self-confidence of their characters appealed to children. What the books achieve is an amazingly precise re-statement of how the middle-class section of society expected its girls to behave, at a time when Victorian restrictions had not wholly given way to successive theories of freedom. To a readership schooled in a belief in hierarchism, the Abbey girls' social position was an added endorsement of the correctness of their behaviour. No one in the books behaves eccentrically; no one questions authority or is disrespectful to social institutions. No one, in fact, has opinions on any subject which does not directly concern herself. The only gesture of rebellion – it is a very minor one – is Rosamund's. Men are everywhere deferred to, though in all cases they are featureless to the point of being interchangeable. The girls enjoy girlhood for as long as they can, but when the time comes they cheerfully marry (the exception is Mary-Dorothy, who is 30 when the Abbey girls discover her, and plain; her books, also, are openly referred to as her "children"). The Abbey books chart the ideal progression of an idealized girl's life, with marriage, typically, as the ultimate fulfilment; they list in the process all the embellishments of an obsolete and pampered existence. There are the lawns and the tea cups and the rose gardens, the chauffeur-driven cars, the piano music heard from the terrace, the picturesque children playing in the sand-pit; and, as a concession to democratic childish taste, the cream buns and the fizzy lemonade. The books constitute in essence a parents' guide, and disseminate none of the excitement or pure enjoyment which attach to certain more disreputable kinds of girls' fiction. But they enforce strongly their own point of view. Girls who read them before the last war tend to remember with affection their definition of "decency" – a concept that vanished along with dinner gongs and the practice of afternoon calls.

XI

Anti-Soppists and Others

> "Were you a prefect and head of your dormit'ry
> Were you a hockey girl, tennis or gym?
> Who was your favourite? Who had a crush on you?
> Which was the baths where they taught you to swim?"
> (John Betjeman, "*Myfanwy*")

THE GIRLS' SCHOOL story flourished between the wars, when old values and traditions were being reasserted in new guise, when the mood in England initially was one of getting back to normality, then of extending that concept to accommodate new trends and institutions. At the beginning of the era the idea of secondary education for girls on a large scale was still progressive enough to be generally interesting. A girls' school at Deptford is mentioned as early as 1617, in connection with a masque which its pupils performed to entertain Queen Anne, wife of James I; but it was not until the nineteenth century that the question of girls' education was taken seriously. Several large schools were founded including the North London Collegiate, 1850, and Cheltenham Ladies' College, 1855. But Mary Kingsley's complaint that "being allowed to learn German was *all* the paid-for education I ever received" was still for a long time a common one among well-off girls of the middle classes. By 1920, however, 185,000 girls were attending recognized grammar schools; this was a rise of 165,000 in just over twenty years. Girls themselves tended to think of school – particularly boarding school – in terms of freedom from the home as well as a later freedom of choice. Even if both kinds of freedom were found to be largely illusory or at least deceptive in quality, they furnished material for a fantasy life which school stories stimulated and reflected simultaneously. This osmotic process quickly led to the formulation of a type of fiction in which the basic structure, moral principles, objectives and characters were the same, and which survived more or less unchanged until after the second world war.

By the 1920s the popularity of the boys' school story had begun to decline. Boys, who were more accustomed to education, were on this account less disposed to accept an unrealistically glamorous view of school life; though an exception was made in the case of Charles Hamilton, whose stories had an addictive quality as well as an inner authority of their own. They had also an added spice since they appeared in weekly papers such as the *Magnet* and the *Gem*, of which respectable adults were almost certain to disapprove. (Corresponding girls' papers are dealt with in chapters 13,14 and 17.) But girls were just beginning to explore and savour the concepts of tradition, "team spirit", even academic prestige (though in most of the stories this is played down), and responded with enthusiasm to the type of fiction which stressed these. The fictional schools constituted *en masse* an enclave of privilege – the ultimate aggregation of the more enjoyable aspects of the experience of being at school. Privilege inevitably involved class-consciousness as well: however much snobbery is frowned on in these books, the girls *are* all of a certain social standing. If a pupil appears who is not, she is treated with conscientious kindness by the better type of girl, and with condescension by the worse; her inclusion in the story is usually for the purpose of separating the upstarts from the naturally well bred.

Schoolgirls had been well primed for the blossoming of the school story by the early books of Angela Brazil (see chapter 7) whose energetic form captains and prefects are silly, exuberant and intense in a way that is highly caricaturable. Though they were taken seriously by several generations of pubescent readers, they have acquired for the non-schoolgirl a laughable quality which was certainly not intended. The schoolgirl as a joke image owes its inception in part to Angela Brazil – an unfortunate result of her efforts to free the girls' story from archaic conventions which had governed it. Silliness in young girls had been ignored altogether by the turgid Victorian writers, such as L. T. Meade, Mrs Molesworth and E. L. Haverfield, or it was used as an occasion for moralizing; Angela Brazil broke deliberately with tradition, by expressing the girls' attitudes from the inside. Instead of boring her readers with a long-winded narrative view of events, she adopted as far as possible their vocabulary and their viewpoint, to achieve a zest and immediacy which the Edwardian schoolgirl must have relished. Her girls can be ruthless, stupid, vain or pig-headed without incurring overt narrative disapproval; the issue is rather the girls' tolerance of one another, than the author's concern to instruct her readers (though that of course is implicit in the stories' outcome, and occasionally *does* obtrude). But her assumption of schoolgirlishness perhaps was too complete; once the novelty of her approach had worn off; it was the laughableness of her stories which came across, because there is no ironic undercurrent, no acknowledgement of inevitable obsolescence.

The image for which she contributed the decisive ingredients was extended in a number of directions. On the one hand it was refined and made slightly more credible by later schoolgirls' writers such as Dorita Fairlie Bruce; on the other it was distorted for the amusement of an adult audience for which the archetypal schoolgirl became a St Trinian's sexpot with macabre inclinations, a grotesque gym tunic and regulation navy knickers which somehow pop into sight. Of course the response to this is a nervous laugh – as it is to the only comparable masculine figure – a choirboy – which also has darkly comic sexual connotations.

The schoolgirl, then, by 1920 was a well-defined image within its own fictional context. The tendency to simplify by a minimum of characterization – schoolgirls all belong to one or other of a limited range of "types" – resulted in the attribution to heroines of certain personal qualities: a sense of fun, well-meaningness, reasonable intelligence, a sympathetic attitude to the school's reputation, respect for at least one mistress (usually the head). Heroines are usually to be found in the Fourth Form (with significant exceptions), as if a medial position in the school was the exact spot where its essence should be concentrated. Certain recurrent episodes take on a symbolic character; the unholy fascination exercised on impressionable girls by the lure of a flat roof, for instance, is used more than once to express the ultimate naughtiness possible within the precincts of a school. The danger of falling over the edge, the mental exhilaration of showing off, the physical adroitness needed to climb out, make this the obvious background for illicit midnight activities. Every good school is provided with a flat roof, as well as cellars, an underground passage, and a large boot cupboard. Elinor Brent-Dyer's "The Prees had found that some of the Middles were in the habit of getting out on the roof at night – it was flat, as you may remember – and disporting themselves ..."; and Dorita Fairlie Bruce's "The Fourth Form Gang had chosen that evening to carry out a long-cherished project, and were ... out on the tiles among Wistaria's chimney pots and gables" find an echo in Muriel Spark's *The Girls of Slender Means* (1963) in which the association of flat roofs with naughty behaviour is expressed with economy: "Nicholas greatly desired to make love to Selina on the roof, it must needs be on the roof. He arranged everything as precisely as a practised incendiary."

Dorita Fairlie Bruce's first book, *The Senior Prefect* (1920; reissued as *Dimsie Goes To School*, when the series featuring Dimsie had become popular) puts across an effective school atmosphere but gets out of hand when the author goes outside the limits of school life to augment her plot. Dimsie's mother, who, in a fit of derangement after the war, has left her husband and child to run off with a set of card sharpers, is found to be living in a house near the school, in a state of bemused remorse: the line of the moral melodrama is followed even to the point of bringing in the old servant who will not abandon her mistress. The climactic sentence of this episode is spoken by naughty Dimsie, who's been dared to break into the mysterious house next door to the school, where she comes face to face with a lady whom she does not recognize. " 'Please, I'm not a burglar' " perhaps cannot compete in lurid intensity with the line delivered by dying William Carlyle to his real (but unrecognized) mother: " 'I am going to heaven ... I shall see Mamma there ...' "; but the situation (which, however, is not typical of Dorita Fairlie Bruce) is as factitious and as self-indulgently sentimental as anything in *East Lynne*.

Dimsie is one of the engaging but outspoken juniors in whom Dorita Fairlie Bruce was to specialize. Later versions of this type – Hilary Garth, Primula Mary Beton, and particularly Nancy Caird of the St Bride's and Maudsley series – are more successful, chiefly because the author is able to present them with rather more detachment. As Kate Douglas Wiggin did with Rebecca, Dorita Fairlie Bruce has loaded on to Dimsie more instinctive goodness than she can comfortably sustain. Dimsie's endearing naughtiness, her candour, her tendency to "barge in" in order to put things right, even her distinctive nickname (composed from her initials: Daphne Isobel Maitland) combine in her to produce a symbol for the author's idea of the perfect English schoolgirl. Obviously, Dimsie's apotheosis was effected at the cost of her credibility as a character: she becomes in the end a force for good which is all but disembodied: "'All the time your influence was quietly permeating the whole school [said the headmistress], so that those who did not respond to it directly were reached indirectly through the others.' " The headmistress's attitude to Dimsie is allowed to transcend favouritism, that most despicable quality of school-mistresses: "Miss Yorke ... [watched] her with a tender expression which she kept for this best-loved of all her pupils"; but the child's extraordinary (and over-drawn) appeal communicates itself even to the hardened, sports-mad seniors of her first term at the Jane Willard Foundation. When the truth about Dimsie's mother comes out (with it, of course, comes the softening statement of the extenuating circumstances which surround Mrs Maitland's odd behaviour) the head girl puts it to them that they should not

"... make it hard for the kiddie, now that you know the truth... ".

The seniors were silent for a moment. ...

"She's a decent little kid, Sylvia," said Primrose, huskily; "none of us would think of giving her a bad time, and what's more, we'll see to it that nobody else does, now that the truth's out."

Dimsie is a study in brown: brown curls, brown eyes, a brown velvet dress; breezy impatience, however, is the aspect of her character which she displays to anyone who loses herself in a brown study. The underlying theme of one book – *Dimsie Among The Prefects* (1923) – concerns the efforts of Dimsie and four friends to

"She had the cheek to say that?"
Illustration by Mary S. Reeve for The Best House in the School.

A midnight feast, drawn by Nina K. Brisley for
The Chalet School and the Lintons *(frontispiece)*

keep the sixth member of their set – Jean Gordon – from indulging too thoroughly her impulse to write poetry:

> "… You must not have more than one death in every three poems."
> "That's too many," objected Dimsie.
> "I know, but we've got to break her of the habit gradually. By degrees we shall get it down to one in ten."

The content of Jean's verse is regarded by her friends as constituting an infringement of the rules of the Anti-Soppist League – founded in book two of the series "to protest against – against a lot of silly rot" ("Rule III: Every Member must solemnly promise not to kiss anyone at all during the term, unless absolutely obliged to"). The touchingly inarticulate statement of the society's function is quickly expanded by the author into a definition which has as its basis the aim to rid the school of unwholesome behaviour, in all its aspects. The League has a frivolous name but deadly serious undertones. Dorita Fairlie Bruce's schools are terribly prone to successive outbreaks of a particular kind of silliness: prefect-worship, midnight gambollings, empty-headed gossip, a preoccupation with aids to beauty – everything, in fact, but an interest in sex in its smuttier aspects, with which many eleven- and twelve-year-olds are obsessed. As Muriel Spark put it: "The year to come was in many ways the sexual year of the Brodie set, who were now turned eleven and twelve: it was a crowded year of stirring revelations." Incidentally, there is an oblique connection between *The Prime of Miss Jean Brodie* and the books of Dorita Fairlie Bruce: all the unmentionable – or at least, unacknowledged – elements of school life which the children's author had no means of suggesting are composed, in the adult view, into a reconstruction which integrates childhood experiences and their later significance. This is true to a certain extent of *all* comparisons of school stories written for children with those written for adults, but in a particular way it is true here: the stringent exactness which Muriel Spark has brought to her view of real-life schoolgirls is paralleled by the exactness of Dorita Fairlie Bruce's assessment of their fantasy counterparts. Of course the wit of one has very little in common with the whimsey of the other; but the comparison *can* be taken further (though here again this holds good as a general statement): Muriel Spark's evocation of Edinburgh in the 1930s has a quality of precise, deliberate nostalgia which approximates to a literary expression of the quality which any memorable children's book will automatically acquire.

The outbreaks of inappropriate or contemptible behaviour at the Jane Willard Foundation and elsewhere are usually dealt with by serious, resourceful and sardonic prefects; but by the time of Dimsie's return to Jane's (1927: Dimsie "goes back" temporarily as Miss Yorke's secretary) the school has completely gone to the dogs: " 'Dimsie, my child, you have come back to a different place. There's no disguising the fact that Jane's is not what it was when you and Pamela and the others left.' " Dimsie's influence, however, soon begins to make itself felt (" 'I've sometimes been at my wits' end, lately, to think what it was the school needed, but now I believe it has been Dimsie all the time' "); a campaign to clean up Jane's is got under way with the attempt to clean make-up off certain misguided girls' faces. The Anti-Soppist League is revived, under the leadership of red-haired Hilary Garth – the most intractable of the juniors at the time of Dimsie's prefectship, but a girl for whom Dimsie has "always stood for an Ideal, someone to be followed and looked up to, whose good opinion was to be coveted and obtained at all costs". Dimsie, of course, at one point has saved Hilary's life, at the cost of serious injury to herself – Dorita Fairlie Bruce has certainly used many of the stock children's-book situations, but she has managed to transcend this to some extent, to compose a carefully worked environment in which heroics, emotional and physical, will be acceptable. A girl indulging in the former will allow herself to be thought badly of rather than explain her behaviour by betraying someone's rather unimportant confidence; the latter may involve keeping one's head when an escaped bear clambers into the open car in which one is driving.

There are seven Dimsie books in sequence, one retrospective story, and one set during the last war, when most of Dorita Fairlie Bruce's principal characters took, unconvincingly, to spy catching. The retrospective *Dimsie Intervenes* was published in 1937 but relates the efforts of Hilary and Co., who are still juniors, to raise money for a piano which is needed by a Guildry company which has been established in the village. (The Girls' Guildry was a rather obscure league midway between the Girl Guides and the Camp Fire movement; Dorita Fairlie Bruce was a Guildry officer.) They form themselves into a syndicate to supply cosmetics, clandestinely, to middle-school members who have developed an interest in their appearances. The enterprise flourishes to begin with; but the author's distaste for precocity of any kind in adolescents asserts itself through the medium of Dimsie's imagined disapproval:

> "I feel, perhaps, that the money we make for the Guildry should be clean – like soap and toothpaste, and even powder. I've only just come to think of it in this way, through imagining what Dimsie might say; but you see what I mean, don't you?"
>
> The others assented, not because they had thought the subject out very profoundly, but because what Hilary said usually "went".

But it takes an accident to one of themselves fully to bring home to the juniors the dangers of dabbling in the marketing of substances they know very little about: someone's hair is inadvertently bleached. (" 'The first question is, what's to be done now? I'm very much afraid, poor kid! it's not a thing we can keep dark.' ") Shortly afterwards, a plump middle-school girl is caught in her underwear: " '… There's no rule, that I've ever heard, against trying on new corsets in the lower music-room' " and Dimsie steps in to dissolve the syndicate; typically, it is the buyers, not the purveyors, of the make-up who are made to look silliest: " '… while you are still at Jane's, please don't try to be anything but schoolgirls. Your recent efforts have only resulted in making you little idiots …' ". For the future, make-up would no longer be fashionable at Jane's.

What *was* still fashionable, in the 1930s, was a nationalist spirit: an aggressive respect for the symbols of British power, the army, the flag, the king. Earlier in this book Dimsie has come up against a disagreeable elderly lady, a Miss Carver (this name is possibly a joke in view of the lady's pacifist opinions), whose strongly expressed views on all aspects of militarism (" 'I disapprove of drill in every shape and form' ") cause Dimsie to react sentimentally and with vehemence: " 'My father is in the Army,' she said, 'and Rosamund's was. They both fought in the Great War for – for all that the Union Jack means – what you dare to call petty and foolish! '… " Actually, Miss Carver's views now seem more reasonable than Dimsie's, and the episode makes odd reading; it's as if the author has become confused between the sentiments of her spirited, intelligent heroine and those of a grim and bigoted old lady. In a book written today, Miss Carver's standpoint would be Dimsie's, and vice versa.

But Dorita Fairlie Bruce, in common with most school-story writers of the period between the wars, had no time for eccentricity in any shape or form. Pacifism, internationalism, vegetarianism, feminism, even intellectualism, for her were dangerous cults which had to be mocked or shouted out of existence. Her ultimate intellectual schoolgirl is Fenella Postlethwaite, the nutty professor in a gym-tunic, a figure of fun and exasperation to her classmates, a girl who is totally unsympathetic to the lighter side of schoolgirl behaviour, until taken in hand by Dimsie and initiated into a proper sense of her own relative insignificance. Fenella Postlethwaite, of course, would have lost much of her impact as a comic character if she had been called, for instance, Mary Jones: her name indicates at once that she is not to be taken seriously. It must be added, however, that the author's four principal characters *do* end up in professions which are just on the right side of orthodoxy: two grow herbs for a living; one is about to be made assistant curator in a museum, and one becomes a church organist: "Nancy was now on terms of great intimacy with her organ, and was never so happy as when she could spend an hour or two alone with it."

In every schoolgirl, the wish not to make herself conspicuous by some kind of gauche or non-conformist behaviour is coupled with a desire to express her individuality by exhibiting at least one notable characteristic. Fictional schoolgirls of this period on the whole were allowed to bypass the indecisions and nervous embarrassments of adolescence, to appear always matter-of-fact and self-assured; but often a particular attribute or deficiency is used to sum up a girl's whole mental outlook. Dorita Fairlie Bruce's schoolgirls are graded, by implication, into three sets: major characters, about whom a great deal is related; lesser ones, who are lucky if they get the one quality which will enable them to stand out (a nose for news in Mabs Hunter; pessimism in Elma Cuthbert, and so on); and the silent majority, which constitutes the bulk of the schools' pupils who are mentioned only fleetingly, if at all. The background aspects of school life, however, are often suggested by means of a single, apposite reference at exactly the right point: the hours spent cycling to and from school, the boredom of lessons in which one has no interest, the time spent in changing one's shoes in the cloakroom or standing aimlessly around on the boundary line at a cricket match, the weekly bath on a rota system, all produce sensations with which most readers were familiar; they could be relied on to fill in the details for themselves. More esoteric customs, like the practice of speaking French in the dormitories at certain times, provide part of the fantasy element which the readers require. (The bastardized Anglo-French chatter in the dormitory at Jane's must have been for many elementary schoolgirl readers of the 1920s and '30s their only contact with the French language.)

The tendency in these books is always to gravitate towards the average: no one is seriously intellectual or completely stupid: no one is ruthless or unreformably *bad*. Several of the more prominent characters are rather unpleasant, for the purposes of the plot – Nita Tomlinson, Sydney Carter, for example – but usually the most bumptious, surly or underhand girl has one mitigating characteristic: typically, it is a geniune wish to promote the good of the school. Nastiness on the whole is confined to members of the upper school; Dorita Fairlie Bruce is inclined to take a sentimental view of children under fourteen and to represent their behaviour and idiom as disarmingly whimsical. Her schoolmistresses are provided with an infallible ability to distinguish between cheek, which must be put down, and coy outspokenness, which should be treated indulgently. Dimsie, in the early books, embodies this type of junior; at Springdale her rôle is split between two eleven-year-olds, Anne Willoughby and Primula Mary Beton, in each of whom an aspect of the prototype is stressed:

kind-heartedness and a dislike of artifice respectively.

One junior who is less than endearing in her unmoulded state is Nancy Caird, who makes her first appearance in *Nancy at St Bride's*. Sent to this school to keep up a family tradition – her mother and aunt had been impeccable pupils – delinquent Nancy organizes one escapade after another, enthralls her contemporaries and disturbs the peace of mind of everyone else. " 'I'm worried to death, and it's all through you, you wicked, tiresome little wretch! I wish to goodness you'd never entered St Bride's! You're a pest to your elders and a positive danger to your own form!' " But there is plenty of "good stuff" in Nancy (" 'I believe she'll be a fine character some day' "), though she has to cause one girl to catch pneumonia, nearly drown another, and get herself expelled from St Bride's before it becomes apparent. In subsequent books it is emphasized that Nancy's early behaviour is thoughtless, never dishonourable. In the second book of the series (*That Boarding-School Girl*, 1928), Nancy has sobered up to the extent of displeasing her new classmates at the Maudsley (a day school where the atmosphere is less rarefied than at St Bride's, a school on an island off the Scottish coast) by her attention to form work: " '... Your work is always being held up as an example to them, and they know quite well it isn't sheer braininess, which can't be helped if you happen to be born that way. I wish, for your own sake, you'd slack off a bit, Nance! It isn't *done* in the Lower Fifth, you know ...'."

The Lower Fifth's main interest is games; in fictional schools, you find a strong tradition of equating philistinism with healthy-mindedness. An enthusiasm for games implies an attitude of fairness, self-effacement and loyalty which is far more to be applauded than any mere intellectual achievement. Playing games is regarded as a legitimate way of discharging energies which might otherwise erupt in a less orderly, harmless or controllable form; nevertheless it is odd that in the books of Dorita Fairlie Bruce and others there should have been so much emphasis on sport. In real-life schools athletic girls are in a minority and at a disadvantage, socially, rather than not. Sweat, mud, and a hefty frame are no substitute for a self-possessed, contemptuous or knowing air, a knack of appearing to advantage in a school hat, or even a degree of acting ability. Sports enthusiasm, like so many other aspects of fictional school life, originated with Angela Brazil – and served a purpose at the time, by indicating that girls were capable of physical activity just as much as boys. The point needed to be stressed; but the distasteful or laughable associations of organized sports were taken over wholesale by girls' writers; the activity was invested with far more significance than its effects can explain. Somewhere around 1880, the more idealistic implications of playing games had crystallized into a metaphor: Playing the Game. This, and its extensions (questionable behaviour is "not cricket"; children who put their own interests first, or who cannot take a joke against themselves, are "unsporting") were soon recycled back into the original, unvarnished activity; so that children who took no interest in games were felt to be incapable of playing the game. (This has a parallel in the persistent equation of social morality with religion.) In fact, children of either sex with a taste for athletics are no more common than those who prefer reading, archaeology or horse-brass collecting. And it is almost inevitable that too much enthusiasm on the part of mistresses or senior girls applied to sport and its moral implications will lead its recipients to take up an anarchic pose like the one adumbrated by Stevie Smith in "Girls!": [1]

> … Miss So-and-so whose greatest pride
> Is to remain always in the VI Form and not let down the side

> Do not sell the pass dear, don't let down the side
> That is what this woman said and a lot of balsy stuff beside

> (Oh the awful balsy nonsense that this woman cried.)

> Girls! I will let down the side if I get a chance
> And I will sell the pass for a couple of pence.

A type of senior whom Dorita Fairlie Bruce allowed to be fairly intellectual is represented by Charity Sheringham (Maudsley): the nonchalant *poseuse* whose affectations really cover a well-developed

[1] *Collected Poems*, Allen Lane, London, 1975.

moral code, cynically resigned to being involved in school affairs but preserving a faint, unmalicious sense of their absurdity. For the author, Charity (a minor character, though she turns up years later in a wartime adventure) clearly embodies the worthwhile qualities inherent in an attitude of detachment; another version of the same type, Rae Merchiston (Springdale: *The Best House in the School*, 1930) is less honourable, therefore less rigidly predictable as far as her motivations are concerned (the outcome is not only predictable, but predetermined). Rae's wilfulness costs her House (the Rowans) a Banner of Merit which they had set their hearts on winning (" 'I'm rather keen on getting that Banner'."); like any normal seventeen-year-old cooped up in a boarding school, she coolly indulges her disreputable instincts to the point where she thinks these will remain undetected. The House Captain, however, finds out that Rae has broken bounds at night to go to a dance: "'It's all up now, Peg! This means expulsion for me, and no Banner for the house! I – I never really believed before that I might be caught, but this is the end of all things!' " Rae's crime is to have transgressed "the unwritten code which prevailed at their school"; but by the same code she is reinstated in everyone's good opinion when she "honourably" owns up to the headmistress, though by this time there is no need to. Where an adult novelist could have related the tale of Rae's escapade in a deadpan, non-committal or satirical way, the children's writer is handicapped here, as elsewhere (from the point of view of objectivity or formalized realism) by having to draw an extremely basic moral conclusion. A system of discipline based on the pupil's sense of "honour" actually became an educational policy at certain moderately progressive schools in the first half of this century: it could be shown to work perfectly, however, only in the Dorita Fairlie Bruce type of fiction, where tensions, complexities of motive or improperly assimilated or contradictory ethical principles do not need to be considered. W. H. Auden, who was educated at a school of this type, claimed that its effect was to turn out a succession of "neurotic innocents".

A recurrent theme in the books of Dorita Fairlie Bruce is the estrangement of two bosom friends in the Sixth Form, due mainly to the pig-headedness of one. Their reconciliation is usually brought about through the intervention of a guileless and perceptive junior, who may admire one or both of them; but always, we are told, in a way which is sane and healthy. Sanity and health – which may include physical health but implies more specifically an uncorrupted attitude of mind – are qualities which the atmosphere of these books is designed to promote and prolong. The clear-sighted innocence of Dimsie and the others is protracted through late adolescence, later marriage – and Dorita Fairlie Bruce has been no more successful in resolving the problem of juvenile characters whom she persists in putting through the motions of "growing up" than other writers who set themselves this task. What results most commonly, and *Dimsie Grows Up* is no exception, is a type of fiction which is in complete discord with the principles of Anti-Soppism, as laid down for children not susceptible to the influence of sentiment. The kind of mental briskness which leads, at twelve, to a contemptuous and high-handed dismissal of any manifestation of "silly rot", it seems, can accommodate a later falling away from an attitude of stringent common sense: "Dimsie awoke from her dream, and turned a radiant face to her friend. 'I'm marrying my mate,' she answered simply, but with a world of joy and content behind the ordinary words." "Dream", "radiant", "joy", "content", are all debased stock words, popular with the type of writer whose function is to sweeten, simplify and diminish every experience by divesting it of elements which conflict, in popular terms, with its idealization. Basically, the genre of light romantic fiction has far less vigour, literary worth or psychological plausibility than that of children's books as a whole; [1] but where the territories of the two kinds of fiction overlap, the children's writer until recently has tended to rely on a formula supplied by the former. This may have come about in tacit acceptance of the fact that the readership for the light romance is essentially simple-minded, but fails to take into consideration the fact that simple-mindedness in an adult is of rather more consequence than

[1] Of course the former is classified instantly by the adjective "light", the latter is spread over the spectrum of values, from the worthwhile to the deplorable.

its equivalent in a child. In a child it is inevitable and therefore quite different in quality; and to palm off on a bright but inexperienced child material which has been devised to satisfy the taste of a lazy-minded or retarded adult readership, is to be guilty of a serious failure of imagination.

In the above case, the author has considered Dimsie's impending marriage, together with the state of being "in love", expressible only in terms of the most soporific banality. Dimsie's uncomplex nature, of course, makes it inevitable that she will fall in with a pre-ordained pattern; she provides the author with more than one opportunity to state the conventional view of women's rôle:

> "And we're all going to live happily ever afterwards!" she cried jubilantly. "Except, of course, Jean and Mabs, and probably they will, too, in the end. Oh, Eric! I was very much afraid you were going to grow into a superior female MP!"
>
> "I hope I shall never be superior or a female," said Erica firmly, "but I may still be an MP even if I do marry Derrick. It isn't impossible, you know."
>
> "No, I suppose not," admitted Dimsie, "but I don't think it's advisable ...".

This was the kind of implicit definition of "fulfilment" which girls' education, traditionally, was expected to produce. One persistent criticism of the whole system of secondary education for girls was based on the charge that syllabuses followed too closely the pattern of those devised originally for boys, that adaptations suited to the peculiar nature of girls' innate abilities had not been considered. John Newson supports this in *The Education Of Girls*: "Education meant boys' education: girls had a right to education, and therefore to boys' education, irrespective of their biological and social differences. ... In the main it is unrelated to their eventual rôles of wife and mother and concerned too much with their 'careers' ..." This of course is based on the fallacy that boys' and girls' intellectual capabilities *are* demonstrably and fundamentally different, and that what will inform and expand the minds of one sex will be a burden to and impose an unnatural discipline on the other. (The fact that "careers" is put in inverted commas implies that the word, in any real context, is inapplicable.) The above author's thesis boils down, in fact, to a mock-serious reassessment of the intellectual status of domestic economy: "... just as much intelligence is required to attain high honours in the domestic arts, and ... to produce an *Homard a l'Americaine* to perfection needs as much wit as to construe one of the more obscure passages of *Bérénice*." "Wit" is an overstatement; skill, perhaps, but skill of an entirely different order. The two attributes are not relatable, and either, or both, may occur in a person of either sex; on this basis the argument is tenable, but when it is applied to a proposed reorientation of the curricula of girls' schools in order to bring them more into line with the girls' "eventual roles of wife and mother", it can hardly be regarded as an objective or relevant assessment. Rousseau's assertion, in *Emile*, that the principal purpose of female education was to render men's lives "easy and agreeable" somewhere along the line had been absorbed into the most pervasive theory of education, so that its import is discernible at a level either subliminal or overt.

It is discernible, certainly, in the books of Dorita Fairlie Bruce and other girls' school-story writers of the '20s and '30s. The girls in these books are usually enclosed within an exclusively female society: characterization, if nothing else, demanded that qualities which had been regarded as "masculine" should be allowed to occur in certain girls – usually the principal characters. These act on their own initiative, are concerned with forging their own position in the society, are shown to be capable of leadership, aggression, inventiveness, intellectual effort. But the implications of this are rarely followed up: where a definite conclusion has to be drawn to a girl's activities, the sentimental equation of marriages with "happy endings" has proved irresistible – and, as in the case of Erica Innes (see above) the idea that the girl's own ambitions should be relinquished at this point is brought out.

Of course feminism, even in its less radical aspects, was completely out of fashion: psychology, the "natural/biological" bias of certain youth movements (in Nazi Germany, for instance), and particularly the economic slump, all appeared to provide their own, and cumulative, arguments for the restriction of women's social rôle. Feminism was as much a crank movement, and seemed as specialized, as any other esoteric cult which could be held up to ridicule. In the 1930s, the issue was considered irrelevant: girls *were* being educated in larger numbers than ever before (over half a million in recognized secondary schools by 1938); women were able to vote; job opportunities in theory were equal. To some extent the beneficiaries of this were at pains to demonstrate that it need not conflict with the traditional function assigned to women in the community; that higher education for girls would not necessarily lead to the "psychological involution" so dreaded by leaders of the American Camp Fire movement. Dorita Fairlie Bruce's *Prefects at Springdale* (1936) contains a character, Miss Peters, who actually *is* a feminist and an ex-Suffragette: " 'She's keen on anything to do with women's education,' said Primula. 'She's what is known as a feminist, and I've heard a rumour that once, in the dark ages, she got sent to prison for scratching a policeman.' " (By using the evocative word "scratching" instead of "attacking" or even "hitting", the futility, "unsportingness", and feline/femaleness of Miss Peters's action are brought out: this is rather too high a price to pay for the mildly comic effect which it produces.) Miss Peters's keenness leads her to organize a competition: each house at Springdale is asked to "demonstrate" the quality of the education provided by the school; a prize is offered for the most effective demonstration. It is won by Wistaria, whose captain, at least, has her educational priorities in order: "It came to me – just came to me – in a blinding flash as I was running back through the grounds … Girls, this house is going all out for domestic science!' " The irony involved in causing Miss Peters to render ineffectual her own position as an educationalist was perhaps not apparent either to the author or the reader; but the speech which she makes on presenting the prize (a dwarf-cedar tree in a pot, to represent – by a further degree of irony – the tree of knowledge) implies a reactionary, fake common-sense approach to the whole question which is out of tune with her stated background – this holds true even if her feminism is conceded to be of the sort which demands a proper appreciation of the tasks performed by women, rather than that which wished to expand the scope of women's activities:

222

"... I'm exceedingly pleased to think that the strongest point in the education at Springdale should be how to cook and serve a meal, – not forgetting the brooms and dusters that led up to it. The rest's all very good of its kind, girls," she added. ... "I haven't a word to say against drill, or science, or languages. ... But, when all's said and done, humanity must eat. ... "

And the anti-feminist position always has been that it is women, by and large, who must feed it. Of course proficiency in domestic science is as desirable as proficiency in anything else; but not all girls are capable of achieving it, just as some boys *are*; in any case it seems a little paradoxical to suggest that the "strongest point" in anyone's secondary education should be how to "cook and serve a meal" – a skill which could be learnt with rather less fuss and expense to the community in the kitchen of any hotel or snack-bar – or even at home. And anyone who *had* a word to say against science or languages would hardly have been affected by revolutionary pressures even to the extent of scratching a policeman.

One exception to the affectedly frivolous or dismissive approach to learning in girls' stories is in the rather sententiously titled *Evelyn Finds Herself* by Josephine Elder (1929), in which a fairly serious attempt is made to express the psychological benefits attendant on mental application: "Evelyn began to feel stimulated, then; to taste the same cold and sparkling joy that came to her when her mind got to grips with a chemistry problem. This was what she wanted – not praise, which made one rest on one's laurels, but criticism, which pricked one on to a greater effort." Unfortunately the japing/madcap tradition in girls' fiction had made it almost impossible by this time to convey a degree of intellectual enthusiasm without sounding priggish or humourless. Josephine Elder, in this book, makes a stand against a glamorous view of school life with its obvious falsification; she gets closer to the atmosphere of a real school perhaps than any other girls' writer of the period, but only by a calculated playing down of the outrageously wilful or naughty behaviour on which other writers tended to rely for their stimulating effects. *Her* effect is to bring out the humdrum aspects of all schools without enlivening these for the reader's benefit by acerbic or epiphonematical comment. Evelyn is a prosaic but intelligent girl who is troubled by qualms of conscience – "Evelyn felt horribly that they were behaving like toads" – which lead to rather earnest bouts of self-examination: "Did she really dislike Madeleine because there was something wrong with her, or was it just jealousy?"

In Evelyn, the process of self-realization is fraught with emotional pitfalls, betrayals, and the perception of unpalatable facts: "although they had been comrades for so long they did not really know each other at all." But it is achieved smoothly enough through a series of straightforward adjustments to altering circumstances: a close friendship which has been allowed to lapse is resumed on a less claustrophobic basis; tolerance for behaviour which she cannot admire is incepted (" 'Don't want to turn into a beastly egotist' "). The author's originality lies in her quasi-realistic approach (misunderstandings arise which are not cleared up); her allusions to standards of behaviour other than those which prevail at the Addington High School: "mothers did not understand things like the dignity of the Sixth, and fathers laughed at it, very gently and kindly, but still, laughed"; and especially in her unemphatic, taken-for-granted conveying of the fact that school work need not be a bore nor impose an intolerable tax upon a girl's brain ("Later, she worked for the sheer pleasure of feeling her mind take a grip on things").

A book which panders rather more to the schoolgirls' demand for easy-going, unflagging entertainment is Winifred Darch's *Heather at The High School* (1924); but here too school work is acknowledged to carry its own rewards. Heather is a scholarship pupil from a poor home ("Her mother had been right when she said all this would cost money. It was perhaps lucky that she had begun to do the Farrells' washing directly they heard about the scholarship"); her situation is neatly paralleled by that of her favourite fictional character, and the story centres on Heather's laughable attempts to conform to an ideal of schoolgirl behaviour which she's acquired from the weekly paper *Schoolgirl's Chum*. This is obviously an amalgam of the *School Friend* and the *Schoolgirls' Own*; and the author's disapproval [1] of what was

[1] Winifred Darch herself was a high-school teacher.

A dog and some rabbits.
M. D. Johnston illustrates Evelyn Finds Herself

considered to be trash is expressed through her juxtaposition of parody with humorous common sense:

> Coralie Montmorency looked dangerous. "So you defy us, do you? I warn you that the consequences will be serious!"
> So they were, of course, but equally of course, as any reader of the *Schoolgirl's Chum* knew, Biddy triumphed in the end. Heather put down the paper.

Heather, too, triumphs in the end. She becomes a Girl Guide and makes a friend of the head girl of the school, whom she has the temerity to invite to her lower-class home:

> "There shouldn't be differences," declared Heather.
> "But there *are*," said her mother. "I don't doubt but she will be very nice and kind and not laugh at us. *Real* ladies don't. But all the same – I'd rather she didn't come here."

Heather's mother conforms to the stock image of the aristocracy-loving ex-domestic servant; but the family's poverty is in no way lurid or overdrawn. It is, in fact, stated but never really conveyed. Heather's fears that she will be persecuted at the High School (based on the treatment meted out to "Bessie Barber" at "Clieveden House"[1]) turn out to be almost groundless; only one girl is snobbish enough to taunt her with her background: "What do you think Helen will think of *your* house and family, you board-school kid?" and she of course has had a council-school education herself. A *real* lady would not have exhibited so deplorable a lack of control or subscribed to so unacceptable a system of personal valuation – and by this implication the author gives away her own belief that *real ladies* exist.

A real lady who amuses herself by pretending to belong to the lower classes is the central character in Christine Chaundler's *The Chivalrous Fifth* (1928). Here, the snobbism which was so much a feature of certain exclusive girls' schools is shown to be ingrained

[1] The author here has hardly bothered to disguise "Betty Barton" (*Schoolgirls' Own*) and "Cliff House" (*School Friend*).

Coming to blows.
Illustration by C. E. Brock for Heather at the High School

even in kind-hearted girls who think they are repudiating it: " 'Look here, we must all be awfully careful what we say to Jane Smith,' Cicily began. 'We must be frightfully careful not to let her feel that it's queer for her mother to keep a second-hand shop. ... The very fact that she's not quite in our set means we've got to be extra nice and polite to her. ...' " "Not quite in our set" takes on an ironic significance when the girls discover that Jane Smith is as much above them, socially, as they had thought her beneath them; the "secondhand shop" turns out to be a Bond Street antique gallery, and Jane's mother is the Viscountess Halmer – family name Smith. "Then Mona spoke in an aggrieved voice. 'But Smith! It's such a common name. How on earth were we to know that she was a member of the aristocracy?' " That question. is answered by the Fifth's most chivalrous member – " 'We hadn't the gumption to see that a girl like Jane had never come out of the slums' " – and the moral lesson (" 'Whatever difference does it make *who* my mother is?' ") is somewhat invalidated by the imputation of undesirable qualities to the general run of girls from the slums.

The theme of the scholarship pupil, with its emotionally dramatic possibilities, was a fairly popular one before the last war. Feelings of inferiority were ascribed – no doubt with justification – to girls whose parents could not afford to pay their school fees. The cry – " 'You horrid, *horrid*, girl! Why, it's an honourable thing to get a scholarship, you know it is! *You* haven't brains enough!' " – was repeated in one form or another in each book of this type, but it had no real meaning until the whole system of values had been reversed. After 1944 [1] it was the non-scholarship pupil who felt herself to be in a position of inferiority, particularly the girl who was accepted reluctantly into a grammar school, and only on condition that she was paid for. Stupidity soon became the focus for a pupil's sense of her own deficiencies,

[1] When the Education Act put secondary school education within the reach of everyone who was thought likely to benefit from it; by the 1950s, according to a sociological study, *Social Class and Education Opportunity*, by Floud, Halsey and Martin, "... the chances of children at a given level of ability entering grammar schools are no longer dependent on their social origins".

superseding a lack of upper-class family connections.

The shift of emphasis in the girls' school story over the past 30 years can be pinpointed in the books of Mary K. Harris, in which a brisk, laconic technique is combined with the fictional expression of certain contemporary preoccupations to produce an effect of integration. Mary K. Harris's principal characters are misfits: a "C-stream" grammar-school pupil who feels herself constantly to be threatened with expulsion on account of her defective brains; a girl who has been rejected altogether by the grammar-school selection committee at the eleven-plus stage; a clever child whose uneasy relationship with the form's most capricious and aggressive personality is both stimulating and impossible to tolerate. This author specializes in expressing the quirks and cussedness of a particular age group, eleven to fifteen-year-olds whose illogical behaviour leads to nothing but difficulties for themselves. If these girls find their own grounds for self-respect in the end, neither the process nor its climax is inflated nor implied to be absolute or irreversible: the C-stream pupil reads Jane Austen for pleasure, writes a prize-winning (not the first prize) essay; the clever girl's impossible friendship is confirmed in the end. Horrid children in these books are not subjected to any old-fashioned character-moulding process; the traits which they embody, moreover, are not contrived for the purposes of the story (to which they are incidental) but are instantly recognizable. Every class contains a child like Jessica's smug little sister who likes reciting in front of an audience; thick-skinned, miserable, jeering Mavis and smarmy, precocious, disobliging Amabel (" 'If Hetty isn't going to stop at school on Friday I don't see why I should. Tyrone – my boy friend – takes me to the pictures on Fridays' ") are equally credible. This increasing credibility is one result of the process of democratization which has been taking place over the last few decades: the emphasis on everyone's "rights" has made everyone, including schoolchildren, conscious of their own identity and anxious to assert it by reading only about characters with whom they can closely identify. Unlike the situation which existed in the 1920s, when elementary schoolgirls were happy to read about the doings of the Earl of So-and So's granddaughter or the cheery exploits of the Hon. Amelia Whatsit, comprehensive schoolgirls today prefer to read about girls at comprehensive schools. There *are* paradoxes involved in this trend: most particularly the fact that books in which schoolgirl behaviour is portrayed most accurately are those which schoolgirls are not supposed to read. (See, for example, the story "Nice Day at School" in William Trevor's *The Ballroom of Romance* [1972]: "At thirteen, in Miss Croft's class, Liz Jones confessed that a boy called Gareth Swales had done her in the corner of the estate playground, at eleven o'clock one night … By the time they reached Class 2 it had become the fashion to have been done and most of the girls, even quiet Mavis Temple, had succumbed to it.")

Mary K. Harris, who died in 1966, wrote over a period of 25 years only six books which come into the school-story category. The advantages of this kind of restraint are apparent when one considers the overall quality of the far better known *Chalet School* series, which Elinor Brent-Dyer wrote between 1925 and 1970. By the late 1940s the possibilities of the series had clearly been exhausted, yet the books continued to appear with dispiriting regularity. The 58th Chalet book (1970) contains its quota of natural and unnatural disasters (a thunderstorm, two floods, and a green dye which falls on someone's head); minor acts of defiance on the part of unruly Middles: " 'That will do. Impudence to the prefects won't get you anywhere, Jocelyn...' "; injunctions which are intended to be mentally bracing: " 'In less than three years you should all be seniors and we don't like seniors who are as weak-kneed as all that' "; and problems and worries for the headmistress: "Then she turned her attention to the list of curtains required for the new dormitories that were coming into being next term. This was not an easy matter to decide, for there were so many dormitories already to take the names of the different flowers that finding new names was something of a puzzle." For all its flavour of a period piece, this was written in the present decade, in the era of the *Little Red Schoolbook,* the Rupert Bear Obscenity trial, teachers' pay disputes, and a great deal of concern over the increasing use of marijuana in schools. Of course this may appear to be a false analogy – one might just as well relate the early Chalet books to the General Strike, the publication of *Lady Chatterley's Lover*, or the controversy over proposed financial aid for Roman Catholic schools – but the point is that although the direct sociological content of the books had always been negligible, by the end of the series they had become absurdly anachronistic, and were no longer explainable even as a queer manifestation of contemporary taste. The mould into which they had fallen, however, was not one which could be modified in any of its essential aspects, even if that had been Elinor Brent-Dyer's aim – and obviously it is the author's view which is being expressed when Miss Annersley says: " 'The longer I live, Mary-Lou, the more horrified I am at the growing wickedness of the world.' "

With the appearance of *The School at the Chalet* in 1925, a new element entered into the "euphoric schooldays" fantasy: this is an international school, the majority of whose pupils are interestingly foreign, but where standards of behaviour and teaching are of a strictly British calibre. It is founded, somewhat impetuously, by 24-year-old Madge Bettany, who has no experience, very little money, and embarks on the project at least partly for the benefit of her delicate young sister's health. Practical stumbling-blocks are swept aside, as the romantic nature of a non-denominational school in the Alpine Tirol is emphasized. It was necessary to the author's purpose that the preposterous undertaking should thrive, and, implausibly, it thrives. Miss Bettany is undaunted by the prospect of language difficulties and racial disaffinities, and steadily increases the number of her pupils until she is running a sizeable and well-organized establishment. The Chalet girls effortlessly become tri-lingual; a new type of slang is invented: "Good enoughsky!". Chauvinism asserts itself only in temporarily undisciplined girls who respond to provocation: " 'I'm not going to be called "pig-dog" by any measly old German!' retorted Grizel." The foreign girls who attend the school are only too anxious to absorb its "English" spirit – basically a compound of exuberance, courage and straightforwardness. This is embodied in Joey Bettany, the headmistress's sister and the moving spirit of the early books, whose literary ancestry can be traced directly to *Little Women*. Like Jo March, Joey is completely "unsentimental" [1]; she also has a healthy contempt for any manifestation of eccentricity: " 'Why couldn't he [the singing master] wear a decent collar and tie like other folks?' " Joey's literary affiliations can be taken further: like John Betjeman's silken Myfanwy, she is "ringleader, tomboy and chum to the weak". Her own physical weakness is soon outgrown; her health responds so well to the stimulating environment that she is able to weather even a series of relapses which are brought about as a result of her remarkable life-saving feats. In the first five books Joey saves the lives of six girls and a dog, coming near to death herself only once, when she catches pneumonia after dragging a foolhardy skater out of an ice-bound river (*Rivals of the Chalet School*, 1929).

> "She is so ill that, candidly, Dick, I doubt if she will see the afternoon."
> Dick groaned. "The chicken! Oh, Jem, old chap! It hits hard!"

The echoes from *Little Women* here are gratuitous: Joey recovers to become head girl of the school, a successful writer of girls' stories and the mother of eleven children. (Like Elsie Oxenham, who also remained unmarried and childless, Elinor Brent-Dyer seems to have felt that her characters' adulthood can best be expressed by supernatural fecundity.) In spite of the eleven children, Joey is psychologically unable to cut herself off from the Chalet School, though her sister has resigned the headship to get married as far back as the third book of the series. When the school is forced to move (initially because of Nazi intimidation, then because of blocked drains, problems of space, and so on) Joey trails after it, moving house with each of the school's successive moves, to the Channel Islands, to South Wales, to an island off the Welsh coast, finally to the Oberland. Her husband and children (including triplets and two sets of twins) are dragged with her. In the last book, the benefits to

[1] It is odd that both these characters, who so thoroughly repudiate sentimentality, should exist in a type of fiction which is innately sentimental.

Joey of a vicarious girlhood are stated: "… she contrived to remain very much of a girl both in character and looks and she always insisted that even if she lived to be a great-grandmother, she would be a Chalet girl to the end."

Of course the series was built up upon the character of Joey: once she is removed from the actual school environment, its weaknesses become apparent. That the author was aware of this is clear from her artificial prolongation of Joey's connection with the school; and when Joey's qualities are distributed among a number of lesser characters in whom the author palpably has less interest, the books take on a factitious and sterile note from which they do not recover. Their continuing popularity can be ascribed only to the fact that the glamour of the *idea* of the Chalet school had taken hold of children's imaginations to the extent that it was able to generate enthusiasm even for the boring intricacies of the old-girl network and the second-generation pupils' family relationships.

This rather crude glamour is derived largely from the school's first, exotic, location; but it is in fact while it is housed in a mansion in South Wales that a number of stories occur which stand up to the usual cannons of school-story criticism. *The Chalet School Goes To It* is one of these, in spite of the sentimentalities of the Chalet School Peace League, with its "hands-across-the-sea" connotations; *Lavender Laughs in the Chalet School* and *Three Go to the Chalet School* are others, though in neither of these is the central theme – the character-developing motif – fully exploited.

A serious weakness of the Chalet School series is the religious sentimentality which accompanies each episode of physical danger: " 'Death – is just falling asleep to wake with God,' she said softly"; and " 'Our Father,' began Grizel dully. 'Oh, Joey, He sent you at last!' " For many children's writers, the expression of such simple-minded Christianity was the logical outcome of the moral function which they had assigned themselves. Its sogginess is the inverse of the bracing, outdoor spirit which they urged upon their readers – and an offshoot of both, in the Chalet books, is the dreadful, arch yet quietly meaningful, way in which weddings and engagements are treated. Social awareness was the last quality which most of these authors wanted to display: the books' most basic assumption is that "all's right with the world" – or at least that only a little faith is needed to make everything all right. God, when properly appealed to, will not let anyone down, neither Dorita Fairlie Bruce's schoolgirls nor Elinor Brent-Dyer's. These tend to pray audibly to be delivered from nasty predicaments, when they are immobilized on the side of a cliff or cornered in an underground passage with the sea lapping round their ankles – unlike Elsie Oxenham's Abbey girls, who turn to God for help in coping with more general troubles.

The names of Angela Brazil, Dorita Fairlie Bruce and Elinor Brent-Dyer have become synonymous with the school-story genre as it was in its heyday; lesser authors, who owed much to these three, failed to achieve anything like a comparable degree of recognition. Dorothea Moore, Winifred Darch, Christine Chaundler, Katherine Oldmeadow, Ethel Talbot, Evelyn Smith, all produced respectable, though ultimately unmemorable, variations on the standard theme, but did not find a coherent focus for the complexity of feelings and images evoked by the idea of school (this is important, irrespective of its degree of realism). At its lowest level, the school story incorporated the pot-boiling elements of tawdry sentiment and far-fetched melodrama; books of this type were mass produced but seldom reprinted, by publishers aware of the ephemeral nature of their appeal. Fashions in trash (which is dependent on fashion: magazine stories have to give the impression of being up-to-date) change more quickly than fashions in most other literary fields. Some of the better-known school stories have survived in paperbacks but these are best read with sympathetic recognition of the fact that they are products of another era.

XII

William and Jane

"He only does it to annoy
Because he knows it teases."
(Lewis Carroll, *Alice's Adventures in Wonderland*)

IN WILLIAM, RICHMAL CROMPTON lumped together all the child characteristics which adults find most abhorrent, thereby ensuring his appeal for a generation of English children whose anti-social tendencies previously had had no vicarious outlet – none, at least, in fiction, where their effects had been presented on a heroic level. For adults, William provides an instantly recognizable symbol for those tendencies: like Cinderella and Billy Bunter, his name has a meaning even for people who have never read the books.

In 1922 William was something new in juvenile literature. A boy who was not particularly truthful, who carried dirtiness almost to the point of fetishism, who was acquisitive, belligerent and opinionated, was bound to make an impact on a reading public whose standards had been determined by the impeccably honourable children of another type of fiction. William listens unashamedly at keyholes – prompted by a "constitutional curiosity"; he will do nothing that does not further his own ends: " 'Do you mean to tell me you want to be paid for doing a little thing like that?' 'Yes,' replied William simply." On one occasion he sets out to be a burglar, stealing what he takes to be an heirloom: in fact it's an old lady's ear trumpet, but his intention is none the less dishonest. The doctrine of kindness to animals, as far as William is concerned, applies only to dogs and occasionally rats; his attitude to cats derives wholly from the idea that there is something effete and untrustworthy about a cat. In one episode he goes so far as to kill one – accidentally – with an air gun ("A Witch in Time", 1950); in another he poisons a stray cat and two white rats with a sleeping draught appropriated from a neurotic visitor. None of these traits, of course, is intended to be unappealing: William is represented simply as a boy whose proclivities are natural and need no justification. But, paradoxically, by making him boyish to an unnatural degree, Richmal Crompton turned William into an archetype. He is the ultimate outdoor child, not *any* small boy with a liking for poking about in ditches and a healthy contempt for books, but an abstraction, a classics mistress's idea of boyhood toughness and resilience.

William appears initially as a disruptive force (a wholesome one: William's direct outlook is always contrasted favourably with the deviousness and misguided values of the grown-ups around him). Hurtling along on a bicycle over which he has no control, with a blackened face and a mat pinned to his shoulders, he crashes into a picnic party and ends in a lake: a feat which prompts his elder brother Robert to remark bitterly: " 'You'd think he wouldn't be allowed to go about spoiling people's lives and – and ruining their bicycles.' " Nearly every character in the William books is activated by a strong sense of personal grievance, usually stirred up by William; but William's own is more pronounced than anyone's. He is constantly involved in promoting one social reform or another: the abolition of school, a return to chimney sweeping (" 'I'd a jolly sight rather work in a mill or up a chimney than in school' "), pensions for boys (" 'Ladies and gentlemen, it's jolly unfair, and we've all gotter work hard to get it put right' "). More altruistically, he is always prepared to lend a hand with other people's causes ("William Clears the Slums"; "William the Salvage Collector" etc.) – and the extent to which William "means well" is usually in direct proportion to the social chaos which he manages to create. " 'I wanted to *help.*' 'But William,' said Mrs Brown [and one can only concur in her bewilderment] 'how did you think it was going to help *anyone* to say that Ethel had epilepsy and consumption?' "

By placing him in a fairly genteel environment, Richmal Crompton highlighted William's peculiarities, at the same time as ensuring that his behaviour would not be taken for hooliganism. His scruffiness would not have been half so effective in a slum ragamuffin – nor would a lower-class child's intractability have brought the requisite expressions of horror to the badly-bred faces around it. William's is the average English suburban family: the irascible father, the breadwinner, complete with strong political opinions and a wife who says "Yes dear"; the featureless mother who does nothing but darn socks, whose complacence borders on imbecility; the vapid elder brother and sister. "Robert and Ethel, glasses of fashion and moulds of form, passed at that moment. At the sight of William, with torn coat and jersey, dirty scratched face, no cap and tousled hair, consuming ice-cream horns among a crowd of his social inferiors, a shudder passed through both of them." The attitude of William's family towards William "was one of apprehension", the Browns' ultra-normality making them particularly susceptible to the embarrassment which William's muddles invariably produce. The terrible child remarks to Lady Atkinson, as she shows him her photograph, " 'It's not as fat as you are. I'm not impolite. I'm being truthful.' " "William's Truthful Christmas", in fact, shows up the unreasonableness of the average Christian precept. William, who has decided to take the vicar's rhetoric literally (" 'What is it that spoils even the holy season that lies before us? It is deceit' ") finds that his efforts at truthfulness merely lead his relatives to conclude that he ought to be exterminated. " 'If it wasn't Christmas day [Robert says] I'd hang him myself.' " In the same story, William, examining a book of Church history which has been given to him as a Christmas present, is so exasperated by the deeds of the saintly Aidan that he is driven to "adorning the saint's picture by the addition of a top hat and spectacles". Elsewhere, however, William, in a weakened condition after influenza, sees himself as "a boy wearing a halo and rescuing those around him from lives of crime" (this is in contrast to his normal hankering after a life of crime for himself). He gets the idea into his head that his sister is a secret drinker with incipient kleptomania; but it turns out (rather flatly) that Ethel's red nose is due to a cold.

William's habitual behaviour in church is to pull faces at a choirboy – an unusual concession to verisimilitude on the part of Richmal Crompton, considering the religious climate of the time when the books began to appear. Clergymen in children's literature were still sacrosanct (though by 1930 there were unorthodox clerics in real life: Dr Barnes, for instance, and the Rev Hewlett Johnson, a Left Book Club enthusiast). The Church was one of those solemn institutions at which one did not – however light-heartedly – poke fun. The village clergyman, however, was a stock farcical character whom Richmal Crompton could not ignore (William's village is made up of just such stock characters); and it is to her credit as a debunker that her vicars are liable to say "Damn" in moments of stress, that her bishops are of the same species as the one who was forever making remarks to an actress. The humour of the William books is firmly in the music-hall tradition, with a veneer of refinement. Children tend to respond to the obvious, and the absurd situations into which William gets himself ("It was, he was sure, contrary to all rules of etiquette to go out to tea accompanied by a cow"; "William stood revealed as the Fairy Queen in the middle of the courtyard", etc.) in combination with the facetious tone which Richmal Crompton adopts to describe them, produce an effect which most eleven-year-olds find irresistibly funny. What subtleties there are are subterranean, gratifying the author's own feeling for satire: and it is not necessary, for instance, for a child to realize that the "Society of Ancient Souls" is a skit on the type of gullible adult who believes in reincarnation – the name is enough to produce the requisite giggle.

Richmal Crompton's response to contemporary social and political events, as reflected in the William books, is always a conservative one: from Mr Brown's wearily sardonic reaction to a noise outside (" 'A revolution, I expect. ... .The Reds are upon us' ") in 1922, to a frightful girl saying in 1954, " 'I'm funny like that, you know, Robert. I can't bear old conventions and ideas' " there is an undercurrent of contempt for the new-fangled. Perhaps that is why, in a world of fluctuating priorities and a universal craving for new varieties of sensation, she chose to create a fictional character whose age, at least, remains static – though changing fads and social preoccupations do provide the starting-off point for more than one episode. There is hardly a cult, in fact, which doesn't come in for its share of ridicule, from Greek dancing (a typical class is composed of "weedy males and aesthetic-looking females dressed in abbreviated tunics with sandals on their feet …

Purple with fury, the General advanced on them.
Thomas Henry illsutrates William the Bold *(frontispiece)*

mostly wearing horn spectacles") to child psychology ("Mrs Gladhill was just beginning the exposition of her third rule for the upbringing of the Perfect Child"). There are a couple of Ruskinites who bake their own cooking utensils and wear nothing which they have not themselves woven on a hand loom. Needless to say, both are vegetarian. " 'Please'm, the butcher's come to see if there are any orders.' The effect of this remark was instantaneous and terrifying. The woman went pale and the man dropped his flute and both assumed an expression of almost unendurable suffering." A Miss Peache's familiarity with the subconscious provides Richmal Crompton with an opportunity to throw in an aside for the benefit of well-read adults: " 'She knows all about what a man called Froude said about dreams.' " The vicar's wife is afflicted with "the sale-of-work mania". As for those ubiquitous societies – for the Encouragement of Higher Thought, the promotion of Perfect Love, and so on – since few women outside the lower classes were employed, obviously it was necessary for the majority to fill in their time with *something*, either meeting to "discuss the burning things of the day such as Communism and vivisection and the longer skirt", or titillating themselves with thoughts of psychic phenomena (" 'I firmly believe that Colonel Henks's spirit is trying to attract my attention'.")

Mrs Brown is sometimes persuaded to attend committee meetings, and meetings of various societies, but her principal function is to darn socks. In one book she is darning on pages 191, 192, 194, 207 and 233. Richmal Crompton eventually lets the reader know that she has noticed the persistence of this occupation: "His mother stopped darning socks. She only did that in moments of deep emotion." Even so, in 1962 "his mother was still darning socks" – by which time it was not only self-sacrificial but perverse. But if Richmal Crompton had allowed her to take advantage of nylon, she would have done Mrs Brown out of her only means of self – or selfless – expression. Of course, for bored women confined to the home there was always "The Housewife's Handy Book" (advertised at the back of *William's Crowded Hours*, 1931) which was coyly "waiting to solve for you all the little problems that crop up in home life. The sections include Dressmaking, Embroidery, Cookery, Etiquette, Beauty, Fate and Fortune, Pin Money, Odd Jobs, How to Dance."

William's sister Ethel is one of the young women who filled in the years between school and marriage in elegant idleness – and it was an indication of her family's social status that she did not need to work. Not that it would have made much difference if she had; male unemployment was causing a great deal of venom to be directed against women who were reluctant to give up the measure of economic independence that they had found during the war, and who persisted in depriving "proper" breadwinners of their daily bread. (Unemployment figures rose from 1,250,000 in 1920 to 2,670,817 in 1931.) However, such questions did not concern the middle classes, and Richmal Crompton dealt thoroughly and in the best school-mistress tradition with Bolshevism, showing, in the most simplified terms imaginable, why it cannot succeed ("The Weak Spot", 1924). Having swept that out of the way, she proceeded to allow the Outlaws to be affected by a less savoury ideology: Fascism. In a startlingly tasteless episode ("William and the Nasties", 1935) William and his friends decide to chase out the Jewish proprietor of the village sweet shop and take his wares. " 'Well, we'd better start bein' nasties straight away,' said William . 'I'll be the chief one. What's he called in Germany?' 'Herr Hitler,' said Henry. '*Her*!' echoed William in disgust. 'Is it a woman?' " Outside the shop they start shouting " 'We're the Nasties and I'm Him Hitler an' we're goin' to take all your stuff so you'll jolly well have to clear out.' " However, "a strange distaste for the whole adventure" soon began to creep over the Outlaws – not surprisingly; the strange thing is that Richmal Crompton should have allowed it to go so far. Perhaps the whole thing evolved from her inability to resist the temptation of a bilingual pun; in any case, having got the Outlaws into a dangerous moral situation, she had to get them out of it quickly – by having them rescue Mr Isaacs from his own storeroom, where he's been conveniently imprisoned by a burglar. Their anti-Semitism is not strong enough to withstand the jars of sweets which the grateful shop owner showers upon them; but in spite of this characteristic ending one is left with a feeling of distaste for the whole episode. So, possibly, was Richmal Crompton; at any rate there are no more attempts to jollify the ethically unjustifiable. Of course, we should

Violet Elizabeth visits the Outlaws.
Thomas Henry drawing for William
the Gangster

remember that Naziism in the mid 1930s had not acquired the opprobrium which fell to it later, though a number of perceptive people could see the way it was going. However, the Outlaws subsequently confine their travestying activities to institutions which are impeccably British to start with – harmless, if esoteric or laughable (The Brains Trust, for instance).

Another nursery character who appeared around the same time as William (1924) was a gift to the parodist, and one which Richmal Crompton exploited to the full. Christopher Robin, that embodiment of childhood qualities which adults are supposed to find endearing, was William's antithesis, smocks, anthropomorphism, and all. Fragments of the Christopher Robin saga, in the context of a superficially less whimsical view of childhood, are transmogrified: "Every morning my new grace is, Thank you God for my nice braces", becomes, in William's friend and second-in-command " 'I had a pair of braces from my aunt,' Ginger said bitterly. '*Braces*!' " The would-be charming corruption of "wasps" into "wopses" is shown up in an unreasonable small naturalist who pursues William with the cry " 'Want wopses!' " (He gets them, too, and William is stung.) Picturesque children – Dutch Boy hairstyles and Georgie-Porgie trousers – crop up from time to time for William to be suitably horrified by; but the most overt caricature of Christopher Robin occurs in *William the Pirate* (1932). Anthony Martin has "*literary* stories and poems, not rubbish" written about him by his mother (" 'Really cultured people buy them for their children,' " he blandly confides).

As if that were not sufficient identification, we are told that one of the literary poems contains a repeated line: "Anthony Martin is milking a cow." Anthony Martin, however, is not a pleasant child (" 'Now drink up your milk, Master Anthony.' 'Shan't,' returned the world-famous infant") and William successfully takes the wind out of his sails by omitting to mention that a man has left recording equipment in the room where the "winsome child" has a tantrum, abusing his downtrodden nurse. William's habitual antagonist in the stories is Hubert Lane, a sly fat boy with a "morbid love of mathematics"; but sensitive children, know-alls and pampered brats are always firmly sat upon. To William, any indication of pretentiousness is anathema. (The most hilarious deflating of a "perfect little gentleman" takes place in "Georgie and the Outlaws" – when the white-suited child is induced to come out with "Damn and Blast" before an audience of shockable ladies.)

William's own pretensions include the inability to admit himself at a loss (much of the farce arises from his efforts to make good his rash declarations) and the belief that he is destined for fame by successfully pursuing one of those traditional masculine-fantasy occupations: intrepid explorer, sinister criminal, ruthless dictator. None of William's ambitions in these directions is to be taken seriously, of course, any more than his glorification of the parallel occupations of chimney sweep and tramp. William and his Outlaws (Ginger, Henry and Douglas) represent a particular phase of childhood in its healthiest and most boisterous manifestation – and the fact that it is only a phase is emphasized by the Outlaws' innocent belief that their present tastes and attitudes are theirs for life. (" 'I'm goin' to have a sweet shop in the house too so's we can get sweets whenever we like … I'm goin' to have switchbacks instead of staircases an' I'm goin' to have swings on the roof ... an' one room with insects all over it – snails an' caterpillars crawlin' all over the walls so's we can watch 'em.' ") William's persistent view of himself as badly-done-by is no more than a ritual response to what he regards as adult privilege and heavy-handedness; his rebellion is not against society as such, but against his own low position in society. "William, Prime Minister" [1930] illustrates one of his attempts to rectify this – as well as the author's usual back-handed presentation of her would-be tough and manly heroes as *cute*. Any enterprising child's adaptation of an adult set-up is bound to be amusing; there is a point at which precocity is reassuring (since it indicates that the child has grasped the essentials of social behaviour) just before it becomes horrific. In this instance Richmal Crompton advertises her own presence by means of a cynical aside:

> "Ladies an' gentlemen," said Douglas, "I'm makin' this speech to ask you all to be Lib'rals same as what I am. ... My aunt's gotter parrot that talks, an' I'll let you come an' listen to it through the window when she's not there if you'll vote Lib'rals. ... I'll let you look at my rabbits too, an' I'll give you all a suck of rock if my aunt sends me a stick when she goes to Brighton same as she did last year." He sat down breathless. There were certainly the makings of a politician in Douglas. He didn't care what he promised.

But even the young readers of the William books must have enough experience to realize that what is being put across is simulated – that is, artful – artlessness. Of course it is done so cleverly that it convinces – which is one reason why William, after 50 years, is as popular as ever.

It is difficult, at first glance, to understand William's appeal for girls – both in the books and out of them. (It's interesting that many boys read and enjoyed the William books without realizing that they were written by a woman.) They might be expected to resent the attitude taken by William – but again the author's tone intervenes between her character's bigotedness and its logical results. And after all, it is all light-hearted – or is it? In the course of the sequence, feminine stereotypes proliferate (twitterers, scatter-brains, eye-lash flutterers, cry-babies, pursuers of culture, proseletyzers, social climbers and so on) – but so do masculine ones; it's not the existence of the former which one has to question but their essence, which admittedly is not attributable to Richmal Crompton, though she does nothing to help effect anything in the nature of a psychological adjustment in her female readers. Still, it's unlikely that all little girls who admire William are emotional masochists; spirited female children, unconsciously androgynous, simply identify with William – or marvel at the fact that all the girls whom he meets are so untypically idiotic. Incidental girl characters tend to fall into two distinct categories: there are those who creep after him, exuding hero-worship, and those who, confronted with William, stamp their white-socked feet or sidle up to the dancing mistress with plaintive expressions: " 'Please, must I have William? He's so awful.' " (An exception is William's cousin Dorita who appears once – in *Just William*, the first of the series – and was perhaps abandoned when Richmal Crompton realized that she posed an effective challenge to William's supremacy. We shall come back to Dorita – or a development of her – later.) As E. Nesbit discovered when she created Oswald Bastable, there was only one attitude to girls which a self-assertive boy with a proper sense of his own importance *could* have: contemptuous incomprehension. ("But boys have to try to take an interest in their sisters' secrets, however silly. This is part of being a good brother.") Anything else would have laid him open to the charge of being what, at the age of eleven or so, he was most anxious not to be: a sissy. (Here we have a double standard blatantly at work again: the word "tomboy" applied to girls below a certain age is usually meant, and is certainly accepted, as a compliment; "sissy" can hardly be articulated without a sneer.) The inconsistency of William's attitude in this respect follows the conventional pattern: for all his loudly professed scorn for girls (" 'They're soppy an' batty an' stuck up an' stupid … They can't play fair or talk sense …' ") he is just as susceptible to a pretty face as Robert is – and like Robert's, the objects of William's infatuations usually turn out to be inaccessible or futile. They have a habit of turning on him for doing what they asked him to do in the first place ("William's Christmas Eve", 1934; "He Who Fights" etc.) – displaying *female* inconsistency and thereby effecting William's justifiable return to his original attitude of disdain. " 'We're not havin' a real girl in it,' said William firmly. 'They mess up everything. One of us'll be the girl. All you've gotter do to be a girl is to put on a sort of silly look and one of Ethel's hats … I'm not goin' to be the girl,' he added hastily." A girl is at the bottom of the one overtly sentimental episode: a sweetly-caustic slum urchin for whom William provides a fairy feast, in the first "William's Christmas Eve" of 1924.

In the early books there *is* a little-girl-next-door – Joan – who manages to overcome William's supposedly natural antipathy to her sex by exemplifying that sex's supposed passivity. This reaches its apex in the following exchange: " 'But I like you better than any insect, Joan,' he said generously. 'Oh William, do you really?' said Joan, deeply touched." William's admiration for the docile Joan – who, we are told, "held no modern views on the subject of the equality of the sexes" – is an example of the traditional masculine tendency to confuse attractiveness with tractability. That this tendency was considered old-fashioned in the frenetic '20s may account for Joan's early disappearance from the series – though she did provide an absurd standard of feminine behaviour which William fruitlessly expects to find repeated. ("As he looked at her, the resemblance to Joan seemed to be fading" and so on.)

More typical of that cinema conscious era, and also more sociologically prognostic, is Violet Elizabeth Bott. "The Sweet Little Girl in White" appeared in 1925, three years before Shirley Temple was born, yet she combines Shirley Temple's appearance and precocity with the significant attributes of Bette Davis in one of her more hard-boiled rôles. The child horror of the 1920s – particularly if it was female – is a potent image; and the more sugary it was the more horrific it now seems. Violet Elizabeth, all frills and curls and a lisp, attaches herself to the Outlaws – who are totally unable to cope with her, because she refuses to meet them on their own terms. ("There was a limpid guilelessness in her blue eyes and in the cherubic curves of her mouth that the Outlaws had long ago learnt to distrust.") Their sense of correct behaviour is not less firm for being peculiar to themselves; her absolute disregard for rules, and her imperviousness to home truths, leave them outraged but nonplussed. Violet Elizabeth gets her own way by threatening to "thcream and thcream" till she's "thick"; moreover, "even at that tender age she possessed the art, so indispensable to her sex, of making her blue eyes swim with tears". Within a few minutes of her first meeting with William she forces him to "kith" her ("William, woman hater and girl despiser, looked round wildly for escape and found none") and later the depraved child inveigles the "desperado and pirate chief" into "playing houthes". Another attribute, also conventionally "indispensable to her sex", is the ability to swop imperiousness for outward submissiveness at a moment's notice. " 'Look here,' said William, stung by her tone, 'don't you jolly well get too bossy. Who's running the night club, you or me?' 'You, William,' said Violet Elizabeth, meekly."

Violet Elizabeth, pert, beaming and irrepressible, and Amelia Tweeddale, scrawny and sanctimonious, represent two sides of a coin which fortunately is no longer legal tender, the idea of coquetry and spinsterishness as inevitable extremes of feminine behaviour having all but disappeared. "Soppy 'Melia", the vicar's daughter, appears in the *Jane* books by Evadne Price, "Just Jane" being the female equivalent of "Just William". Jane seems to have borrowed her favourite word, "soppy" – as well as other qualities – from William's cousin Dorita (see p. 245) and the rather unusual predicament in which William and Dorita find themselves – forced to appear as child attendants at a wedding – is a frequent one with Jane. Surrounded by adults who are bent on violating the dignity of childhood by tying it up in white organdie ribbons, Jane is often driven to desperate measures: on an occasion when a bouquet is to be presented to a duchess, Jane is found "crawling along the drainpipe twenty-five feet above street level, clinging like a fly to the side of the house, and – horror of horrors – she was stark naked". Since Jane, by virtue of her sex, is more prone to this type of persecution than William (" 'Jane, go upstairs and tell Nana to curl your hair and get your fairy frock out' ") her gestures of defiance need to be even more extreme.

Extremeness, in fact, is the keynote of the Jane books, where each character displays its peculiarities to an excessive degree. Like William Brown, Jane Turpin lives in a village which has its quota of standard inhabitants; and the village's name, Little Duppery – notwithstanding the extra "p" – is an immediate indication of the line which the stories are going to take. Someone or other is always being got the better of – and Jane, again like William, is all the more effective for being done down occasionally.

Duppery's inhabitants include a back-biting spinster (Miss Baldock), a good-for-nothing gardener (Arnie), a plain-speaking cook (Vilet), a number of venomous social-climbing middle-class ladies (mothers of Jane's companions), the odd brash honourable or two (Evelyn Tulk and Lady Medway), a spiteful grown-up sister (Marjorie Turpin). A great deal of the background humour is derived from an application of that old masculine-initiated myth: women's nastiness to women. Verbal abuse between ladies, as a laughter-raising device, is as much overworked here as its physical counterpart was in '30s Hollywood films, when the most depressing social drama had only to include a shot of two women grappling together, to have the audience roaring in its seats. Whereas William's mother has no personality of her own and very little function in the stories beyond forming part of his background (we are told that William likes his mother but never shown why he should), Jane's is an exemplification of feminine viciousness, alternately smarmy and snarling. Mrs Turpin is beaten at her own game of carefully modulated rudeness only by the vicar's wife: " 'Small?' she had echoed. 'Small? Probably you are unaccustomed to *real* emeralds, my dear Mrs Turpin, but let me assure you that this is *large* as *real* emeralds go. This did not come from Woolworths, you know. I believe the sixpenny variety is really enormous! Probably you can endorse this.' " Mrs Tweeddale, however, is " 'always out to make a sensation. What Frood calls a Sensualist, I am sorry to say' ". When Jane – who is fascinated by false teeth – compliments Miss Baldock on hers, Jane's mother weighs in joyfully with a back-handed apology: " 'You should be glad you're a spinster, Miss Baldock, with no husband and children to worry you. Children can be so distressingly frank and embarrassingly truthful.' "

In the midst of all this bickering and bitching, it's not surprising that Jane's ideal is "a real, manly woman, devoid of all feminine weaknesses". A Miss Pitts, "six feet high in her golf shoes, utterly indifferent to fashion's whims ... hair brushed back and cut short like a man's, a long nose adorned with gold-rimmed pince-nez ..." seems to fit the bill – but Miss Pitts reverts disgracefully to feminine behaviour when pursued by the Rev Archibald Crimm. A disillusioned Jane is left to endorse the observation of Oswald Bastable and others: "Women, Jane told herself bitterly, were all alike. They all went soppy sooner or later."

Jane's feminism, unfortunately, is derived from the cockeyed outlook which causes her to invert all common attitudes and judgements – and therefore is not to be taken more seriously than her envious contemplation of Miss Baldock's teeth (" 'I wish they were mine. I'm always wishin' that.' "), or her excited anticipation of an operation ("Dr White would … cut her to pieces with sharp, shiny knives to the accompaniment of much flowing red blood, which, unfortunately, she would not see, being unconscious …"). It is precisely by stressing this naïve perversity of Jane's that Evadne Price manages to infer that the adults' standards of behaviour are not so unreasonable as they appear to Jane – thereby upholding the *status quo* at the same time as ensuring a sympathetic reception for her heroine's amusing eccentricity. In her own view, Jane is "handicapped by golden hair, a pink-and-white skin, and regular features" – and while there is no doubt of the sincerity of Jane's repudiation of these – to her – liabilities, no reader, however young, can be unaware that in conventional terms they represent considerable assets. As it is, their shock value is persistently exploited: "Jane, a truly charming vision in white organdie and a blue sash, complete with bluebell wreath, received them in the hall. " 'Jus' you laugh at this ole' wreath an' I'll swipe you one' was her greeting"; " 'You blue-eyed kids what look as if butter wouldn't melt in your mouths are something fierce, blast you' ", and so on. If Jane's appearance gets in the way of the kind of image she wants to present, it succeeds in driving home for the reader the extreme character of her behaviour – which includes setting a barn on fire and hitting a soppy "little Lordship" on the head with a stone, which causes him to bleed. Jane, for all her prettiness, is "everything every mother doesn't want her little girl to be": over-active, self-assertive, outspoken, unhampered by a sense of class distinction; but always straightforward and resourceful, and incapable – so far – of fluttering her eye-lashes or simpering.

Frank R..Grey illustrates Jane at War

Violet Elizabeth Bott – who does both – is four years younger than Jane; but whereas Violet Elizabeth is a parody of a certain type of adult, Jane is the archetypal child, male or female. She and William, in this respect, are not so much complementary as interchangeable, with one important distinction: William's contempt for girls is not paralleled by a corresponding attitude in Jane. She is simply opposed to "soppiness", wherever it occurs; and it is incidental that its principal embodiment should be Amelia Tweeddale. It says much for Jane's indomitableness that she has succeeded in imposing her own aversion to Amelia on the entire juvenile population of the village – where merely to speak to the odious, tale-bearing child is to lay oneself open to the serious charge of "going 'Melia". 'Melia, however, an embryonic missionary, thrives on her ostracization; the little masochist "would thoroughly enjoy being eaten by cannibals provided they tortured her enough first". Her smugness is unshakeable; her erudition is of the sort that is bound to infuriate: " 'Mushrooms,' piped Amelia, 'are the spore-bearing fruit of a fungus.' " When Jane hauls Amelia out of an icy river, she realizes that she will never live down the shame of having saved Soppy 'Melia's life, and quickly persuades Arnie the gardener to take the credit for her brave action – possibly Evadne Price was fed up with all those fictional young life-savers whose courage was duly and durably applauded. The ubiquitous juvenile aptitude for burglar-foiling comes in also for its share of parodying: Jane blithely directs an intruder to the glass under which the key to the silver cupboard is kept hidden.

A burglar with a conscience features in an episode in which Jane's vicissitudes are typically represented. The affair of the blue tulle poke bonnet quickly becomes a case of "now you see it, now you don't" – with the offensive garment, which is doubly obnoxious to Jane because of Soppy 'Melia's identical poke bonnet, taking on the character of a nightmare object which haunts its unwilling possessor. Jane's mother locks up the bonnet to keep it out of Jane's clutches; Jane retaliates by hiding 'Melia's bonnet, so that she and 'Melia will not have to appear in public similarly dressed. When a thief walks off with the contents of the Turpin cupboard, including the bonnet, Jane restores Amelia's in the happy belief that her own has gone for good. It comes back by post, with a touching letter: "I am a burglar, but I hope a man, and sooner than rob a little child of her hat I'd give myself up to justice." Jane, for once, is completely vanquished by the magnitude of the burglar's misapprehension.

Jane's appearance in 1928 can hardly have been fortuitous, since the timing, sociologically at least, was exactly right – though curiously the books don't seem to have been all that popular (although William is still avidly read, Jane has been out of print for several decades), nor was Jane ever accorded the status of a stereotype. It is true that Jane had an overt predecessor in William, which obviously lessened her impact, but there was certainly room for a corresponding female figure – particularly one whose exploits were related in an equally lively and entertaining fashion. It is possible, of course, that there was a subconscious reluctance to accept in a girl behaviour which seemed normal in a boy. By the late 1920s, women had had a measure of emancipation – which, apart from the vote, boiled down in theory to the right to earn their own living (by virtue of the Sex Disqualification [Removal] Act, 1919). But because this right was not bolstered up by tradition, and because social attitudes are not easily accessible to modification, appreciation of this reform by both sexes at a practical level was wearing a little thin. The "womanly woman" was still held at a premium – and "womanly" had, as it still has, a great many connotations which were mythical rather than physical. The gaiety of the flapper (which had a veneer, though only a veneer, of liberation) was seen as having been merely a reaction to wartime constriction, natural but necessarily fleeting; and the female emancipation which paralleled it was thought also to have had its fling. Since areas of social concern go in cycles, the current reaction was against emancipation. It became statutory to applaud women who had achieved success in the professions, or otherwise made their mark, by stressing that they had retained their femininity – as though *that* were the achievement. So, *Home Chat*, describing in the home life of an ex-"intrepid explorer", remarked that she "has proved herself to be a thoroughly domesticated woman, in spite of all the masculine deeds she has done". In all seriousness, it added "she has an adorable six-months-old baby called Ocean – isn't that a lovely, original name?" (The implication was that her exploring had been worthwhile because it had enabled her to handicap her daughter with a pretentious name.)

Children, however, had benefited from the post-war emphasis on freedom of various kinds. Girls were no longer expected to break

"Well, watts it matter ..."

in their brothers' boots, nor passed over in favour of boys when it came to "paid-for" education. They were neither secluded nor openly belittled: pre-pubescent girls of the middle classes were treated in much the same way as boys – though pulled up sharply from time to time by the bogey of the femininity which would sooner or later overtake them. (Girl readers of popular papers were advised to familiarize themselves with the properties of Rinso, since "the girl of today" is "the housewife of tomorrow" – a pronouncement whose ominousness lay in its inexorability.) Against a background of lessening parental control (in 1931 the authorities blamed this, in conjunction with the influence of the war, for the wave of juvenile crime which had hit England), both Jane and William are believable, if occasionally overdrawn, figures. Though still superficially under their parents' thumbs, each manages to circumvent the more outrageous of the grown-ups' dictates – and Jane in particular is something of a breakthrough, as far as the presentation of a ten-year-old girl is concerned. Rampaging through the village, tying up Soppy 'Melia and covering her in black shoe polish, to be exhibited as a captured Abyssinian, she represents a kind of freedom for the female child which would have been unthinkable in any previous decade. She is also inflexibly rooted in a particular era: ten years earlier her hoydenism would have been tempered with something more easily recognizable as sweetness (as it is, the only overt sentimentalization is of Popeye the Pup); and a post-second-world-war ten-year-old would have been more knowing, less ready to believe in fairy tales. (The few stories involving "magic", from a technical point of view, are the least successful; Jane's gullibility in this respect is not in keeping with her general character, and it's impossible not to feel that the author has faltered here in her efforts to keep up with the convolutions of incident and coincidence which constitute the best of William.)

Jane's innocence is pinpointed for the reader in a hilarious episode which consists of a letter from Jane to her Grandmother Pilk (*Jane the Unlucky*, 1939). Jane, staying with her family at an exclusive hotel ("Mother says this hotell is nice corse you dont have to dress and its the Cimple Life. But Granma they dress all the time") becomes friendly with a young man who takes her fishing. The plot revolves around a pair of tarry drawers – Jane's, which the young man offers to wash to save her from the wrath of Nana. "So he put them in his pokett. And I went back to the hotell. And Nana was so bussy with Babby wat had a Stomicake thank goodness. And was cryen in biter pane poor little thing for witch I was glad." Unfortunately the drawers fall out of Mr Antony's pocket in public, and Miss Bird, the hotel receptionist with whom he has also been friendly, is asked to leave. "Well said Katie its terable that any girl no mater how Lo would give a man a Shocken Mascop like that for luck. And fansy the man boasten about them. No said Nana not boasten for he pulled them out by accident with his pipe." This story is an expression of current attitudes to sexual misbehaviour (a subject more often treated in Whitehall farce) and the clichés which bewilder Jane – "Them Quite ones is alwus the worst"; "the woman alwus pays" – are only too intelligible to the average reader. For all the distraction of the idiosyncratic spelling, it was a terribly risky theme for a children's story – but paradoxically, it is successful in this context, while elsewhere it might have seemed vulgar. ("That was Miss Bird I said. And Nana said Birds the right word for her.") Jane, exasperated by Nana's and the chambermaid's gossiping, and completely misinterpreting the subject of their concern (" 'Youd think Nanad be greatfull to him about taken the tar off my new drores but no' "), comes out with, " 'Well watts it matter so long as the drores is all right and bean wore now' " – a sentiment more reasonable even than Jane could realize. Miss Bird's character is finally vindicated, of course, and the rumour about her ownership of the knickers is traced to its source – Marjorie Turpin. As Jane's father puts it, " 'All ages Womens damn cats. Rewen your golf and karakter too' " – the perennial judgement of the experienced male. Jane is left with her incomprehension: " 'And I was very pusled corse no one said a thing about my tarry drores and that was watt it was all about' " – and the moral about youthful ignorance being bliss in conjunction with adult uncharitableness is rammed home. (It might be thought that Evadne Price had exhausted the humorous possibilities of knickers in this incident, but they appear effectively again in *Jane at War*. Orris the evacuee cannot keep his hands off Nana's underwear: " 'My knickers seems to fascinate him, they do. Can't leave 'em alone. He wore my navy directors into the High Street yesterday' " – a proclivity which the sender-up of "Frood" *must* have seen in its most obvious interpretation.)

Jane's character is established decisively with the first lines of repartee in *Just Jane* – " 'If you were my child I'd – I'd wring your neck.' 'If you was my father I'd be glad if you did' " – but it was perhaps never so highly developed as William's. It is difficult, for example, to imagine Jane carrying out so complex a piece of obstructionism as William does in the following exchange with a school lecturer:

> "I incline to the theory that the plays of Shakespeare were written by Bacon."
>
> "How could they be?" said William … . "How could that man Ham—"
>
> "I said Bacon."
>
> "Well, it's nearly the same. … Well, if this man Bacon wrote them, they wouldn't put this man Shakespeare's name on the books … ".
>
> "Now, boys, I want you all please to listen to me. … There was a man called Hamlet—"
>
> "You just said he was called Bacon," said William.
>
> "I did *not* say he was called Bacon."
>
> "Yes, 'scuse me, you did. … When I called him Ham, you said it was Bacon, and now you're calling him Ham yourself."
>
> "This was a different man. … *Listen*! This man was called Hamlet and his uncle had killed his father because he wanted to marry his mother."
>
> "What did he want to marry his mother for?" said William.
>
> …"It was *Hamlet's* mother he wanted to marry."
>
> "Oh, that man that you think wrote the plays."
>
> "No, that was Bacon."
>
> "You said it was Ham a minute ago. … I tell you what," said William confidingly, "let's say Eggs for both of them."

But since there are only ten Jane books – compared to nearly 40 about William – her occasional lack of solidity may be due to a failure on the part of the author to ensure that the subject matter is sufficiently concentrated.

Only one book of the Jane series, *Jane the Patient*, is consistently tasteless. By confining her to a bed, Evadne Price wantonly ignored a fundamental aspect of Jane's appeal: her physical overactivity. Essentially a running-around child, Jane's faculty for self-expression had never been developed to an extent where interest in her could be sustained, even when she was immobilized, without resorting – as the author has done – to a lurid over-delineation of the hospital setting. The two frightful old women in the beds next to Jane's are blown up to the point where, artistically, they quickly explode – and the incident where Jane convinces them that they are dead sadly fails to convince the reader.

However, the ten books are extraordinary; they have a liveliness and singular interest. They stand out remarkably from the rest of Evadne Price's work. Like Richmal Crompton, she also wrote books for adults, though of an even more ephemeral character (their obsolescence seems to have been built in even to the titles, which read like the contents page to a bygone magazine: *My Pretty Sister*; *Strip Girl*; *Glamour Girl*; *Escape to Marriage*; and so on). It may have been their familiarity with the family romance which predisposed both authors to social comedy, with adults playing a larger part than is usual in children's fiction. Together, William and Jane form a complete genre on their own – with a radical distinction, however, in both execution and status. William is firmly in the tradition of English humour, mid-way between Denis the Menace and Basil Seal (his universal appeal is indicated in a gratuitous tribute from E. M. Brent-Dyer: in one of her Chalet School stories it is the staff, not the pupils, who are queuing up for the latest William book); while Jane is artistically unclassifiable – out on a limb – unpolished and clumsy at times, but as a curiosity at least as deserving of attention as that other literary oddity, Fanny Hill.

XIII

A Superabundance of Schoolgirls

" 'Honour bright is honour bright,' said Clara
stubbornly. 'I know what boys are. You think that a
girl's bound to give the game away. Well I won't. Not
for anything – not for wild horses.' "

(The *School Friend*, 1927)

THE 1920s AND '30s saw the heyday of schoolgirls' fiction not only
in books but in weekly twopenny papers, [1] which originally were
offshoots from the boys' publications of Lord Northcliffe. As Alfred
C. Harmsworth he had crusaded against the "penny dreadfuls"
brought out by other publishers in the 1880s, which in his opinion
incited youth to debauchery. His own early boys' papers contained
a fair share of blood and thunder, but Northcliffe's code for decent
living underlay them all, and this moral tone was refurbished when
in 1919 the first Bessie Bunter weekly, the *School Friend*, appeared.
The *Magnet* had been the launching pad in 1908 of Billy Bunter,
the overweight anti-hero whose name has become an addition to
the language. In 1919 readers' correspondence indicated that it was
as popular with girls as with boys. Many girls were reading the
more exciting material produced for their brothers, because in the
first two decades of the century girls' fiction on the whole remained
unstimulating, with emphasis on feminine duty and domesticity.

Reginald Thompson Eves, who in 1919 was editor of the *Boys'
Friend*, felt that the time was ripe for the Amalgamated Press to

[1] The *School Friend* (May 1919 to July 1929) was originally
published at 1½d [½p] but cost twopence [1p] for most if its
existence.

bring out a girls' paper which would echo the exuberance of the *Magnet*. The phenomenal Charles Hamilton (Frank Richards) was asked to write the main weekly story for the new magazine. Undeterred by the fact that he was then also producing two 20,000-word stories every week for *Magnet* and *Gem*, and one of 5,000 words for the *Boys' Friend*, Hamilton as "Hilda Richards" accepted the assignment: Bessie Bunter, a female counterpart of her "fat, shiny, greedy and conceited" brother, and the other pupils of Cliff House School for girls began their adventures in the *School Friend*. (Hamilton had sketchily created Cliff House as long ago as 1909 in the *Magnet* and it was in the boys' paper that Bessie first made a brief appearance in 1919.)

It soon became apparent that Charles Hamilton after all had not the right touch for girls' stories: his bossy, lying, skirted version of Billy would have to be mellowed to satisfy the wishes of Bessie's female audience. Her brother had buffooned his way through the *Magnet* for eleven years to the delight of boy and girl readers, but obesity in a girl produced quite a different effect, making her a figure of sympathy rather than contemptuous amusement. Hamilton's other Cliff House characters were ciphers rather than believable schoolgirls, either overdrawn embodiments of squealing femininity or, at the other extreme, tomboyishness. Charles Hamilton came off the paper after the first few issues: ironically his creations were then developed by other writers into realistic personalities, attractive to several generations of schoolgirl readers, and Bessie Bunter's grotesque aspects were gradually eliminated until she became a still fat but loyal and lovable duffer.

The *School Friend*'s early success was due largely to Horace Phillips, who had previously been editor of the *Scout* and *Cheer Boys Cheer*, and contributed women's stories to the *Sunday Circle* and *Sunday Companion*. Phillips continued under the pseudonym of Hilda Richards and wrote dramatic, emotional stories about the Cliff House girls. These so effectively boosted the *School Friend*'s circulation that in 1921 he was given the opportunity to create his own fictional school (Morcove) for a new paper, the *Schoolgirls' Own*. The Cliff House stories were then taken over by R. S. Kirkham, a young writer whose style was less dramatic and often amusing. The *School Friend*, which in 1919 had advertised itself as "The Only Schoolgirls' Paper in the World", went from strength to strength to be joined by other long-lasting magazines, the *Schoolgirls' Own* (1921 to 1936) and *Schoolgirls' Weekly* (1922 to 1939). In 1929 the *School Friend* was superseded by the *Schoolgirl* which survived until 1940.

Paradoxically the whole girls' enterprise was conceived, created and sustained by men. Editors, writers and artists changed during the two decades of these Companion Papers, but they were nearly always male. Notable exceptions were Alma Buley, who contributed fiction in the 1920s, and Alice Stafford, a sub-editor who wrote some stories in the '30s. Isobel Winchester was responsible for the "chatty hints" pages of the *Schoolgirl*. R. T. Eves was convinced that men were more sympathetic than women with the aspirations of pubescent girls. He saw every woman writer as a potential mother whose protective and occasionally repressive attitudes might colour her stories; he also believed that she would consider her own life and personal tastes as typical and expect all right-minded schoolgirls (even though of a different generation) to share her views. Whether or not R. T. Eves's assessment was accurate, there is no doubt that his team of male authors was not content merely to reflect the activities of contemporary schoolgirls and the mood of the period. They projected a new image of responsible but lively girlhood, in which pompous adults – and assertive boys – were thoroughly debunked. Editorial policy demanded that the heroine of every story should be active in her own interests and not simply, as in many earlier books, a victim of events; femininity although not forgotten was enlivened by adventure and enquiry. Girl readers began to consider not only fictional heroines but themselves as initiators rather than shuttlecocks of fate, or backers-up of men.

In the early *School Friend* stories a girl might have to pursue dubious characters by riding surreptitiously on the luggage grid of the villains' car. By the mid 1930s heroines were more adventurous and technically competent, like Kit and Joan Fortune "… the intrepid Flying Sisters, whose daring flights over the jungle have made

THE
SCHOOL FRIEND
Every 1½D. Thursday

No. 1. Vol. 1. | Three-Halfpence. | Week Ending May 17th, 1919.

THE ARRIVAL OF BESSIE BUNTER! (An incident from "The Girls of Cliff House!" Complete in this issue.)

School Friend *cover, No. 1, Vol. 1, 1919;*
the artist was G. M. Dodshon

261

history". These were created by Ida Melbourne and their exploits appeared in the *Schoolgirl*. On one occasion when Kit is piloting, with Joan and an African princess as passengers, a typically challenging situation develops. The princess's sacred leopard, Lobo, breaks loose and starts savaging the control column. The plane goes into a spin and begins to loop as Kit has to abandon the controls – but all is not lost, for "... Joan kept her head... climbed over her seat, caught the princess and dragged her backwards. Clinging to her from behind Joan took the liberty of pinching the royal person ..." – whose screams then brought the sacred leopard to her rescue, thus successfully diverting him from tearing the joy-stick to shreds. So once again the Flying Sisters were able to negotiate a happy landing.

These Amalgamated Press papers were especially popular with girls from poorer homes because they were inexpensive, crammed with small-print stories and attractively illustrated. (Hardly any space was wasted on advertisements and none on the type of turgid religious feature which was found in some of the dearer magazines.) To many children and young teenagers the *Magnet* and the *School Friend* seemed natural continuations of the comics which they had enjoyed when very young. Like comics, street games and skipping-rhymes, these papers were part of the unsentimental, spontaneous folk-lore of twentieth-century childhood, often frowned upon by adults who wanted to improve their offspring by foisting "good" literature on them – just as they tried to prevent them from playing in the street, which was considered "common". Parents, teachers, aunts, uncles and librarians mistakenly assumed that all juvenile hard-back books must inevitably be superior in moral and intellectual content to the story papers. In fact although the Amalgamated Press authors were in business primarily to entertain (and to sell the magazines) their fiction was not only gripping but well written and constructed, and in accordance with an impeccable moral code. Northcliffe himself imposed a censorship, rather surprisingly even barring the word "rotten" in girls' papers at one time. R. T. Eves established certain rules to be observed by all his writers. Cheats, liars and spiteful girls were not allowed to prosper: smoking, swearing, drinking and tale-telling were beyond the Pale. Hundreds of thousands of girls in the 1920s and '30s lived out the Northcliffe code, and the example of Cliff House's honest and robust pupils was often more effective than advice from schools and churches.

Readers became so identified with the fictional characters in the *School Friend* that the Amalgamated Press used to receive postal orders for forwarding to Bessie Bunter. (In the stories she was always – like brother Billy at Greyfriars – vainly awaiting the arrival of imaginary remittances and tuck hampers.) To sustain the illusion that Barbara Redfern & Co. of the Cliff House Fourth Form were real people, the paper devoted one or two pages regularly to "The Cliff House Weekly", which consisted of articles supposedly written by different girls attending the school. This provided an acceptable method of imparting domestic hints – "Cookery Notes" by Annabel Hitchins, "How To Make A Crochet Hair Tidy" by Mabel Lynn and "A Dainty Perfumed Sachet" by Marjorie Hazeldene as well as building up a detailed picture of Cliff House, which many readers felt they knew as well as their own schools. Individual pupils' homes, hobbies, pets, hairstyles, party frocks and holidays were featured,

" Keep that basket shut, Bessie ! " called out Clara Trevlyn, as she pulled at the oars.   " I'm only counting the tarts ! " said Bessie Bunter.   " Think I was eating one behind this sunshade ? "   " I believe you'd eat the sunshade, if there wasn't anything else to eat ! " replied Miss Trevlyn.

and a weekly diary of events, "This Week At Cliff House", was signed "Your Chum Barbara Redfern". High spots in earlier stories were recalled in a "Do You Remember" series, and Bessie Bunter contributed "Extrax From The Clif Howse Ensyklopedier" in her own startling spelling. (This described the tuckshop as the most important "eddifiss on the Clif Howse sight" and explained that Bessie's "graitest athletick triumfs" took place in a "spayshus" room that had been built by a man called "Jim Nazeyum – hense its name".)

In spite of the fact that most of the fictional heroines came from affluent backgrounds, enabling authors to set their stories in expensive boarding schools or to create exotic travel series, elementary schoolgirls had no difficulty in identifying with them. Perhaps these readers enjoyed a sense of sharing in what went on behind the portals of privilege but, more probably, they simply responded to the naturalistic language and likeability of the leading characters. In common with other successful writers for children the Amalgamated Press authors managed to convey the feelings and jargon of schoolgirls as if from the inside, without the obvious imposition of adult ethics or comment. " 'They stung me fearfully for the new hockey stick but it's a real ripper.' " Above all, the stories created an atmosphere of feasibility. Girls who read the Companion Papers often found that their own out-of-school adventures were modestly confined within the framework of the Girl Guide movement or weekly tap-dancing lessons. For most of them, participation could never be other than vicarious in the ice-skating, horse-riding, regattas, cruises and country-house parties taken for granted by their magazine heroines. However, the male writers were so inventive and convincing that they managed to involve readers as well as fictional girls in the vivid situations which they created. Using a wide variety of feminine pseudonyms, they transported their audience for twopence a week through endlessly successful school themes, "tales of bygone days", ghost stories, mystery and detection, exploits of gipsies in disguise, poor little rich girls and rich little poor girls. (The Cinderella theme had greater popularity in the 1920s than the more democratic '30s, with mill-girls making good in public schools, or an impoverished orphan having to work in shop or sewing room to support younger brothers and sisters.) There were Girl Guide stories, dangerous enterprises in Africa, India and the South Seas, plots set in film and broadcasting studios, young girls driving racing cars, speedboats and aeroplanes, jungle and Wild West adventures, and so on, and on and on, for thousands of millions of words.

Horace Phillips's first Cinderella series in the *School Friend* began in number 21 (4 October 1919) with *Only A Scholarship Girl*. The paper's sales increased enormously, suggesting that thousands of readers from ordinary homes were very much in sympathy with the mill-girl scholarship-heroine, Peggy Preston, who underwent shocking tribulations during her early days at Cliff House. She was dubbed "Pauper Peg" and "Pawnshop Peg" by the snobbish element led by the richest girl in the school, Augusta Anstruther-Browne, who was as pretentious as her name implies. Augusta's behaviour reflected rigid Edwardian class distinctions rather than the increasingly liberal post-war attitudes of the period in which she was supposed to exist. (Horace Phillips, like some authors of greater distinction, was a generation out of date in many of his assessments of social conventions. Juvenile readers were generally tolerant of this kind of anachronism as long as characterizations were intense, and the stories strong in either dramatic or humorous content. Similarly adult readers accepted P. G. Wodehouse's Bertie Wooster as a contemporary character in the 1920s – when in fact he was rooted in the young men-about-town who had hung around the Gaiety Girls a decade earlier. The indolent activities of most of these "Stage-door Johnnies" had been abruptly ended, like many other social patterns, by the shake-up of the first world war.)

Augusta Anstruther-Browne not only tormented the scholarship girl but tried to get her expelled by false accusations of theft. To resolve the social dichotomy and effect the desired happy ending, Horace Phillips had to resort to one of the stock contrivances of children's fiction: Peggy saves her implacable enemy's life in a fire, with the result that "Pawnshop Peg" is transmuted into " … brave Peggy Preston, as bright and fun-loving as any, a girl endeared to the hearts of all!" – including the ungracious Augusta. During the 1920s Peggy's poverty and worthiness were frequently exploited by the Amalgamated Press writers, who considered her more closely akin to the average *School Friend* reader than other Cliff House characters. Working-class girls who identified with Peggy Preston must have found gratification in the fact that she was always described as "the prettiest girl in the Fourth Form". During the '30s Peggy, though still occasionally referred to as "the scholarship girl", was an integrated and popular member of the school.

For several years after her advent Peggy played the part of circulation booster. The *School Friend* got carried away by the rags-to-riches motif when in 1921 it attributed to Peggy Preston, its fictional Cinderella, the authorship of a serial called *The Minstrel Girl,* which featured Nina "… a girl who wore ragged clothes and played a violin in the streets for her bread and butter …" Nina too was more reminiscent of Edwardian than post-war heroines: in squalid lodgings, she supported her sick mother and loyal dog, against a background of snobbery from local high-school girls and drearily frequent visits to the pawnshop so that blankets and bangles could be exchanged for food. *The Minstrel Girl* was actually the first contribution to the *School Friend* by a very young writer, L. E. Ransome, who was to become the next Hilda Richards and write the weekly 20,000-word Cliff House story from 1924 to 1929, when the paper was replaced by the *Schoolgirl*. He is best known as Ida Melbourne, in which name he demonstrated his flair for amusing fiction and inventiveness throughout the 1920s and '30s. (L. E. Ransome wrote girls' stories under several other pen names, including Elizabeth Chester – for dramatic fiction – Stella Stirling, Barbara Ransome and Evelyn Day.)

His most popular heroines were iconoclasts, who overcame adult bigotry with disarming exuberance. By the '30s he had inverted the maudlin Cinderella syndrome into humorous vehicles for the rebellious characters in which he excelled. *Her Harum Scarum Highness,* [1] the Princess Tcherina, or "Cherry for short", provides a typical example. Cherry is an "Imperial Imp" living temporarily in England under the repressive guardianship of a pair of countesses who personify the "Ugly Sisters": they are fat Olga and angular

[1] In 1935-36 this series ran for 35 weeks in the *Schoolgirls' Own* and then transferred to the *Schoolgirl* for eighteen issues.

Katzi. Unfailingly Cherry manages to outwit them and engage in forbidden games of cricket and other democratic activities with Ginger Potts, the butcher's boy, whom she also accepts as "her chief guide and instructor in English". Another of Ransome's "poor little rich girls" was Gipsy Joy, whose long-running adventures continued in the *Schoolgirl* for 54 issues from 1937 to 1938. Lively, orphaned Joy Sharpe lives with her kindly but impractical grandfather, who leaves her in the charge of Miss Retcham, an acid-tempered governess. "She was the complete home Hitler and Mussolini rolled into one." Miss Retcham's prescribed régime for Joy is one of Victorian seclusion, especially from association with "vulgar" children from poorer homes. Joy quickly finds ways of overcoming these restraints: she joins the ranks of Amalgamated Press teenage heroines who, in the simplest of disguises, can successfully hoodwink their nearest and dearest. Easy-going Grandpa and hawk-eyed governess are fooled week after week by Joy's transformation into Nakita, the impertinent, dashing gipsy girl. Joy is certainly adept – "In a few seconds only every part of her skin was covered with dye", which is applied also to her mongrel dog Tinker who similarly escapes recognition. As Nakita, the disguised schoolgirl finds freedom and many opportunities for skirmishing with Miss Retcham, whom she manages to manipulate like a puppet on a string.

Resourceful juveniles who could undermine adult authority made attractive reading for girls in the 1930s. They intended to demand more from life than their often overburdened mothers who, according to a famous twopenny library's report, were still addicted to the escapist sops of Ethel M. Dell, Elinor Glyn and Marie Corelli. Many young girls influenced by the more emancipated characters in their Amalgamated Press papers saw themselves as embryonic Amy Johnsons, film-stars or at least career girls, rather than future housewives. The decade provided glorified girl cult figures in Shirley Temple, Deanna Durbin, Judy Garland and the two little princesses, who were very much in the public eye when their father, George VI, came to the throne after Edward VIII's abdication in 1936.

Ida Melbourne was also responsible for "the irrepressible and the lovable" Hilda Manners of Vere Abbey School who became a frequent attraction in the *School Friend* from the mid 1920s. Breezy Hilda, abetted by her languid chum, the Hon. Theresa de Travers, gently but firmly kept their rather inefficient form mistress, Miss Timms, in her place. "Hilda gave her a friendly nod and an encouraging smile. 'I'm just hopping it now, Miss Timms. I mean departing,' she corrected herself." Happy rebels were also created by Ronald Fleming, using the pen-name of Renee Frazer. (See chapter 17– Peter Langley.) His Tess Everton, "Madcap of Templedene School", had, improbably, inherited from her "Oirrish" great-grandmother not only the traditional heart of gold, mischievous blue eyes and dark curly hair but the thickest possible accent. " 'Shure, an' phwat is so curious darlint? … it's meself – is wishing I hadn't done it … it's agrayin' with ye entoirely I am!' " The "begorras" and "spalpeens" which punctuate her conversation are the trademark of Tess's individuality – though in moments of crisis they are abandoned for more orthodox English. She suffers no nonsense from bullying staff or seniors, whose humiliation she engineers by elaborate and comical stratagems. The first Tess Everton stories were published in the 1925 *School Friend* and later she appeared in the *Schoolgirl* of the early 1930s. Renée Frazer's next iconoclastic character was Sally (Sunny) McAllister, who began life in the 1927 *Schoolgirls' Own* before transferring to the *School Friend* in the following year. Sunny is occasionally a schoolgirl, but more often seeks excitement beyond the confines of school life. She is the sort of girl for whom even an innocent, suburban bus-ride can develop into a surprising escapade, involving the discovery and unmasking of an imposter who plans to defraud teenage "ex-Princess Nina of Betania, who has fallen on hard times".

In the 1920s the "freedom-loving flapper" had symbolized girls' craving for wider horizons. Short hair, boyish flat figures and knee-length skirts became fashionable. The Amalgamated Press writers had reflected this by wholesale bobbing and shingling of their heroines in the middle of the decade. Eton cropped, enigmatic and bemonocled Jemima Carstairs must have seemed the ultimate in modernity when she entered the Cliff House saga at the end of 1925. (She first appeared as a new girl at Morcove School in four

Schoolgirls' Own stories towards the end of 1925 when L. E. Ransome was relieving Horace Phillips for a few weeks.) Jemima was an adolescent incarnation of the "intelligent ass", a popular convention in adult detective fiction and the theatre of the '20s, when the assumption of an inane façade concealed a razor-sharp mind revealed only in the final stages of the book or play. According to L. E. Ransome, her creator, Jemima's inception was partly inspired by a contemporary actress named Heather Thatcher who wore a monocle; her appearance might equally have reminded readers of Beatrice Lillie. There were touches of Wodehouse, Edgar Wallace and Charles Hamilton in Jemima's vocabulary and demeanour, but most of all her appeal lay in her representation of the desire inherent in most schoolgirls to "be different", to express individuality.

Alternating between indolence and astuteness Jemima Carstairs was distinctive – superior but likeable, and a refreshing change from the usual sporty heroines of the genre. (Bessie Bunter was the only member of the Cliff House Fourth Form who vigorously protested her dislike of games, contrary to "the true sporting spirit of a great school".) John Wheway took over the "Hilda Richards" stories in 1931, when the Cliff House saga began again in the *Schoolgirl*, and he successfully sustained Jemima at her enigmatic, burbling best. Jemima dresses with panache whenever she can abandon the regulation gymslip in favour of "a little wisp of a black velvet frock" and "crinkly Russian boots under a mannish short coat". As well as the much publicized tortoise-shell monocle, she often carries another bizarre accessory in the shape of a light cane. Jemima remained popular until the *Schoolgirl* ended in the wartime paper shortages of 1940.

The readers of the Companion Papers were generally between ten and fifteen years old, and it must have been satisfying to them to see what Jemima, a schoolgirl in her mid teens, could achieve. She unmasks spies, baffles international jewel-thieves, resists torturers, defeats scheming schoolgirls, befriends the underdog and drives "fast cars, speed-boats, aeroplanes and most things mechanical", as easily as she can give an exhibition Charleston, "looking quite the Society hostess" with "her sleek hair gleaming in rivalry to her shining monocle".

269

Jemima's pet phrases are often affected but amusing: she never walks but always "totters" or "staggers": of her mental processes she is inclined to say, " 'Funny little tangles this old brain puddle of mine gets into at times' " or " 'A rather feeble notion flickers across my cranial vacuum' ". Enquiries about her health might well bring the reply, " 'All merry and bright, and chirping like a row of trilling robins on a Christmas morn' ". When considering a weighty problem Jemima addresses herself as "Jimmy Old Top", or "Jimmy Old Spartan" and concentrates on polishing her already spotless monocle "as though that task were the most important thing on earth". She remains outwardly cool, even flippant, in moments of distress. " 'Oh, chin up – chin up!' Jemima muttered fiercely. 'Chest out, old thing! Remember the bulldog spirit.' "

Jemima was a calculated combination of elements which would appeal to schoolgirls who wanted to assume fashionable and rather adult poses. Another popular Cliff House character, Barbara Redfern (Babs), might well have been an unconscious expression of the anima images of her various male manipulators. For the ten years of her *School Friend* existence she was – except for one or two "catty" actions attributed to her by Charles Hamilton at the beginning – the epitome of every conceivable virtue. (When John Wheway started work on the Cliff House stories he deliberately set out to make Babs less perfect and more likeable to his readers.) It is of course important to remember that each generation of readers probably remained faithful to one story paper for only two or three years and that Babs's repeated ordeals and triumphs would therefore have some freshness for each one. Even so, Barbara Redfern's unswerving sweetness, courage and loyalty must

Barbara Redfern.

occasionally have seemed overdone to girls whose own characters were less consistently wholesome. Barbara was not only the captain of the Fourth Form and the lower school, but is frequently described in early stories as "the idol" of her form-mates. This too must have jarred on readers, as real-life schoolgirls hardly ever make heroines out of their exact contemporaries: "crushes" are reserved for older girls, cult figures or members of the opposite sex. However, rôles at Cliff House are reversed with startling rapidity; outcasts become heroines during the course of one hockey match – "Cliff House, sports loving, could forgive much of a girl who could play the game, and play it well. But Cliff House would *worship* a girl who could save a game!" – and conversely idols could be reduced to nonentities overnight. Babs maintained resolute calmness and integrity in face of all adversities and reversals of fortune. In the 1920s, story after story ends with her deposition from the captaincy by lying, conniving villainesses. Their deviousness is blatantly obvious to the dimmest reader, though utterly unsuspected by everyone at Cliff House, even Barbara's best chums, who, like the teachers, mean well, try to be fair but never, never learn from endlessly repeated experience that Babs can do no wrong. "Barbara Redfern, once the idol of the Fourth, lay curled up in a chair in her study alone with her thoughts, while far across the quadrangle excited girls were toasting their new Form Captain's health vivaciously in ginger beer ...". This pathetic situation of course will be redressed a few issues later as "Barbara Redfern comes into her own again", having once more proved her worth and the baseness of her enemies.

Barbara's sterling qualities are well illustrated in her duel with Sheba Stanton, the wayward girl from the USA with a "loud and unmusical voice", who throws herself on and off horses with abandon and tries to intimidate the Fourth Form corridor with her riding whip. (Americans were not popular in Northcliffe's juvenile papers during the '20s. Charles Hamilton had established the brash, conceited, money-making Fisher T. Fish from "Noo Yark" at Greyfriars in 1910, and other writers perpetuated these unappealing attributes in their American schoolboys and girls. More sympathetic portrayals appeared in the '30s when tolerance towards "foreigners" became fashionable.) The main object of Sheba's family in coming to England is to take away Babs's home and fortune (under false pretences, naturally). The Redfern family loses everything and Babs remains at Cliff House only because she wins a scholarship. Sheba constantly taunts the impoverished Babs and tries to bring about her expulsion, but expectedly even ruthless Sheba has to acknowledge Barbara's strength and her own weakness in the end. They are both threatened with death in one of those frequent and timely interventions of the elements and natural catastrophes that so often occurred in and around Cliff House. On such occasions showy characters usually collapsed under the first onslaught of freak tidal waves, avalanches, consuming fire or other equally dramatic "Acts of God" – but Babs never wavered. Trapped in a cave the two enemies share the conciliating experience of water creeping up to their waists. Significantly Babs and Sheba do not pray like the fictional schoolgirls of Elinor Brent-Dyer or Dorita Fairlie Bruce in identical predicaments. Religion was taboo in Northcliffe's papers for girls, to avoid offence or embarrassment – and really Cliff House did not require divine intervention when it contained the resourcefulness of Barbara Redfern.

"Have courage!" whispered Babs.

"Courage! Oh it's all very well for you to say that!" burst out Sheba. "You can swim!"

"I won't swim without you, Sheba – I promise that!" Babs answered. [Sheba sobbingly has to admit that this is bound to be true, and at last she surrenders to Babs's relentless virtue.]

"I must say it – I must! ... It's a struggle, but I – I will do it. You're wonderful ... ".

"Sheba, I love you for saying all that!" Babs whispered. ... "Don't say any more, dear. I'm sure I understand now."

And Babs of course, with astounding nobility of spirit, always *does* understand.

Less cloying and far more human than Babs was Clara Trevlyn, another member of the Fourth Form at Cliff House. The character was conceived by Charles Hamilton, and first appeared in *Magnet* stories in 1909. Clara and Marjorie Hazeldene remained staunch "girl chums" of Harry Wharton & Co. of the Greyfriars Remove from the Edwardian era of their inception until the 1960s, when Hamilton featured them in some of his post-second-world-war "Bunter" books (published first by Skilton, then Cassell). Charles Hamilton enjoyed a long-standing love/hate relationship with the Suffragettes and the New Woman, whose campaign attracted so much public interest in the early days of the *Magnet* and *Gem*. Apart from providing him with comic material for his boys' stories, they inspired the creation of Clara, his most vital feminine character. She was a fourteen-year-old version of the New Woman. Like many fictional tomboys Clara was overdrawn, especially in the 1920s' *School Friend*, to create an adventurous atmosphere in stories which, because of their all-girl cast, might otherwise have seemed unbalanced and insipid to readers. Hamilton had envisaged her as the young "sport", getting on well with boys and speaking their "slangy" language. In spite of her boyish ways, Clara in the *Magnet* has to fulfil Hamilton's basically sentimental picture of young girls, by being "… charming … with golden curls and vivacious blue eyes…". (The later *School Friend* authors did not wait long to cut off the curls and give her an Eton crop.) Although Clara is supposed to meet boys on equal terms – even challenging a Greyfriars bully to a fight for insulting the pupils of Cliff House – Hamilton cannot resist lumbering her with all the undesirable attributes which he considers exclusive to women: calculated duplicity, illogicality, craven fear of mice and insects and an obsessional interest in pretty hats. (In fact most girl readers of the *Magnet* in the '20s and '30s probably wore hats only under pressure from parents and teachers.) Clara's behaviour towards her Cliff House friends swings like a pendulum from feline huffiness to mawkish reconciliation, which Hamilton seemed to consider the quintessence of relationships between girls. Of course the *Magnet* was written primarily for boys who enjoyed the perpetuation of the concept that "girls are soppy", which enhanced their own sense of superiority. Fortunately L. E.

Ransome and John Wheway in the *School Friend* and the *Schoolgirl*
realized that "kissing and making up", as well as cattiness, should
be treated with extreme caution if their readership was not to be
alienated. Charles Hamilton was unable to sustain tomboy
characterizations because essentially he had a Victorian resistance
to "strong-minded" women, and also found something funny in the
idea that girls were as fit as boys to take part in organized sports. (It
is significant that when writing for girls in the early *School Friend*
and in *Bessie Bunter Of Cliff House School* as late as 1949, Hamilton
persistently used "cat" as a term of abuse; women school-story
writers during the same period – Angela Brazil, Dorita Fairlie Bruce
and Elinor Brent-Dyer – rarely used this epithet.)

The men who took over the Cliff House saga from Hamilton and
Horace Phillips knew that their readers expected integrity in feminine
characterizations. Clara Trevlyn was built up into a lively schoolgirl
whose amazing courage and athletic prowess became acceptable
because of her counter-balancing weaknesses. Her bluntness and quick
temper added credibility to the *School Friend* stories and endeared
her to readers who recognized the same qualities in themselves.
Dismissing affected and mushy behaviour as "piffling rot", and always
essentially down to earth, Clara became one of the most acceptable
embodiments of fictional schoolgirl honour and "team spirit".

She was also, to some extent, a proponent of sexual equality.
Although sex, like religion, was a forbidden subject, Babs & Co.
were allowed to have social contact with the boys of Lanchester
College (Jack Tollhurst & Co.) in the '20s, and Friardale School
(Jimmy Richmond & Co.) in the '30s. (The Cliff House writers who
succeeded Charles Hamilton in the *School Friend* were not allowed
to bring the Greyfriars boys into their stories.) Clara's particular
friend was Ginger Hawkins. The relationship was wholesome and
sexless, and Ginger, who considered Clara a "top-notcher", really
put up with an awful lot. One day when Clara is late getting back to
school (after enjoying a Douglas Fairbanks Senior film) Ginger offers
her a lift in a motor bike and side-car combination. She firmly
announces that she will ride the bike, and Ginger can get in the
side-car: " 'You don't think I'd trust my life with you driving?' said

Clara scornfully. 'Boys can't drive motor bikes. I'll give you a few tips as we go along.' " And so they proceed, in spite of Ginger's initial protests. Jemima Carstairs in 1927 expressed the opinion that " 'Boadiccea was a tame lamb compared with Clara' " and the tomboy's closest chum, Marjorie Hazeldene, constantly takes her to task for her hoydenish activities.

> "I don't agree with girls doing that sort of thing; [when Clara wants to sail a boat on her own] they may be strong as men, but they haven't the nerve."
> Clara went positively red, and her face clouded with rage. "Well of all the silly Victorians!" she retorted angrily. "You mean to say a girl these days hasn't as much nerve as a boy?"

To prove her point Clara hires a sailing boat and takes it out to sea, where the inevitable and devastating storm immediately blows up. Clara, who swims several miles to shore when her boat capsizes, discovers and eventually effects the capture of a nest of smugglers. She returns triumphant to her friends, expecting to be the heroine of the hour. " 'That sort of thing's all right for boys,' said Marjorie, 'but not for girls.' "

Marjorie's gradual development in the girls' papers into a milksop is disappointing: she was another early *Magnet* personality and Hamilton, though overdoing her worthiness, had endowed her with vitality that dwindled away in the *School Friend* and *Schoolgirl* – possibly because she had to become a foil for Clara's strength.

Like Clara, Babs had a special friend at Lanchester College. Jack Tollhurst was referred to as Barbara's "boy chum", this description having fewer sexual implications than the term "boy friend". At times the relationship is a study in stilted chastity:

> "I say, might I trot by the side of your bicycle as far as the gates of Cliff House School? I want to get in a training run tonight."
> "I shall be pleased for you to accompany me, Jack," Babs said.

It is reasonable to assume that curiosity about sex in adolescent readers was even stronger in the 1920s and '30s than today, when the subject, both in theory and practice, no longer remains a mystery to many young people. But the Amalgamated Press's juvenile papers were not lifting any veils: its artists were instructed to play down female breasts and buttocks, and in swimming-costume scenes the water should, if possible, come almost as high as the girls' armpits. In spite of these restrictions T. E. Laidler, the Cliff House illustrator in the *Schoolgirl*, managed to suggest physical development in his attractively pictured fourteen-year-olds. (G. M. Dodshon who illustrated the *School Friend* stories drew younger-looking girls with strangely oriental faces.) Authors had the equally difficult task of conveying the beginnings of emotional maturity, as well as schoolgirlishness, in their heroines. On the whole they succeeded. L. E. Ransome, who also wrote for boys, has said that " ... the war heroes of boys' papers are nominally grown men but in fact a schoolboy's fantasy of himself as a man ... without the girls and beer element". Similarly girls liked to identify with fictional characters who, although youthful, suggested appealing future adult capacities.

Only the slightest glimmerings of sexual awareness were permitted in the friendships between Babs and Jack, or Clara and Ginger. More usual boy/girl relationships in the 1920s papers were those based on another pattern established by Charles Hamilton in the *Magnet* as early as 1908. His Marjorie Hazeldene was always propping up her wayward and vacillating Greyfriars brother Peter. In the *School Friend* Barbara Redfern played a similar self-sacrificial rôle in the life of Raymond Bannister, her weak-natured cousin from Lanchester College. Brother and sister themes were popular. Dolly Jobling, who shares Marjorie and Clara's study, is normally a light-hearted girl whose great hobby is toffee-making, which she pursues with singular lack of success. (Her culinary efforts usually end in disaster – with chimneys set on fire or unsuspecting teachers accidentally sitting on trays of runny toffee which have been left on chairs to set.) Overnight Dolly is transformed from a cheerful member of the Cliff House "chummery" into a haggard outsider, because of brother Arthur's being charged with theft, which disgrace she cannot bring herself to confide to her friends. (There is a convincing "before" and "after" drawing of Dolly on the front cover of the first story in the series.) The melodramatic nature of this series is conveyed by the titles: "Dolly Jobling's Secret", "The Girl Who Kept Silence" and "Her Brother's Peril". Just as the magistrate is about to sentence her brother, Dolly rushes into court and establishes his innocence. The last paragraph of the story typifies the self-sacrificing sisterly theme that was so liberally served to girls in the 1920s: " 'Arthur, my brother!' she muttered, her eyes filling with tears. 'What a wonderful lot I have learnt! Even if it all happened again – yes, I'd be willing to do twice as much – for his sake!' "

In the 1930s the *Schoolgirl's* boy and girl relationships were more robust. Overt sexual interest was still taboo, but appreciation of male and female qualities in each other could be hinted at. Girls were no longer expected to subjugate their own interests for their brothers, cousins or boy chums – and they were often permitted to deflate juvenile male pomposity. One of the happiest examples of this was an Ida Melbourne series in 1938 called *Cousin George And The Imp*, which must have been especially appreciated by girls who had suffered from bossy elder brothers. Hetty Sonning, the fourteen-year-old "imp", was their mouthpiece: " 'We've got to skittle those boys out,'[at cricket] insisted the Imp 'or they'll blow to pieces with swank.' " As her parents are in India, and Hetty has been forced to leave boarding school (for showing too much "originality") she goes to live with stuffy Aunt Miriam and her sixteen-year-old son George. Lordly and rather slow-witted, George sets out to make Hetty "serious-minded and guide her thoughts" but though he "boomed and woofed his commands, she could manage him easily". With subtlety and assumed meekness Hetty always gets her way, goading unadventurous George into many exciting situations by comparing him adversely with "Bob Biggs", a completely mythical "fearfully strong and brilliant" character whom she pretends she knows. Hetty becomes extremely fond of George in spite of his "somewhat up-stage, haw-haw big brother manner", but she constantly gets the better of him. For instance when George insists on taking Hetty on an educational visit to a museum she soon makes him abandon the project, by whispering to the attendant that he is unstable and will smash the glass cases with a walking stick which he is affectedly carrying. They end up on the river – as Hetty has intended from the onset. Ingeniously contrived, and getting away from stock situations, these stories are so fast-moving that it is difficult to predict how Hetty will manage to exploit every new situation to her advantage. But she always does.

The *School Friend* heroines are distinctive, and there is no understatement about its abundant bitchy girls. At Cliff House in the '20s Marcia Loftus and Nancy Bell (collaborators rather than "chums") were the most consistent "sneaks and toadies" in the junior school. (They were superseded in the *Schoolgirl* by rich Lydia Crossendale and her parasitic "cronies" Freda Ferriers and Frances Frost.) In common with bullying prefects Connie Jackson and Sarah Harrigan, Marcia and Nancy are unscrupulous by nature and unprepossessing in appearance – illustrations show them with lank hair, greasy complexions and general lack of style. Much more fascinating to readers, and holding greater sway over the inmates of Cliff House, were the "bounderesses", who resisted the conformist pressures of *esprit de corps* with panache and a dash of vulgarity. Their philistinism was augmented by a plentiful supply of money and smart clothes, usually supplied by doting, unscrupulous, self-made fathers. ("Bounderesses" never seemed to have mothers.) Augusta Anstruther-Browne, who had so odiously persecuted "the scholarship girl" in 1919, was the most intriguing expression of this type in the *School Friend*. She smoked, played cards for money and broke bounds at night to attend local dances. It was a safe bet that every weak or wilful Cliff House character would succumb to the dancing craze at least once during her schooldays. Seemingly innocent romps in the gym and music room, if not immediately quashed by disciplinarian prefects, would inevitably lead to *risqué* trips to the local Palais de Danse. " 'You will go back to the dormitory and wipe off that powder and change into your drill frock. Then, as you seem to have nothing better to do, you can write me out fifty lines.' " Lines never deterred Augusta, who was defiant of all adult authority, which she flouted by the use of strong scent and make-up, and being seen with jazzy friends in fast cars. Augusta was a fantasy representation of the slightly ruthless modishness and freedom from parental restraint for which lots of young girls in prosaic circumstances yearned. Possibly to prevent her from exerting too strong an influence over her readers, the Amalgamated Press writers suddenly plunged her into poverty, when overnight her father lost his fortune – to the last penny and stick of luxury furniture in Augusta's study. This was particularly tough on his daughter, who had just been thrown out of Cliff House for her headstrong ways, and as her father went abroad she was figuratively "out in the cold, cold snow". With unconvincing and melodramatic repentance, she returns to Cliff House in the false and humble-sounding name of Olive Wayne. By the simple expedient of cropping her hair, assuming a pair of spectacles and twisting her ankle so severely that she develops a chronic limp, Augusta escapes recognition from her former classmates – even in the close confines of dormitory life when presumably the spectacles have sometimes to be removed. Eventually forgiven and restored to her former glory, Augusta alternates between recklessness and reform for the next nine years.

A decade later John Wheway delighted pubescent girls in search of glamour with an up-dated bounderess who typified the tawdry brilliance of the 1930s. More flamboyant than Augusta and sharing with her that affected double barrelling of a commonplace surname, as well as a go-getting father, Diana Royston-Clarke – "the firebrand" – was a schoolgirl evocation of Hollywood's Jean Harlow. Her "glorious mass of billowy platinum blonde hair" was tossed around haughtily in protest at the imposition of any constraints. Whenever Diana was irritated by what she considered the "goody-goody" aspects of Babs & Co. she would alarmingly flash her violet eyes and dilate her nostrils. Quick tempered, with a curious habit of yelling "Yoicks!" in moments of emotional stress or exhilaration, Diana was her own worst enemy. She arrived at Cliff House in a "magnificent" chauffeur-driven car – " 'Nice bus,' Jemima Carstairs commented critically, 'Three thousand if threepence – what?' " – dressed precociously in a flashy sable coat, silk stockings and high-heeled shoes, which must have endeared Diana to schoolgirls of the '30s who resented their own encasement in regulation serge gymslips, wrinkled lisle hose and velour hats. When she is unable to achieve her ends by exercising personal magnetism, Diana tries to buy power and whatever else she craves. Of all his fictional creations Diana Royston-Clarke was John Wheway's favourite.

He managed to make all the Cliff House juniors credible, from teenage firecrackers like Diana to "dear old Fatima" (Bessie) who in the *Schoolgirl* had become plump rather than fat, and genial instead of grotesque. She was a popular member of the Fourth Form, in spite of her many foibles, which included habitual boasting about titled relations who had absolutely no existence outside Bessie's imagination. " 'You don't mean to say Sir Dustbin de Dishwater de Bunter has turned up trumps at last,' " says Clara, when Bessie receives one of her rare remittances. Bessie Bunter's wistful appeals – " 'I sus – say Babs!' " – always bring out Barbara's protectiveness for her weaker chum. Barbara by this time is less of a paragon. She laughs more, and seems a straightforward schoolgirl with "clear blue eyes" and short chestnut hair, usually described as glossy, waving or crisply curling. (Most of the Cliff House "baddies" had straight hair in the 1930s.)

A general lessening of insularity had prompted the inclusion in the stories of some foreign girls, the most attractive of whom were the excitable, diminutive French student, Marcelle Biquet, and Leila Carroll from the USA. Leila is the daughter of a Hollywood producer and numbers famous film stars amongst her friends. She says "shucks" frequently and convincingly to generate the appropriate trans-Atlantic atmosphere.

Readers responded to the naturalness of the Cliff House girls and tried in many ways to emulate them. At times this must have been daunting as their heroines were unusually competent for their age. Horse-riding, hockey, cricket, tennis, swimming, diving, skiing, sledging and skating presented no difficulties for them. (In one story Babs and Diana are described as adept performers of Morris dancing – *on ice* – anyone who has mastered the leaping lolloping Morris step on firm ground will boggle at the degree of skill required for that.) Babs is a highly talented artist, and Mabs (Mabel Lynn) such a brilliant actress and playwright that, at fourteen, she has already turned down offers of West End stardom in order to remain a member of Barbara's coterie. Even "duffer" Bessie excels at ventriloquial tricks which help her out of many tight corners, and she is a cook of Cordon Bleu standards. Leila Carroll, with characteristic American confidence, no more than a passing qualm and without any prior toning up, is able to deputize at short notice for a sick circus-high-wire trapeze act. Equipped with such a variety of accomplishments, the Cliff House juniors almost casually can entertain orphans and refugees, nurse ailing old ladies, and arrange fetes or festivals to raise funds for local charities.

Their commendable activities were brought to a sudden end when, like several other juvenile magazines, the *Schoolgirl* ceased publication abruptly in May 1940, because Hitler's invasion of Norway had cut off Britain's main supply of "pulp" paper. The Amalgamated Press resurrected the *School Friend* after the war in a different format (see chapter 17), but Cliff House School was not revived. Bessie Bunter appeared in the "dummy" for the first issue but was rejected in favour of Dilly Dreem – a duffer but not a fat girl. In 1950 Babs & Co. must have seemed anachronistic to the Amalgamated Press policy makers: strangely however their only survivor has after all been the most retarded member – Bessie. She inspired John Wheway's Tilly Tuffin in IPC's *Princess* during the early 1960s, and Bessie Bunter, fatter and more of a buffoon than ever before, existed as a comic-strip caricature until 1974 in IPC's *June*.

XIV

And Still More

"Eeet hard when people do not play the game. I zink everybodies should go to school in England. Zen they learn to play the game, yes."

(Schoolgirls' Own, 1928)

WHEN HORACE PHILLIPS relinquished authorship of the Cliff House stories in 1921, he soon achieved the distinction of creating a group of fictional schoolgirls who, though convincing to readers in the 1920s and '30s, owed their inspiration largely to the Victorian melodrama of Mrs Henry Wood and the aura of romantic novelettes. Vigorous " ... 'hockey on the halfers!' " and cosy study teas " ... 'after you've come in out of the rain' " seem reluctant afterthoughts rather than essential ingredients of his stories. Morcove School's highly-charged emotional ambience was further enhanced by regular visitations from Rose of the Desert, a mysterious Arabian girl, to whom adventure and intrigue clung as tenaciously as the insubstantial veils and draperies which she never supplemented, even in the coldest of Devonshire moorland mists and sea breezes.

Using the pen-name of Marjorie Stanton, in the first issue of the *Schoolgirls' Own* (5 February 1921) Horace Phillips plunged his readers immediately into the harrowing story of plucky Betty Barton's endeavours to keep together her poverty-stricken family. The beginning of *Scorned By The School* suggests a reversion to the early twentieth-century tear-jerkers of Mill and Home Life, directed at sentimental adults rather than down-to-earth schoolgirls. Chapter One firmly sets the scene: fourteen-year-old Betty, wearing leaky boots and shabby shawl, runs home from the council school in teeming rain to prepare a midday meal for her small brother and sister; Mother is out charring because Father, disabled in a factory accident, can now earn only a pittance. The inadequate meal is interrupted by the rent collector, who brings the threat of eviction and removal to the workhouse unless arrears can be settled; and – in case readers might still be expecting schoolgirlish frivolity – Betty's already crippled father gets run over in a street accident. Horace Phillips's industrial Lancashire is every bit as grisly as that described several decades earlier by Mrs Gaskell and Mrs Hodgson Burnett (see chapter 4). But heroine Betty Barton is soon transported from murky Ribbleton (Manchester?) to an expensive boarding school on bracing Exmoor, thanks to an uncle who, having made good in America, whisks the Barton family into a new luxury home before the gates of the workhouse can close upon them.

In spite of Morcove School's upper-class tone, it soon becomes apparent that most of its inmates would be better placed in a reformatory. Betty Barton is subjected to thuggery and intimidation even worse than that endured earlier by the Cliff House Lancashire scholarship girl, Peggy Preston. Betty is stigmatized as "a washerwoman's daughter" and "a common skivvy", and her humiliations – " 'She can't really be a council school girl. Why, her face is clean!' " – were presumably intended to endear her to the real-life council-school children who would be likely to buy this new twopenny paper. (It is possible that many working-class girls did not think of themselves as "council-school" pupils until the authors of popular fiction hammered home the difference between their environment and that of more wealthy families. Children who knew only the conventional confines of working-class life in the early 1920s accepted attendance at council schools as the norm, because their activities rarely impinged on those of boys and girls at "posh" and "paid-for" schools.)

In spite of her humble origins Betty soon demonstrates that she is the only member of the Fourth Form who is "a lady". Being ladylike is an accomplishment dwelt upon by Horace Phillips lovingly and repeatedly during the fifteen years that he was responsible for the Morcove saga. (Horace Phillips wrote almost all of the weekly Morcove stories in the *Schoolgirls' Own* from 1921 to its last issue, no. 798 in May 1936. Serials about Morcove then appeared in the *Schoolgirl* until February 1938 but probably some of these were written by other authors using the Marjorie Stanton pen-name.) Like many writers of girls' fiction Phillips had a weakness for the aristocracy, whose female members might be expected to be "ladies" in every sense of the word, and therefore provide an example of commendable behaviour for girls from less favoured homes. Constantly popping in and out of Morcove School is the daughter of the Earl and Countess of Lundy from neighbouring Barncombe Castle. Lady Evelyn Knight is " ... a girl of eighteen, no more ... not in the least affected, but just an exquisite specimen of true British girlhood" who, of course, becomes a staunch chum of Betty Barton. In 1928 Horace Phillips introduced Pam Willoughby, his favourite character, always known as "the little Lady of Swanlake" (Swanlake being her elegant home). Pam was frequently described as tall and stately, but "little" in this context can be taken to imply youth and feminine limitations. Despite the success of Cliff House's tomboy Clara Trevlyn, about whom Phillips had written many *School Friend* adventures, he could not bring himself to create a similar character at Morcove: instead he compromised with "merry madcap" Polly Linton, the first of Betty's form-mates to befriend her. "Wonderfully pretty, full of high spirits and evidently a girl of character" Polly nevertheless was to be kept on a tighter rein than Clara, with a more socially acceptable manner of skylarking which conveyed skittishness rather than independence.

Horace Phillips of course had established the untarnishable virtue of Barbara Redfern in the *School Friend*, and Betty Barton was similarly endowed. Week after week "Marjorie Stanton" expatiated on Betty's courage and resolution – " 'Never mind; I'll manage!' Betty cried, forcing a cheery note" – and she soon becomes Captain of the Form, as more and more of its weak-willed members succumb to her worthiness and indulge in repentances of a lurid type. The early Morcove stories struck a censorious note, and without the editorial ban on religion Horace Phillips would almost certainly have alienated young readers with his religiosity. His maudlin tendencies were redressed at first by restraints imposed by the Amalgamated

Press rules for its juvenile-fiction writers. Later, Phillips's delineation of the boarding-school framework strengthened, bringing discipline and credence to his stories.

The *Schoolgirls' Own* soon became popular in spite of "Marjorie Stanton's" emotive style: the paper's success was partly due to the excellence of Leonard Shields's illustrations. The *School Friend* had once declared that Barbara Redfern & Co. were "The Most Famous Schoolgirls in the World", but the Morcove girls could have claimed to be the most beautiful. Shields was best known as a regular illustrator of the *Magnet*; adolescents of both sexes positively radiated vitality in his drawings, and the attractive blue and orange covers which he designed tempted many girls – and some boys – to buy the *Schoolgirls' Own*.

Humour was noticeably absent in its early issues and when at last Phillips succeeded in producing one of his comical set pieces he repeated it regularly over many years. Trixie Hope emerged as a distinct personality in the middle of 1921. She had been promised a foreign holiday by her parents (a thrill for schoolgirls then, though now a commonplace) and was therefore practising her French at every conceivable opportunity. Rather like Robert Browning's "wise thrush" who, in "Home Thoughts From Abroad",

> Sings each song twice over
> Lest you should think he never could recapture
> That first fine careless rapture

Trixie has to repeat herself all the time, speaking first in French, then in English for the benefit of the elementary-school readers who of course were not taught any foreign languages. " '*Vous êtes une cafarde* – a sneak!' " This mildly amusing contrivance soon becomes tedious. " '*Cela ne fait rien* – that doesn't matter!' Trixie said obstinately. 'If you go getting into fresh mischief I shall be *forte triste* – very sad!' " Madge Minden, one of Trixie's chums, not surprisingly breaks in "with an exasperated stamp of the foot. 'You and your silly French jabber – I'm sick and tired of it. Just hold your tongue, Trixie!' " But Trixie keeps it going for six years until 1927 when, happily for readers who must have shared fictional Madge's irritation, she was shipped off permanently to France on a long overdue language scholarship.

Although Horace Phillips produced a few vivid characterizations, he was incapable of developing their potential: consequently even in the mid 1920s the Morcove girls must have seemed old-fashioned. Phillips himself has expressed surprise at the life-span of his schoolgirl creations, whom he had expected to be ephemeral, and it is difficult to understand how they survived for so long, especially in the more liberal psychological climate of the 1930s. The school story was still, of course, the stock-in-trade of popular fiction for girls, and the intensity of Phillips's writing may have appealed to the more emotional type of reader.

Madge Minden began promisingly. In 1921 she was the form musician – inevitably "temperamental" but at least not a witless conformist. (She didn't even follow the general trend in 1926 and shingle her hair, which remained long until the Morcove stories ended.) Madge is described as "no blue-stocking", though possessing "something in her – some fine spirit – that impelled her, now and then, to withdraw from the society of even her dearest chums". Unfortunately Phillips didn't explore further the predicament of the talented individualist, forced into continual relationship with "average", even philistine, girls in boarding-school communities. Madge, though despising Mendelssohn and preferring what her reactionary form-mistress dismisses as " 'that ridiculous Russian modern music' ", is not allowed to depart too drastically from the straight and narrow path of sporty schoolgirlishness. Horace Phillips effects one of his typical compromises: "Madge Minden, a cricket bat in her hand, and carrying batting gloves, was strolling down the passage whistling a César Franck Sonata."

Slightly bizarre vignettes abounded in the Morcove adventures. In December 1921 Betty Barton & Co. encounter some Moorish figures, walking in procession through the quiet North Devon seaside town of Barncombe. (However great their need for concealment, the henchmen of Rose of the Desert – so often forced to operate nefariously in England – never seemed the least bit concerned that their Arab garb might give them away.) The male leader wears "rich jacket and knickerbockers all quaintly spangled with ornaments that flashed in the setting sun" and the women are veiled from head to foot. Initially the Morcove coterie cannot guess their nationality and Madge conjectures,

> "They must belong to some race that doesn't like its women to be seen by the world too much."
> "Well thank goodness we are British!" said Betty. "We play hockey and ride bikes ... "

and self-consciously rejoicing in schoolgirl liberation through athletics they are soon on their way, with "a merry ting-tinging of bells". But Betty & Co.'s Christmas cosiness at Linton Hall, Polly's home, is abruptly curtailed. From falling about happily on the ice-covered lake they are diverted overnight to camel-trekking across the North African desert, to the marble minarets, fountains and pools of a vicious sultan's palace, in search of Madge and Tess, who have been kidnapped.

This is the first of a long series of improbable Arabian adventures, all of which involve Rose of the Desert, who frequently champions the Morcove contingent although her tribe are enemies of the "Breeteesh". Betty and her friends are generally accompanied by Jack Somerfield, a 28-year-old explorer who is the younger brother of their elderly headmistress. (Like many Amalgamated Press writers, Phillips seems vague about the customary period of fertility enjoyed by women. Age differences between brothers and sisters suggest that it was not uncommon for fictional mothers to continue child-bearing for 45 years.) Jack had saved the life of Rose of the Desert some years earlier, but her passionate devotion to him is rooted less in gratitude than sexual attraction. Although Lord Northcliffe rigidly barred sex from his schoolgirl papers Horace Phillips came perilously near to producing full-blooded love stories whenever his characters were anywhere near the vicinity of the desert. (He might well have been influenced by the success of E. M. Hull's *The Sheikh* in 1919.)

Restricted by editorial policy Phillips has to content himself with

The Schoolgirls' Own

2^D

NOT WANTED! "You can clear out, Betty Barton!" exclaimed the snobbish girl. "We've no use for Council School kids here!" (See "Scorned by the School!" in this issue.)

No. 1. Vol. 1.]   PUBLISHED EVERY TUESDAY. [Week Ending February 5th, 1921.

The MORCOVE PEERESS

by Marjorie Stanton

A FINE STORY of the EARLY DAYS of BETTY BARTON and Co. of MORCOVE SCHOOL

4D

5-10-39

The SCHOOLGIRLS' OWN LIBRARY No. 701

290

allowing Rose and Jack, for a period of fourteen years, to exchange pleasantries like " 'O Engleeshman with the heart that never quakes!' " and " 'I never will forget how, in the breast of my little brown maiden, there always beats a heart of gold' ". In their very first North African trip Betty confides to Polly " 'Isn't it pretty clear that he loves her just as much as she loves him?' " and Jack frequently alludes to Rose's "secret longing", implying that it will one day be fulfilled. However Rose of the Desert's most axiomatic utterance turns out to be 'Kismet – it is fate. I know East is East, and West is West and never the twain shall meet ... ' " etc. for the "little brown maiden" does not really get a lot of sustained romantic encouragement, especially considering the number of occasions when at grave risk to herself she rescues Jack from slow and horrible death. He has no compunction at fobbing her off with " 'Well done!' " and a casual kiss on the hand. Possibly Phillips had been instructed by his editors to cool the relationship: in the 1920s and '30s schoolgirl fiction was hardly progressive enough to permit marriage between a white man and a coloured girl. So when frustrated Rose eventually bows out of the saga in 1935 Jack has for four years been the husband of a European aristocrat, who is "a vision of radiant loveliness".

The spate of novels emulating the garish prototype of *The Sheikh* suggested that the mere presence in the desert of fair-skinned English girls provided an irresistible invitation to their capture and rape by oversexed but pseudo-sheikhs. (These turn out to be disguised Europeans who eventually fall in love with, and respectably marry, their victims.) Virginal British girls, who might in consequence have been expected to give the desert a wide berth were, apparently, either incapable of learning from the sordid exploits of their predecessors or eager to copy them. Similarly the Morcove girls were off to the desert for the hols year after year, in spite of contrary resolutions arising from experiences of sandstorms, slavery, harsh imprisonment and hairsbreadth escapes from death. (Rapist sheikhs, however – either real or synthetic – were lacking, thanks to the Amalgamated Press taboo on sex.) Possibly too Horace Phillips sensed that long camel-back journeys across the desert were more likely to produce enteritis than to act as an aphrodisiac, and the Morcove girls' appraisals of their North African adventures are realistic rather than rhapsodic. On one occasion when fleeing for their lives they are asked by Jack Somerfield " ... with the cheery humour of a Britisher in a tight corner. ... 'Which of you are the most tired – the camels or yourselves?' " and Paula Creel, the affected "swell" of the Fourth Form, replies " 'Weally, it is cwuel! ... Talk about being pwostwate, geals! This is worse than fifty hockey matches wolled into one!' "

Soon after the desert trips began Phillips introduced into the stories another "dusky" character – Naomer, fourteen-year-old Queen of Nakara. In her case there was no possibility of sexual entanglements in the all-girls-togetherness of Morcove, so Naomer was permitted to function on terms of equality with Betty Barton & Co. However her high spirits and greediness occasionally have to be curbed so that she can learn the impeccable Britishness so beloved of Horace Phillips: " 'Naomer darling, it isn't usual to eat all the sugar out of the sugar-basin!' " Naomer is a good-natured chatterbox, addicted to meaningless ejaculations like " 'Bekas – what ze diggings – oo gorjus!' " and making life a misery for the languid, pretty but vain Paula Creel. Polly adds her "madcap" energies to Naomer's teasing and Paula constantly complains about their "insuffewable tweatment" in "wuffling" her hair and hats, or inadvertently squirting her "dainty fwocks" with lemonade. They usually catch her at her lowest ebb, "wecupewating" from "stwenuous gwappling with the work in class, yes, wather!" These triangular romps joined Horace Phillips's repertoire of stock slap-stick situations.

The Amalgamated Press had featured many coloured juveniles in their story papers since the first decade of the century. (See chapter 8, Coosha and Pete.) In the days when most English children had never seen an African, an Indian or a Chinese, these characters represented "the mysterious East", and were often extravagantly overdrawn. Socially, they ranged from fabulously rich oriental princes to subservient South-Sea islanders of the "Me Klistian ... me missionary girl" variety. Other writers were probably impressed by Charles Hamilton's Hurree Jamset Ram Singh, the teenage Indian nabob who came as a pupil to Greyfriars School in 1908 and remained extremely popular until the *Magnet* ended in 1940.

Hamilton thought "it would have a good effect" on his readers to make a "coloured boy" an equal and valued member of Harry Wharton's group of friends, known as the Famous Five. At first Hamilton's presentation of the lithe, inscrutable and intelligent high-caste Hindu is believable, but later he is allowed to degenerate into an amiable but archetypal personality, chiefly memorable for his flowery habits of speech and mixed metaphors: " 'The superfluousness of the idiotic Bunter is terrific!' ... 'The ancient and ludicrous flame of friendship burns undimfully in my breast' ... " and " 'Perhaps there will still be a stitch in time to save the cracked pitcher from going longest to the well.' " In his own boyhood Charles Hamilton had been a "constant reader" of "Cheerful Ching Ching", a Chinese created by Harcourt Burrage in the *Boys' Standard* of 1881. Hamilton introduced a Chinese boy to Greyfriars, but his Wun Lung was a caricature, infinitely less attractive than Hurree Singh (and militating against good race relationships). Cliff House School, at first a girls' version of Greyfriars, never had an Indian student, though an unobtrusive Persian girl appeared in one or two stories in 1921. However the *School Friend* was able to infuse an exotic element into the serials which ran alongside the Cliff House stories during the first few years of the paper's existence. In "Julia Storm's" *The Girl Crusoes*, readers become acquainted with two "daughters of head hunters and savage warriors from Solomon Islands": they are Melita whose "face could only be compared to the sole of a black india rubber shoe" and Chrissie who "was more of a coffee colour". "Melita's hair was wonderful. It stood right up on end a foot high. ... " Not to be outdone by Melita's dramatic appeal, the first issue of the *Schoolgirls' Own* two years later produced a Julia Storm serial called *Castaway Jess*. By this time the editors of Amalgamated Press girls' papers must have been convinced that English schoolgirls enjoyed reading about bizarre characters of different races. *Castaway Jess* features, as well as its English heroine, six kow-towing Japanese girls in traditional dress, Sin, a Malay servant, Nareo and Baloo who are Pacific islanders, some Chinese pirates, a French school-mistress "Mademoiselle", an Irish girl and, to up-stage them all, a monkey. Stories of adolescent girls, or whole schools, cast away on South-Sea islands were just as popular in the *Schoolgirl* of the 1930s, though by then the sarong-clad native girls seemed to owe more to film-star Dorothy Lamour than Harriet Beecher Stowe's Topsy.

Despite changes in social attitudes brought about by the second world war, and the influx of West Indian immigrants to Britain soon after it, the Amalgamated Press resurrected in picture-strip format the teenage-white-castaway/girl-Friday theme with *Jill Crusoe* in its new *School Friend* (1950). Deference on the part of M'lani, the native girl, was possibly made more acceptable to readers because Jill's shipwreck was supposed to have taken place 50 years earlier. (In the 1920s servility from native girls had been taken for granted. "Topsy", a Kaffir girl in *The Ivory Seekers* by Gertrude Nelson in the *Schoolgirls' Own* in 1921, "came near to worshipping her young [English] mistress".)

It could be argued that the Northcliffe story papers used "coloured", or indeed any foreign, characters less to encourage racial tolerance than to boost the image of British fair-mindedness. In a 1923 *Magnet* Harry Wharton consoles a Eurasian student who has been rejected in India by both white and native communities:

> " … India isn't the only country where that sort of rot makes people uncomfortable. I've heard that the darkies in the United States get the same stuff, only much worse. Anyhow, we don't bother our heads much about such piffle in this little island. A fellow's taken for what he's worth, not for the shade of his giddy complexion."
>
> "He is all right, if he plays the game, as you call it," said Da Costa [the Eurasian]. ...
>
> "That's it."

Read retrospectively this claim seems platitudinous but in the 1920s it carried conviction.

Horace Phillip's touches of "Hurrah for England" in snatched and slightly embarrassing dialogues between schoolgirls are as sincere as Hamilton's. His stories constantly reflect the seriousness of his own

THE "WHITE QUEEN"
from MORCOVE

By Marjorie Stanton

A STORY
OF THE EARLY
ADVENTURES OF
BETTY BARTON & CO
*telling how Betty once became
Queen of a North African Tribe*

7·11·35

4ᴰ

The
SCHOOLGIRLS'
OWN LIBRARY Nº 515

295

MORCOVE'S CHRISTMAS PROBLEM

AN ENTHRALLING STORY of the early ADVENTURES of BETTY BARTON and Co. of MORCOVE SCHOOL

by Marjorie Stanton

4D

1-12-38

The SCHOOLGIRLS' OWN LIBRARY No. 661

nature: as soon as Betty Barton's form mates abandon their snobbish prejudices they form wholehearted friendships with her. When describing chummy feelings between girls Phillips has no reticence about evoking deep emotions. Betty tells Madge Minden that she will enjoy meeting "poor ailing Nell, coming forward with her limping step", and hand outstretched: "but handshakes were not good enough, Madge felt. She kissed Nell as if she was already quite in love with her. And perhaps she was!" Readers who felt out of their depths when faced with such intense friendships probably preferred the Morcove bad hats. They were numerous. Ursula Wade appeared in the second number of the *Schoolgirls' Own*, as a sneak, liar and thief: she never reformed. Teresa Tempest in *The Girl Who Swanked* (September 1921) was spoiled and self-willed. In the dormitory "Teresa stood radiant, with her (permanently waved) hair up, in orange charmeuse dress, and silk stockings [at twenty-five shillings – £1.25 – a pair] and suede shoes". (Teresa was actually created by L. E. Ransome who wrote a few Morcove stories as "Marjorie Stanton".)

Cora and Judith Grandways were Betty's main tormentors in her early days at Morcove. They had no saving graces whatsoever, and particularly resented Betty's improved social position because back home in Lancashire their family had employed Betty's mother as charwoman, their father owned the factory where Mr Barton had been crippled, and also he was landlord of the slum dwelling which used to be the Bartons' home. (Horace Phillips never baulked at creating cliché situations if they added pathos to a story.) "Cora's brazen conduct and reckless escapades caused a backwash of trouble for the whole Form" and, as with Ursula Wade, even Phillips could find no believable loophole for achieving her transformation. But Cora's sister Judith eventually inspires the climax of his mawkishness. Phillips enjoyed creating girls who were easily swayed and influenced by others, either for good or evil. Judith Grandways gradually comes under the spell of Betty Barton & Co. though she is tortured by a sense of disloyalty to her sister. After several weepy episodes the problem of how she can acceptably repudiate Cora is solved. Phillips decides that she has never been a Grandways after all – but an adopted child. Mrs Cardew, a beautiful and understanding lady who has worked up an acquaintance with Judy, and to whom the Morcove junior is strangely attracted, turns out to be her mother – of course. "And Judith, as she flew to those loving arms that had been longing to hold her through the years said all that was in her happy heart when she voiced the one soft word: 'Mother!' " Not content with restoring one orphan to the maternal bosom, Phillips similarly transforms the status of Dave Lawder, who had been featured in the saga for some years as a friend of Betty & Co. He turns out to be Judy's brother. (Perhaps Horace Phillips had read *Pollyanna*?)

A year or two earlier in 1930 Judith had displayed similar intensity over Ronnie Helder, a young film-star who worked with her when a film unit came to Morcove. Their parting was touching, and even without the erotic aura of the desert Phillips once again seemed to be going beyond the frontiers of the permitted boy/girl healthy friendships: "Even if she should never see him again, to have known him in the last few weeks was to have had a tide of happiness started in her young life that was silent, strong, running fathoms deep."

In 1926 Grangemoor School for boys sprang up a mile or two away from Morcove, conveniently housing Polly's brother, jolly Jack Linton; Jack had appeared in the *Schoolgirls' Own* from 1921 but at first he was not a schoolboy, but a young man of nineteen. In 1926 he was about the same age as Polly – fourteen or fifteen – and he and his Grangemoor colleagues became regular companions for Betty & Co. Possibly it was felt that boy characters would inject vigour into the Morcove stories and make them more natural and up-to-date. The girls had their favourites – ladylike Pam Willoughby was drawn to Jimmy Cherrol, the boy who claimed an inferiority complex; Naomer had a rapport with Tubby Bloot, a Billy Bunter type who shared her passion for cream puffs; and lively Polly preferred Jack's "grave" friend, Dave Lawder (later Cardew). Polly and Dave have their coy moments: after a typical North African adventure in 1926 when the boys and girls are being transported to safety across the desert in a lorry Polly declares that she doesn't want Dave to sit next to her – as she will be tempted to "tease" him. Dave indicates that he would welcome this but Polly plays safe: " 'Nothing doing! I want Naomer on one side of me, and Pam on the other; then it'll be just like going home on the school bus after a match! Hurrah! Hockey next term!' "

In spite of occasional lapses into sentimentality the keynote of the Morcove/Grangemoor relationships was hearty decency, as typified by Jack Linton's interest in "handsome" Madge, in the first Christmas series (1921). Jack and Madge were then "getting on very well, these two, in a nice, honest chummy way". Chumminess certainly overflowed in the festive season. Possibly, after Dickens, no one succeeded more fully in conveying the spirit of Christmas than the Amalgamated Press writers. All the trappings of rollicking, good-time, old-world celebrations prevailed. Tremendously high-spirited parties of bosom friends assembled in stately homes whose lakes unfailingly froze solid for skating, as snow quickly covered the surrounding countryside to make possible sledging and snowballing. Inside, beneath the gaze of ancestral portraits, blazing logs crackled in panelled halls hung with paper garlands, holly and mistletoe. Here the chums would enjoy their orgies of roast turkey and Christmas pudding, taking time off from eating for an occasional ghost hunt or fancy dress dance. They were likely to stumble on buried cavalier or monastic treasure, from clues hidden amongst the rare books which invariably lined the library from floor to ceiling.

To many of the girls who bought the *School Friend* or the *Schoolgirls' Own*, Christmas, in their semi-detached or terraced houses, just would not have been Christmas without vicarious participation in the Morcove and Cliff House girls' festivities.

XV

The *Girl's Own Paper* Goes to War

"It's farewell to the drawing-room's mannerly cry
The professor's logical whereto and why
The frock-coated diplomat's polished aplomb
Now matters are settled with gas and with bomb."
(W. H. Auden, "Danse Macabre")

THE *Girl's Own Paper*, after many pedestrian years, began its Indian Summer when in 1930 it divided into two publications. At last the "G.O.P." actually became a journal for girls, and its former women readers were diverted to *Woman's Magazine*. The Religious Tract Society, now functioning under the name of Lutterworth Press, was perhaps inspired by the success of Northcliffe's girls' fiction papers throughout the 1920s, which appealed especially to readers from working-class homes. The "G.O.P." soon became popular with middle-class parents who wanted "good" literature for their daughters. Its fiction kept alive the honour and duty themes of "untrashy" annuals like *British Girls'*, *Mrs Strang's*, the *Empire*, and *Blackie's*. Angela Brazil, Elsie Jeanette Oxenham, L. M. Montgomery, Baroness Orczy, Elinor Brent-Dyer and other accepted writers contributed regularly to the paper during the 1920s. Each issue contained a religious article, usually occupying a whole page, and interest in careers, needlework and sport was encouraged.

Many working-class girls dismissed the magazine as "prissy", resenting its educational overtones: more words of lively fiction could be bought for twopence in the small print, pulp-papered *School Friend*, *Schoolgirls' Own* and *Schoolgirls' Weekly* than for sixpence [2½p] in the glossy-looking and suspiciously upper-class offering

Girl's Own Paper *Cover, December 1940*
featuring a W.R.N.S. Officer

from Lutterworth Press.

Physical culture movements currently in vogue became almost a fetish with the *Girl's Own Paper*. Its pages were full of articles like the following: "A Hiking We Will Go" and "Youth On The Road" (Youth Hosteling and hiking); "Margaret Morris Movement As A Career" by Betty Simpson – "I am going to tell you about an all-British and pioneer school of recreative dancing and health exercises ... ", illustrated by exhilarating photographs of girls in abbreviated tunics dancing on the sands against a background of breaking waves; "How To Keep Fit" by Prunella Stack, leader of the Women's League of Health and Beauty – showing smiling exponents leaping about in their familiar white tops and black satin knickers. Hints on how to improve prowess at hockey, tennis and all organized outdoor games seemed never-ending: it is remarkable that sports' writers Marjorie Pollard and Sid. G. Hedges did not grind to a halt long before 1940, but obviously they were able to attract the interest of a new generation of readers, and the games were to some extent evolving. "You must bully with the flat of your sticks. ... " Hockey inspired not only technical advice but verse as in "The Hockey Match" by Thelma Hamilton-Jones (*Girl's Own Paper*, 1940):

> With hair and girdles flying free,
> The eager Forwards ran,
> They seemed like rushing infantry,
> Each one marked by an enemy,
> In the opposing "clan".

For many young people sport and speed were the keynote of the early 1930s. Records were broken by Malcolm Campbell on water and the Cheltenham Flyer on land (78 miles an hour by train) and aviation history was made repeatedly. The media responded to the exploits of Amy Johnson, Amelia Earhart and Jean Batten in prose, poetry and song. Flying implied liberation and control of the elements: female aviators by their achievements and in their own personalities were symbolic of the widening spheres of activity sought by women and girls. Broadcasting after her Gipsy Moth solo flight from England to Australia in 1930, Amy Johnson said: " 'There is nothing more wonderful and thrilling that I can imagine than going up into the spaciousness of the skies in a tiny light plane where you feel alone, at peace with everyone, and exactly free to do what you want and go where you will ... '." At the same time she was disturbingly aware that the phrenetic admiration which she attracted resulted less from her technical achievement than the public's surprise that a woman could meet the challenges of long-distance aviation. " 'I do not want it to be unusual that women should do things ... '."[1] In spite of catching the world's imagination and receiving tributes from international aviators, statesmen and royalty, the "Amy Wonderful Amy" of popular song, "Heroine" and "Queen of the Air", could not obtain a serious flying job until 1940 when she became a wartime member of the Air Transport Auxiliary. Women pilots might be acclaimed wonders of the air, but society doubted their capacity to assume sustained responsibility.

The *Girl's Own Paper* of the 1930s struggled to echo the popular mood and to become airborne. In 1936 it enthused over "A New Career Open to Girls", and described the first British air stewardess. She was photographed at work in a polka-dot dress with a large frilled organdie collar: unlike their American counterparts, early British air hostesses wore no uniforms. Dorothy Carter contributed several flying stories. Her "Lizzie of the Bush" (1939) dealt with the heroism of upper-crust Australian Elizabeth who "swam, sailed, flew her own aeroplane and played a good game of golf". During a bush fire Elizabeth saves whole flocks of sheep by ferrying them out of danger in a De Havilland Dragon: to control this against the "currents and turmoils which threw [it] about like a piece of paper in a high wind", she maintains a vice-like grip on the wheel of the control column and braces her feet firmly against the rudder bar. (Fiction writers of the period were lavish in their use of technical jargon to create atmosphere.) One instructor tells another in *Sally's Solo* (1940) " ' ... she's as keen as anything, but she just won't take any trouble. She laughs and pushes the [joy] stick about as if it were a hockey stick.

[1] Constance Babington Smith, *Amy Johnson*

You can't treat a plane like that. One day she'll get into a spin through her outrageous treatment of the rudder bar. ... ' " (But Sally made a good pilot in the end.) "Turning into the wind, Marise opened the throttle full out for the take off. As they reached the middle of the lagoon the flying boat came off the water and soared into the air. 'I must get that tear [in the wing] mended at Honolulu,' said Marise mechanically." Marise Duncan is the heroine of *Mistress Of The Air*, a serial by Dorothy Carter which ran from 1937 to 1938. She is "the youngest girl ever to compete in the King's Cup Air Race", flying her own plane, the Vega Gull. She wins, naturally, but the course of female aviation never does run smooth. " 'Very nice dear,' said Mrs. Duncan [her mother] when she was shown the cup, 'But is it going to help you get a post? Flying is all very well for fun, but I really think you'd better make up your mind to find a job as a secretary or something, don't you?' " However, fictional Marise found responsible aeronautical work rather more easily than the infinitely better qualified, real-life Amy Johnson: Marise became the only "lady instructor" at a flying school, presumably because she took to heart the male proprietor's advice – " 'no girl learning to fly is going to have the least bit of confidence in you unless you are wearing a smart set of white overalls, looking like Myrna Loy ... setting off to fly the Atlantic. ... ' " Marise later becomes involved in a Pacific island treasure hunt, in company with a general and a Lady Wilhelmina. (As well as fearfully affluent girls who piloted their own aeroplanes, titled people and high-ranking service officers appeared frequently in "G.O.P." fiction.)

One of the most successful women in aviation during the 1930s and '40s was Pauline Gower, the author of *Women With Wings*, who ran an air-taxi service with Dorothy Spicer before becoming commandant of women ferry pilots in the Air Transport Auxiliary, and a board member of British Overseas Airways Corporation. She wrote fiction for the "G.O.P." about girls flying their own biplanes, and later became its regular air correspondent. When Pauline Gower died in 1948 the magazine recorded in a whole page obituary "so keen was she on her 'G.O.P.' work that her last aviation article was written the day before she died".

The *Girl's Own Paper* was proud of its internationalism and its large circulation abroad. A world-wide club was organized, whose members saw their own photographs reproduced in the paper: they were invited to correspond with one another and to take part in varied literary, sewing, craft and gardening activities and competitions. Little of the disturbed political atmosphere of Europe in the mid '30s was reflected. Awareness of the true meaning of Fascism was growing at home through the activities of Mosley's British Union of Fascists and the influx of Jewish refugees escaping from persecution in Nazi Germany; yet in 1937 the "G.O.P." published a surprisingly enthusiastic article about the girls of the Hitler Youth organization in a series "Schooldays at Home and Abroad". As Stephen Spender has said in his book *Citizens In War – And After* (1945): "The Vicarage and the Women's Institute did not wake up to Fascism until the time of Munich." The "G.O.P." describes "The German Girls' League" as "the greatest in the world", having high aims "with regard to uniformity and self-denial". (Accepting guns instead of butter, in accordance with Göring's promises, perhaps?) Readers are introduced to "the rugged contours of the romantic valley of the Rhine" where the Gerdas and Grizelas in their youth camps are selflessly helping the Third Reich on its triumphant way by practising handicrafts, taking courses in physical education and household management, and spending much of their leisure time in making clothes for needy families. The *Girl's Own Paper* comments that "the sphere is of unquestioned feminine character", and " ... this organization helps to realize the Führer's programme with regard to his view of life".

In fact Hitler's philosophy was the ultimate expression of anti-feminism. He certainly believed that a woman's place was in the home, to produce numerous children to maintain his militaristic vision of an "Aryan"-dominated world. Birth control clinics in Germany were closed and the sale of contraceptives made a criminal offence. Hitler's sentimental glorification of motherhood – a bronze medal for four or five children, a silver for six or seven and gold for eight or more – was matched by his brutal repudiation of the idea of careers for women. Addressing the Women's Congress of the Nazi Party in 1934, he said: " 'We National Socialists have for many years guarded against the intrusion of women into political life, which in our view is a disgrace.' "[1] German women were forced out of political and professional life, jury service, trade unions and local government. The Nazi régime partially solved the unemployment problem of the early 1930s by taking work away from women, and giving it to jobless men. " ... the National Socialists who ... turned women out of their jobs to the derisive chant of 'Go back to pot and pan, then you will get a man', tried hard to put a halo round the heads of their Hausfrauen." Woman's only value, it seemed, was "to preserve the blood and to propagate the race". Hitler hated "emancipated" women as much as "effeminate" men, Jews, democrats and negroes, all of whom he saw as contributing to cultural and political decline.

Possibly because of its international readership the *Girl's Own Paper* seemed reluctant at first to take the war seriously. It was not alone in this: women in England and Germany were convinced in the autumn of 1939 that their men would be home in time for Christmas. Music-hall entertainers and schoolchildren adopted cheerful catch-phrases during the "phoney war"; spirits were kept up by the thought of hanging out one's washing "on the Siegfried Line" in the not far distant future. And as late as April 1940 the monthly editorials of the "G.O.P." were still philosophical, even dismissive, about the war: reference was made to a letter recently received from a Finnish girl, who wrote about the daily Russian air-raids. (Russia and Finland were then at war with each other, although of course Russia was not yet fighting Germany.) These were " ... nothing very awful. ... It is quite comfortable to have a pause of an hour or so, to sit in the shelter and to do handwork, knitting or something. ..." It was probably reassuring for readers to consider the air-raids to which they might one day be exposed in this casual light, rather than in terms of the slaughter at Barcelona and Guernica during the Spanish civil war. In January the editor had rallied her girls, in case they were inclined to "grouse" at the inconveniences of war: " ... I am going to imagine you all with expansive grins bearing 'it', if there is anything to bear, in true 'G.O.P.' style." There

[1] Katherine Thomas, *Women in Nazi Germany*, Gollancz, London, 1944

306

WORRALS FLIES AGAIN

by Captain W.E.JOHNS

Author of The "Biggles" books

HODDER & STOUGHTON LIMITED LONDON

Title page, 1942

was one inevitable wartime function which the paper did not underplay, and that was knitting, which could be recommended without reservation. Apart from the comforts it produced for various social groups (balaclavas for soldiers, blankets for refugees, etc) knitting, to girls' magazine editors, seemed an almost mystical rite which imbued its teenage participants with virtue. "If you have some spare wool and time to spare KNIT." Two months after the first appeal, when possibly its editorial offices had been almost buried under the "stacks and stacks" of six-inch-plain-knitted-squares-for-evacuee-blankets which it had solicited, the "G.O.P." diversified suggestions for ways in which girls could help the war effort. It stressed the value of vegetable growing.

This paper, with its interest in fact, fiction and pictures, provides the social historian with a fascinating record of life for girls growing up in wartime Britain: obviously conditions were far more austere than in pre-war days, but underlying hardships, destruction and fear was an extraordinary sense of excitement and community involvement. Pubescent girls were fortunate in lacking the mature person's deeper understanding of the implications of war. Aerial "dog-fights" were spectator sports to many children, for whom the Battle of Britain also provided the new and enthralling hobby of amassing collections of shrapnel from anti-aircraft shells. Reports of oppression and semi-starvation in Nazi-occupied countries merely served as a rallying cry for more knitting, sewing, allotment digging, salvage collecting, help for the Red Cross and with family shopping. (Young daughters were very useful when someone was required to wait in queues for foodstuffs and other articles in short supply.)

The shake-up of war brought people from widely differing groups into close social contact. Class barriers usually broke down in wardens' posts throughout the country and neighbours sharing fire-watching rotas often spoke to each other for the first time. Evacuation emphasized the incredible squalor in which many children from industrial areas had been living; for some of them, moving to safe areas in the country provided a decent environment and new opportunities, but it frequently highlighted the class-ridden structure of English life. In reception areas, rooms in "upper-class" houses often remained empty of evacuees, in spite of their being crowded into poorer homes. Angus Calder pin-points this in *The People's War*:

> In another case, the council protested that the town was full up and could take no more immigrants, but an official investigation showed that while working-class districts were, indeed, full, twenty-three town councillors had between them no fewer than seventy-six rooms to spare. There is no doubt that most working-class children and adults were happier to stay with their own kind of people. But there were places where this literally meant sleeping in double shifts. ... The moral was that status remained status, power remained power, and class remained class.

In June 1940 the "G.O.P." published "Other People's Ways", a story about wartime evacuees in a country village. The author was Joan Verney. An editorial note tells readers that "Lady Joan Verney [had been] a Woman of the Bedchamber ... from 1920. Her hobbies are photography, embroidery, and travel." Superficially this story is a plea for mutual tolerance between country hosts and town visitors. However the evacuated heroines are, of course, from well-to-do backgrounds, and soon on matey terms with fellow evacuees in the nearby home of the local squire, Sir Arnold Thompson. " 'We've been planted on poor Uncle ... it is hard on him, but if he didn't have us he might get dirty children with fleas, so he has to bear it!' " This is not exactly a touchstone of the national unity exhorted by the government. Lady Joan was fairly safe in the assumption that few of the "dirty children with fleas" would be buying the *Girl's Own Paper* at sixpence [2½p] a time: but perhaps she was unaware of the existence of free public libraries where the same flea-ridden juveniles were allowed access to reading rooms that took in the "G.O.P.", considered by many librarians to be more edifying than the cheaper girls' fiction papers.

In the first three years of the war the *Girl's Own Paper* excelled in its cover designs, which usually featured colour photographs of attractive adolescents. These cover girls exuded wholesomeness and vitality, whether they were peering laughingly through the strings of tennis racquets or wearing gym tunics with blouse sleeves purposefully rolled up and "Digging for Victory". "Typically English" models with golden page-boy bobs unruffled by their dog-walking, horse-riding, swimming, hockey or lacrosse, they might equally have symbolized the fictitious "racially-pure Aryan" ideal of the Hitler Youth. Complexions became even more glowing when in September 1940 the paper changed its covers from photographs to coloured illustrations (mostly by McKinlay). Against a Union Jack background each issue carried a vivid and glorified portrait of a young woman in uniform: the Red Cross, Auxiliary Fire Service, WRNS, WAAFS, ATS, Land Army and WVS were featured. This was part of the *Girl's Own Paper*'s recruiting drive which suddenly and passionately intensified after the Dunkirk evacuation at the end of May 1940.

Under the threat of invasion greater solidarity developed in Britain between different classes and different groups of workers. Writers of popular songs told us that in common with Mr Smith and Mr Brown, "the King was still in London Town", and the "G.O.P." endeavoured valiantly to emphasize this trend. "Most of you ... have evacuees in your homes or at your school. ... Well, here is something you can do at once. You can make life pleasanter for somebody else, whether you are an evacuee or a hostess." Fleas could now be ignored and attention given by rich and poor towards working together for survival. The sense of unity extended also to civilian immigrants from countries which Hitler had overrun, and to the "Free" Forces who escaped with them. Co-operation between the allies at a teenage level was expressed in the "G.O.P." in "Ici On Parle Français", a story by Frances Cowen showing how a refugee French girl was initially resented for her alien ways, but soon enthusiastically accepted by an English family. As children in various parts of England suddenly found that they now had school-mates from Belgium, Holland, the Scandinavian countries and France, emotive songs with which the BBC had familiarized them took on new meaning.

My sister and I remember still
A tulip garden by an old Dutch mill

And the home that was all our own until—
But we don't talk about that. ... [1]

In fact wartime children, both British and refugee, *did* "talk about that" – "that" being life in other European countries, before and after the imposition of the Nazi régime. For the first time in their lives English girls were meeting "foreigners": in our present multi-racial society it is sometimes difficult to remember that, before the last war, many children in working-class communities had never actually been in contact with anyone from abroad. Solidarity was later to embrace the awe-inspiring Russians, who unexpectedly became Britain's allies in June 1941 when Germany invaded the USSR. Whatever his political doubts, Churchill hastened to assure the Russians that their struggle was " ... the cause of free men and free peoples in every corner of the globe", and Mrs Churchill's Aid to Russia Fund raised £8 million. The average British man and woman were impressed beyond measure by the Stakhanovite efforts of Russian factory workers, the resistance of the Red Army and, most of all, the determination of peasants who burned their crops and homes rather than leave them for the invaders. "Russian Rose" was one of the more memorable pieces of popular music to come out of the war years. It reflected the warmth of the British people's response to Russia, as well as hinting at the future second front constantly demanded by Stalin. Variety artists could always be certain of thunderous applause when they sang about the ally who so uncompromisingly "scorched the earth that gave them birth ... ".

But before Russia's entry into the war, when Britain was on her own and facing the imminent possibility of defeat by German armies which had so far proved invincible everywhere else in Europe, the *Girl's Own Paper*'s editorial of September 1940 had expressed the country's total commitment to the elimination of Nazism. It was Dunkirk, that "victory in defeat" and mixture of humiliation and heroism, that finally shattered the last vestiges of the magazine's complacency. (Although the September issue was not published till three months after Dunkirk, the June, July and August issues were

[1] "My Sister and I", Campbell Connolly & Co., London

THE HOCKEY MATCH

WITH hair and girdles flying free,
  The eager forwards ran ;
They seemed like rushing infantry,
Each one marked by an enemy
  In the opposing " clan."

And close behind came halves to drive
  Or chase advancing foes ;
Then anxious backs would also strive,
The goalkeepers would " come alive "
  When any need arose !

All eyes were fixed upon the ball ;
  The sounds which filled all ears
Were hockey sounds known to us all—
The click of sticks, the captains' call,
  The whistle, and the cheers.

A tackle here, a bully there
  (This ever-changing sight !)
A pass, a dribble everywhere,
A corner, when all stand and stare,
  Then rush with all their might !

With every goal excitement grew,
  With each fresh bully came
Another chance to strive anew
To keep the ball and shoot it through
  And score to win the game.

*A Poem by Thelma Hamilton-Jones,
from* Girl's Own Paper, *January 1940*

almost certainly printed in advance of the Dunkirk evacuation and therefore unable to reflect its impact.) The editor's page carried a poem, "Dunkirk", commemorating the "little ships" that helped to bring home the British Expeditionary Force – "You'll be battered by bullets and riddled by shell, Are you ready to take an excursion to hell?" – and several exhortations to readers to help "the British come into their own, shed their aloofness and throw themselves with great gusto into this war for freedom". The "G.O.P." certainly abandoned its own aloofness with this issue: "We have all been shaken out of our ruts and we have all got to show what we are made of today as never before."

Flora Klickmann's Flowerpatch (see chapter 5) had been transformed into a vegetable-growing, salvage-collecting, fire-fighting, women's-services-recruiting battlefield. As well as being up against the bloody-mindedness of the British with their backs to the wall, Hitler now had to face the crusading vigour of the *Girl's Own Paper*. This was directed not only at Hitler but towards the male-oriented establishment at home, represented by Mr Ernest Bevin, who was then Minister of Labour. At a British and Professional Women's Luncheon one of the speakers pointed out that " ... many women ... still waiting for war-work ... had offered their brains and skill to Mr Bevin". The diners were told by the Minister of Labour " ... that the trouble lay in the fact that women had no talent for organizing". Ernie Bevin should have known better, and apparently Lady Astor, who was present at the luncheon, tackled him in "very spritely" terms. ("She looked very smart, by the way, in a well-cut black suit and a jolly little white hat.") The "G.O.P." editor endorsed Lady Astor's protests by saying, "Personally I think we should be conscripted like our brothers. Now I shall bring some brickbats on my head. Well, let them come ... ". (Her wish was eventually realized when in December 1941 desperate labour shortages forced Bevin to conscript women between the ages of twenty and thirty: they had the choice of entering the services or industry.)

The high spot of the paper's recruiting campaign for the women's services was its serialization from October 1940 of Captain W. E. Johns's *Worrals Of The WAAF*. Although every war produces its spate of heroic children's stories, Worrals was one of the few clearly defined fictional idols to emerge from the 1939-45 war. W. E. Johns, prolific author of the "Biggles" books, was a pilot in the Royal Flying Corps during the first world war, and a recruiting officer for the RAF during the second. To the *Girl's Own Paper* he represented an admirable compound of orthodoxly-accepted values and aeronautical panache. Worrals was created at the request of the Air Ministry to encourage girls to join up, and the "G.O.P." readership provided a fruitful source of new recruits. "Most of you ... have often wondered why your brothers have such fine, exciting stories as Biggles to read while you have to put up with dull stories about insipid females. Well, goodbye to all that, for the 'G.O.P.' which has blazed the trail through the ages, has persuaded Captain Johns to step in and give us something new for girls, something worth reading! Behold Worrals – she's emerged to do her bit in this war. ... " This announcement obviously was not only an indictment of the entire range of fiction provided by other girls' books and magazines, but of every previous issue (and woman author) of the *Girl's Own Paper.* Whether or not the advent of Worrals heralded the end of fictional "insipid females" in the "G.O.P.", Captain Johns's heroine aptly personified the patriotic fervour and frustrations which the war aroused in many teenage girls.

Worrals Of The WAAF was reprinted in book form, and sequels followed rapidly, many of which were first serialized in the "G.O.P.". The opening instalment introduces Flight Officer Joan Worralson (Worrals) bemoaning the fact that " 'Men can go off and fight, but girls – oh no' ". Worrals, only eighteen, is already fed up with her routine duties: " 'Four or five times a week for five months I've been taking battered Tiger-Moths back to the makers for reconditioning. It's about as exciting as pedalling a push-bike along an arterial road ... '." (She is suffering the same disillusionment as Amy Johnson and other skilled women pilots who in their early days with the Air Transport Auxiliary were allowed to ferry only old-fashioned machines: the advanced models were reserved for male aviators.) Flying an old Reliant, Worrals pushes her luck by shooting down a grey monoplane after intercepting a radio message urging British fighters to bring it down at all costs. Captain Johns's terse narrative always gives a sense of pace. Worrals – like Biggles – is not given to philosophizing or introspection: she gets on unemotionally with the job in hand. However, knowing that he was writing for girls whose work in the services would normally be non-combative, Johns frequently felt obliged to justify the killings or violent actions performed by Worrals, even at the expense of slackening his stories' tempo. Therefore when Worrals shoots down the monoplane she is portrayed with appropriately dry lips, parched throat and cold hands as she presses the machine gun button. " 'I've got to do it – this is war ... '."

By the time she is grounded Worrals has overcome her qualms, and is able to face her commanding officer with equilibrium. Squadron Leader McNavish, who resents women's participation in the services, receives her coldly: " 'As one pilot to another I congratulate you on your skill and initiative ... but officially, I must warn you that you simply must not do this sort of thing. ... Think what propaganda the enemy would make of the incident if it were learned that – er – ladies were now manning British fighter aircraft.' " Worrals retorts that the guns fired as well for her as for any male officer, and her CO is reduced to muttering, " 'Yes – er – no doubt, no doubt. Guns are like that; they have no discrimination.' " Captain Johns's colourful essays in feminism added spice to Worrals's adventures and struck responsive chords in girls who resented the fact that their brothers were allowed greater participation in the war than themselves. "G.O.P." readers too must have enjoyed his descriptions of Worrals grappling with the technicalities of aviation. "The machine lifted, hung for a moment, wallowing as if it might stall, and then went on as the engines picked up." At a time when the Battle of Britain fighter pilots had invested aeronautical achievement with Olympian splendour, the imagination of girls who had never ridden anything more demanding than bicycles must have lifted like the tails of Worrals's machines as she eased throttles, roared engines and sped her aeroplanes like arrows through the skies. Worrals constantly puts her technical knowledge to good use. When trapped in a plane with desperate German spies who are threatening her with an automatic, she grabs the controls and flies so low that they dare not touch her, knowing she would then suicidally crash the machine and kill them all. (She has nothing to lose, as she is being flown to a German concentration camp, " 'where they know how to control impetuous young women ... ' ".) In this first story Worrals successfully uncovers and captures a German spy ring, unaided by RAF officers to whom she confides her suspicions. These are contemptuously dismissed as a " 'woman's intuition getting out of control' ".

Thoughout the series Worrals's companion is another teenage WAAF officer, Betty Lovell (Frecks). Like so many English girls in the 1940s, Betty is addicted to Hollywood films, "the flicks", whose jargon she uses constantly in uneasy juxtaposition with RAF slang. Frecks is slower-witted than Worrals – " 'Say! ... Sure that goes for me, too ... ' " – and less intrepid – " 'I'm getting the heebie-jeebies ... ' ".

In the *Girl's Own Paper*, *Worrals Of The WAAF* was followed by *Worrals Carries On*. When it begins Worrals and Frecks are suspicious about a "Free Belgian" pilot at their base, whom they "tail" to Soho.

> "Funny place for him to come to, isn't it?" queried Frecks.
> "Not at all. After all, he's a foreigner," Worrals pointed out.

The next time they shadow him the girls are less successful. Fog, a 50-mile-an-hour wind and somewhat inexpert navigation bring about their forced landing in Occupied France – when they think they are near their own aerodrome. Surrounded by "coal-scuttle helmets", "guttural voices", jack-boots thumping "a sinister tempo on the roads" and other menaces, Worrals and Frecks take part in a further killing – that of a German soldier guarding the plane by which they hope to escape to England. Captain Johns sensed that a further bout of justification was required so Worrals confides: " ' ... people who barge into a war must expect to see something of the seamy side. Frankly, I'm only concerned with getting home, and if a few Huns get hurt on the way I shan't saturate my pillow with tears on their account.' " These were natural enough sentiments in wartime days when well-brought-up British girls *were* encouraged to "be beastly to the Germans".

Later in this book Worrals and Frecks volunteer to be parachuted back into France to rescue stranded British Army and Air Force personnel. This dangerous mission brings into the saga its first hint of romantic love – which Worrals vigorously and immediately extinguishes. Although romance flourished in wartime England, often bringing together unlikely couples, it apparently was not to be allowed to disrupt the image of wholesome virginity which Worrals projected to "G.O.P." readers, nor to inhibit the pace of her anti-Nazi activities. Flying Officer Bill Ashton, a dashing Spitfire pilot, desperately tells Worrals: " 'You know, kid, you mean an awful lot to me. If anything happened to you, I should never forgive myself.' " Worrals dismisses what Frecks calls " 'this sob-stuff' " by speaking sternly to her admirer: " 'Be yourself. You'll laugh at this nonsense in the morning.' "

Subsequent books take Worrals and Frecks to many theatres of war. Whether confronted by the Gestapo, the Japanese, swearing "Aussies", Middle-Eastern gun runners, slave dealers or mad white queens on remote Pacific islands they retain their sangfroid and, perhaps even more surprisingly, their virginal state. " 'They'll think twice before they murder a white woman ...' returned Worrals crisply," and " 'We don't deal with crooks' " (when threatened with slow death by a spear-hurling African tribe in *Worrals In The Wilds* [1947]). As well as human "baddies" the girls take in their stride rats, sharks, wild buffalo, rhinos, lions, bears and crocodiles. After particularly nerve shattering escapes from the Gestapo they steady themselves, not with cigarettes or tots of whisky, but with a packet of raisins or some "pre-war nut-milk chocolate". Action is all important and Messerschmitts, Zero fighters and Mitsubishi bombers enliven the atmosphere if things begin to flag. Some of Captain Johns's most arresting passages describe war in the skies, which are frequently "alive with flame and hurtling metal" or being scissored and quartered by searchlights hunting raiding aircraft.

Of course the *Girl's Own Paper* would not want healthy-minded girls like Worrals and Frecks to remain in uniform after the war had ended, but Captain Johns resisted establishment patterns of happily-ever-after domestication and allowed them to continue their adventures as flying private investigators. Equipped only with an obsolete aeroplane, an automatic and camping gear they take on the most hazardous assignments with enthusiasm, and there is never any mention of fees. Worrals's resentment of men becomes perhaps more intense as the series progresses: " 'To call a man by his first name is to put all sorts of conceited notions in his head' ", and " 'Who started the war, anyway? Men. Take a look at the world and see what a nice mess men have made of it. No wonder they had to appeal to women to help them out.' " (*Worrals In The Islands,* 1945.) And her attitude to killing became less inhibited. " 'I'll shoot you, you scum. I've killed far better men than you' ", (*Worrals In The Wilds*) and, when asked to find and arrest Anna Shultz, the Nazi "she-devil of the Sternberg Internment Camps" who was obviously based on real-life Irma Greese, "the blonde beast of Belsen" – " 'I'll hang her for you if you like – and so would any other woman who knows her ghastly record' ". (*Worrals In The Wastelands,* 1949.) Otherwise, when her adventures ended in the early 1950s, Worrals's character had not matured from the naïve, unswervingly British, overgrown schoolgirl of the first story in 1940.

Girls who read the *Girl's Own Paper* must have realized that if they joined the WAAF they were unlikely to have adventures as exciting as Worrals's. For those who wanted factual information there were endless articles describing life in the various women's services and voluntary organizations. But the WAAFs were given the most space (pictured handling barrage balloons and packing parachutes, etc.). As well as "Worrals", the "G.O.P." ran aviation features every month, sometimes covering four pages. Even when recruiting for the WAAF was temporarily suspended "owing to the rush of recruits", "Pilot" and Captain W. E. Johns were writing flying gossip in "The World On Wings – Between You And Me And The Joystick". Someone on the editorial staff must have been a flight addict: the June 1942 issue not only gave its readers the regular instalment of Worrals and "The World On Wings", but a further one-and-a-half pages on flying in "The Romance Of The Carrier

Pigeon" (and its vital war work). Even the religious page in that issue became airborne, under the heading of "The Winged Life" (the spirit winging its way to God, etc.) and it included Fay Inchfawn's poem "Power To Fly".

As early as June 1941 the "G.O.P." had drawn attention to the fact that although there was an Air Training Corps for boys no similar organization existed for girls, although individual, unrecognized units of a group calling itself the Women's Junior Air Corps were springing up. The paper encouraged pre-service-age readers to join this spare-time activity, and by 1942 was appealing for more and more leaders to meet the growing demand for officers from all over Britain. Another organization for girls who were too young to join the women's services was the Girls' Training Corps. The training it offered was similar to that of the WJAC, but many girls preferred the latter, whose uniform of airforce blue and grey suggested the *Per Ardua Ad Astra* image. In fact the WJAC volunteers who expected to become acquainted with the intricacies of navigation and aerodynamics were almost certain to be disappointed. Technical instruction was often confined to basic aircraft recognition and study of the Morse Code. Also a great deal of time was spent in the questionably useful pursuits of marching, drilling and saluting. The WJAC, in common with most other organizations for girls and women, naturally encouraged training in first aid and nursing but, however commendable, these courses seemed far removed from the world of aviation immortalized by "The Few". Just as WJAC members usually never saw the inside of an aeroplane, neither did their participation in this junior service bring them into contact with legendary RAF heroes: instead they had to make do with the company of adolescent boy enthusiasts in the ATC who linked up with WJAC recruits for joint church parades, sports days and dances.

The *Girl's Own Paper* in the 1940s contained fewer conventional school stories than in the previous decade, as girls at an early age were tending to lose interest in schooldays. They wanted to grow up and start work, which they felt would give them a greater sense of involvement in the war, with its indefinable energy and purposefulness. During 1941 and 1942 the paper published articles stressing the importance to readers of continuing their education so that they could help to rebuild English life after the war. But to many girls this seemed a remote and insipid prospect compared with joining one of the services, going into a factory or on the land. Britain was beset by official slogans which were designed to increase the war effort and maintain security. "G.O.P." heroines embodied these attitudes as they conscientiously strove to "Go To It", "Make Do And Mend" and "Dig For Victory", never forgetting that "Walls Have Ears", "Careless Talk Costs Lives" and they should "Be Like Dad And Keep 'MUM' ". (In fact fewer Mums were being "kept" by Dads than in pre-war days: government control of female labour from 1941 made it compulsory for most women, except those looking after small children, to undertake some form of war work, so plenty of mothers were now contributing wages as well as house-keeping energies to their homes.) "G.O.P." stories describing the restrictions created in young girls' social lives through blackouts and bombing conveyed an atmosphere far more authentic than the wish-fulfilment world of Worrals. School leavers starting work *did* have opportunities to get out and about, in spite of parental fears for their well-being in a Britain that was becoming increasingly packed with service-men of many different nationalities, who naturally looked for companionship and sex from local girls. It was the ten- to thirteen-year-old readers, still at school, who longed to do something more challenging than chopping up vegetables for British Restaurants or collecting paper for re-pulping. Phyllis Cooper, Frances Cowen and other regular "G.O.P." writers expressed their restlessness in a series of fictional cameos about girls chafing against domesticity and bursting to do their bit.

In Phyllis Cooper's "Black-out", the pixie-hooded heroine, illustrated in earnest conversation with a tin-hatted air raid warden, gives vent to this frustration: " 'I *hate* sewing, and I *loathe* knitting. ... I want to do something. Join the WAAFs or the Red Cross. ... Oh why, oh why, am I not a few years older.' " The kindly warden, whom she encounters when helping an old lady in the black-out, solves the problem of how to apply her excess energy – which she is soon throwing wholeheartedly into the production of vegetables from an allotment.

Illustrations by Phyllis Cooper to her story "Black-Out"
Girl's Own Paper, *December 1940*

" 'I do really think, Babs, that life's a howling wilderness,' " confides the leading character in Phyllis Mathewman's *Nancy And NARPAC*. Her outlet is eventually found in working for a "National ARP for Animals Committee", which gives first aid to pets hurt in the Blitz. (Even dogs, the hoary perennial tear-jerkers of girls' fiction, were invested with wartime heroics by the "G.O.P." Elizabeth Cross's "Paddy Finds A Family" describes how an unwanted dog finds himself a new family by digging out a grateful survivor who has been buried under the bombed rubble of a cottage.)

"A Matter Of Opinion", by Joan Rowland, is a slightly bizarre story about a mother and teenage daughter who are both staying at home, each for the other's sake. The daughter can eventually hold back no longer and signs on for the WAAF. At first terrified to tell her mother, she is amazed when that staid, domesticated lady reacts by "whirling her madly up and down the garden path", shedding "ten years in as many seconds" and announcing her own intention of rushing out immediately to join up.

However dramatically patterns of family life and society were disrupted by war, the *Girl's Own Paper* never lost its enthusiasm for the aristocracy, whose members in fact seemed even more appealing to authors when they abandoned tiaras for uniforms and welfare work. In the 1940s the "G.O.P." perpetuated the Victorian tradition of creating middle- and upper-class backgrounds for most of its heroines. In Joan Rowland's "Wanted A Job", eighteen-year-old Sally Gray says, " 'I haven't any experience in running a club ... but I do know how to run a large household, and I can manage a large staff of servants.' " Lady Joan Verney's *The Country Is So Dull* deals with Pip, the seventeen-year-old daughter of General Burnett. She is a WVS driver who is being sent to Devon to escape the London bombing: " ' ... really what upset Daddy ... I was out dancing at the Savoy and we had to stay in the shelter till nearly three, and when Robin Darcy took me home there was Daddy raging up and down, and the *things* he said to Robin! As if he could have helped the bomb ... '." Separated from Robin, Pip has to fall back on the companionship of a young army officer, Sir Maxwell Garner. It is not evacuees who preoccupy Lady Joan this time, but Polish refugees. Pip's aunt and hostess says plaintively, " 'I don't know why we let our houses to foreigners at all; I daresay they're all spies'." This story contains several stock ingredients of children's war fiction: the local conscientious objector, who naturally has to be portrayed as a weak and shifty character, a dog who instinctively recognizes and snaps at disguised fifth columnists, and foreign refugees who turn out to be working for the enemy.

"Siren Cinderella", by Frances Cowen, shows readers how Jennifer finds herself war-work, in spite of an over-protective guardian: " 'Remember [when Jennifer is going to a party] that if there is a siren you must return at once.' " Jennifer disobeys this curfew because she drives a slightly injured army officer back to base. He is not only a general but a "Sir" and using rank and personal prestige he manages to convince Jennifer's aunt that the girl should leave home to become his regular chauffeur. Frances Cowen produces further titled people for the delectation of readers in a spy story, "The Man In Air Force Blue", when they meet a Home Guard and the "stout, pleasant-faced woman by his side", who are Lord and Lady Morrow. And in her "Adventures Of A Ruby Pendant" the same author creates Lord Chesterfield, who organizes broadcasts for the troops, and Lady Muriel, whose forte is Red Cross concerts.

In "Sonia's Stolen Days" Frances Cowen leaves lords and ladies aside and features a Sixth Form girl who is simply "very, very rich. She took private riding lessons, had a visiting music master and actually a professional to train her in tennis." The war, to Sonia, seems at first nothing more than a nuisance, and an interruption of her socializing: " 'We were going to the South of France for Christmas, and we can't now. I don't suppose we shall even get any decent hunting.' " She finds herself stranded in London for a few days, leading the simple life at the Strand Palace. (She avoids the Savoy and the Berkeley where so many of her family and friends stay, as she wants to be on her own.) The theft of her handbag in the black-out throws her on to the mercy of two working-class sisters, whose worthiness transports Sonia from permanent, upper-class boredom to enthusiastic participation in the war effort. She joins the sisters in their work at a Forces canteen – not for officers but "poor ordinary people whom she had never met before".

Although the "G.O.P." occasionally gave a pat on the back to factory girls who made munitions, it preferred to set its stories of patriotic achievement in more easily glamorized occupations. The editor probably considered that her fairly affluent readers would be less likely than working-class girls to gravitate to the factory floor. They were encouraged rather to join the women's services, the Red Cross, WVS or Civil Defence. In spite of their sympathy with high-born characters, "G.O.P." fiction writers might have found it difficult to create situations where teenage heroines could hob-nob conveniently with honourables on the assembly line. It was easier to sprinkle them amongst officers in stories of service life, or voluntary helpers in fictional home-front adventures. Munitions work made heavy demands on its operatives: routines were tedious but exacting, and shifts were as long as eleven hours a day, especially during the months that followed the collapse of France. With desperate urgency the British army needed re-equipping and RAF losses during the Battle of Britain had to be made good. But if factory girls were the Cinderellas of the *Girl's Own Paper,* at least they were not forgotten by two other British institutions – Gracie Fields and the BBC. Gracie Fields jollied up their image in "The Thing-ummy Bob" song; the BBC endeavoured to enliven factory monotony with regular programmes of "Music While You Work", "Workers' Playtime", in which professional variety artists visited factory canteens, and "Works' Wonders", when workers themselves were able to perform on the air.

Women took to wearing trousers when working in factories, Civil Defence or turning out at night into their air-raid shelters. If the war can be credited with producing any fashion in women's clothes, it was the popularizing of trousers for women of all ages. This fashion has survived and become a way of life, in spite of the reversion from austerity to femininity in clothing in 1947, when Christian Dior's "New Look" was widely adopted. The paper's wartime fashion pages provide an interesting record of padded shouldered utility suits, wedge-heeled shoes, trousers, zippered siren-suits and scarf-turbans to protect hair from factory machinery. Complying with government exhortations to "Make Do And Mend", the "G.O.P." advised its readers to "Get to work on that tired wardrobe, and make it look brand new", with boleros cut from old frocks. These were decorated by crochet and daisy-stitch embroidery, or ric-rac braid trimming, which really came into its own during those days when clothes were rationed and constantly being remodelled.

Whatever the difficulties, readers were encouraged to improve their appearances. "War or no war, bombs or blitzes, there comes a time when a girl just has to make an extra effort" – and tackle lacklustre hair, necks grimy from heavy coat collars, dingy teeth, spots, blackheads and other perennial teenage beauty problems.

Because of paper shortages, the "G.O.P." became smaller and smaller as the war progressed, until it was a pocket-sized magazine with very small print. After the ending of hostilities in 1945 its tone changed and some of its wartime vitality disappeared. Girls were soon urged to turn their attention back from service life to more domestic realms. Religious homilies remained a regular feature, and in 1948 the Rev Henry T. Wigley's answer to a correspondent wanting to become a film actress was reminiscent of the rigid Victorian attitudes expressed in the *Girl's Own Paper* of the 1880s. (See chapter 5.) "Again and again in history the theatre has been corrupt and a source of moral damage to the Community." The Rev Wigley was particularly concerned about "the emotional disturbance inherent in the constant acting of scenes of intense love-making".

In 1948 the "G.O.P." changed its name to *Heiress,* and no longer attempted to cater for schoolgirls, but for young women in late teens and twenties. It was still a rather upper-class magazine: " 'I was thrilled when Ralph telephoned inviting me to the Hunt Ball' "- but, later – to Guy, another admirer -" ' ... dancing isn't everything. You ride much better than Ralph ...'." (Christine Pullein-Thompson). *Heiress* soon became a tired and watered-down women's magazine, without sufficient romance or glamour to last, and it finally ceased publication in 1956. The *Girl's Own Paper* had survived the war but not the peace.

XVI

New Vistas

"The bright, explosive carnation of a ballet-skirt projected under the edges of a face towel. In a corner the white blouse and pleated skirt of Madame hung behind a faded gray curtain. The room reeked of hard work."

(Zelda Fitzgerald, *Save Me The Waltz*)

TOWARDS THE END of the last century, the theatre began slowly to shed its loose-living associations. By the time of King Edward VII, children from all sections of society were encouraged to attend elocution and dancing classes, though in most cases these were expected merely to provide a gloss for their everyday behaviour. The small proportion of those who were being trained full-time at drama or ballet schools, in fact, were likely to be more serious and better-behaved than the majority who were not, since their careers – always a serious topic – had been decided on and had to be kept constantly in their minds. The well-chaperoned child star of impeccable propriety had been a feature of American film studios as far back as the early 1900s; but it was not until the 1920s in England that the middle-class images of model child and child actress or ballet dancer began to coalesce. Noel Streatfeild was the first children's author to express the theatre's increasing social respectability (despite the *Girl's Own Paper* which, as we have seen, maintained a contrary view as late as 1948) in a book which is respectable also from a literary point of view; and *Ballet Shoes*, which came out in 1936, remains the best example of the type of fiction which began with it – the family story with a theatrical bias.

It is appropriate that this book should use conventions of the media which provide its subject matter. It is stagey in the obvious sense of being about the preparation for careers on the stage, and also in the sense of being contrived; but the contrivance is that of a fairy tale, which is appropriate both for a children's book and for the theatre. The limitations imposed by a theatrical form are made to work here as a valid part of the author's whole disciplined approach. In the theatre, for example, every line must be relevant, and it is from the strict relevance of Noel Streatfeild's expression that much of her humour derives, since the most direct conclusions (particularly when reached by a child) usually are also the wittiest. The three orphaned children who are the book's central figures have been acquired as babies by an eccentric gentleman in the course of separate fossil-hunting expeditions: when they are in need of a surname they decide to call themselves Fossil. This emphasizes their relationship with this person (who is an unstated old fossil); so does their nickname for him, Gum (a contraction of Great Uncle Matthew; he has left them to be brought up by his great-niece, Sylvia).

Gum fails to return from an expedition and money is running short, when the children are offered places at the Children's Academy of Dancing and Stage Training. The title *Ballet Shoes* perhaps is not the most apt one for this book, since only one child – Posy – has ambitions to be a dancer; but it is to Posy's ambitions that everything in the end is subordinated, including the artistic integrity of the oldest child. Pauline,

A picnic.
Drawn by Ruth Gervis for Ballet Shoes *(frontispiece)*

who is a better stage than film actress, signs a five-year contract to work in Hollywood so that she can pay for Posy's training in Czechoslovakia. In Posy, the economy of the author's method of presentation is seen at its most stringent. Posy not only has no characteristic which does not relate to her dancing, she has no existence outside of a ballet-school context. She is simply the most basic idea of a ballet dancer embodied, and for this reason the author cuts out the "sensitive", soul-searching, self-realizing processes which so weakened the presentation of other theatrical or musical children (Kit Haverard, for instance, in Elfreda Vipont's *The Lark In The Morn*). Posy is ruthless, exhibitionist, and these qualities are implied to be an effect of her startling ability. She remains, however, a charming fairy-tale figure. Noel Streatfeild often introduces a clichéd image or character trait only to give it an enlivening twist: here, the Russian child, Petrova, is the one who is *not* a dancer; "Madame" is there, imperial Russian to the soles of her dancer's feet, but she does not speak in the dreadful broken English common to most children's-book foreigners; Gum reappears in the last chapter, but is not in time to keep the family from splitting up, nor to prevent the sale of their orderly and sedate house in the Cromwell Road. Nana, bulky, respectable and insular, is the person who will accompany Posy to Czechoslovakia.

Not the least feature of the book's skilful construction is the character of Petrova Fossil; she is of a mechanical turn of mind, which provides a balance for the stage enthusiasm of the other two, without in the least upsetting the theatrical bias of the book as a whole. Petrova "thought the rehearsals a frightful bore, but she brought her handbook on aeroplanes with her, and when not wanted for the fairy scenes, or to work at one of the innumerable ballets, she would curl up in a corner, and study it".

Petrova's obsession with cars and aeroplanes is an offshoot of the short-lived adulation which, in the '20s and '30s, was accorded to women who made their mark as aviators, explorers, engineers: the glamour of these as professions for women was related to their apparent unsuitability, to the potent attractiveness of the exception which is held to prove the rule. Naturally women who succeeded in these fields were exceptional; so were men, for that matter, but in their case success did not have the additional spectacular quality of a dog on its hind legs, walking *well*. Women sometimes had to pay for the disproportionate prestige which surrounded their achievements in unlikely professions by having it obscure its source: Amy Johnson, for instance, found herself unemployable in a "serious" aviational capacity. (See p. 304). The idea of women as mechanics or electricians lost much of its singularity during the war, when it became a commonplace; and in the post-war rash of propaganda designed to promote the return of all those working women to the home, occupations involving a high degree of technical skill became unfashionable.

With the three Fossils, however, Noel Streatfeild has managed to indicate a whole range of occupational possibilities open to girls; she even suggests that Petrova's ambition may be the most worthwhile:

> "Fancy," Petrova said, "me. You'd think I'd be the one to do nothing at all."
>
> Pauline shook her head. "I wouldn't. I've always thought you were the one that might. Film stars and dancers are nice things to be, but they aren't important."

What *was* important, to Noel Streatfeild and her readers, was an image of child stars – Wintle's, or Lila White's, or anyone else's, Wonders – which had fascinated the author since the time when, as a child, she had been taken to see a matinée on the pier at Eastbourne. Speculation about the origin and lives of the glittery, sequined little performers ("From where did these extraordinary children come, who led such different lives from their own?"[1]) provided the germ for many of her books; her own experience of drama school and as a repertory actress (described in *Away From the Vicarage*, 1965) ensured a background authenticity which imposes order even on the least realistic of her plots. *Ballet Shoes* consciously avoids realism in its treatment of character; *Tennis Shoes* (1937), which followed

[1] Noel Streatfeild, *A Vicarage Family,* 1963

it, contains as its star the first of her series of difficult, self-opinionated, prickly children who *are* real, in the sense that even in outline they are recognizable. (She was to perfect this type in Jane Winter in *The Painted Garden*, 1949.) Nicky Heath trains to be a tennis champion in secret; she cannot bear it to be known that she requires training: "If anybody came out she would lie down on her racket and pretend to be doing nothing. ... She wanted them to think she was just as lazy as ever, and became good by luck."

Noel Streatfeild took something of a risk with Nicky Heath: readers at the time were not used to heroines who behaved in a way which was consistently opposed to the principles of team spirit, self-effacement, thoughtfulness for others, and so on. None of the other characters is strong enough to shift attention away from perverse Nicky. She is surrounded with siblings who are superficially more attractive; but these too are less than understanding in their treatment of their sister. Susan and Jim are twins, wrapped up in one another; David is the prototype for another character, this time a minor one, which Noel Streatfeild was to use as a recurrent motif: the eccentric toddler. (One, in *Party Frock,* 1946, prefaces every sentence with "My dear", so that he sounds like an old quean.) In this case his distinctiveness takes the form of using long words:

> "Nicky has a nat'ral aptichude."
> ... Nicky turned to the twins.
> "What's an 'aptichude'?"
> Neither of them had the least idea.
> "I should think it's another word for conceit," Jim suggested. "And about right, too."

The important point that *Tennis Shoes* makes is untypical: it is that "team spirit" is not conducive to individual achievement. Nicky comes out on top because of her perky, unsuppressible egotism; she has a self-assured disregard for conformist pressures which exasperates her sister:

The school was divided into four houses. The marks of

everybody in each house ... were added together and a cup was given to the top house every term. The result was that St. Clair's was full of girls struggling to get to the top of their class and to win their colours. In fact, almost all the school but Nicky. Susan did her best to make her try.

"But you must see how you are letting your house down by always being at the bottom of your form."

Nicky would look aggravatingly vague.

"What house?"

"You know quite well it's St. Catherine's, Nicky. ..."

This was written at a time when girls were being inundated with fiction which urged the suppression of one's own objectives and the promotion of everyone else's. The mythology of the best house in the school, the best team in the neighbourhood, the best school in the country, implied above all a concerted effort in which every girl was expected to do her bit, but in which no one personality was conceded to be of more ultimate importance than any other. As a corollary, other people's achievements could be applauded, but it was "bad form" to relish one's own. Nicky's "unsporting" behaviour culminates in an incident which takes place when she is playing in a county junior championship match: she serves a double fault, flings down her tennis racket, and stamps her foot. Her family is outraged: "As one person they got up and walked out."

The lecture from her father which follows fails to subdue Nicky, who has won the match: "She helped herself to a piece of bread and butter. She took a bite. Then she grinned at her father. 'Miss N. Heath, the pocket star, is very grieved. It won't occur again.' " This is the nearest she can come to admitting herself to be in the wrong – we're a long way here from the remorseful, reorientated outlook of the usual puffed-up child who's been made to see the awfulness of her behaviour. The whole book, in fact, is an argument for the special treatment of special people – in spite of the explicit denial of this which occurs on the last page:

"Meringues! For all of us?" asked David anxiously. "Or

just Nicky?" Annie snorted.

"All of you, of course. ... There's no favourites in this house."

Tennis Shoes was followed by *The Circus is Coming* (1938). Again, the background is meticulously observed; again, the two children who are its chief characters are treated fairly – so fairly, in fact, that they are not endowed with any special capabilities. Peter and Santa, brought up to be "a couple of ninnies" by a misguided aunt, have run away to join their uncle, Gus, who is a clown in a circus. Gus is off-hand, non-committal about what he plans to do with them; they are hardly aware of the disruption which they have caused in his well-ordered existence. In the end, they are fitted out with training schemes: Peter prepares to be a groom, Santa a gymnast – but only because in that environment there is no place for anyone who does not work.

That principle can be shown to apply with equal force in a wider social context: almost all Noel Streatfeild's books are concerned with children who make the most of their abilities, in order to earn money or simply as a means of self-expression. (Her performing children may be of either sex, though usually they are girls; no distinction is made between girls' ambitions and boys', and unlike most other "career" stories, there is no reference in Noel Streatfeild to the matrimonial advantages of any profession. Even pretty girls of sixteen or so never consider that they may be other than self-supporting, and certainly no ambitious child sets an artificial limit to the duration of her chosen career.) Two exceptions are *The House in Cornwall* [1] (1940) an unremarkable adventure story involving a kidnapped prince, and the more successful wartime *Children of Primrose Lane* (1941), in which a group of resourceful working-class London children capture a spy: the actual capture is effected by two girls who wrap him up in a rug and sit on him. If spies have to be caught, this is obviously the way to do it: with panache, exuberance, and a dogged British

[1] This was serialized in the *Girl's Own Paper* 1939-40; it was also written at a time when Noel Streatfeild's own war work left her with no time to carry out her usual thorough research.

determination: " ' ... if six English children aren't as good and better than one German man we might as well give up fighting the war.' " This type of thumbs-up, Dad's Army phraseology was used widely as part of the national effort to keep up morale. The mood in this country in 1941 was very much one of doing one's bit, the blunter aspects of which are likely to be conveyed in a light-hearted children's book: "Since he had been permanently a soldier, he had changed a lot, and had become cheerful and funny about almost everything." However, patriotism here is as muted as possible; only once is the business of spy-catching acknowledged to be more than an

Over the wall.
Marcia Lane Foster
illustrates The Children of Primrose Lane *(frontispiece)*

exhilarating romp: "It was on the tip of her tongue to stop Millie, with her play-acting and her posturing, and make her think. Then suddenly she knew that that would be both silly and wrong. It was good that people of nine and ten should be able to think of things as games when they were not."

The character of Millie Evans, the child horror in this book, is adjusted precisely to the requisite social level. Where the middle-class children of the other books are self-assertive and contrary, Millie is pert, self-satisfied, curled and frilled by the kind of mother who likes a good cry at the pictures. "Our Millie" whines if anyone speaks crossly to her: " 'There's no need to be unkind: I'm only little, and I've done everything so far.' " She can behave like a slightly less crudely comic version of Violet Elizabeth Bott (see p. 246); but the other five children, who conform more or less to an ideal of childhood unpretentiousness, will not put up with any kind of showing off:

Millie looked silly and spoke in a lisp which she had not really got: "I do think that cream buns are the nicest nice fings."

Sally answered for them all: "There's nothing wrong with cream buns, Millie Evans, but you don't need to talk in that sloppy voice about them."

It is an index of Noel Streatfeild's skill that she can create awful children and proceed to make them likeable, without altering their characters in any radical way. (Incidentally, the qualities which *make* Millie awful are precisely those which tend to be imposed on pretty little girls by adults who subscribe to the most conservative theory of femininity: coyness, sugary sweetness, flirtatiousness, an ability to simper and a habit of trading on their good looks. Millie can be as sensible as anyone, but because she *is* clever she understands that in certain circumstances it pays off to appear silly.) Nicky, Millie and the others come off not simply because they are amusing or true-to-type; they are acceptable almost on their own terms. (The qualification is necessary because their own terms *are* inflated: this is part of their awfulness.) Technically, this is achieved because their positive qualities are shown in action, not merely stated; on a realistic level because often they *do* have something to be conceited about; and morally, because the origins of their ill-adjustment are suggested. Jane Winter (*The Painted Garden*, 1949) suffers from acute resentment of the fact that her brother and sister are more obviously talented than she is: "She couldn't do anything, not anything at all, and she was the only plain Winter." When she is chosen to play the part of Mary in a film version of *The Secret Garden* she makes herself insufferable by lording it over everyone, on the set and off. She's not treated with the respect which she considers her due: "Unfortunately for Jane her way of trying to keep her end up when she felt it was down was to be truculent and unpleasant."

Jane does not blossom into an accomplished actress. She's been considered suitable for this part only because of her natural resemblance to spoilt, cantankerous Mary at the start of Frances Hodgson Burnett's story; she is able to convey the sulky aggressiveness of Mary with a minimum of acting. The transformation effected in Mary's nature is not repeated in Jane; the book's moral implications are more subtle than that. "Rachel had plenty of time to notice Jane and be surprised about her. 'How queer,' she thought, 'now she really is acting Mary and they're pleased with her, she's nicer instead of worse.' " It is, of course, the satisfaction which Jane gets from having done something well which makes her nicer; there is no suggestion that the niceness will remain. What she really craves is appreciation; this is a common, but not a "nice" trait. At its most tangible, vulgar and extravagant level, appreciation takes the form of orchids – " 'Hundreds of them! Real, film star flowers.' " It is at the point when these are presented to Jane – incidentally, the end of the book – that her isolated acting success and her sense of personal worth can crystallize, to become something that is safely over, but which has had its effect. Jane's original ambition was to train dogs; even here, there is no pandering to the readers' expectations of easy fulfilment. The boy who plays Dickon in the film, one of the few people whom Jane likes, presents her with a reed pipe like the one he uses to tame wild animals. However, "To play pipes needs patience and a certain natural ability. Jane had neither." She makes no progress with her pipe playing, and obviously is in for a disillusionment when she tries it out on real animals.

The setting for *The Painted Garden* is California; two minor characters in the book are Pauline and Posy Fossil, who have grown up without any of the fuss, mawkishness or annoying unrealism which has attended the ageing of innumerable other children's-book characters. They remain fantasy figures, self-sufficient and unbothered by emotional troubles. Again, if people in children's books must grow up, this is one of the two ways in which it can be done: complete artificiality is necessary, or complete realism (the latter need not involve explicit physical detail; its success can be measured by what it can convey by suggestion, so that its effect on each reader will depend on the reader's experience. Two writers who excel at this kind of children's-book realism are Alan Garner and William Mayne: see chapter 19). It is the in-between course which tends to result in over-blown sentimentality, hesitancy, or falseness of tone.

After *The Painted Garden* there is a slight but perceptible falling off in Noel Streatfeild's style. (Perhaps this was inevitable; *The Painted Garden* provided a standard which could not easily be maintained.) *White Boots* (1951) is a lightweight but competent tale of two young ice skaters. One has been brought up to be a champion – " 'Pushed here in a pram, she was, by her nanny' "; the other builds herself up steadily by unostentatious hard work. The author's admirable restraint is still in evidence: there is no spectacular success for Harriet, merely one or two indications that she *may* do well. *White Boots* is less successful than some of the earlier books chiefly because its subject matter to a certain extent has had an influence on its treatment; the kind of light, superficial glamour which adheres to ice skating, ballroom dancing, circus or music-hall performances, certain types of water sports such as surfing, has crept into the writing of this book. The author's detachment has receded by several degrees, which makes for a lessening in the sharpness of outline. Even the name Lalla Moore is almost too authentic in this context for an ice-skating child: it is neither outrageously idiosyncratic, like Posy Fossil, nor determinedly unpretentious, like Jane Winter. It imparts to the book its own philistine connotations.

The encroaching vulgarity in Noel Streatfeild's books culminates in the sleeveless black plastic mini-dresses which are worn by Gemma (another unfortunate name, this time because it was unfashionable at the time when the character was conceived) Bow, an ex-film star, and her two cousins, during performances of the sub-pop group into which they have formed themselves. In the four Gemma books there is hardly a memorable episode: you get the usual near-fatal accident (near-fatal this time in terms of career, not life); the usual end-of-term play in which actress Gemma shines; the usual singing and ballet-dancing children; and a boring small boy whose only enthusiasm is for "swirling" tunes (perhaps it is because this word is unusual that it seems to be spattered all over the text). The Gemma books are propped up by their many references to contemporary facts of life: Headstone Comprehensive; kidney machines; television advertising. The children even speak occasionally in a diluted pop-world jargon: " 'I don't need a room for my thing and Lydia does' ". For this reason they may acquire a sociological interest. *Ballet Shoes* and certain other of Noel Streatfeild's better books, however, were not at any time considered out-of-date.

This is not to minimize the effect of their historical evocations, but simply to suggest that these are not detachable from the themes of the books. The victory atmosphere of *Party Frock,* the mood conjured up by the idea of a circus at Carlisle on a wet Saturday afternoon in the 1930s, have a mysteriously compelling, cohering function. Perhaps the flashy, grease-paint ambience of a stage training academy needed to be balanced by a way of life as highly regulated as the Fossil sisters'. This, in its turn, is part of a wider orderliness which has all but disappeared, and this makes a similar theme more difficult to treat effectively in the 1960s, without a great deal of literary adjustment.

Other writers who took the stage, ballet dancing, concert playing or an associated profession for their basic theme include Pamela Brown, Kitty Barne, Elfrida Vipont, Lorna Hill. The most notable thing about Pamela Brown's first book, *The Swish of the Curtain* (1941), is that part of it was written when she was fourteen. This may explain, but hardly justifies, the book's persistent tonelessness. Pamela Brown has not exploited her age but she has been unable to get away from it, so that the book has neither the quality of consciously indulged precocity which makes, for example, *The Young Visiters* acceptable, if only as an oddity, nor the competence which can come only from experience. In *The Swish of the Curtain* characterization is of the most rudimentary; the seven young people (of both sexes) who are the book's chief characters are scarcely differentiated: each may have a particular theatrical ambition, but this is hardly sufficient to communicate a sense of their separate identities. With the would-be horribly comic Mrs Potter-Smith, Pamela Brown fails completely; this lady's gushing viciousness is wooden and implausible, as though the author had observed and reproduced the verbal mannerisms of a common farcical type, without having the least grasp of the technical backing needed to support it. Similarly, Maddy's way of dealing with Mrs Potter-Smith, a zany, free-association rudeness, is put over with self-conscious stylization.

The doings of Maddy, the youngest and most outspoken member of the Blue Door amateur theatrical company, are the subject of Pamela Brown's next book, *Maddy Alone* (1945). Like Jane Winter (see above) Maddy is chosen to play the leading part in a film; unlike Noel Streatfeild, Pamela Brown has not bothered to enliven her film-set background with one convincing detail. Neither is her heroine capable of the sustained, logically assessed behaviour pattern of Jane. Twelve-year-old, untrained Maddy never falters in her presentation of a difficult, sixteenth-century character; her aesthetic judgements are unrealistically pointed: " 'It's not a very nice castle. It's a terrible castle. And if you think I'm going to act in the same film with it you're very much mistaken.' " She refuses to yield an inch, is the despair of her stage-Dutch director (" 'At effery turn a headache she gif me' "), barges her way into the home of the local lord-of-the-manor (an archetypal old body in gardening trousers) and persuades him to hand over his castle to the film company (" 'Zis is too true to be goot' "). The film is a splendid success: "New Child Star – Madelaine Fayne Makes Hit."

Maddy's brashness is on a par with the author's brash approach to the whole business of presenting character. Every conceivable stereotype[1] puts in an appearance: at drama school (*Golden Pavements*, 1947) there is Auriole, the gold-digging beauty in "scarlet jumper and emerald slacks" who ensnares impressionable Nigel until Lyn steps in to tell her that Nigel's money is running out:

> " ... Anyhow it will *have* to stop soon, because Nigel is absolutely broke."
>
> "Well thanks, dear, for telling me. Saves me wasting my time, doesn't it?" And Auriole sailed down the stairs to lavish her attentions on one of the old Etonians from the beginners' class.

There is the fierce, ugly but talented girl who works as a waitress to pay her way through drama school – "The only one who showed

---

[1] Other writers, notably Richmal Crompton (see p. 244-45), have used stereotyped figures to comic effect; Pamela Brown merely records the most banal constituent of each.

any spark of genius to warm Mrs Seymore's heart". In *The Swish of the Curtain* the most important character after the children is a bishop, complete with gaiters and liberal opinions: "I consider, Mrs Fayne, that there is no more evil in the theatre than in any other walk of life."

Perhaps there is a sociological point in having a bishop come out in favour of acting as a career: the Church's ultimate seal of approval stamped finally on this traditionally amoral profession. The farcical association of bishops with actresses persists, however, overlaid with faint echoes from Trollope: Fenchester (really Colchester, where Pamela Brown grew up) has at least a syllabic connection with Barchester (the only *literary* quality of Trollope's to which Pamela Brown approximates is his dullness). The fusion of the two, Victorian author and Whitehall clergyman, is in the endearing remark of the real-life bishop who announced that he liked nothing better than to spend an hour or two on the bed with his favourite Trollope. The nearest Pamela Brown can come to this is in the episode when Maddy tells two nosey old "spinsters" that this particular bishop is her father: "It's all right ... when father's sober. But when he's not – my goodness!"

What is evident in the Blue Door books is the characters', and by extension the author's, heartfelt enthusiasm for the stage. This is not converted into an enhancing undercurrent, however – which would have required a disciplined approach of which Pamela Brown was not capable – but is presented crudely. A common result of an author's imputation of "sensitivity" to a character is a piece of insensitive prose: "They walked home through the dark streets, arm in arm and in an uplifted mood. The stars were out, and there was a shaving of a moon. Lyn gazed up into the sky. 'Please God,' she prayed, 'make me an actress.' "

Kitty Barne and Elfrida Vipont also get carried away by their heroines' artistic pretensions. (This, of course, is where Noel Streatfeild triumphs: she is able to convey enthusiasm, even total dedication, without the least suggestion of rapture or intensity. Any manifestation of either in a Noel Streatfeild character would lead her friends, in the author's succinct phrase, to "make noises as if they were being sick".) Karen, in Kitty Barne's otherwise unexceptionable *She Shall Have Music* (1942), has an unfortunate tendency to "soar to the skies with joy"; this, however, is balanced by the book's main point, which is that ostentation on a concert platform is deplorable. Musical Karen gets into the hands of a well-meaning but vulgar pianist:

> Aunt Anne, knitting by the fire, was wearing her watchful parrot expression.
> "What do you go screwing up your poor handkerchief like that for? You're making it very dirty."
> "It's for my nervous tension," replied Karen.
> "Your *what*?"
> Unable to explain further, Karen took refuge in: "That's what Rosalba said."
> An enormous sniff shook Aunt Anne from stem to stern.

And she has to go through the traumatic experience of being given no marks in an open contest – "terrible style" – before her talent can find an appropriate outlet.

Kit Haverard, in Elfrida Vipont's *The Lark in the Morn* (1948), has a similar set-back: another "silly fool of a woman" encourages her to stand up in public and sing a difficult song ("Voi Che Sapete") before she is ready. This book gets off to a fairly lively start, but quickly deteriorates after the first few pages. Depressing Quaker undertones are matched with an enervating lushness which creeps into the prose: "The song came to an end, but the singer still held the room. Papa Andreas turned the page with a smile. 'Terry, my boy,' said he, 'some day you may be an artist!' and slipped quietly into the first bars of 'Nacht und Traume'. Kit closed her eyes. It was almost too lovely to be real."

"Quietly" is a key word; in *The Lark in the Morn* and its sequel there is a great deal of quiet, too-deep-to-be-expressed, emotion. When it *is* expressed, it is, unfortunately, shoddy in style and meaningless in content: "Cousin Charles reminded them all of the adventure of married life, and how all experience, whether of joy or sorrow, should enrich and beautify it." Everything in the books is sweetened and laid on thick, including the martyrdom, in *The Lark on the Wing*, of "Crazy" Laurence Cray, an updated guitar-playing missionary who is stabbed to death in "the stony wastes of Chihar": "Laurence was alone no longer. He was part of the great multitude who had fought the good fight, fearing no evil because they walked with God. ... The house of the Lord was eternal, and Laurence Cray was living in it still, as he had always lived in it." This reads like a throwback to the "moral" tale of the last century, which persistently sentimentalized, in spiritual or affectedly innocent terms, the fact of death. In spite of its 1940s London setting, *The Lark on the Wing* luxuriates with Edwardian intensity in all the plushy feelings which are the literary equivalent of Kit's songs. Even the hard core of the books, Kit's determination to be a singer in spite of discouragement from relatives, is subjected to unnecessary dramatization:

> "Well?" smiled Papa Andreas, as he took her hand. "Now can you tell me what is in your mind?"
>
> "And now do you know what you want to do?" asked Miss Priestly.
>
> "Yes," answered Kit with her head held high. "Yes, I know now. I'm going to sing!" She looked very like Janey. Her eyes were full of tears.

This carries with it a negation of its own point: all the implications of self-awareness, discipline, intelligence, which should have accompanied Kit's decision are lost in the inflated emotionalism of its expression.

Girls with a feeling for ballet dancing, an emotional attitude to horses and a taste for magazine fiction of the fluffiest type, can gratify all three simultaneously by reading the books of Lorna Hill. These romanticized tales of Sadler's Wells must owe their continuing popularity to the scope which they offer for an orgy of self-indulgence; by concentrating on the most common adolescent fantasy images the author has made sure of appealing to the most widely dispersed qualities in her readership – that is, the least discriminating.

In America, the theme of the stage-struck adolescent was particularly relevant; from 1920 on, thousands of girls with acting ambitions converged on Hollywood, where only a handful could hope to achieve any kind of recognition. As in England, however, a distinction was made between acting on the "legitimate" stage and acting for films; much of the opprobrium in which the former had been held during the last century was transferred to the latter, and persisted as long as the cinema could be regarded as a new-fangled medium, disseminating nothing but its own brand of trashy glamour. Stage actresses in children's books were sometimes allowed to be "great"; while film stars were represented as bitchy, wide-eyed and stupid – an unreasonable assessment, since without at least basic intelligence they would hardly have succeeded in an overcrowded profession. A whole set of moral implications was grafted on to a weakness for the cinema; girls who aped film stars were subjected to incessant criticism from Church, family, educational or other authoritarian sources. As far as an actress was concerned, her moral worth could be assessed directly in proportion to her preference for the stage, which was "real", down-to-earth, and implied a willingness to work. By contrast, the nature of the cinema was to impress by a kind of trickery; it involved a professionalism which was ethically suspect. Noel Streatfeild's Pauline Fossil retains a faint but ineradicable contempt for film acting [1], and Pamela Brown's Madelaine Fayne high-handedly dismisses the vehicle of her astonishing success (see above) as "only" a film.

Helen Dore Boylston, in *Carol Goes on the Stage* (1943; the American title was *Carol Goes Backstage*) and its sequel, *Carol in Repertory*, contrived to make her heroine at once archetypal and exceptional (this, of course, is what all successful "career" stories do): she provides a convenient literary embodiment for all those amorphous hankerings after a dramatic career. This does not follow automatically with every theatrical heroine; it requires recognition of the most basic qualities with which young theatre enthusiasts can identify, and the technical expertise to weld them together in a

[1] She expresses it, however, in *The Painted Garden*, a book which presents one of the least biased views of the film industry.

well-structured setting. Helen Dore Boylston's facility in these areas is matched by her deficiency in another: she can't resist cliché, both of expression ("Carol had already learned that theatre people are the kindest and most warm-hearted of any profession") and situation: her light-romantic relief centres either on a featureless young man who is pleasant to begin with, or one who is sullen, ill-mannered and sardonic, but gradually reveals a more attractive facet of his personality. Mike Horodinsky in the Carol books is an example of the second type:

> "But my *dear*," said Julia, shocked, "he's up from the *Peo*ple! I mean, he's risen above his environment."
> "He hasn't risen above any environment that I ever heard of," Carol said. "And he's got a long, tough pull before he even reaches the level of the People. *I* think he's disgusting, and the less I see of him the better!"

Readers of magazine stories will realize at once that this is a prelude to "Oh, Mike! Do you really think so?"

The first type of male lead, which provides less scope for crude dramatic development, is represented by Dr Barry in the same author's Sue Barton series. That Sue Barton was even more popular than Carol, both in America and England (more than half a million English hardback copies sold, according to the blurb of a recent edition), may be attributable simply to the fact that the nursing profession is open to a far wider range of applicants. Where the successful actress *has* to be exceptional, the nurse is essentially ordinary; she is also essential, in a fundamental sense, and bound up in her everyday life with matters of life and death. When nursing is invested with a degree of glamour comparable to that of the theatre, this is bound to go a long way towards making it attractive to readers, either as a profession for themselves or as one whose members are particularly deserving of respect, and also to effect an upgrading in the social position of nurses. Their moral status is already inextricable from a definition of nursing: "to care for the sick" is one of the seven beatitudes of the Catholic Church. "Our Lady" in this context carries a lamp; and Helen Dore Boylston has just managed to squeeze a supporting first-hand reference to Florence Nightingale into *Sue Barton – Student Nurse* (1939). A 92-year-old patient, once a drummer boy at Balaclava, remembers: " 'I seen her – on her knees – in th' dirt beside us – dressin' our wounds – hours at – a – a stretch – lovely young thing – she was – slim – an' gentle ...'." (Florence Nightingale was over 30 when she went to the Crimea, and on the stout side.) This is the traditional view of Florence Nightingale, expressed with tear-jerking simplicity, and the author has brought it in to reinforce her own glorified version of hospital life. Nursing is never treated merely as a *job* – and often a pretty revolting one at that; an effect of the emphasis on its vocational, almost holy, aspects, is the suppression of all the distasteful facts of life on the wards – bedpans, blood, guts, vomit, the shocking processes of dying. Rather, these are absorbed into the sweetened whole ethic of nursing, implicit in the esteem in which its practitioners are supposed to be held.

However, the gap between the reality and the cleaned-up, children's-book view is more irritatingly apparent here than it is, for example, in books which deal with acting – which lends itself more readily to glamorization. Nothing is *less* glamorous than sickness; yet almost every kind of cheap serial featuring hospitals proves enormously popular, and not only with adolescents – *Dr Kildare* and *Emergency Ward 10* on television, for instance. There are, of course, a number of obvious reasons for this: hospital personnel are concerned with "ordinary people" whose problems have suddenly assumed tremendous interest; there is the unpredictability factor, which relieves nursing from the routine dullness which can deaden occupations such as banking or clerical work; there is the potent "hospital romance" aspect: in popular terms, a partnership of doctor and nurse may represent the ideal marital alliance, in which each party fulfils a predetermined function, responsible, skilled executor and helpmeet respectively. Nursing has always been considered a "proper" women's occupation (Florence Nightingale simply helped to have it recognized as an official, rather than a private, one); the "ministering angels" fantasy existed before Sir Walter Scott (in *Marmion*) gave it a permanent literary form.

The Bodley Head, who brought out the English editions of Helen Dore Boylston's books, shortly afterwards launched a series of "career" novels for girls by different authors; these, however, for the most part were less skilfully put together than the prototypes. The practical information contained in the Sue Barton and Carol series is integrated into the text; in subsequent career books it tends to stand out like a peg leg – and performs more or less the same propping up function. *Pauline Becomes a Hairdresser*, *Clare in Television*, *Mollie Qualifies as a Librarian*, and so on, are no more than fictionalized handbooks, in which the soft sell, the job's provision of matrimonial opportunities, is supported by the technical facts of each occupation. Naturally enough, the result usually had no more cohesion than a badly animated cartoon.

These career books tend on the whole to fall in with one pervasive view of employment for the school leaver: that a girl's job expectations will be satisfied by a little money, for titivation, a little leisure, to display its effects, and the opportunity to retire gracefully into marriage after no more than a year or two of work. The choice of career, in fact, usually is not for oneself but for one's husband: the implication behind a girl's choosing to became a dental nurse, for instance, is that she wants to marry a dentist. Nevertheless, by the late 1930s women *were* making some headway in the professions: among others, in the diplomatic service, in engineering, aviation, chemistry, oceanography, most branches of industry, and, of course, the civil service. (Which, however, continued to dismiss women employees upon marriage.) But the two professions which, in the 1930s, lent themselves most readily to an up-to-date, popularized interpretation were those of girl reporter and girl detective – interestingly enough, these carry with them implications of initiative, mental alertness, deductive ability, physical mobility, courage, technical skill and personal ambition – qualities previously considered out of bounds to women. Of course, this reversal wasn't by any means straightforward: stories featuring these classes of occupation were hedged around with compromise, traditionally feminine back-biting or sentimental dialogue, conventional endings involving strong arms and wedding bells. The image of the 1930s girl reporter belongs indubitably to the cinema, where it was redefined, enlivened, shown in accelerated motion and embodied in Rosalind Russell or Joan Crawford. The young detective, however, first appeared [1] in America in Carolyn Keene's [2] Nancy Drew books for adolescent girls.

Eighteen-year-old Nancy Drew is the daughter of a lawyer; she is always getting involved in one of her father's cases, only to find that it ties up with one which she's been asked to tackle herself. This is a minor element of the books' pattern – which *is* repeated. As tales of detection, these are extremely simplified; though often the background – which may require the description of a glass-making factory or the events leading up to a complicated property deal – is surprisingly accurate. Description of any kind, however, is kept to a minimum; the stories are incessantly on the move, and the author's sentences are of the shortest possible length. The only superfluous words occur in the euphemisms which Carolyn Keene persists in using: people pass away instead of dying, an old lady's hair is snow-white, not just white.

The fast-moving style of the Nancy Drew books obviously holds an appeal for readers who demand continuous sensation. Suspense, however, is not so much built up as whipped up over one alarming event after another. The books generate exhilaration rather than excitement, the feeling of being driven along in a very fast car. Dramatic incidents are over almost before the reader can grasp what is happening. In *The Secret Of Shadow Ranch* (1935):

> ...part of the muddy bank collapsed, sending a huge surge of water over Nancy and her horse! Keeping a firm grip on the reins, Nancy stuck firm to the saddle. In a few moments her mount steadied himself and began to swim towards Bess's horse. When they drew close, Nancy seized Choo-Choo's reins. While the frightened girl clung to the saddle, her horse

[1] A lady detective (for adult readers) had been created by Anna Katharine Green (1846-1935); but the stories featuring Violet Strange were not this author's best.

[2] Carolyn Keene is a pseudonym covering several authors in the Stratemeyer Stable, principally Mildred Wirt, who wrote the earliest (and the best) Nancy Drew books.

was towed to the shore.

"Oh, Nancy!" she exclaimed. "You were wonderful. You saved us!"

Like all good heroines, Nancy is an accomplished life-saver: on one occasion when a sleep-walker slips off a narrow ledge high above the ground, resourceful Nancy is ready with her lassoo at an upper window. Nancy takes bumps on the head, kidnapping, ghostly manifestations and blunt threats in her stride. She manages to appear phlegmatic and quick-witted at the same time. Of course the stories cheat all along the line. Everything is made easy for Nancy; her "hunches" always pay off; clues are literally blown into her face. There are no startling revelations; crooks are identified from the beginning and sometimes prove surprisingly tractable when confronted by Nancy, in her rôle of righteous and denunciatory citizen. In *The Hidden Staircase* (1941): "Nancy and Helen were amazed – Willie Wharton, with little urging from them, was confessing more than they had dared to hope." (The adult detective-story pattern is followed far more closely by Enid Blyton in her *Find-Outer* series – see chapter 18 – in which the suspects are eliminated one by one until the real culprit is left.) As a fantasy figure, Nancy Drew's impact comes chiefly from the fact that, in the books, she is taken seriously: sober and intelligent adults engage her to solve their problems, and she is completely unrestricted by home pressures. The Dana girls, detective sisters created by the same author, are younger than Nancy Drew and still at school, which makes the point even more telling. (It loses its point, however, when we get to Enid Blyton's youngest "detective" who is eight; she calls clues "glues" and is confused about their purpose. But she is one of a group which collectively fulfils the same function.) The "mystery" quality of these mystery stories is largely a misnomer; their basic theme is that nothing *is* mysterious; everything has a prosaic explanation, usually an economic one. They are written to a formula which will allow for no deviation in the presentation of character or let-up in the incessant production of thrill after thrill. Since the thrills are all of the same kind and since one *knows* that there is no need for alarm on Nancy's, or the Dana girls', behalf, their effect depends entirely on the extent to which the reader goes along with the author's implication that the heroine's life, or liberty, or reputation as a detective really is in danger. This is more a voluntary process than it is in stories where the outcome is less predictable.

In Margaret Sutton's Judy Bolton stories, which began with *The Vanishing Shadow* (1932), the appeal to the reader's imagination is more subtle; the author's basic purpose is to create an atmosphere in which the supernatural may effectively be suggested. One result of this, however, is that its ultimate repudiation stands clear and incongruous from the books' main themes, and it is from the prosaic explanations which she has provided for properly unaccountable happenings that their lurid quality derives. "The ghosts of dead Indian warriors" (*The Ghost Parade*, 1933) are stronger in their evocations than a commonplace little bank robber called Slippery McQuirk.

Judy Bolton's position as a detective is less official than Nancy Drew's (but even Nancy has an authoritative figure – her father – behind her). She is less than sixteen when the series opens, and cherishes her detecting ambitions "in secret". When she mentions them to a friend, she is put in her place: " 'A detective!' Pauline gasped. 'Why, Judy, only men are detectives. Can you imagine anyone taking a mere girl on the police force?' " The "mere girl", of course, proceeds to demonstrate her flair for elucidation by getting to the bottom of another friend's "baffling" disappearance. In *The Yellow Phantom* (1933), however, the author's style is seen at its most tawdry; the plot is far-fetched to the point of meaninglessness.

Judy ages by a year or two in the course of the series; she acquires a pilot's licence so that her image may be brought into line with those of other detective figures whose omnipotence is symbolized by their control over so complex a piece of machinery, and by the fact that the most extravagant means of transport is at their disposal. The association of a certain kind of detective with aeroplanes quickly became a matter of course: it was used in types of fiction (children's or adult "thriller") where the impact on a reader has to be immediate and forceful. Judy, however, is far from being the showy kind of detective; when, in *The Voice In The Suitcase* (1935), she turns up

Nancy Drew in The Mystery of the Tolling Bell.
Drawn by R. H. Tandy

Judy Bolton views The Haunted Attic.
Illustration by Pelagie Doane

in an aeroplane to visit a reactionary old couple and is told off for it, she speaks up for herself in a way which isn't typical:

> "If the Lord had intended girls to fly," he said, "I reckon He'd been after putting wings on their shoulders."
> This was a bit too much for Judy. "Perhaps He put brains in our heads for the same reason," she called back flippantly,

and spends the next few pages regretting her rudeness. She is more "real" than Nancy Drew to the extent that she has problems of her own: friends are sometimes difficult – "Lorraine's studied mannerisms prevented her from enjoying life as completely as Judy did" – and she displays a typical adolescent indignation about social distinctions: "Nice girls never associated with the mill workers on upper Grove street."; "There was a dividing line as sharp as the dividing line between sin and virtue."

The Nancy Drew books, which are still being written, were not widely available in England until the early 1970s. There is no English edition of Judy Bolton. The "girl detective" pattern worked out by Carolyn Keene and Margaret Sutton was evolving simultaneously in England in a slightly different medium: the weekly papers of the Amalgamated Press.

XVII

Girl Sleuth to Brainless Beauty

"But where is the penny world I bought
To eat with Pippit behind the screen?"
(T.S. Eliot "*A Cooking Egg*")

THE FIRST AMALGAMATED Press girl detective was Sylvia Silence, who appeared in the *Schoolgirls' Weekly* in 1922. In the early stories, you find no trace of the verve or exuberance which became important aspects of the girls'-paper detective in the '30s. These qualities, moreover, were applicable both to the flow of the later stories and to their protagonists' behaviour: the emphasis on a detective's "skill" loses half its point if it is expressed in a clumsy way. The main defects in the writing of *Sylvia Silence* are carried over from a slightly earlier age, when women's notorious "softness" was represented by a softening of any activity in which a woman was involved. However consciously this is done, it is bound to determine the form of the whole product, which becomes flaccid. Deliberate "feminization" can only make anything worse, given the conventional attributes of femininity. Sylvia Silence calls her clients "dear" and is motivated chiefly by an emotional attitude towards them. There is no question of payment: usually it is the other way round, as she saves some poor person from complete financial ruin. As far as dialogue in the stories is concerned, the author, "Katherine Greenhalgh" (John W. Bobin), has tended to confuse clarity with stiffness. The word "mortgage", for instance, needs to be defined for the readers' benefit, but this is done in a way which underlines the artificiality of the whole format:

" ... unless Little Boy Blue takes the first prize at the show to-day we shall have to go."

"I am sorry to hear this, dear," Sylvia said, with genuine sympathy. "You mean that you have raised a mortgage on the property, and not been able to keep up the payments on the interest, and that, unless you can now pay off the whole amount you owe, the person who advanced the money will foreclose and claim the house and shop?"

The story's structure fails to support the weight of this; also it is out of key with the lightness of the times. (Melodramatic themes in schoolgirls' fiction, however, continued to flourish until the end of the decade: see chapter 13.) But Sylvia Silence is very much a rudimentary figure; neither the papers nor the image of a girl detective had acquired the cogency which was to characterize them later. The *Schoolgirls' Weekly* had just begun publication and was obviously feeling its way; *School Friend*, the first paper of the lot, was less than three years old.

There had been some attempts to create "lady detectives" for adult readers in the 1890s: Catherine L. Perkins's *Experiences of Loveday Brooke, Lady Detective*, was published in 1894; George R. Sims's *Dorcas Dene – Detective* came out three years later, followed by *Dora Myrl: The Lady Detective* (M. McDonnell Bodkin) in 1900. A sleuth named Miss Van Snoop appeared briefly in the first volume of *Harmsworth's Magazine*, also in 1900. But these seem to have been devised simply to give an eccentric twist to the "mystery" theme: the least-likely-person here is not the criminal, but the detective. Women's actual social position made it difficult for anyone to take seriously a woman claiming to be a criminal investigator, and the device became actually an annoying distraction from the technicalities of the plot. As a gimmick it defeated its own ends. It is interesting that (before the 1960s) we find *no* straightforward, competent, run-of-the-mill woman detective in the whole of the genre (the two who come closest to filling this rôle, Harriet Vane in the Dorothy Sayers books, and "Nicholas Blake's" Georgia Strangeways, are not in fact detectives). The least-likely-person again determined the creation of Agatha Christie's Miss Marple and Patricia

Wentworth's Miss Silver. The difference between these and earlier woman detectives is that it was no longer sufficient to make the chief character simply a woman: she had to be elderly, unmarried, white-haired and fond of knitting, and these particulars somehow helped to make her acceptable, chiefly because they imply a strong "human interest" angle on the business of detecting. This takes away a great deal of its intellectual, puzzle-solving appeal and makes it generally more palatable. Also, the shock to the criminal of being bowled out by a seemingly innocuous person is one from which the reader can get some obvious satisfaction. The old-lady detectives' approach, indeed, is neither clinical nor aggressive; they are concerned only to see that justice is done, and through them the authors can take a facile view that "old-fashioned" virtues are still the best. These may include caustic common sense and a disbelief in degrees of culpability: a person is either guilty or not guilty.

At the other end of the scale the "lady detective" is a child, or at least a young person, created for children. Here the image gelled instantly; it captivated readers and its total disregard of plausibility was its most enchanting feature. The angle on life which it provided comes nearer to meeting the child's requirement for acute sensation than anything a real-life experience could supply. The general line of fantasy which runs through the girls' papers, moreover, is acceptable precisely because it is mundane. It is exact enough within its own terms of reference, which admittedly *are* limited; associations in any kind of popular literature are bound to be superficial and loosely spun. The authors have no high purpose of which they can fall laughably short. The purpose is plainly to entertain; the style of the stories is usually unpretentious and brisk. It is also consistent over the whole range of subjects treated; the rules laid down for Amalgamated Press writers were explicit enough to produce a uniformity of tone. This cuts out "originality", but also the concept of "spiritual uplift" and all the awful ways in which it can be expressed. Amalgamated Press fiction is mostly dulcet in tone, there is no central point or allegory or objective of the author to turn it into "good" literature; and of course the stories do incorporate elements of "bad" writing: coincidence, contrivance, deficient imagery ("it was a ghostly-looking place with its crumbling walls covered thickly with ivy") and husky emotionalism (" 'He's – 'she struggled with a sob – 'he's a cripple!' "). Even a simple statement can get its author into difficulties: of a character in a Noel Raymond story (*Girls' Crystal*) we are told that "he lives alone with his daughter". Supporting characters are built up only to the point where they will behave in a way necessary to the plot; even the heroines of long-running serials are fitted out from the beginning with qualities which are immutable. Characters do not "develop", they react predictably. But the authors have already predicted the readers' tastes; by falling in with these, they insured themselves to a large extent against criticism. A reader who identifies strongly with a particular character is in no position to pull its construction to pieces.

If it *were* pulled to pieces it is unlikely that it would be capable of reassembly, since there is no central force to hold it together. More than most fictional creations, the girls'-paper heroines demand to be eked out by the reader's imagination. The stories provide a guideline: each reader will get out of them as much as she is prepared to put in. They have a particular function: to furnish crude fantasy images to amuse the reader while her critical responses are being evolved. It is only in cases where these fail to develop that her taste in reading goes on being self-indulgent; when the formula is repeated with sexual or motherhood fantasies grafted on to it, it has become totally infelicitous. The stories are meant to be grown out of.

This is one reason why the Amalgamated Press was able to go on using the handful of authors whose style had determined the quality of the papers. On the assumption that the readership would change completely within a three-year period, their themes were infinitely repeatable. Creativity in these writers was largely a matter of efficiency: they were skilled to the point at which any one of the small main group (which included L. E. Ransome, John Wheway, R. S. Kirkham, C. Eaton Fearn, John McKibbon, Horace Boyten and Draycott M. Dell) could turn out 10,000 words of perfectly competent fiction at a single sitting. Modifications in prescribed social attitudes, naturally enough, were slow to be effected, but it is possible now to pick out the shifts of emphasis in successive decades.

Themes in the '20s were predominantly murky or sentimental; the whole tone was one of lavender rather than spice. The '30s were altogether more brisk; these were the years of the economic depression, but the undertones in Amalgamated Press fiction of the previous decade were far more depressing. The "mill girl" theme was brightened up in 1935: "Elise Probyn's" (John McKibbon's) *Susie, The Pride of The Factory* (*Girls' Crystal*), however, is simply a schoolgirl, only with a foreman substituted for a headmistress. This series is hardly convincing, but it constitutes at least a gesture of recognition for the paper's working-class readership. As a general image, the sweetly emotional '20s heroine with her small pursed lips was superseded by the breezy, cheery, late '30s sports girl; a wave of the arm now carried more weight than a throb of the heart. Carnivals, bandits, the Near East and boating on the Thames were popular motifs. The war years had their own quality, which has been discussed elsewhere; in Amalgamated Press terms this could be expressed only through the *Girls' Crystal,* the one girls' paper to keep going. The war had little direct influence here; perhaps it was considered unsuitable as a background for girls' stories until it was safely over, when the wartime heroine in occupied France quickly became a stock figure. The *Cruising Merrymakers* (created by G. C. Graveley, as "Daphne Grayson"), which ran from 1939 to 1952, typifies the kind of illusion which was fostered by the paper at that time: that of a sunny, carefree, privileged, intrigue-ridden, and wholly enviable existence. Hiking, swimming, boating and tennis continued to absorb both characters and readers. The incidence of boys in girls' stories was increased; a principal boy was usually a mocking, perverse character who is really on the side of "justice", or a smooth, charming type who captivates everyone but the perceptive heroine. By the mid-'50s Amalgamated Press fiction was at its most bland: girls with short pony tails, wide under-skirts and flat-heeled shoes exemplified the "teenage" ideal, shortly to be complicated by a whole gamut of social undercurrents which the girls' papers failed to come to terms with. In 1960 the Amalgamated Press was taken over by the International Publishing Corporation (IPC).

A schoolgirl detective named Lila Lisle was the first to follow

Sylvia Silence; she had a short run in the *Schoolgirls' Own* in 1930. Both characters were created by John W. Bobin, who by now had adopted the pseudonym of "Adelie Ascott". Lila Lisle is described throughout as a "problem-solver" or "problem-investigator"; her status is entirely amateur, and in fact she has only to apply herself to the solving of a "crime" for it to turn into something else, usually a muddle which has been caused by someone acting out of the highest of motives. There is nearly always a sense of anti-climax in her solutions. Bobin's next girl detective was altogether more effective, though she had to acquire a new author before she began to emerge as a distinctive type.

The long series of Valerie Drew stories began with *That Amazing Room of Clocks* in the *Schoolgirls' Weekly* of 7 January 1933 (no. 542). It was written by "Adelie Ascott", and this name continued to appear under the stories until no. 653 (1935) when Bobin died. ("Adelie Ascott's" last appearance was in the 1936 *Popular Book of Girls' Stories*, when Valerie Drew followed up *The Clue of The Persian Perfume*.) The next 115 episodes were issued anonymously; then in July 1937 the character was taken over by "Isabel Norton" (this author may well have been responsible for the unsigned stories, however). Three series of twelve separate episodes were followed by four serials; the last, *House of Hidden Peril*, ended in the final number of *Schoolgirls' Weekly*; the magazine was incorporated with the *Girls' Crystal* in May 1939. Valerie Drew was transferred to the *Schoolgirl* where "Isabel Norton's" stories had a brief run; in March 1940 this paper also was merged with the *Girls' Crystal*, which became the only Amalgamated Press girls' weekly to survive the war. (It shrank, however, to 6½ inches x 9½.) The *Girls' Crystal* already had a popular detective figure in Noel Raymond; Valerie Drew was dropped. She reappeared in 1948 in no. 47 of the *Schoolgirls' Own Library* (second series); but this was a reprint of a serial (*Valerie Drew's Holiday Mystery*) which had run in the *Schoolgirl* from August to December 1939. The last original Valerie Drew serial was left unfinished when the *Schoolgirl* folded. Two short and unexciting episodes, however, appeared in the 1941 *Popular Book of Girls' Stories*.

The girl detective's first impact on readers was ensured simply by the extravagant tone of the opening story. Valerie arrives on the crest of a wave which throws her on to a lonely island off the Cornish coast, a place about to be infested with a number of oddly behaving people ("Who was the veiled woman up by the weird clock in the turret?"). Having just escaped drowning, Valerie proceeds to step on a rotten branch 50 feet above the ground (she prefers to approach top storeys from the outside). Before the mystery is solved two people have had sharp knocks on the head, Valerie is trapped in an airtight safe, the housekeeper, a "sinister-looking woman" named Mrs Grimmet, is imprisoned in the chicken-run, and three blameless characters (including Valerie) are bound hand and foot, gagged, and left in the toolshed. The mood of the story is reinforced conventionally by time and weather; the action takes place during the course of a wild, stormy night.

The most obvious distinction between children's detective stories and those written for adults is the former's necessary lack of restraint; the authors are at liberty to use every stage prop (except an actual body, which is considered more than "nice" children can take), every trick of language and overt manipulation of events, on the assumption that for most of their readers the effect produced *will* be to startle and intrigue. Young readers have to become familiar with clichés before they can reject them. The authors' problem is chiefly to devise a reasonably plausible explanation for the outlandish occurrences with which they have saddled themselves; this often results in "innocent" people being exposed as neurotic or obsessional. A lady in the above Valerie Drew story, for instance, allows her relatives to believe her dead and hides out in a secret room in her own house, simply on the off-chance that she may be able to discover what became of a necklace which had disappeared a year earlier. Obviously, no sane person is going to act in this way, but there is no suggestion that this lady's behaviour is abnormal.

In the early stories Valerie Drew's age is important to her characterization; she is eighteen, and able to pass herself off as a schoolgirl when the need arises. She is not yet a "detective" in her own right: "Girl detective – she had earned that title by helping her father ... before his recent retirement." Sylvia Silence and Lila Lisle also had fathers whom they "helped"; but Valerie Drew is so quickly established as a brilliant, suave and self-possessed heroine that the support of a father-figure becomes unnecessary. The only accessory which she needs is her alsatian, Flash, of whom the author actually *says* "he seemed to know almost every word she said". The implication that Flash is almost capable of solving mysteries himself is made explicit when he actually *does*: "Detective Flash" was the title of an episode which appeared in April 1934. Valerie's father, who is much less important to the series than Flash, fades out completely after featuring as the victim in an early story (" 'My father was brought from the house either bound or gagged or drugged' "). This is one of the few occasions when the object of persecution is not a distraught young girl.

The removal of Valerie's father from the stories was part of the tendency in the 1930s to emphasize the independence and proficiency of leading girl characters. At first glance it may seem that all those girl racing drivers, aeroplane pilots, deep-sea divers, explorers, mountaineers, lumberjacks, lion tamers, and so on, represent the actual extent of women's emancipation, or at least the Amalgamated Press policy-makers' willingness to promote it; but this view is over-optimistic. The authors' purpose is simply to crystallize the ten-year-old's image of herself at twenty; the author, if not the reader, is fully aware of certain "socializing" pressures which will alter the child's view of herself as she gets older. Thus, fantasies of rounding up a gang of thieves or a herd of cattle, or becoming an aerial photographer, are likely to give way gradually to the more limited, but more sensible and socially approved fantasy of "getting married" – but by this time the girl will have shifted to reading papers of another type. However, by pandering explicitly to the child's view of her own grown-up state instead of attempting to impose a muted realism on stories involving intrepidity or hardihood, the Amalgamated Press writers avoided the softening distortions of writers like E. M. Brent-Dyer, for instance. Occasionally there is a softening of a particular incident, but usually this is done so skilfully that it is unnoticeable. Amalgamated Press rules did make provision

Valerie Drew and Flash.
Cover for the Schoolgirls' Weekly, *February 2nd 1935*

for what were thought to be differences of attitude in boy and girl readers. As L. E. Ransome put it:

> In a car race – if one is injured the other boy goes on to win. When it comes to girls you've got to have that girl stopping and losing the race and you show what a fine girl she is not to care about winning the race, but to stop for the male rival who's crashed. Different angles – that's how you have to do it. If you don't do it that way, you know, she drives heedlessly on although the dog's injured at the roadside, the readers wouldn't take it.

By concurring in this general policy, Bobin could have made Valerie Drew completely ineffectual; as it is, her development into a "forceful" character is slowed up. In 1933 she is still calling her friends "dear"; and some pretty strange emotions are mingled with the cold-blooded business of investigating crimes: "Some of the torment left Grace's white face. It was replaced by a blind, unreasoning trust as her moist eyes met those of the girl detective." Characters are still allowed to speak in the language of an old-fashioned popularizing convention; it is surprising that this was acceptable to readers, but the story line may have been so strong that they could disregard it:

> "Now, why after working hard in Sanders' emporium all day, must you come home and strain your eyes over typing work?"
>
> "Because of one I love," Gladys answered involuntarily.
>
> "I don't understand you," murmured Valerie. …

This is consciously stilted, as though the author had been taught to express pathos in a particular way, and of course it has become laughable. Increasing naturalism in the girls' papers, however, forced Bobin to modify his novelettish touches, although outmoded "literary" phrases go on recurring in the stories. The most ingenious and entertaining "Adelie Ascott" serial was undoubtedly *Valerie*

Drew – Schoolgirl Detective, which ran from November 1933 to March 1934; but even here, members of the "secret society" which plagues the school are "clad in the raiment of a bygone age". As an antidote to this kind of high-flown banality there are plenty of banal colloquialisms. People are "ghosts of their former selves"; "cold thrills" run through them; scenes "tense with drama" meet their eyes. Occasionally we find grammatical, as well as stylistic, lapses: " 'You could hardly expect either Miss Ware or I to advertise who I really am.' "

While she is playing the part of a Sixth Former, Valerie naturally enough gets into difficulties with the other girls who accuse the headmistress of showing favouritism towards her. She has been caught breaking bounds at night, and her classmates are indignant when Miss Ware fails even to hand out a reprimand. They confront the headmistress who is completely at a loss until resourceful Valerie indicates to her the attitude which she should take up – by means of the deaf-and-dumb language. This is just one of the many accomplishments which the girl detective has cultivated: "she had neglected nothing which might help her in her profession".

"Adelie Ascott" may have been under editorial pressure to keep her heroine strictly up to date; Valerie Drew's professed enthusiasms sometimes fit oddly with the manner of their expression: "I take a great interest in motor-racing events." (A few years later a girl would have been "keen" on motor-racing, or found it "tophole".) "Isabel Norton's" first achievement was to effect a fusion of the character with the framework; in the later stories also the emotional and atmospheric murkiness is largely dispelled. The tone of these is altogether more bracing; "the old dark house" as a setting becomes less popular than the holiday camp, though people behave no less deviously in the open air. The detective wears a divided skirt whenever she can, and carries a walking stick. But this development is not effected abruptly enough for the reader to be aware of the change of author. New qualities in Valerie Drew are built up gradually, until she appears as a type of detective far more efficient and high-powered than the near-schoolgirl prototype. She acquires a private aeroplane and a Park Lane flat, and progresses from helping girls who are being cheated out of their aunts' legacies to tracking down international criminals like the "sinister" Colonel Mar (*Valerie's World-Wide Quest*, July-October 1937). Like Noel Raymond in the *Girls' Crystal* and the later Terry Brent (post-war *School Friend*), she is provided with a "clever jewel-thief" antagonist, Marcelle Dauphine.

All three of these "audacious" girl criminals are French – Rosina Fontaine and Claudette Morel are the names of the other two – which is a simple way of suggesting qualities of sophistication and unscrupulousness, and also of allowing these to appear more attractive than they could be in an English girl. The foreign "adventuresses" have not had the benefit of a British upbringing; at French schools, as Marie Corelli's *Boy* is told, they teach pupils to "tell lies prettily and to cheat with elegance". The girl jewel thieves also provide a device for highlighting the detective's moral qualities by embodying exactly the opposites of these. Marcelle Dauphine is clearly Valerie Drew in reverse, and shows what can happen when remarkable capabilities are not allied to a steady moral core. Marcelle is equally quick-witted and self-possessed, and it is only because right must be shown always to triumph in these stories that she is constantly foiled by Valerie. She is a version of the complete individualist type, whereas Valerie conforms to a social code of conduct. The author finally manoeuvres them into a dramatically symbolic confrontation, when they meet on opposite ends of a ledge which runs round the outside of a high building: "Grimly they faced each other across the gap – girl detective and girl criminal. The decisive moment had come at last." Marcelle, however, escapes down a rope-ladder and dashes to a waiting aeroplane – the series makes full use of all the twentieth-century technical aids to crime.

There is a serious flaw in Marcelle's characterization – she is reformed. This is brought about partly because she has been made so attractive to readers that *their* moral standards may have been considered in danger, and partly in order to show Valerie's ultimate triumph as complete, morally as well as technically. But from the moment when Marcelle's criminal activities are shown to have been undertaken for a sentimental reason, her impact is lessened; the reader is prepared now for the weakening reformation which still suggests, when it comes, that the author has abandoned the original scheme in favour of a tear-jerking conclusion to Marcelle's career as a jewel thief. The reader, whose interest has been stimulated all along by the ingenious techniques which Marcelle and Valerie employ to outwit one another, is suddenly appealed to on another level: a sentimental one. She is asked to swallow a sad tale of a dying fiancé who needs expensive medical treatment in order to be kept alive. Obviously the combination of girl detective and girl readers had been too much for the author: something softening had to be thrown in. Marcelle becomes Valerie's devoted friend and assists the detective to solve at least one mystery, in *The School on Haunted Island* (April-July 1938). This is essentially a rewrite of *Valerie Drew – Schoolgirl Detective*; the school has been modernized but the plot lacks the intricacy of the earlier version. Valerie has aged sufficiently to pass herself off as a games mistress, rather than a pupil; Marcelle comes along to help out with French and cookery lessons and to instil into the hearty schoolgirls a sense of "chic".

Valerie, of course, as a *girl* detective is several degrees less ethically ruthless than Noel Raymond, who is intrinsically a "good sort" but has no compunction about handing criminals over to justice. The aspect of both detectives which is emphasized is their concern for victims, but in Valerie this is extended to apply even to wrong-doers: "Criminal the woman might be, but Valerie could not see her in danger without helping." "Rosina the Baffling", Noel Raymond's most elusive and persistent antagonist, has a superficial likeness to Marcelle but is really a far more amoral and poisonous type. In her lighter moments she is equally attractive, mocking and exciting and self-assured in a way which only an archetypal French girl can be; but when she is at a disadvantage her characterization becomes heavy, overburdened with melodramatic traits, one of which is a tendency to address the detective as "You fool". "Stand back, you fool" is not noticeably different from "Kiss me, my fool" and Rosina is clearly derived to some extent from an image of the original "vamp", Theda Bara, in her most celebrated rôle. The point is that Noel Raymond is *not* a fool, and also he is completely unsusceptible

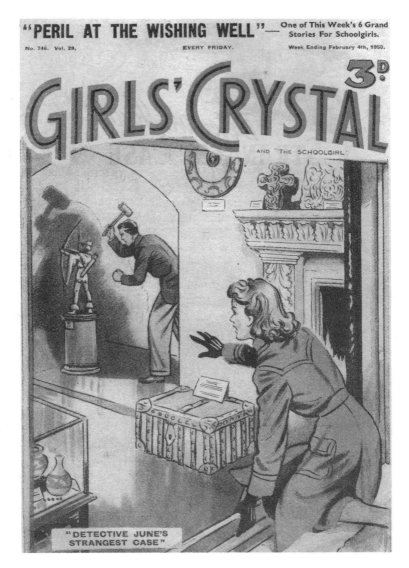

"Detective June" going about her business.
Girls' Crystal *cover, February 4th, 1950*

to Rosina's attractions, sexual or otherwise; he can see that she has "a face of almost flawless beauty" without allowing it to have an effect on him. In the tradition of wilful and ruthless female characters, Rosina has violet eyes which "glitter with excitement and avarice", "swift wits and amazing resource". Since Rosina's adversary is not a girl detective, the nastier aspects of her character can be called "feminine": "It was several moments before the young detective could recover from the smarting effects of the powder – a typically feminine weapon that Rosina had obviously kept for such an emergency." Rosina's "femininity" more than once comes near to causing her downfall. Her wits are not swift enough to lead her to take the obvious step of changing her brand of perfume, whose distinctive smell enables the "young detective" to sniff her out, even when she is heavily disguised. She is, of course, impossibly adept at impersonation, and her facility in this respect reaches a climax of absurdity at the point when Rosina, disguised as a countess, is bowled out by Noel Raymond who has got himself up as the real countess's butler.

Noel Raymond provides the only example of a male character who appears as the central figure in a girls' paper series (Terry Brent, who featured in a picture strip in the 1950s *School Friend*, is simply a less subtle version of the original detective: like Noel, he has a schoolgirl helper, named Trix Preston). The author, "Peter Langley", was also the only Amalgamated Press girls' writer to use a masculine pseudonym (he was Ronald Fleming, who also wrote under the names of "Rhoda Fleming" and "Renee Frazer"); probably it was felt that the character would lose in conviction if the author were thought to be a woman. The Noel Raymond stories began with the first issue of the *Crystal* (the title was changed first to *Girls' Crystal Weekly* and later to *Girls' Crystal*) on 26 October 1935. The detective story remained a weekly feature for nine years, until 11 March 1944 (no. 438). Between 1945 and 1951 Noel Raymond appeared intermittently, and interest in the stories came to be focused increasingly on his niece June Gaynor, the detective's "assistant".

Like Valerie Drew, Noel Raymond is always stumbling on queer goings-on which arouse his curiosity. His method of elucidation is

366

precisely the opposite of the process which William Empson in *Some Versions of Pastoral* (Chatto, London, 1935) has called "putting the complex into the simple": he has to extract the simple explanation from a situation of the most preposterous complexity. The starting-off point for one episode is the appearance, on the detective's doorstep, of an agitated girl who mistakes Noel Raymond for his own valet. She presents him with a note, written in his own handwriting, which requests that he hand over to the bearer a stag's head complete with antlers which he has bought recently at an auction. Without disclosing his identity the detective produces a stag's head (not the correct one, as it turns out), but follows the girl who proceeds to bury the object in a public park. To come up with a fairly acceptable reason for this behaviour must have involved the author in a mental effort similar to that demanded of participants in the radio game *My Word*, when two contestants have to devise an imaginary but plausible origin for a current phrase.

Oddly enough, the author was so fond of this girl's name, Joan Gelding, that he uses it twice in less than a year (December 1936 and November 1937); there is possibly a Freudian analogy to be drawn between the name "Gelding" and the fact that the girl has to be helped; that is, she lacks some essential attribute which could have enabled her to help herself. The "victims" in the detective stories form a necessary exception to the Amalgamated Press tradition of allowing girl characters to be purposefully active in their own interests. It may have been felt, however, that insufficient provision had been made for the reader's need to identify with a strong female character; the detective gets a "Fourth-Form Assistant" in October 1937, and June Gaynor is an important fixture in the series from this time on. By 1938 she has become "Detective June"; her partnership with Noel Raymond lasts until the final episode in the *Girls' Crystal*, "The Vanishing Statues" (May 1951). The two detectives are then fused into a single figure, Vicky Dare – who is, however, a resurrection of Valerie Drew, complete with alsatian dog named Rex. (Vicky Dare was created by Reg Thomas under the name of "Judy Thomas"; he is perhaps better known as "Jane Preston", see below.) This series ran until March 1953, when the

Noel Raymond in the Girls' Crystal
Girls' Crystal Annual *1942*

Girls' Crystal became a picture-story paper. The detective feature was dropped altogether, possibly because a successful picture-strip detective already existed in the *School Friend*: Terry Brent.

Terry Brent, who wanders through the English countryside from one village to another, solving mysteries out of the kindness of his heart, is the most leisured and philanthropic of the girls'-paper detectives. (He was created by Stewart Pride, who at this time was the paper's editor.) Many of his "cases" have as their starting-off point a childish object; a snowman, a bag of sweets, a kite or a walkie-talkie doll may have a sinister import. The reader is addressed directly throughout this series ("Did you spot it, readers?"). Obviously the picture story has less power to absorb its readers, it demands less concentration and provides an altogether more superficial kind of entertainment; as John Wheway has said "You can't get under their hearts with the picture stuff". The above device puts the Terry Brent episodes into a category of their own, midway between a puzzle and a story.

Terry Brent soon comes to grips with his particular girl jewel thief; Claudette Morel is introduced into the series in September 1950. This character is intrinsically as ruthless as Rosina the Baffling but much more light-hearted: " 'So I didn't completely bluff you after all, my dear Terry! Too bad! Just as I was about to open the safe, too! ...' " Claudette's alter ego is a monkey, which represents the light-fingered and mischievous aspects of her nature. Like Rosina's perfume, the monkey can be a dangerous accessory: "By Jove – I know that monkey! It's KEEKO!" Claudette specializes in mystifying her intended victims: as one of them puts it, "Daddy and I and the servants are baffled!" Incidentally, social priorities in that line are clearly indicated; there was a tendency in the early '50s, in the girls' papers and elsewhere, to pretend that life had reverted smoothly to what it had been for the moderately privileged, the great middle-class social mean, just before the war. It was not until the end of the decade that democratizing or "liberating" influences began to make themselves felt: "boy chums" became "boyfriends"; "Mums and Dads" were acknowledged to be imperfect ("even the best of them fall out sometimes"); schoolmasters took to wearing luminous maroon socks; and fourteen-year-old girls were allowed to be obsessed with their complexions.

As a "debonair detective" Noel Raymond furnished an outlet for the faculty of hero-worship which undoubtedly existed even in the *Girls' Crystal*'s first generation of readers, though it was not exploited openly until much later. Other stereotypes which fulfilled the same function were enigmatic young sports masters, skiing instructors, sheriffs and travel couriers: it was confined to young men who were in a position of authority, and the innumerable boy "outcasts", blameless and misjudged characters who are "helped" by heroine after heroine, come into a slightly different category. They are more to be commiserated than admired, and are in an interesting and untypical state of vulnerability as far as their relation to their "girl helpers" is concerned. One of these is "Hazel Armitage's" *Lonely Boy of Lonely Isle* (post-war *School Friend)*; "Lonely Laurie" has bought an island off the Scottish coast solely for the purpose of establishing his innocence of a robbery which had taken place in the district four years earlier. The story's heroine, Lynne Benson, persists in helping him in spite of his initial brusqueness; she is motivated by an attraction which remains unnamed: "Lonely Isle, in spite of its grim aloofness, seemed to be calling her. She wished she could think up an excuse to visit Laurie again."

Carol – the Last of the Lincolns (also by "Hazel Armitage": *Girls' Crystal* 1945) is in a similar position with regard to another victim of a cruel plot, Andy Felton; this story has a nonsensical ending which has no function other than to give an ironical point to the title. Carol is *not* the last of the Lincolns, since Andy turns out to be her long-lost cousin; and this puts too great a strain on the reader's willingness to suspend disbelief. " ' ... Terry Lincoln did not die. He was carried downstream and there picked up by a family of kindly gipsies ...'."

Rita Marsden, the *Girl Helper of the Hooded Four* (*Girls' Crystal*: this was written by Reg Thomas, as "Jane Preston") is concerned first of all to get herself accepted as a useful accomplice by the "Four" whom she intends to "help". These belong to a nearby boys' school, and the usual boys' mock-chivalrous, contemptuous assessment of a girl's abilities is exaggerated here in order to heighten the impact of its inevitable retraction: "Rita flushed. They were her very good friends, yet just because she was a girl they were not going to take her any further into their confidence. Very gallant of them, of course! She could understand their refusal was because they did not like the idea of her running risks. But—" This story combines two highly-charged girls' papers themes: the "secret society" which is formed to expose a case of injustice, and the girl who repeatedly makes good her claim to physical and intellectual agility. The former, with its mystifying rituals, its masked and hooded members, its whole romantic import, will naturally appeal to the child reader on a very basic level (*The Fourth Grey Ghost* and *The Silent Three* were series which exploited this fact). The latter sidesteps the convention that girls are endowed with some endearing weaknesses which must be deferred to. The convention is taken for granted, however, and it's largely from the unexpectedness of each heroine's efficacy that the reader's gratification arises. These heroines are shown to be exceptional girls, for maximum effect. The boys' contempt must seem to have a base in fact; this is important to *their* characterization, since they are not usually stupid or boorish, merely slow to recognize the surprising nature of the girl in question. A comparable theme in boys' fiction is the "muff" who makes good, but in this case the qualities of a muff are clearly defined; *every* girl who demands to be taken seriously by a group of boys is subjected to rudeness, at the very least, before she is allowed to win her point. We find constant by-play between the girl who thinks boys silly for thinking *her* silly, and the boys who remain convinced of their own "superiority" or grudgingly acknowledge themselves to have been, in this instance, mistaken. The relation in every case is riddled with unnecessary – but essential in terms of story – complexities. The girls, moreover, find the boys' attitude generally an understandable one, but each insists on an exception being made in her own case. The heroine of *Freda's Daring Double Role* (*School Friend*, May-August 1950), however, has to impersonate a boy in order to overcome the prejudice of three members of a "gang" which she wants to join:

"...You mean to say that any girl – even a jolly nice one – is barred just because she's a girl?"

The tall boy heaved a sigh. "I don't want to seem rude, and I don't want to argue," he said. "But that's it. You've hit it. So far as we're concerned, girls are barred. No girls by request."

"Not at any price," added the boy with the round face.

Conveniently, as it happens, Freda's hair has been cut during an illness; she can effect a superficial sex change at will by slipping off and on the "golden wig" which her "Aunt Sarah" makes her wear. This, in fact, is one of the most lively and ingenious of all the post-war *School Friend* serials. It achieves a tone of sustained exuberance, but one has only to consider what would have been its effect if the sex rôles had been reversed, in order to realize just how radical the double standard still was. A boy got up as a girl, for the purpose of helping a group of schoolgirls who'd scorned to have anything to do with him on account of his sex, would have been an offensive figure, eccentric to the point of perversity. Freda, however, gamely scrambling down a rough cliff path in a pair of sun glasses and an old belted raincoat, is merely dashing. This, of course, is because she is "living up" to something, whereas the boy would have been "climbing down". There was never any question of a boy having to "prove" himself in the same way, unless he'd been handicapped initially with the most ludicrous disadvantages; but in most girls' stories a girl who is confronted with a number of boys is put at once on her mettle, forced into a defensive position.

L. E. Ransome, who wrote the Freda serials (there was a sequel in 1952, *Freda's Quest at the Boys' School*) under the name of "Stella Stirling", was the Amalgamated Press writer who most consciously exploited this theme. He is best known as "Ida Melbourne" and as a humorous children's writer is on a par with Richmal Crompton: both can be applauded for the effrontery of their farcical pile-up of disaster on disaster, each managing just to keep the whole structure from toppling over. "Ida Melbourne" established the pattern for a particular boy-girl relationship with the 1930s *Schoolgirl* series,

Cousin George and the Imp (see p. 279). This was so successful that it was repeated first in *School Friend*, only with the names of the principal characters changed to *Babs and Cousin Bill* (beginning in November 1950) and later in the same paper's *Sue – the Girl Next Door*, though there were significant variations in the latter series. "Cousin Bill" is a lofty but slightly dense sixth former, Babs the ebullient girl who gets the better of him week after week. The deflating of Bill is always a gentle process, however, and his cousin's "fondness" for him is stressed. Babs's methods of self-assertion tend to be underhand in a traditionally "feminine" way: "she had found that meekness was the best way of getting him to go her way", and she is quick to turn her cousin's foibles to her own advantage: "When he was out with Babs, Bill had a way of adopting the manners of a Zulu warrior to the extent that he walked ahead and let her follow a few suitable paces behind." Naturally enough, Babs falls further and further behind, until she is able to scamper off on a jaunt which she has planned on her own.

Babs unfortunately is a younger version of the "little woman" of women's magazine fiction who gets her own way by a combination of flattery and astuteness, but the package in this case is far more neat and attractive since it does not have to accommodate the mawkish embellishments necessary for the older age group. Babs is quintessentially sensible; she has summed up the situation and seen at once the best way to manipulate it. The nastier implications of her behaviour are socially derived and affect the reader only at the most subliminal level; they are obscured by the surface comedy, and in any case arise from a premise which was widely accepted: that of feminine deviousness.

The tone of *Sue – the Girl Next Door* is even more extreme since the masculine "butt" in this series, Archie, is an overt misogynist. The narrator of the stories is a boy, Hugh, who is caught in an unfortunate position between his friend Archie, who hates girls, and his friend Sue, who *is* a girl: this basic situation furnishes limitless provision for farce. Hugh is the archetypal "good-natured chap", a boy who bends over backwards to see everyone's point of view: "Fact is, Archie has a 'thing' about girls. He seems to regard them as inferior beings, and is usually ashamed to be seen with one, even with Sue, who's a jolly nice girl, and better at most things than the average boy." L. E. Ransome considered this attitude perfectly natural in boys of the ten-to-fourteen age group; he regarded it as typifying the aversion which sometimes precedes a strong attraction, and this estimation is socially justifiable, though no less pernicious on this account. It turns the girl into a passive figure, awaiting her transition from nonentity to nymphet (always in someone else's view); and although this is explicitly contradicted in most girls'-paper stories, where the girl must act on her own initiative, it is still an underlying force in so far as there is never any serious questioning of the *status quo*. Perhaps this is not to be expected from a popular girls' paper, however, whose function is rather to reflect than to challenge the mood of the times. The '50s, in many ways the most retrogressive decade of the century, had a spokesman in Archie's uncle, whose age might have been expected to give him a more balanced outlook than Archie's: " 'Well, it wouldn't be fair to take your brother and not you,' said Uncle Sam, jovially. 'But I'm not taking any other girls along. They're not usually very brainy and they're often a drag on the company.'" This is the kind of low comedy which works by having a very stupid person say what everyone else thinks might be true but which they consider themselves far too enlightened actually to state. As a balance to the fanatical Archie, in the above series, there are the two "normal" characters, Hugh and Sue; but the comedy arises from their efforts to humour Archie's prejudice or to circumvent it; to them his attitude is a nuisance, not an anomaly. Of course Sue always comes out on top in the stories; but, like Babs, she has to simulate in the process a degree of acquiescence in Archie's views which she is far from feeling:

"Well, you don't want your uncle to think you're the kind of boy who makes pals of girls, do you?" asked Sue amazed.
"No," admitted Archie, rather guiltily.

But the reinforced conservatism of the '50s may have been another case of "withdrawal in order to jump better". The pressures which

"Hetty chuckled in delightful anticipation ..."
Girls' Crystal *Annual 1947*

were working towards the surface in English society have been described as "revolutionary" (see Christopher Booker's introduction to his book *The Neophiliacs*, Collins, 1969); the decade which followed quickly and forcefully established its own character. By the late 1950s the girls' papers, which the discredited conservatism had contained within its compass, were on their last legs, at least in the format in which they had been evolving since the 1920s. The Hulton Press's *Girl*, the female equivalent of *Eagle*, had attempted to provide a supply of fiction which was midway in style between *School Friend* and the old *Girl's Own Paper*, combining the entertainment value of one with the respectability of the other. Its first cover serial featured *Kitty Hawke and her all-girl air crew* (November 1951): " 'Well, here we are again, gang, with one more job chalked up to the all-girl air crew – to prove to Dad that we can operate his 'planes as efficiently as the glorious males.' " Kitty Hawke was soon replaced by a conventional pair of schoolgirls, Wendy and Jinx, and the paper's bright colours, as well as its whole bright image, eventually began to jar. It never had the addictive quality of the cheaper papers. The deterioration of the latter may be pinpointed, however, in a dreadful *School Friend* picture-strip serial, *Anita – Beloved Princess* (1956), in which all the worst aspects of the decade were aired: princess worship, vapid romanticism, a teenage dreamworld more gaudy than glossy. Later efforts to incorporate into the rigid structure of the papers two adolescent enthusiasms which previously had had no place in the well-bred fantasy world of their readers, fashion and pop music, had an immediately disastrous effect. The style of the Amalgamated Press had depended upon a set of formulae which its writers were expected to adhere to: these produced a structure which was highly developed in its own way, and even restrained in comparison with what was to follow. The relaxations of the '60s were expressed in girls'-paper terms in sheer indiscipline: initially this was confined to the dropping of the apostrophe from the phrase *Schoolgirls' Own Library*, but themes soon became more and more extraordinary as writers were allowed a freer rein. Instead of following a positive, progressive line of development, once it became obvious that the old stand-bys were played out, Amalgamated Press fiction suddenly spattered out in every direction: its subjects began to range from science fiction at its crudest (*Cathy the Cat Girl*), to the discotheque scene at its least convincing (*Last Dance at the Disco*). The line of demarcation between the content of publications like *School Friend* (changed to *June and School Friend* in 1965), *Girls' Crystal*, and so on, and the *Romeo*, *Mirabel* tradition of mindless romance, becomes less distinct. There was a sudden return to the "Cinderella" syndrome of the '20s: girls who were treated cruelly by money-spinning guardians began once more to feature prominently in the serials. These may have been seen as "rebels" against, or at least as victims of, an existing social order, thereby fitting in with a current line of thought. Among them was Clementine Miller, who "has been orphaned and left to a pauper's fate but for the intervention of her awful Aunt and Uncle ... who promptly put her slaving away amongst the coffins in their Undertaker's shop." For the past ten years the girls' papers have been full of awful aunts and uncles, whose sadistic behaviour towards their charges is completely unrestrained. The no-holds-barred policy has resulted also in a number of death-bed scenes as lurid as anything the Victorians devised; and, in one of the most tasteless serials of all, a girl is told that she has six months to live and decides to devote them to looking after a crippled child at a nearby orphanage. The only kind of disability which so far has not been foisted upon a heroine is mental deficiency. Leading characters are often blind, crippled or otherwise handicapped. This clumsy device is obviously intended to heighten pathos and drama; it is interesting that it was first used widely in children's fiction in the most repressive era of all, the mid-Victorian period. However, the troubles of Mrs Haliburton or anyone else at that time were nothing to those of one recent girls'-paper character: as the result of a train crash, Kay Green has "lost her parents and the use of three limbs. Determined to remain independent, Kay gathered up stray dogs and trained them to pull her along in a wooden cart." (*Kay for Courage*, *Bunty*, 1970).

Enthusiasm for fashion found a straightforward outlet in some of the girls' magazines, but one serial at least (in *Bunty*, 1970) shows how it can get out of hand: "Jill Wade and all her chums from the school sewing class had been kidnapped by a strange woman called

Miss Adams ... ". "Strange" is not too strong an adjective: Miss Adams has the girls chained to sewing machines, so that they can turn out a constant stream of fashionable garments for her boutique.

A more conventional character is *Wendy of Bramvale*, who was created by "Hazel Armitage" in the late 1950s. Wendy is important because she is a transition figure: she has a natural originality which successfully resists the conformist pressures of a large school, she is impulsive and simple in a way which was to become socially desirable; in fact she presages a type which flourished in the late 1960s, the "child of nature". The author, however, was not altogether at ease with this creation; there is a suggestion of hesitancy in the writing, and he is still harping, perhaps for reassurance, on the "kindly gipsies" image which he had used before (see above, p. 370); in this case the "gipsy" is the heroine's aunt in disguise. L. E. Ransome also brought a bizarre note to his use of contemporary enthusiasms, notably the mania for pop music which began to develop into an adolescent obsession in the mid-'50s. The tone of the early rock singers was essentially explosive, expressing juvenile dynamism and discontent; usually it affected its hearers in an explicitly sexual way. Mr Ransome allowed his Fourth Form members of Queenscourt co-educational school (created in the '50s but updated later) to share in this enthusiasm, but presented it in a way that deprived it of its innate vitality. His *Pop-Singing Schoolmaster* fails to integrate its central image with the merrymaking, japing background; and the result is a distortion of both. Even the name of Mr Ransome's pop singer is wrong: "Rooty Smales" is more suggestive of a crookbacked old villain.

The Queenscourt stories contain as one of their principal characters the dreariest of feminine stereotypes: the brainless beauty. It is, of course, Leonora Varden who makes a fool of herself over Rooty Smales. Leonora is no groupie, however; her emotions are all in her head:

> "Oh I'm so thrilled, so madly excited," said Leonora clasping her hands and doing a little dance. "To think we shall actually see Rooty Smales – perhaps touch him—"

"I can lend you a quid if you're short. No need to touch him," came the voice of Lionel Mortimer-Fawksley.

The element of dry common sense imposed by the second half of that exchange is quickly abandoned: to the silly hero-worship of Leonora (" 'He's fabulous – a dream come true,' she said huskily. 'Oh, it mustn't ever end! Tell me it won't, Kitty' ") is added a rip-roaring comedy situation (" 'It's false. He's here in disguise. He's Rooty Smales,' howled Snyder!"). All that's missing at this point are secret documents and international gangs, and these are soon supplied.

The lack of control in the later Queenscourt stories and their rather desperate use of current imagery (of a French girl we are told "Brigitte made a point of being odd, novel, unorthodox – because she enjoyed the shock it caused others") are typical of what was happening in the genre as a whole. The papers were being deformed by their inability to incorporate demotic trends into an original and proven framework. For a period of roughly 25 years – 1930 to 1955 – they did have some oblique relevance to contemporary life, and provided at least a basic combination of reassurance and entertainment for the adolescent reader. They also succeeded in compelling acquiescence, at least for a time, from all their adherents, cutting across levels of intelligence and social class. It is too easy to dismiss them as trash; their preoccupations all along had a conservative bias, which resulted in impoverishment of their fantasy content but guarded them at the same time against the excesses which have come to characterize present-day papers (D. C. Thomson's, *Diane*, *Judy*, *Jackie*, and so on, are no more restrained than those issued by IPC). The writing may have been pedestrian but it was rarely florid; occasionally it attained a light-hearted distinction of its own. It is fortunate that the decline of the girls' papers has occurred at a time when they are most dispensable; it has been paralleled by an unprecedented diversification in "reputable" children's books.

XVIII

Swallows and Ponies

"A girl whose spirits have not been damped by
inactivity, or innocence tainted by false shame, will
always be a romp. ..."
(Mary Wollstonecraft, *Vindication Of The Rights Of
Woman*)

1930 WAS THE year of Arthur Ransome's *Swallows and Amazons*; this
book had an extraordinary effect, and its theme was taken up by other
writers to produce a new type of children's novel, the "holiday
adventure" story (see *Tellers Of Tales* by Roger Lancelyn Green). As
elements of the Arthur Ransome saga were dispersed through other
books, however, their quality was diluted; this was inevitable as
"adventure" began to imply specifically the tracking down of
criminals. In the twelve Arthur Ransome stories which feature the
Blackett, Walker and Callum children, the author is concerned to
pursue to its limit the kind of enjoyment to be got out of quite ordinary
activities: sailing on Lake Windermere, keeping out of sight of an
aunt, building an igloo in a snowbound wood. Their effect is bound
up with the author's quirks of style; he can be whimsical, for instance,
in a way that's quite acceptable, because its form is unexpected and
because it fits into a context of practical activity ("Wet work was
being done in Octopus Lagoon"). The humour in the stories is sedate
and low-key. More than most children's books these are full of matter,
but they are not in the least weighty. Ransome works best within a
reasonably formal framework, and there's usually a fairly subtle
objective at the centre of his plots: the saving of a rare bird from
extinction or the prevention of the spread of a forest fire. Usually

something *is* saved, even if it's only the faces of the two Blackett girls, Nancy and Peggy, who have to cope with the inconvenient arrival of their great-aunt. On one occasion, it's a kitten which is found floating on a chicken coop in the North Sea. Of course, Arthur Ransome's major preoccupation was with boats and sailing; some readers may find the emphasis on these excessive. The stories have appealed persistently to "bookish" children, although their protagonists conform without exception to a type of the outdoor child. (This may be due as much to an interest in the unfamiliar as to the author's balanced, "bookish" style.) The type, however, is extended in the Callums, Dick and Dorothea; each provides a special viewpoint for out-of-doors events. Dick is the prototype for a character which flourished later: the clever bespectacled boy who is none the less physically active. Dorothea does have a "literary" bent, but its outlets never seem pretentious or obtrusive:

> The snow had changed everything. ... A whole jumble of things was in her mind, Good King Wenceslaus, the Ice Queen, Ib and Little Christina, the little girl who sat on her wedding chest in the winter forest, waiting for the coming of Frost. It was not much good talking about these things to Dick, whose mind worked differently. Why, the first thing he had done that morning when they had run out into the glittering snow had been to put a scrap of snow on a bit of glass, so that he could look at the crystals under his microscope.

Incidentally, this juxtaposes the traditionally "romantic" outlook of the girl with that of the archetypal "scientific" boy. However, Arthur Ransome's stories come into the small category of those which appeal equally to children of both sexes; in them, moreover, sex rôles are not insistently differentiated. Girls do the cooking, but are also "Amazons"; a boy is nauseated by the practical business of skinning a rabbit.

The holiday had already been recognized as the most obvious background for children's adventures, by E. Nesbit and others (see chapter 5). A holiday is a break in ordinary life when anything may happen; it is also a time when two or more families are thrown together.

An island camp.
Drawn by Clifford Webb for the first edition of
Arthur Ransome's Swallowdale

Certain combinations of children, their authors imply, generate a kind of excitement which must find an outlet in this or that "mystery". These stories follow the same pattern: a group of children, abnormally high-spirited because they are on holiday, notice that something "odd" is going on and poke their noses into it, thereby rendering invaluable assistance to the police: " 'Well, these children seem to have done most of the work for us,' said the Inspector, shutting his notebook" (*The Secret Seven*, by Enid Blyton). Within this structure the adventures range from the reasonably plausible (most of M. E. Atkinson's stories, for instance) to the laughably eccentric (Enid Blyton when she writes about foreign princes and secret mountains).

Between 1936 and 1950 M. E. Atkinson wrote fourteen stories about the exploits of the Lockett family, Jane, Oliver and Bill. Although she has handicapped herself with a rather cumbersome framework – the stories are supposedly written by the children's aunt, who occasionally appears in them – the feeling of children coping resourcefully with the unexpected is articulately conveyed. The force of the stories comes largely from the characters' efforts to overcome their special weaknesses: "Jane munched her scone in silence. ... She could not, with honesty, show fierce enthusiasm over a night that promised to be full of the things she hated most – darkness, cold ... and the even chillier dread of the unknown. But loyalty to the Secret Society and to their far-distant host kept her pledged to the enterprise." (*Mystery Manor*, 1937.) Someone is always exhibiting stamina and determination, gritting her teeth and plunging in head first, and this creates a kind of tension which reacts productively on the reader. It savours faintly, however, of the Victorian idea that it is always of moral benefit to have accomplished whatever one has been most reluctant to do, that this, in fact, is a necessary part of the process of character formation. The character of the M. E. Atkinson children on this level is bound to be striking, since they so resolutely set out to cultivate it. Anna Angel, for example, is a poor swimmer but forces herself to cover the distance from one flooded house to the next: "As she hauled herself up onto the doorstep her legs and arms might have been made of lead, so heavy had they become. Her breath came in painful gasps. She felt sick. Only the knowledge that she must get back as soon as possible with her report spurred her to further effort." In this book (*Crusoe Island,* 1941), the children are stranded in a deserted house in a flood; their difficulties are increased when one catches pneumonia and another breaks his leg. The unfortunate Anna is forced to undergo further degrees of physical exertion: "Blood poured down both shins. Her blistered hands were raw. One plait had come undone. A mane of ungovernable straw-coloured hair swept across her face, catching in the twigs and adding to her general distress." But the end of the book produces a general maxim for the genre: "You had to put up with the rough along with the smooth, for adventures are not real adventures without a spice of danger and anxiety."

Throughout the series there are occasional endearing touches of realism. For all the children who have been irritated by the fact that characters in their favourite books are never inconvenienced by having to go to the lavatory, there is finally an acknowledgement of this necessity (in *Crusoe Island*), though only in relation to the mongrel Angelina. " 'We can't put her outside. It's a bit awkward.' It was more than awkward. The problem was not one about which one usually writes in the polite type of book, but it was a problem all the same."

In *Problem Party* (1945) the author brings together many of the subordinate characters who had appeared in the first nine books. The party is organized by Evelyn Standish, for whom these *are* characters in books, but also real people: she has read the stories written by the children's aunt, which of course are the nine Lockett family books; and this fictional overlapping of fact and fiction has an odd effect; it seems unnecessarily convoluted, like one of those labyrinthine books featuring a character who is writing a novel about a character writing a novel. But the series as a whole fits in with one idealized view of childhood: it depicts children as straightforward and unaffected, and is at pains to emphasize their concern with personal integrity. As far as adventures are concerned, M. E. Atkinson has steered a middle course between the preposterous and the mundane. The books are satisfactory, though never strongly evocative of time or place.

It is possible to trace a decline in the adventure story which culminates in the books of Enid Blyton – possibly the most widely read children's books of the twentieth century. Blyton pushed the

A game of cards.
Drawn by Harold Jones for Mystery Manor

"mystery" theme as far as it could go in one direction: that of simplification of style and crude dramatization of content. Her approach was almost precisely the obverse of Arthur Ransome's. His effect in one sense is to bring out the significance of commonplace childhood experiences; hers to present a string of "significant" occurrences in a way which is totally commonplace. She is consistently trite. She "writes down". She introduces herself coyly into the stories in the form of a disembodied benevolence: "What fun they were going to have!" "They certainly would have fun!" Yet few children seem to resent this approach; the Enid Blyton combination of cosiness and excitement has proved almost irresistible, and parental disapproval and library bans have actually helped to keep her books in circulation. Their popularity has never waned. They have been criticized for shoddiness of style, for a too-conscious play on the child's gullibility, for a specious jollity; with less justification, perhaps, for colour prejudice and for their promotion of a "middle-class ethic". None of these has affected the books' appeal, which is located centrally in the characters' enthusiasm, their constant sense of being "on holiday" and "in the thick of things". Enid Blyton's objective is essentially philistine, her method simply to shear off layers of meaning or ambiguity, so that only the most superficial expression of "involvement" or "enjoyment" remains. She has made sure of the reader's support by a number of obvious devices. Natural, but slightly anti-social, qualities of children – greed, for example, intellectual laziness and conservatism – are presented in such a way that they appear wholly justifiable, even attractive. Readers are told at once of each character's particular foible, so that this will raise a laugh when it is next referred to – and references to it thereafter are constant and plain. An artificial limit is set to everything else in the books, including the author's vocabulary. Writing, for Enid Blyton, became so mechanical that she could complete an 80,000-word book (*The River of Adventure*) in five days: she began it on Monday and finished it on Friday of the same week. She was unforgivably careless, and many of her inconsistencies, surprisingly, have not been picked up by editors or proof-readers. In one book there is a cat which is referred to as "he" and "she" indiscriminately; its name is changed gratuitously in the following book of the series. A character who has been described as someone's sister suddenly becomes the same person's niece. This disorder implies a kind of arrogance in the author which contradicts the image of a thoughtful and reasonable older friend which she tried to project; it is backed up, however, by her assertion that she took no notice of critics over the age of twelve. The order in the books is of another, quite unrealistic, sort. The impetus of each story is towards a nursery-world tidiness; criminals are tidied away in gaols, unruly or selfish children have these traits straightened out of them, and this is effected with a disingenuous ease.

The Enid Blyton "adventure" and "mystery" stories involve five main sets of characters: the "Famous Five", the "Adventurers", the "Find-Outers", the "Rockingdown – Rat-a-Tat" group, and the "Secret Seven". *Five on a Treasure Island* was published in 1942, and its impact was immediate. It contains one fairly strong character, and it is this girl, George, who has carried the series; the other three children are as unmemorable as the author can make them. Of Dick we are told only that he has a large appetite; Julian, the oldest, has a sense of responsibility and a smooth approach. Anne, as a foil to George, is the archetypal "feminine" girl, fond of dolls and cooking and "playing house". She is "babyish" to begin with, but becomes less so. In George, on the other hand, there is something for the reader to come to grips with: fierceness, resentment, the wish to have been born a boy. George is always in a false position; like all tomboys she can be "as good as", but this implies a basic deficiency. She never can be the genuine article. Anne, in an unusual moment of spite, points out " 'They're *real* boys, not pretend boys, like you' " and this crucial deadlock has a force which transcends even the author's bland treatment of it. For Enid Blyton the whole complex business of social rôles and attitudes is thoroughly simple, on the surface. George wants to be a boy and behaves as if she were one, and that is the end of the matter. This is George's "character", and to go deeper into it would be to impede the flow of events in the stories. Character is the least of Enid Blyton's concerns; the lightest indications of one tendency or another are enough to fit in with the lines of the plot. One child is fond of animals, another of birds; one girl is meek, another hot-tempered; one boy is a scamp, another fat and brainy. In the "Secret Seven" books, which are intended for younger readers, the author has hardly bothered to provide the seven with distinguishing marks more interesting than their names. It is the plots which are important, and these all move towards the point at which the children's effectiveness can be manifested, when the criminals are recognized and outwitted. These wrongdoers metaphorically wear striped jerseys and eye-patches; invariably they lock the children up in some uncomfortable place, usually underground, and make the usual threatening gestures, but the reader has to make a mental effort to be taken in by these. When the sense of adventure is expressed by a child it becomes inarticulate in a way that's meant to be touching:

> "Oh, George, don't be silly," said Julian. " ... Anyone would think we were in the middle of a big adventure!"
> "Well, I think we are," said George unexpectedly, and she looked rather solemn. "I sort of feel it all around me – a Big Adventure!"

This is the extent of the children's emotional reactions to danger and intrigue: they sort of feel it all around them.

It was probably the author's pursuit of the highest common factor, in a social sense, which led her to locate her characters firmly in the middle class; this represents an aspect of the "normality" which her books are constantly striving to express. Her moral sense is entirely clear-cut: she is on the side of law and order, and is at pains to uphold all the conventions and traditions which these may involve. She depicted a world in which social boundaries *are* clearly marked; her books are full of urchins who know their place, whom the principal characters befriend. These have names like Sniffer, Nobby, Tassie, and Ginger, and express themselves in a series of expletives: "Cor!" "Lovaduck!" "Coo!" They are not naturally as brave or resourceful as the middle-class children. If they stay to tea they eat in the kitchen; they are cheeky, shrewd and reluctant to wash. The latter trait is also foisted on to foreigners in general, even if they belong to the upper classes:

> "All his clothes of the Very Very Best, even his pyjamas –

but did he wash? Not he! And if you said you'd pop him into the river he'd run a mile, wah-wahing!"

"Lots of foreigners are like that," said the third boy, munching away. "We've got two at our school. One never cleans his teeth, and the other howls if he gets a kick at football."

This is a type of chauvinistic humour which many children enjoy, and incidentally it sums up two objectives of British education: to instil an acute sense of cleanliness and to teach the pupils to take their punishment like a man. The former may be still socially valid but the latter has a jingoistic connotation which has very little relevance at the present time. There is no sense that Enid Blyton has dissociated herself from the more vulgar or untenable opinions of her characters; her own viewpoint, her teacher's ethic, is everywhere conveyed. Her morals may not be pointed, in the sense of sharp, but they *are* pointed. In general they may be related to the seventh commandment of the Christian Church, though it is simply convenient that this ties up with the usual ending of the adventure story. Thieves cannot prosper, but neither can people who are selfish, thoughtless, slovenly or lazy. It is plain that Enid Blyton was conscientiously aware of a responsibility to her readers. Beyond a belief that childhood ought to be a time for "having fun", however, she had few liberal or progressive opinions. It is because of her way of expressing this "fun", a jokey, chatty, reassuring tone, that her books have thrived. Most children will respond, at least for a time, to the undemanding jolliness of her style. Children who read nothing else quite often will read Enid Blyton.

Her conventionality is nowhere more clearly apparent than in the distinctions which she makes in her treatment of boy and girl characters. Her boys are consistently "chivalrous" in the most rigid way:

"I'm not taking the girls," said Jack, firmly. "I don't mind any risk myself – but I won't risk anything with the girls. You can come, of course, Philip."

* * *

"O Gracious! what a queer place," said George.
Eileen Soper illustrates the Famous Five
*(*Five on Kirrin Island Again)

"Well, decent boys like looking after their girl cousins or sisters," said Julian. "And oddly enough decent girls like it. ..."

* * *

The girls cried bitterly at this. They thought it was very unfair. They couldn't know that Andy didn't feel at all certain of ever getting home, and was very much afraid of the girls being washed overboard when big waves came. He and Tom were strong – and besides they were boys – but the girls would never be able to stand tossing about on a raft for days and days.

Only in George are the girl's instinct for self-assertion and her demand for equality adumbrated. The author has withheld complete approval from George, and for this reason George is one of her most interesting creations. It is the characters of whom she approves most who are the nonentities – Julian, Dick, Jack, Larry, Roger, Peter. George is not quite fairly treated: there is no suggestion that her fantasy of being a boy is just as "normal" as Anne's acceptance of a "housewifely" rôle. Her cousins go along with George's eccentric behaviour for the sake of peace, and because they like her: along with the "masculine" qualities of recklessness and aggression she has cultivated those of loyalty, courage (" 'You're the bravest girl I know' ") and truthfulness. In *Five Go To Mystery Moor* (1954) George is brought face to face with another girl who behaves as she does; for comic effect the author makes them dislike one another on sight:

" ... That awful girl Henrietta too. Why do we have to put up with her?"
"Oh – Henry!" said Anne, with a laugh. "I should have thought you'd find a lot in common with another girl like yourself who would rather be a boy, and tries to act like one!"

George and Henry react to one another "like a couple of idiotic school*girls*", and this makes George's well-adjusted cousins laugh. It also underlines the fact that they are *not* boys, and Henry herself is forced in the end to accept this fact, with its more hateful implications. When she is at a loss to know what to do, she thinks, " ... there's no grown-up here tonight except Mrs Johnson. ... I'm going to dress, and then get William. He's only eleven, I know, but he's very sensible, and he's a boy. He'll know what to do. I only *pretend* to be a boy." This, one feels, is the author's view of girls who "pretend to be boys": that they are pretentious and silly. They will "grow out" of it; the growing out is a process of adjustment. "Real" boys who are forced to take notice of the trait are inclined to sound dismissive, smug and obtuse: this is in spite of the author who plainly felt that she was giving the reasonable, balanced view: " 'Hold your horses, George, old thing,' said Julian, surprised. 'After all, you've often been pleased when people have taken *you* for a boy, though goodness knows why. I thought you'd grown out of it a bit. ... ' "

George is "difficult", but her quirks, her originality, are excusable because of her age. Grown-up female characters in the books who do not conform to the traditional, cosy image of "a mother" are shown to be utterly shallow and worthless. The two types – maternal and worldly – are contrasted most explicitly in *Six Cousins at Mistletoe Farm* (1948): the "hard-working, cheerful, sensible" farmer's wife, and the spoilt, high-heeled, whining, vanity-ridden "Aunt Rose". Aunt Rose is "brought to her senses" only when she is faced with the prospect of losing her husband and children; she resolves to subjugate her own interests and inclinations to theirs, thereby fitting in with a pattern of self-effacing domesticity which the author considered admirable.

Her recurrent use of the "happy family" as a fictional motif has a direct relation to her own experience. Her adolescence was insecure; she disliked her mother, whom she saw for the last time in the 1920s (Mrs Theresa Blyton died in 1950). The author's father walked out on his wife and children in 1912; the episode was re-created nearly 40 years later, in *Six Bad Boys*. This is perhaps Enid Blyton's nastiest story; she has taken, unusually, a "topical" theme and sentimentalized it, bringing to the problem of juvenile delinquency an attitude dispiritingly retrogressive. Of the six boys, four are unredeemably lower class, outside the author's pale; the two whose "downfall" is related have problem families; we are told that they are good boys at heart but emotionally deprived. The father of one has deserted his family, driven away by his wife's querulousness; the other boy's mother wilfully creates the vacuum in her son's conscience by her decision to *go out to work*. At the time, in the early '50s, there was a great deal of public concern about latchkey children and the morally deteriorating effect on a child of coming into an empty house. A mother's place quite literally was in the home; she could leave it only at the expense of her children's ethical well-being. Of course Enid Blyton's own childhood experiences had predisposed her to accept this debatable view; it is stated over and over again in *Six Bad Boys*. Having got hold of what she believed to be a serious, psychological truth, the author could not leave it alone. The pathetic "bad boys" find a way into the cellar of an empty house; they try to manufacture in this dismal setting a measure of the home comforts which they all lack. By this simple device the author emphasizes the nature of their moral deficiencies. Of course they soon steal money to "furnish" the place. They are caught, brought up in court, and some are sent to approved schools. Enid Blyton's ultimate remedies, however, are as weak, exasperating and implausible as her causes: " 'Coo – I shan't be bad again, now I've got a proper home!' " The diminishment of "badness", the banality, the whole cotton-wool lack of sharpness or insight are typical of the author at her worst. Here, she has subordinated characterization entirely to an endorsement of her own point of view. The book is an addition to the anti-feminist propaganda of the time. This was compounded largely of the findings of popularized anthropological and psychological studies. Women's "natural" functions naturally were stressed, and the gloss was in the lipstick, shining kitchen equipment, the bright magazines whose golden girl typically renounced her birthright for a home in the suburbs.

The guilt which society imposed on working mothers is likely to have had an effect more psychologically damaging to their children than the mere fact of a temporarily empty house. The "villain" of *Six Bad Boys* is Bob's widowed mother, who insists on her right to work: 12-year-old Bob, however, expects her to sit at home all day keeping the house warm for him:

"I think I shall soon find a job to do," said his mother.

"I'm bored now. And I want a bit more money."

"Don't do that," said Bob, suddenly filled with panic, though he didn't know why. "I like to think of you at home all day. I don't want to think of an empty house – and no fire – and no kettle boiling. Don't you get a job, Mum. ...."

Enid Blyton's poor, ill-treated Bob is in fact self-pitying, destructive, a thoroughly unsympathetic emotional blackmailer. His whining has a solid, socially-approved backing, however " 'He is your only child,' [said the magistrate] 'Don't you think you could give up your work and care for him again?' " Few mothers in that situation would have the gumption to answer No, as Bob's mother does; this is presented as the final evidence of the unfortunate woman's hard-heartedness. The story has a happy ending, of course: Bob is adopted by the "proper" family next door: " 'I used to envy them because I hadn't a family too,' he thought. 'But now it's *my* family. ... I belong! Here I go walking in, to join my family!' "

It is odd that the need to be employed, usually so serious, dignified or forceful a topic, should be made here to seem frivolous, indicating in its subject a flighty nature. But it is not grim financial necessity which drives Bob's mother out of the house but boredom: the point seems to be that it is morally justifiable for mothers to be employed only if they would *prefer* to be at home. However it is looked at, the tedious, restrictive concept of "women's work" was always basically illogical.

When character is made the focus of interest in an Enid Blyton book the author's dormant sentimentality is given a free rein. In the adventure stories there is a certain coarse exploitation of the sense of danger, the *frisson* of a mock Gothic thrill. The castles, lighthouses, rocky islands, underground caverns, waterfalls, deserted valleys, cliff-top buildings, secret passages, Elizabethan manors, lonely farmhouses, have a significance for the reader which the author does not need to analyse. They work their own effect, which is to involve the reader in an uncritical response to the situation. Of course Enid Blyton cannot avoid the attenuation of everything which comes within her compass: nothing is allowed to retain an element of the sinister, tragic or unexplainable. Her colours are taken straight from the nursery paint-box; it can only be within the context of the nursery itself that she has cultivated an awful habit of speaking to her characters: "Good night, Ern and Bingo! You're quite safe, though Somebody has peeped in at the window, and knows you are there! Don't worry, it was only the black cat next door – and she fled as soon as she saw Bingo! Sleep tight!" Structurally, her most successful books are those which involve the five "Find-Outers"; the series began with a number of stories which imitate a detective-story pattern, with "clues", a list of suspects, the step-by-step elimination of all but the culprit. The children's detecting efforts are obstructed by the preposterous Mr Goon, a comic-strip policeman of heavily drawn irritability. The "Find-Outers'" baiting of Mr Goon often verges on the spiteful; the children are not altogether pleasant, they are obsessively inquisitive in a way which is "not British": they simply cannot mind their own business. They do not "fall into" an adventure, they poke one out. This of course involves an unseemly kind of prying into the "suspects'" lives. The central figure in the books is "Fatty" – Frederick Algernon Trotteville – a plump boy who is boastful, self-assertive, clever, but essentially truthful and kind-hearted. Again, it is the author's reservations about Fatty's personal qualities which have made him notable; but he stands out at the expense of at least three of his friends. These are totally recessive, merged with the village background. The fourth, Bets, is occasionally allowed a measure of limelight: she is the "baby" whose innocent observations often put Fatty on the right track. Fatty is what the servants call a "caution"; he thinks too much of himself, but always with reason. The author's precarious hold on plausibility, however, slips altogether when it comes to the presentation of Fatty's relation to "Inspector Jenks" – a "high up" policeman who is in every way the antithesis of Mr Goon. She may have uncovered the common children's fantasy of being accepted on equal terms by elders whom they wish to impress, but to present this as if it were feasible instead of containing it within a *Billy Liar* situation is to have an effect precisely contrary to the one which is intended. By going all out for the reader's gratification, as it were, the author has underlined her own tongue-in-cheek condescension:

" ... What a fathead that fellow Goon is, isn't he? [said

Inspector Jenks] Still, I'm glad I came over here. I'd like you
to take a hand now, in this mystery, Frederick."

"Oh – thank you very much, sir," said Fatty, thrilled.

"I'm not telling Goon this, because he's such a blunderer,"
said the Chief, "but I have a distinct feeling that the Lorenzos
are back in Peterswood for some reason or other. ... "

This is going too far, even for the most rabidly self-confident or
unimaginative reader. However, the early stories do have an
inventiveness, an intelligent extension of the basic motif – the burnt
cottage, spiteful letters or whatever – into a well-reasoned plot which
is deadened only slightly by the ponderous or self-conscious quality
of the humour.

The final "mystery" in this series, however, is wholly nonsensical.
In *The Mystery of Banshee Towers* (1961) all the weakest elements of
the earlier stories are thrown together. The author's tendency to
moralize is everywhere indulged. The age of her audience appears to
have dropped by several years, moreover, perhaps because her own
powers were in a state of decline: "Ern stared at Fatty. What queer
things Fatty sometimes said – but they were worth remembering. Ern
thought, 'Nothing like trust in a family.' That meant trusting one
another. There was quite a lot in that idea. Ern decided to think about
it when he was in bed." A softening, a deflation, has overtaken Fatty,
Ern, Mr Goon, even Buster the dog. The dialogue is depressingly
silly: " 'Real or unreal, that banshee is MOST mysterious' ". The
tone of fey mock solemnity which the author usually reserved for her
own intrusions is extended here to the characters: the effect is one of
slackness and affectation: " 'Do begin the Meeting, Fatty,' she said.
'We're LONGING to hear about this new Mystery. Is it *really* one?' "
This puts the characters, and the readers, inescapably in their place.

Malcolm Saville's concern for place, his meticulous establishment
of a precise location, suggests a thoroughness and imaginative density
which his books do not live up to. In them the sense of anticlimax is
fostered by the conventional resolution of the elements of each plot.
His criminal characters are hardly less "flat" than Enid Blyton's, his
children "detectives" scarcely more clearly defined. His own progress

as a writer has followed the most usual course: a kind of spirited, middle-of-the-road competence at the beginning has given way gradually to the production of fantasy of the most routine kind. His recent "secret service" books (for older readers) have achieved the quality of a *Honey* serial. They take up the theme of bright romance at the point where the Lone Pine books – out of consideration for the readers' age, perhaps – were forced to leave off. Their failure to take account of emotional complexity or to suggest even a superficial realism has made them completely sentimental. There is no hardening, no ironic or even whimsical detachment to provide an alternative viewpoint for the author's derivative sequence of events. Social problems like drug addiction are represented in terms of a distorting extremism. Drug pushers are crackpot anarchists who speak in clichés – this is itself a cliché – or simply belong to the category of bad-tempered villains whom children and animals conveniently dislike.

The author's first book was *Mystery at Witchend* (1943); in this, however, a number of wrongdoers are deceptively charming.

> "Is it a camp?" the stranger asked. "It's a grand place for one. ... Can't you tell me all about it, and then I'll tell you about fighting in a Spitfire, if you like?"
>
> Dicky began to weaken. A chap like this couldn't be a real enemy.

But this "chap" turns out to be "one of the worst", and Dickie is made aware of the nature of spying: " 'I say,' Dickie broke in, 'spies are awful liars, aren't they?' "

In this wartime adventure the Morton family, whose father is in the RAF, moves from London to a farmhouse in Shropshire; the whole district, however, is crawling with German spies. Five children form themselves into a "Lone Pine" club: this has its own "Rules", its confidential documents including a declaration of membership which must be signed in blood. The older members go along with the club's more childish trappings for the sake of Mary and Dickie, the nine-year-old Morton twins, a touchingly eccentric pair for whom the author has a special sympathy.

"Are you frightened, twin?"

"Not ... not 'zactly *frightened*, Dickie," Mary gulped. "Just something in my throat. This old fog, I 'spect."

The twins are sturdy and self-reliant, and Malcolm Saville has conferred on them an odd forthrightness, a constant rush to verbalize their feelings in an unlikely way: this in fact became the dominant aspect of his characterization. His children are painfully concerned to get things clear in their own minds, and the technique enables the author to present their characters in their own terms, but it shows up the lack of variety in the quality of their perceptions and moral assessments. The last thing these children suffer from is an emotional block, though their emotions sometimes cause them to act unreasonably. They are often caught in a circular phase of development, with touchy or aggressive behaviour followed by an apologetic effort to explain its causes, which may lead to a resumption of the first state: "Peter suddenly realized that she was being snubbed. She still did not find it easy to accept leadership from anybody else, and although she was sorry that she had been rude again to David, she resented the way in which the two boys made their plans alone if she didn't happen to agree with them."

It is generally his girl characters who are given to the kind of self-analysis which makes them seem embarrassingly outspoken. (" ' ... I like wondering what I shall be doing in an hour's time, and I specially like to-night because it's Christmas and the end of an adventure – and to tell you the truth, Guy, which I think may be very bad for you, I like this necklace you gave me and I like you and Mark being here. ... Don't spoil everything by being sarcastic, Guy! I can't bear it to-day and this is such fun. ... ' ") Boys are more taciturn, abrupt, emotionally straightforward. Usually they are dominant. Typically, the least controlled person in the Lone Pine books is a girl, Jenny Harman, who's impressionable, easily excited, and unintelligently stirred by romantic fiction. She is inclined to gush: " 'We'd like to say thank you very much for such a wonderful welcome and for taking all this trouble, Trudie. I expect we've all had a lovely day, and now this is just the right beginning to a thrilling evening.' " Jenny's light-headed approach to life is balanced by that of Tom, a stolid farmer's boy who likes nothing less than to look a fool. These two comprise one of Malcolm Saville's incipient sexual partnerships. Like many other children's authors he has put himself in a false position by confining a group of adolescents in a setting which will allow of very little acknowledgement of the peculiar strains and tensions of adolescence. The children *are* paired off, they are aware of "special" attitudes to one another, and this is conveyed by a coyness, a weakening, sanctimonious note in the writing. There is a withholding of truthfulness which is mitigated only slightly if one remembers the inhibited, nice girl's conventional resistance to romantic involvement. The girls here, even more than the boys, have to vindicate themselves by a courageous standing up to experiences of physical danger: this conveniently defines their "worth".

All the children, however, are called upon to make a right decision at one time or another. The basic fascination in all adventure stories lies in the involvement of innocent bystanders in a situation apparently beyond their control, but which they are really, against all odds and by virtue of sheer moral grit, inexorably changing. It is from the confrontation of innocence with duplicity that the sustaining force derives, but obviously the richness of the story's texture will depend upon the author's representation of each. A rare lightness of touch is needed to build up a convincing villain (Antonia Forest comes near to creating one in *The Marlows and the Traitor*); there are too many tempting conventions, stylized criminal mannerisms, shorthand notations which have lost currency through over-use. One simple trick is to establish a person's moral character by relating it to an animal's reaction to him, the implication being that the animal is responsive only to the most fundamental human condition which is either "good" or "bad". But the most old-fashioned and idiotic type of criminal is the foreign one.

Malcolm Saville's peculiar Englishness has had a strengthening effect when it is expressed as a feeling for the picturesque, bound up with a knowledge of country lore or contained within his evocations of Shropshire or the Sussex Downs. He has only to include a single "foreign" element in his plot, however, for the story to take on an undercurrent of absurdity and stiffness. Those which have foreign locations (*The Sign of the Alpine Rose*, for instance) are the worst of all. "Abroad" has a dangerous romantic appeal of its own which needs to be played down and disciplined before it can become thoroughly effective. Like the romance of the past it tends towards the florid and exotic, its seductive quality is shallow and obvious, and to play on this is to make an appeal to the least subtle part of the reader's perceptions. Naturally, as the geographical range of an author's associations is widened, these are more thinly spread.

An adventure story which has an imaginary setting is Mary Treadgold's *We Couldn't Leave Dinah* (1941). There is no Channel Island named Clerinel, but the author's invention of one is entirely convincing, even when the island is invaded by Nazi troops. The plot is fairly simple: two children, a brother and sister, get left behind by accident when the rest of their family is evacuated; they camp out in a cave, and finally succeed in securing an important document which they hand over to a British agent. Within this rather limiting framework, however, there is an unusual subtlety of characterization, an emotional consistency and a low-key ironic note which hold the story in place. As a story it is thoroughly interesting; quite simply, the author is in control: there are no simplifications of the English language or melodramatic swoops of action or feeling. There are the usual heroics, but even these are ironically placed. The quality which most obviously confers heroism upon a character is a disregard for personal safety, an obsessive feeling for a kind of abstract of justice or social order: this is found to exist in a person of whom the children have been rather contemptuous. *Their* view of the war is straightforward, militaristically patriotic like most children's; but the end of the book brings with it, at least for Caroline, a positive psychological advance to back up the strategic one. The title is a thoughtless child's exclamation: "Caroline turned away from the window, her face set in long mournful lines. Even her pigtails drooped dejectedly. 'And what about the ponies? Oh, Daddy, what about Dinah? We couldn't leave Dinah.' " But Caroline finds that she *can* leave Dinah, her attitude to Dinah is modified by the forces of necessity, she can even hand over the pony cheerfully to the bumptious but pathetic German child Nanerl. The book provides, among other things, a view of the "pony club" from a proper perspective.

The horse has become a powerful symbol in girls' fiction, a central image in which snobbism, display, and the doctrine of kindness to animals are blended. Kindness to some animals, at least: a natural extension of the horse theme is the hunt theme, for which only the most facile moral justifications can be provided. " 'We killed a fox which had been slaughtering chickens,' " the narrator of *I Carried the Horn* (Christine Pullein-Thompson, 1951) smugly remarks, but her own taste for slaughter is immediately expressed: " 'It seemed dreadful that the whole of August must pass before we could even begin cub-hunting.' " The thoroughly distasteful business of fox-hunting is presented with a characteristic bluffness, a hearty, outdoor disregard for its bloodier implications. The book, however, is littered with bloody

Caroline and her pony evade the Nazis.
Illustration by Stuart Tresillian
(We Couldn't Leave Dinah)

images: the fox hounds are out of control, they nearly kill one another and are known to have killed a corgi and a pekinese. This is made the subject for several grisly jokes: " 'Keep an eye on Conscript ... or else he'll be eating up someone's best French poodle.' " The dogs unearth a carcass from a dustbin and fight over it. The obtrusively carnivorous children live off meat sandwiches. Dialogue in the book is horribly authentic but its horror is social; it is bloody in the metaphorical sense and crudely funny, largely because humour was not the author's intention:

"Mummy's already thought of the most wonderful eats," said Kate.

* * *

"I know, we are awful," said Valentine. "I'm sure no one else lets their hogged manes get in such a state."

* * *

"I'm hopeless on shoulders," said Laurence. "I never know a good shoulder on a horse when I see one, much less on a hound."

Someone comes out with an observation which sounds like a pop-song lyric, gone wrong: " 'Hounds will eat all the eats at the meet like they did last season.' "

The children's attitude throughout is firmly backed up by that of their elders, aggressive unthinking country gentlemen who are preoccupied with tradition, stupid in a way which is too easily caricaturable: "But Major Sunderland waved our thanks aside. 'It's wonderful to find such young enthusiasts in these days of anti-blood sports bills and all the abominations of modern civilisation,' he said." This type of snorting, blue-blooded bluntness is only moderately effective as satire because its inversions of judgement appear to be too complete; the author has added to its comic effect here, however, by presenting it with a straight face. Her adhesion to one point of view is so unwavering that she has not even found it necessary to state that the fox enjoys the foxhunt as much as anyone. This weak defence implies at least a defensive attitude on the part of its purveyor. The fox's feelings here are completely irrelevant, and this is odd in a type of fiction in which horses and dogs are endowed with near-human characteristics.

The stock type of pony story features a central character who longs for a pony but can't afford one; usually she is connected with a group of superior girls – relatives or school-fellows – who do have ponies but are not "natural" riders like the deprived heroine. She, however, by luck, pluck, or sheer determination, gets hold of a horse, a seemingly inferior animal which turns out to be a champion. In the less sophisticated stories she wins all the prizes at the county gymkhana; more restrained authors are content with allowing her to ride off with a couple of rosettes. Diana Pullein-Thompson's *I Wanted A Pony* (1946) sticks closely to this line of development, but the author has an unpretentious style and a quality of detachment which her sister (see above) lacks. The narrator's independence and the author's approval of it are conveyed with economy: "they were very scornful about anything they did not agree with and they often told me that *honestly* I was *queer.*" This strikes a note of clarity and observant good sense which is kept up throughout the book. Pony books on the whole are bound to bore anyone who is not fascinated by ponies; they have also a built-in riling effect because of the exclusive nature of pony owning: " 'Decent ponies are never given away – they are worth too much. That is why there is an old saying, 'Never look a gift horse in the mouth,' said Jill."

The odd tendency of certain young girls to identify strongly with horses has provided a profitable fictional theme. This may be worked out in terms of a central idea of poor-pony-girl-makes-good, or show the girl in command, subduing a refractory animal by her kindness to it, or identify one kind of dumb throughbred with the behaviour and mannerisms of another. The image of a girl on a horse may be presented as heroic or conventional, depending on the author's viewpoint; but naturally the reader's own tastes will supervene. The inelegant costume, the out-jutting coat and fattening jodhpurs, have a style which is firmly rooted in tradition. It is not only the horse, however, which is affronted by the rider's whip hand. It is difficult for the uncommitted reader to dissociate any pony book from the absurd, exasperating connotations which the genre has acquired. It is Enid Blyton, with her talent for heavy outlines, who has depicted the horsey girl at her most strident – Jane in *Six Cousins* and Bill in the *Malory Towers* series, for instance. The pony is effective as a symbol only when it is neither overloaded with crude associations nor sentimentalized, when it is integrated into a fictional scheme which would be depleted but not laid waste without it.

Bertram Prance illustration for Seven White Gates

XIX

"Time Present and Time Past ... "

"Even while the dust moves
There rises the hidden laughter
Of children in the foliage."

(T. S. Eliot, "Burnt Norton")

CHILDREN'S BOOKS IN recent years have become more open, more daring, episodic, highly charged; there has been a blurring of the rules which separate boys' fiction from girls', even adult literature from that intended for children. *Good* children's books, of course – classics, "cult" books, simply anything that is unusually well-written – have been enjoyed all along by adults, just as lightweight adult fiction is often appreciated by children. (It is not so much lack of judgement as lack of experience which enables them to respond to the Angèlique-Georgette Heyer type of romancing.) There is at present a tendency to represent childhood in terms of its emotional complexities; this, obviously, has led to a deepening of characterization, a stressing of each character's individuality and a merging of childhood with an extended social and psychological consciousness. It is no longer cut off, idyllically unrealistic or simply the unresponding vehicle on to which certain impossible chunks of adventure can be loaded. The adventure as such, the unfolding of a tale, is less important than the characters' reactions to it, but stories on the whole are no less eventful because of this. There is a subjective approach, and with it a shift to idiosyncracies of style and subject matter: in the better type of story, however, these are not mannered or self-indulgent. Childhood has been probed and investigated by writers like Lucy Boston and William Mayne, evoked with dispassion by Philippa Pearce and Gillian Avery; dissolved and dispersed by Alan

Garner and inflated triumphantly by Joan Aiken. For some authors it has been a question of thinking themselves back, for others an external summing up of some of the fundamental qualities of being a child. Philip Larkin's line – "Smaller and clearer as the years go by" – has a relevance here: the further back in childhood one goes, the greater is the necessity to confine oneself to clear, precise, diminutive images. "At night he dreamt of Christmas. He found the fieldmouse foreman decorating the Christmas tree. … His eyes were brimming with twinkle and his cheek was full of nuts." (L. M. Boston, *The Children of Green Knowe*, 1954.) William Mayne has managed to convey the endearing quality of extreme youth without being whimsical: " 'Don't catch a rabbit,' said Mary. She always hoped that a rabbit would one day invite her into its burrow; and how could it invite anybody who went rabbiting with Hewlin?" Mary "doesn't know yet which things are real and which unreal"; in her, the author has imaginatively reconstructed an expectant, egocentric, almost voluptuous state of feeling. It is a voluptuousness with the lushness removed: "Mary went in. Adam had not understood that she thought anyone would like to be lost in a cloud if they could; and that a cloud on a hill was the best place to lose yourself in."

William Mayne has devised a kind of dialogue in which the character speaks principally to himself to clarify some facet of his personality for his own benefit. His children are surprisingly articulate, but leave much unsaid. The possibilities for ambiguity, for private interpretation, are endless here, but the device is used also to project unequivocal feelings and uncertainties. Peter, in the same book, for instance, dissipates self-consciousness by focusing incessantly on his dog: the refrain "Come by, Hewlin", "Our Hewlin again", "All bangled, like our Hewlin" serves to divert attention away from himself and at the same time indicates his idea of himself as a boy with a dog. In *Earthfasts* (1966) the author's concern with psychological effect is everywhere apparent: he has got inside the characters who are confronted with a variety of phenomena, in order to express more explicitly their efforts to extend conventional definitions to accommodate their experiences of the supernatural.

There did not seem to be a link between the Keith and the

David who had ridden up Arkengarthdale that morning and talked with a drummer boy, and the Keith who was eating bread and butter by a house window in this afternoon. ... It was all black and strange. Keith was far away from the morning, at times, and far away from the afternoon at others. There were two distinct modes of being going on at once inside him; and the mood he was in was caused by the first mode playing against the second.

The author's explanations are entirely convincing; his reordering of "natural" events has in it a matter-of-fact quality and controlled tension which combine authoritatively. Everything is worked into this book; legend, superstition, a "scientific approach", psychological detail, a surface interest, a powerful evocation of scene; and everything *works,* because it is given just the right degree of emphasis. The characters are driven to extremes of feeling and experience (one even "dies") but there is no note of hysteria, no sense even of make-believe. The kind of striving-after-effect which has marred books like John Gordon's *The Giant Under the Snow* (1968) is completely absent here. The exactness, the lack of fuss, the logical strength of *Earthfasts* say much for the author's restraint.

Restraint is the last quality which has guided the composition of Joan Aiken's "unhistorical" adventure stories, but these have an exuberance, a pantomimic largeness which is equally effective. There is nothing original about her plots, but she has brought to bear on them a sensibility which *is* original, if only because of its ability to assimilate, re-channel, enliven, send up, make good use of elements and conventions already traditional. She has effected a fusion of Gothic with Baroque, set off by a manneristic flair for detail, both idiomatic and ornamental. Her books have reputable antecedents in *Uncle Silas*, the novels of Thomas Love Peacock, Dickens, the Brothers Grimm, *Treasure Island* and John Masefield's "Kay Harker" stories. But Joan Aiken's Nightmare Abbeys are all her own, her "Midnight Folk" are given an unexpected location – they are *Night Birds on Nantucket*, "Hanoverian" plotters, whose drastic design is to fire a gun across the Atlantic, in an attempt to slaughter the English king Jamie III at St James's Palace.

Joan Aiken has created, for her own purposes, a period in English history which never existed: the time is around 1832, but she has placed a Stuart king on the throne, infested the countryside with wolves and disgruntled Hanoverians, and erected a castle, a folly along the lines of the Brighton Pavilion, in Battersea Park. This device has a great economy: events which take place in an imaginary era are not governed by restrictions of plausibility, either social or temperamental. The period's non-existence serves mainly to emphasize that the stories are not meant to be pegged to the ground; their purpose is to take off as stylishly as possible. In a time that never happened anything *can* happen: wild dashes by air balloon; encounters with flirtatious pink whales; rides to London on an elephant named Rachel.

In the first book, *The Wolves of Willoughby Chase* (1962), the Gothic mood predominates.

> It was dusk – winter dusk. Snow lay white and shining over the pleated hills, and icicles hung from the forest trees. Snow lay piled on the dark road across Willoughby Wold, but from dawn men had been clearing it with brooms and shovels. There were hundreds of them at work, wrapped in sacking because of the bitter cold, and keeping together in groups for fear of the wolves, grown savage and reckless from hunger.

The principal girls in this story, Bonnie and Sylvia, are spirited but uninspired. Things happen to them, they have to deal with wolves and wicked governesses and suffer awful privations in an orphanage, but their characters are not developed; they lack the sheer perverse charm of the back-chatting urchin Dido Twite, whose appearance (in *Black Hearts in Battersea*) is unheralded by the conventional build-up for a heroine. Dido "was a shrewish-looking little creature of perhaps eight or nine, with sharp eyes of a pale washed-out blue and no eyebrows or eyelashes to speak of. Her straw-coloured hair was stringy and sticky with jam and she wore a dirty satin dress two sizes too small for her." She is, however, an archetypal scene-stealer, but the author *has* built up qualities in her which make for an expansion of this rôle. She is emphatically not a cute or beaming child in the Shirley Temple tradition. She is forthright, scornful, tough; knowing in the usual way of a London street-child; completely "modern" in her lack of emotional encumbrances. She has no use for her relatives, just as they have none for her. She is resourceful, intolerant of any kind of dithering, and prone to encounter and get the better of a whole cast of villains, including a spidery West Indies witch and a sinister "Mr Mystery". Miss Slighcarp, the awful governess of *The Wolves of Willoughby Chase*, turns up again in *Night Birds on Nantucket*; she is passing herself off as the timid Pen's Aunt Tribulation, and sits up in bed exactly in the manner of Red Riding Hood's wolf. Pen (short for Dutiful Penitence), befriended by Dido on board a whaling ship, is a slender-reed type of person who needs the irrepressible, sensible Dido to prop her up.

Joan Aiken's one failure is with Simon, the central figure of *Black Hearts in Battersea*. Simon has a whole pastoral tradition behind him, which to some extent has had a flattening effect. He is a type of rustic, noble-natured boy who has made a success of bringing himself up in a wood, living on chestnuts, who turns out to be a prince – or at least the Duke of Battersea. With Simon there is a slackening of the author's controlling amusement; she almost presents him seriously. She has given him no quirks of temperament, no interesting rough edges. He is an amalgam of Dick Whittington, a babe in the wood who survived (his sister survived too, as it turns out) and Oliver Twist. He sets out for London with a donkey and a kitten, to study art at Dr Furneaux's Academy in Chelsea, and is embroiled at once in a situation of Hanoverian intrigue. He is, however, played off the stage by Dido Twite, whose heart he has won, incidentally, by providing her with a new dress, a replacement for the dirty satin one, "two sizes too small". The new dress serves its purpose, is ruined in a shipwreck, and Dido takes to dressing like a sailor boy. By now her character has evolved sufficiently to fit this costume. She and Simon lose sight of one another for a couple of years, but are reunited up a Cuckoo tree – a scene, however, which is left to the reader's imagination.

The richness of the books is underlined by their dramatic contrasts.

There is opulence on the one hand and squalor on the other, and the characters are subjected to the most extreme experience of each. *Midnight is a Place* (1974) has its Midnight Court, a vast, stately, gentleman's residence set in a park, from which its hero, the boy Lucas Bell, goes out to work in the sewers of Blastburn. There is of course a comic sense, an unseriousness, which informs even the most horrific of Joan Aiken's events: horror is all on an extravagant level, which makes it less threatening, though it continues to stimulate. The books have a fairground kind of grotesqueness which is forceful and decorative. The fantasy which these stories contain is in no sense personal or nostalgically retrogressive; they are fanciful in a way that is formal, lucid and objective.

The sense of history has been important to many children's writers in the 1960s, whether their context is factual or – like Joan Aiken's – factitious. "History" is a thickening, an enriching agent, which needs, because of this, to be approached with caution. Often the most would-be factual writers are the most romantic: Hester Burton, for example, whose characters behave no less sentimentally for being placed against a background of "stirring" political or social events. And Rosemary Sutcliff's thorough documentation is, unfortunately, less noticeable than her glossy simplifications of character and scene. Her overall view of the past is unrefined, teeming with more significance, more villainy and nobleness than she can contain. Her people are merely glittery and dressed up; her melodrama can only have a wrong effect because she presents it with a straight face. It's true that she always has a story to tell, an elaboration of some idea of social progression or moral worth or physical agility, but even the suspense which this generates is of the most bland kind. The historical periods which she has imagined are unrelated in a productive way to the present, but fail to transmit a sense of their own authenticity. There is about the books a damning suggestion of fancy dress.

The most obvious way to play off the past against the present is to dream up a character who is impelled by some mysterious force from one to the other: these are the "time travellers", a band of children who need little further definition, in whom such uncanny elements are so concentrated that they seem always on the point of explosion.

Pat Marriott's wolves.
The Wolves of Willoughby Chase *(above)*;
Black Hearts in Battersea *(below)*

The idea has a power, an odd fascination; it has passed into the category of exterior or detached fantasy: fantasy, that is, which is common to everyone, which has its own framework, rules, everything but mode of expression. The latter, however, is the crux: E. Nesbit's style was suited to the theme, others' less so. Alison Uttley's famous *A Traveller in Time* (1939) is basically successful but tends towards the emotional; the author's own involvement has made for a slight weakening, a drop in tension. Levels of interest which ought to work separately are almost fused. It is Alison Uttley's sense of the particular which saves the book, her detailing of Elizabethan milk pails and leather jugs and warming pans and bunches of herbs: this gives it a quality of precision, a domestic quaintness which is acceptable because of its down-to-earth effect. The book has gathered up, and then discharged, the kind of imaginative concern which is felt with the minutiae of other people's lives. It provides also the ultimate rationalization of one kind of frustration: its unfortunate heroine falls in love with a person whom she meets frequently; the problem is that he belongs to another *time*. The emotional refinements of this situation are not stressed, and the basic emotion *is* sweetened, by the hushed reticence with which the author approaches it.

Gillian Avery's ground is intrinsically safer: the period which preoccupies her – the late Victorian era – is nearer to the present time, and less prone therefore to romantic inflation. Few historical writers, however, have seemed less inclined to glorify, or even prettify, their chosen setting. Psychologically Gillian Avery's books have a modern tone, constructively they have a stringency, a narrowing down to one basic objective or mood. The objective of her characters, usually, is to assert themselves in some particular way, the mood is usually one of embarrassment, and the books' drama comes of course from the conflict between these. The author has made good use of twentieth-century effects to project her view of the nineteenth century: she has simply presented the past *as* the present, by emphasizing its unevenness, prosaicness and normality. For us, of course, the past *is* strange. The sense of another time is conveyed externally, through the stories' props (which, however, are far more incidental than Alison Uttley's): the pantechnicons and copper boiling pans and knickerbocker suits. There is nothing retrospectively smooth, faded, or all of a piece about the author's view. The books in fact have a low-key irregularity, almost an irresolution, which is just kept under control.

Her characters are comically awful – James Smith, Amy Gresham – or politely, diffidently, but purposefully intelligent – Maria Hennicker-Haddon, Harriet Jessop, Julia Gresham. Some of the comedy comes from the confrontation of the two types. The embarrassment which the latter have to endure has nothing "refined" or staid about it, which might have been expected from the 1870s or '90s; it is spasmodic, irrational, mixed with teeth-grinding irritation. When conventions were more rigid, of course, the possibilities for social unease were frequent and its effects acute: in this sense the author has related her narrative tone exactly to the time in question. "At this point, overcome with horror, and hardly knowing what she did, Maria plunged down on her hands and knees under the table. ... Maria, not looking to right or left ... went on crawling up the room under the tables and bookcases." But it says much for Gillian Avery's effectiveness that one has to *remember* that eleven- and twelve-year-olds were not supposed to go about alone; it is, of course, their recentness, their independence, which is immediately striking about these children. Everything in the books is seen from their point of view: this is itself a recent tendency. Adults – usually eccentric or pompous – have had an oddness projected on to them by the children; their characters are conveyed in pieces, mannerisms, catch phrases, *idées fixes*, as these affect each child in succession. No adult is quite rounded off, viewed as an entity; their function is simply to alarm, exasperate or support the children.

The Warden's Niece came out in 1957; the period of its publication was in a sense more reactionary than that of its setting. The mid-'50s was a time when girls' aspirations were fixed to an almost unprecedented extent on early marriage, which was regarded as a mixture of liberation and achievement. In the 1870s feminism had at least a kind of dignity about it; it was a "cause", however freakish, waspish or esoteric its promoters were made out to be. It was accorded a certain degree of public recognition; it attracted supporters, its momentum was increasing. In the 1950s, in fact, the whole idea of feminism, with its connotations of the old-fashioned and the sexually repressed, appeared to be directly opposed to the kind of freedom which girls *were* seeking: freedom to leave home, to flaunt themselves in the manner of actresses and heiresses, to marry young. Women who followed careers seemed under some compulsion to write letters to magazines pointing out that they managed to keep house as well.

Gillian Avery, however, has no feminist axe to grind; it is simply an accident that her *Warden's Niece*, created in the 1950s, should stand out against the prevailing mood of that time. It is not that Maria is in any way fanatical, a child prodigy, or that she has been devised at all for a sociological purpose. She is merely unusually, creditably ambitious, without priggishness and without any kind of moral heroism. She has run away from school because she is "bad at geography" – yet she hopes to make her mark as a lecturer in Latin and Greek. There is no fuss about this ambition, either from the author or the other people in the book. The book contains an outrageous clergyman, a temporary tutor; the three Smith boys – lordly, conciliatory and bumptious respectively; and, offstage, a seventeenth-century boy who died at fourteen: the story involves Maria's efforts to piece together the history of this person. Her imagination has been set to work by a scrawled inscription on the wall of a stately home: "Begone ye foul traitors." This, with its suggestion of *a story*, is one of the book's most plausible touches: it is exactly the sort of thing to intrigue an intelligent child. Maria's research is impeded by tradition – " 'I should like to make it clear that I disapprove of women in the University' "; her own diffidence; and helped on by a bull. She almost gives up the project when she finds that it leads to "house-breaking, playing truant, gatecrashing into the Bodleian, and being a receiver of stolen property". She does, however, assemble an interesting collection of facts, only to meet with a final setback: "the trouble was that nobody seemed to care". But Maria is allowed to read her "learned paper" at the end, to the Kentish Historical Association.

Harriet Jessop, in *The Elephant War* (1960), has a mother who

414

takes an interest in Women's Rights, but wishes herself that "nobody had ever thought of improving girls' education". Harriet is bored, mildly discontented, fascinated by the Smith boys but unable to impress them (the action of this story takes place slightly before that of *The Warden's Niece*). As a heroine she is altogether less impressive than Maria, though no less convincing. Her formidable aunt involves her in a "cause", a campaign on behalf of Jumbo, an elephant at the London Zoo: this leads to a succession of farcical events. Harriet is not clever, but she has a kind of conscientious self-assertiveness which passes for intelligence. She is as prone as Maria to find herself in situations which are socially embarrassing: these are usually created by eight-year-old James Smith, who in this book is at his worst (" 'You're the most hateful boy that ever lived. ... And the stupidest' ").

In *The Greatest Gresham* (1962) two at least of the children accept the value of embarrassment as a means of broadening their minds: they force themselves to do things which their conservative parents deem "unsuitable", riding in a hansom cab, for instance, or accompanying the milkman on his rounds in fancy dress. They are made aware of their limitations of spirit by the "independent", attractive, motherless brother and sister next door – but these in their turn find things in the Greshams to admire. This is a conventional enough theme, but its treatment here, its edginess, hesitations, played-down ending, has given it an unusual psychological validity.

In the 1960s a "social problem" genre of children's literature began to develop: delinquency, child neglect, teenage pregnancies, juvenile vagrancy, "disturbed" secondary modern schoolchildren, children whose parents are getting divorced, the influx of West Indian boys and girls, all become suitable subjects for treatment. The results are mostly facile in tone and unhelpful in the kinds of solution which they offer. The dreary seduced girls have mums who turn up trumps in the end and agree to take in the unwanted babies; the girls find they love the babies after all; or the babies' fathers, having solved their own emotional problems off-stage, come back prepared for marriage. Josephine Kamm and Honor Arundel wrote several books of this type.

The tendency of girls to become infatuated with unsuitable, intense, misunderstood young men also has had extensive treatment. Catherine Storr used it as her basis for *Thursday*; an uneven, on the whole unsuccessful, story. In *The Chinese Egg* (1975), however, she has written a book which takes in many facets of contemporary existence: class distinctions, difficulties in communication between parents and children, the intricacies of teenage relationships. *The Chinese Egg* mixes fantasy and social comment with a more conventional police hunt for a group of kidnappers: it is exciting in the usual, superficial way of any thriller, but its concurrent themes move towards a point of integration which gives it a technical interest.

"Elsie, do you happen to have your smelling salts ...?"
Dick Hart illustrates The Warden's Niece

The adolescent girl is difficult to present unsentimentally. Typically, she has a feyness, an attractive self-consciousness which lends itself either to a kind of flowery abstraction – "The girl ... whose eyes were blue, green, brown? You do not know, only you know the girl was real, as real as day" – or to a chatty, smug, would-be realism – "You see, although Mum's nagging and old-fashioned views have got me down, I've never had any real reason not to shrug and at any rate pretend to go along with them. Now, for the first time, I had." These effects have been largely unnoticeable in the kind of story in which "action" is most important: it is only when the drama is social or emotional that they become obtrusive. The problem *is* being tackled, however: writers like Nina Beachcroft,

Penelope Farmer, Penelope Lively, Jane Gardam and Nina Bawden have presented heroines who are complex, unaccountable, capable of irony, judgement, self-realization. Jane Gardam's Jessica Vye (*A Long Way From Verona*, 1970) is articulate and perceptive; she has a wry sense of her own oddity, but suffers from all the frustrations and enthusiasms of the normal, intelligent thirteen-year-old; and her evocative, piecemeal existence is recreated with subtlety.

This book derives a great deal of its character from its wartime setting. More and more children's writers who grew up at this time are turning to the war years as a source of inspiration; and of course the disruption caused in people's private lives, the adjustments which everyone had to make, the driven, unnatural excitement, have a fascination now that they can be seen as safely, and quaintly, over. It takes about 25 years for a period to progress from dullness or desolation to absorbing interest.

Nina Bawden, in *Carrie's War* (1973), has brought to her depiction of a couple of evacuees clarity, unpretentiousness and disciplined imaginative resources; the book has a kind of condensed ordinariness which becomes in the end extraordinary. Its "odd" characters, Hepzibah and Mrs Gotobed and Mister Johnny, are, from a child's point of view, strange but comfortable, no more peculiar than most grown-ups. The story's climax, its dramatic point, comes as one of those startling coincidences which *seem* to have proved something totally unacceptable: in this case the connection is, effectively, neither pushed nor explained away. In *The Peppermint Pig* (1975) Nina Bawden has gone back further in time; to the Edwardian era, in fact, and the book begins with an Edwardian stock situation: a father wrongly accused of theft. In this respect it resembles *The Railway Children*; but Nina Bawden is less whimsical and far less sentimental than E. Nesbit. (*The Railway Children*, in any case, is not one of E. Nesbit's better books.) There is no dramatic resolution in *The Peppermint Pig*, nothing retrogressive or self-indulgent in its style. It is simply beautifully, meticulously observed throughout; its details of place and character are exactly *right*. Nothing much happens in the course of the story; a child is frightened by a mail coach near a haunted pond and comes to certain conclusions about the nature of fear; a couple of antagonistic boys make a silly bargain with one another; Johnnie, the "famous pet pig", is invited out to tea in the drawing-room of the manor house. Poll Greengrass, for a children's-book heroine, is presented with unusual fairness and detachment. The book's moral point, if it has one, is that change is inevitable. " 'We are carnivorous animals', " Poll's Aunt Sarah remarks. The pig is not saved.

Extremely odd things happen in *Charlotte Sometimes* (Penelope Farmer, 1969). Charlotte, a new girl at a present-day boarding school, finds that her identity is split between herself and someone called Clare, a girl who lived (and died) in 1918. This is an impressive fantasy: its elements are so cleverly structured that it appears plausible, and the reader is put in possession of just enough facts, successively, for interest to remain at a high level. You also get a supernatural element in Nina Beachcroft's *Cold Christmas* (1974); a ghost story which is marvellously astringent, delightfully chilly.

Penelope Lively's sixth and seventh novels are concerned with time, memory, continuousness, perceptions that are constantly and unconsciously shifting. The past does not "stand still"; its function is to affect, enrich, inform the present. This has always been the author's central theme; but in *The House in Norham Gardens* (1974.) and *Going Back* (1975) she has achieved a degree of refinement and integration that the earlier books, for all their excitement and inner rationality, lack. Overt fantasy in the books has become progressively less important; in *Going Back* it's done away with altogether, but the author has retained its quality in an extraordinary way: each small incident has its own significance, its place in a general pattern, and because of these an added power of suggestion. More is implied than is said, though it is the book's images rather than its characters' experiences that are memorable.

But it is perhaps *The House in Norham Gardens* that shows most clearly Penelope Lively's achievements. More substantial than *Going Back*, this is also less archetypal: its heroine, Clare Mayfield, has presence, individuality, humour, a kind of rashness. Oxford in winter, austere and sharply defined, is set off by brief evocations of violent green jungle – another time, an unimaginable civilization, recreated

A school meal
from Charlotte Sometimes, *drawn by Chris Connor*

in the pedantic notes of an Edwardian anthropologist. Clare's great-grandfather (dead) and her great-aunts (with whom she lives) represent something which she cannot altogether grasp: a process of accretion, a reconciliation of inner and outer experiences. For Clare, time is unbearably fluid, for the old it has crystallized, but Clare learns how to impose her own kind of order on both modes of experiencing.

The point about the above heroines is that they are all *there*, on their own terms, not to fulfil any symbolic or socially integrating function. The difficulties, moods, obsessions of adolescence *are* episodic, quickly changing; they cry out for a form of expression which is both sure and swift. Children's writers have been helped, basically, by the ending of restrictions on what they are allowed to mention – fifteen, twenty years ago sex could not be referred to, for example, even obliquely. But freedom of expression has its own dangers, as the dreadful unmarried-teenage-mother syndrome shows.

Alan Garner's five (so far) children's novels can be seen as a movement in one direction: towards increased internal pressure and thematic compression. The two earliest (published in 1960 and 1963) attracted a great deal of attention but seem now to be less satisfactory than the three which followed: of these, the latest, *Red Shift* (1973) has reached an extraordinary level of intensity, a merging of the most telling kind of realism with controlled hallucination.

Conversely, of course, there is a slackening of intensity as one proceeds backwards through the books. The 1960 *Weirdstone of Brisingamen* is a story of magic; of elves, trolls, wizards, dwarfs, a whole imaginary universe at the back of the real one, and the two children who are brought in to play their part in shoring it up. The book's central issue is the most general one, a conflict between "good" and "evil". The mythological background is expanded and in a sense flattened; the fantasy is external to the author's real preoccupations – continuity, repercussion, the affective power of symbolic objects – and the children's characters are much less important than the things which happen to them. In the sequel, *The Moon of Gomrath*, there is a slight shift towards particularization, a classifying of *kinds* of power: " 'The High Magic was made for a reason; the Old Magic is a part of things. It is not *for* any purpose.' " It is the girl whose personality is dominant here: " ' ... it is a woman's magic, too ... ' ". (It would be: it is natural, organic, secret, "a part of things".)

Taken together these books have an authority, a compelling effect; they are *imaginatively* believable. For his subject matter the author has drawn on a common store, a whole primitive oral heritage of embodied natural or emotional forces, but he has imbued the books with his own peculiar sense of these. His approach is more subtle than, for instance, William Croft Dickenson's (author of *Borrobil,* 1944), and the context which he provides for his supernatural images – that immaterial "other world" – in fact carries more weight than, for example, C. S. Lewis's. The author of the Narnia books had a weakening, Christian-allegorical tendency which he failed to contend with: the increasingly overt religious symbolism in the series has made for its overall deterioration. The use of Celtic or Norse mythology in children's books has a validity, a stimulating or enhancing effect of its own which the use of Christian mythology does not, chiefly because the latter is not generally accepted *as* mythological. In the first case it is the reader's imagination which is brought into play, though her moral sense may be indirectly involved; the richness of the reader's response will naturally depend upon the author's powers of suggestion and interpretation. Magic – in the form of legends and superstitions – is a significant part of everyone's experience. When it is used, however, to express a kind of Christianity which it parallels, it is robbed of its imaginative effect: it becomes merely a version of a myth which most children are expected, in the real world, to believe. It is impossible at the present time that a serious children's author could produce a "straight" story of religious conviction, but to dress up the theme in magical clothing can only have an odd, emotionally-strained effect. With C. S. Lewis the subject dictated its own conclusion: the children *had* to be killed in a railway accident so that "Narnia", or its extension, could turn into "heaven"; this is distasteful, a subjective fantasy which has got out of control.

In *The Weirdstone of Brisingamen* and *The Moon of Gomrath,* magic has a traditional, woodland setting. It emanates from stones, trees, grassy mounds; and the creatures which embody its blacker aspects are contained within a rabbit-warren of underground passages, caverns, and swamps. With *Elidor* (1965), however, comes a more conscious attempt to play off the prosaic world against the supernatural; the story has an excitement which derives from the queerness, the unexpectedness of events which take place in an ordinary house in suburban Manchester. There is not the complete acceptance of magic which is a feature of the earlier books, and because of this the peculiar things that happen are actually more effective:

> Mrs Watson's scream interrupted him. They rushed through to the kitchen and found her staring at the electric food mixer, which was spinning at top speed.
> "Switch it off!" cried Mrs Watson.
> "It is switched off, Mum," said Nicholas, and he took the plug out of the socket, to be certain. The mixer did not falter.

In *Elidor*, nothing is quite what it seems: four "Treasures" turn into a cracked cup, a bit of iron railing, a keystone from a derelict church, a couple of splintered laths nailed together like a sword. Magic is either magic, or static electricity. "Elidor" is a dead land: only by four children's efforts can its "light" be restored. The youngest child, Roland, is the most emotionally committed; but again it is the girl, Helen, who must work out the connection between two worlds. She is the "makeles mayde" who can pacify a unicorn.

There are no elves or wizards in *Elidor*. Its fantasy is more delicate and remote; the undertow of unexplainable forces is more important than a fairy-tale rationalization of these, though explanations *are* proffered. The children's brushes with the supernatural are fleeting and ambiguous, except for the first. The "shapes" which are oddly manifested from time to time have no form which is predictable or accountable, merely an ominous, intrusive presence. No crude moral effort is demanded of the children; they have to act simply in accordance with a set of rules which will – symbolically – put an end to a kind of disorder. Even Helen's "makelesness" is natural, since she is a child.

There is an explicit relation of one world to another in *Elidor*, and "natural" and "supernatural" are stressed alternately. "Magic" in *The Owl Service* (1967) has receded further from the surface; it is bound up with emotional pressures and its effects are disruptive. It is sparked off by a violent, lyrical story from the *Mabinogion*. There is no definable "other world" here, merely the creeping, inexorable, threatening overflow from a Welsh myth. The compulsion towards a form of re-enactment which overtakes the book's protagonists is rooted in their own natures but brought into play by powers external to them, by the heady contrast, within the myth, between Lleu's bride of flowers and the murderous sexual jealousy which her creation has unleashed. They are projected into an extremity of tension not their own, which comes near to taking them over; a kind of annihilating shift of feeling and purpose which is experienced subliminally. A ghostly, fatal pattern begins to impose itself.

The stresses, the irritability and bloody-mindedness of the characters, however, are explicable on the most rational, psychological level. The relation of each to everyone else is "difficult"; class-consciousness is involved in the most defensive, incommunicable way. Exasperation in each person is followed by the need to exasperate. A great deal is expressed by a gesture or exclamation. Of the three adolescents the most interesting is the "scholarship" Welsh boy, Gwyn; Roger and Alison, step-brother and sister, are smooth, moody, or simply reluctant to commit themselves. It is Alison who responds most unquestioningly to the indefinable, residual *sensations* which she perceives: there is a certain vacuousness in her nature which makes her malleable, receptive. She remains passive throughout.

She discharges a kind of sexual poignancy, however, which has a great deal of charm. *The Owl Service* is perhaps the first really *adult* children's book; the first book, that is, in which childish sensibilities are not deferred to, in which the author has not felt that his audience needs, above all, to be protected. In *Red Shift* the mood is even starker; there is no "romance" in the sense of a rarefied or fabulous dimension, only a movement backwards, a paring down of violence, of states of intensity, to the bare bone. This is in no sense an easy novel; its own concentration, its layered quality, demands a reciprocal degree of concentration from the reader. It has a density which must be allowed to work its own effect. In a remarkable way, the author has expressed the *depth* of the past, as well as its immediacy; each period of time has a distinctive quality which is established with extraordinary conviction. There is a tangible object, a stone axe head used by a disorganized Roman Legion, built into a seventeenth-century hearth and unearthed by the book's present-day characters, Tom and Jan, which links each period with the others; but the intangible forces which it symbolizes are pervasive and continuous. It has been an instrument of slaughter and rape, and connected extrinsically with a massacre in a church during the Civil War. Near the place where it was walled up someone has scrawled an ambiguous, disturbing phrase: "not now never not any more"; this is made somehow to have a connection with the degrees of betrayal and emotional failure which are the book's subsidiary themes.

The fact that it revolves around an adolescent sexual relationship has given *Red Shift* a sociological importance which has nothing to do with its value as literature: this is considerable, in spite of the kinds of criticism which the book has already attracted. Obviously, it is an *intelligent* children's book; it demands a certain knowledge, and a positive receptivity to the underlying subtleties of its composition. Moreover, it is not aimed in an exclusive way at a particular readership; like adult novels beyond a certain level of intelligence, its appeal is unlikely to be affected by considerations of sex, or, on an upward scale, age. This is one reason why we have ended a study of girls' fiction with a book not written specifically for girls: it is becoming obvious that it is better, less restricting, more related to quality, in the end more economical, to write books which may be read by anyone. The term "women's fiction" has always had a derogatory implication which brushed off to a certain extent on girls; we have tried to show which stories deserved the dismissals involved in this, and which did not. The standard plots and characters that flourished twenty or fifty years ago are now obsolete: at best they show a kind of innocence that's related to their unconscious humour, at worst they are boring or stiffly melodramatic. The school story, the pony story, girl detectives and girl Crusoes have merged in a genre which exploited the light-headed aspect of childhood, and also its silliness. There *were* exceptions, but they stood out: the qualities that made them notable have suddenly proliferated. Techniques of presentation have become more subtle, more idiosyncratic. Children's books are no longer something to be grown out of: they have acquired a literary standing, with its attendant glamour; they can be criticized as seriously as anything else. Their characters at all levels are complex: maladjusted, nervous, stolid, perceptive or sedate. Various kinds of emotion have been analysed exhaustively, with results that are rarely tiresome. The best children's authors tend to see childhood in relation to adult experience: the characters' potential is implied, with all the interrelating facets of personality and situation. It is clear too that the classification of a book according to the sex of its author or its protagonists can only have a limiting, a cutting-off, effect. It is perhaps significant that the books which are truly imaginative – *Alice's Adventures in Wonderland*, the E. Nesbit stories, in recent years the books of Alan Garner – cannot be pigeon-holed like this. In the end it is the polarities of "good" and "bad" that are important; and distinction in writing for children, or anyone else, is a quality which, like all others that have involved the exercise of reason or imagination, is not sexually determined.

POSTSCRIPT

Into the Eighties

The ten years following 1975 have seen some unprecedented developments in the field of children's books. For one thing, the sense of moral obligation, which governs all writing for children, has acquired a new bias. It used to entail keeping your stories as anodyne as possible; now, if anything, the opposite holds true. Painful topics have become virtually *de rigueur,* as far as children's fiction is concerned. It's as if contemporary authors are terribly afraid of lumbering their audience with a false belief in the essential snugness of the world. No subject is now considered out-of-bounds to an impressionable readership. Snobbery, racist bullying, inner-city violence, dyslexia, sexual deviation, trouble in the home, unresolved miseries at school, bed-wetting, the political situation in Chile, epilepsy and mental deficiency have all received a showing. A recent, cheery novel by Betsy Byers, *Cracker Jackson,* concerns wife-and child-battering. Authors like Robert Cormier have written about dying teenagers, in a way far removed from the Victorian handling of the theme.

The trick is to keep the narrative tone pretty palatable, while allowing the events of a plot to get grimmer or racier than they used to be. Delinquent, inadequate or simply absent parents loom large in recent works for children — perhaps conceived in reaction to all those bland parental figures of the '40s and '50s — but usually there's a lesson about tolerance or resourcefulness implicit in the central characters' eventual attitude to them. 1983, indeed, was the year of the absconding father in juvenile fiction, while in 1984 a slight shift of emphasis occurred. Adultery (the favourite sub-plot of that year) was in the minds of many heroes and heroines worried by unusual behaviour in a parent. Other foibles on the part of parents included undue social consciousness, and the resultant installation of a couple of unmanageable boys in the family home ("It's our duty to help the underprivileged") — an episode blithely recounted by Gene Kemp in her novel *No Place Like*. Among the more outré adolescent anxieties envisaged by authors we find a dread of spontaneous combustion, and a fear that one's father has gone round the bend. Ordinary worries continue to proliferate. Is one's bust expanding at a too-rapid rate? What's to be done about one's horrid schoolfellows? Why is one endowed with insufficient cheek?

There are many pitfalls for the social realists among children's authors. It didn't, for example, take the whole high-rise, multi-racial, adventure-playground syndrome too long to acquire a faintly risible overtone. An impeccably rational or liberal approach, unfortunately, doesn't always rule out earnestness. You notice this, perhaps, especially in those novels featuring a blameless heroine who suffers on account of some flaw in the social system, or some obtuse attitude on the part of an adult. There are still, it seems, too few authors like Gillian Avery who treat fashionable causes in the most effective way: with amiable and high-spirited mockery. *The Elephant War,* which was set in the 1860s, goes in for this stimulating tone; and it does just as well for an Avery novel of the 1970s, *Huck and Her Time Machine*. This particular piece of time-travelling (a long-lasting device) is perfectly attuned to the present. There are, however, other inveterate motifs of the genre which — in the hands of authors bent on striking an up-to-the-minute note — can take an infelicitous turn. One example is the old "bosom friends" theme, with a lesbian dimension added.

Naturally, among the books applauded for showing social enlightenment are those which take a firm feminist line — it's no longer amusing or admirable, if you're a girl, to attain your ends by devious means (we remember those story-paper serials from the '50s, like *School Friend's* "Sue—The Girl Next Door") or to opt for marriage in lieu of a career. As with all fiction designed to foster some desirable social adjustment, though, the best of the feminist tales keep their implications subtle — we have Jan Marks's *Handles,* for example, with its motorbike-enthusiast heroine foisted for the summer on some charmless relatives, and the discovery of a motor-

Retold by Alison Lurie

CLEVER GRETCHEN
AND OTHER FORGOTTEN
FOLKTALES

Illustrated by Margot Tomes

cycle workshop nearby to cheer things up. We find, too, a revival of bygone stories which conform to feminist requirements of the present time: Alison Lurie, for instance — in *Clever Gretchen* — has assembled some "forgotten folktales", all of them featuring heroines to whom a "Sleeping Beauty" type of passivity is utterly alien. In the same genre is K.M. Briggs's wonderful retelling of the old *Kate Crackernuts* story (first published in 1963) — another timely reissue.

In the midst of all this progressiveness it's somewhat surprising to find a strong resurgence of interest in the traditional girls' school story — but there it is. Schoolgirl heroines continue to have a ripping time, to be cut off (by the tide) or cut up (at someone's sneaky behaviour) in reprints of past best-sellers like Dorita Fairlie Bruce's Dimsie books, Elinor Brent-Dyer's Chalet School series, and Enid Blyton's tales of Malory Towers and St Clare's. And the sporting, plucky schoolgirl has received some new incarnations. Anne Digby's Trebizon School series, launched in 1978, now runs to nine titles, all of them harking back in atmosphere to the pre-war *School Friend.* Trebizon is one of those fictional boarding-schools that are colourfully located (this one's at the mouth of a huge bay fringed with golden sand), and come complete with a tall clock tower in the grounds to generate goings-on.

Balcombe Hall (created by Harriet Martyn), like Trebizon, makes a school series which reproduces the flavour of the past while keeping its details firmly up to date. The heroine of the Trebizon stories, for example, is obliged to board at the school because her oil-expert father has secured a post abroad — not in the outposts of the British Empire, to be sure, but with the Saudis. At Balcombe Hall, the girls are fearfully keen on Jeremy Irons, watch soap-operas like *Dynasty*, understand the principles of word-processors and can boast a headmistress who sports moon boots.

Peter Glidewell's stories of St Ursula's — first produced for BBC TV and now available in narrative form — include spies and secret panels among their inspiriting ingredients. Glidewell's *Schoolgirl Chums* has a new girl, Alison Dayne, falling for delectable Miss Anastasia Devine and falling foul of putrid Miss Prosser — not to mention performing a familiar life-saving feat when the school

429

catches fire. (The author of these stories disowns any impulse towards burlesque.)

The resilience of the British schoolgirl, as an evocative figment, is further illustrated by the success of Denise Deegan's Brazil-inspired send-up, *Daisy Pulls It Off* (winner of the 1983 "Best West-End Comedy" award); and by an exhibition of schoolgirl stories and artefacts put on in 1984 at the Bethnal Green Museum of Childhood (*Jolly Hockey Sticks* was the title). Whom do we find among the audiences for these entertainments? Adults looking back with relish, naturally enough, but also innumerable Comprehensive schoolchildren tickled to death by the gymslip genre.

However, it's undoubtedly the Grange Hill Comprehensive adventures which have proved to be the most innovatory and addictive school stories of the present decade. Featuring girls and boys in more or less equal measure, these began as spin-offs from the TV series launched in 1978, which stimulated controversy by virtue of its extreme realism, but quickly started to look like a national institution. Some of the Grange Hill books appear under the name of Phil Redmond (creator of the television series), while others are the work of Robert Leeson and Jan Needle. The books provide, for Grange Hill's heroes and heroines, experiences rather more complex than the small-screen programmes can encompass; and, partly because of the publicity arising from their media links, they attract an enormous readership including children who aren't habitual readers. Robert Leeson — in *Reading and Righting,* his history of children's fiction — states firmly that "if you do not appear in the stories of your society's culture, you do not exist". Certainly the multi-cultural Grange Hill books offer a sufficient range of characters for almost every kind of child to find in them a focus of interest.

Leeson has a keen ear for the rhythms and resonances of school and playground dialogue, and a knack of communicating working-class robustness and humour. Because they go all out for undiluted topicality, the stories tend to stress such facts of modern life as shortage of resources, bullying at school as a reflection of urban violence and decline, and the problems that many young people experience in finding work, or existing on the dole.

GENE KEMP

THE TURBULENT TERM OF TYKE TILER

A Carnegie Medal Winner

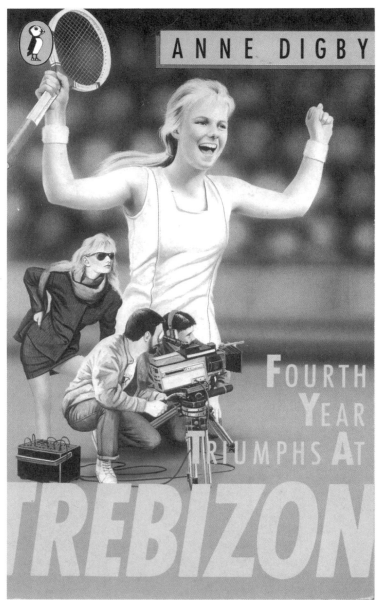

ANNE DIGBY

FOURTH
YEAR
TRIUMPHS AT
TREBIZON

Still in the day school context, Jan Marks, in a story called *Chutzpah* (from her collection *Hairs in the Palm of the Hand*), has a good deal of fun with the doings of an emphatic Comprehensive schoolgirl who leads a campaign for women's rights (wood-and metal-work lessons to begin with) in the classroom. And Alison Prince, in her stories of Mill Green School (five titles to date) gets to grips with arson, theft and various other dramatic occurrences, all designed to show how life at a country Comprehensive can be every bit as eventful as it is at Grange Hill.

In *Save Our School* and *The Mintyglo Kid* Gillian Gross has produced a schoolgirl heroine who embodies the sharpness of the 1980s, while at the same time bringing to mind the irrepressibility of Evadne Price's Jane. Strongly feminist Clipper, who is black, takes the lead in a group consisting mainly of white boys. Sturdily written, and with a progressive tone throughout (but without banging the drum of social awareness too loudly) these books take a clear-headed look at some community and personal issues afflicting present-day children.

Two further stories with school settings must be mentioned, each of them centred on an unlikely friendship. Posh Becky, in *Cora Ravenwing* (by Gina Wilson) befriends quaint, rather farouche Cora in the face of disapproval from everyone around her. And in Gene Kemp's diverting book *The Turbulent Term of Tyke Tiler,* a bright child forms an alliance with a rather dim one. In a sex-role reversal twist to the story's tail (giving an exhilarating boost to the feminist cause), Tyke, the iconoclast and rebel, quite literally raises the roof of the school. Even in the face of strong competition from new and established children's authors, Gene Kemp, with this novel, puts herself at the forefront of the school genre.

Turning to the girls' weekly papers (or, to be exact, comics, as stories seem to have been replaced altogether by picturestrips), we find frequent and desperate attempts to come up with new themes and formats. However, in essence, the papers of the '80s are repeating the old plots of thirty years ago. There are minor adjustments, of course. Girls now aspire to be pop-singers rather than screen actresses, and their relations with boy friends are less staid than they used to be. Photo-strips, in many cases, have taken over from line drawings — conducive to realism of a kind, perhaps, but also restricting activities available to heroines. Only in the D.C. Thomson paper of the late 1970s, *Spellbound,* along with I.P.C.'s *Misty,* was there any attempt to break new ground. Both papers (now defunct) went to town on the preposterously supernatural, presenting ambulant Egyptian mummies, reluctant teenage witches, all-girl interplanetary air crews, and the like. In 1981, a new version of the 1950s Hulton *Girl* was launched by I.P.C.; however, this proved to be rather less addictive in quality than the prototype, despite the odd memorable injunction like the one which occurs in "Sally's Dance of Sorrow" (the statutory ballet story) — "Right, now, girls. Let's have you in the first position ..."

Ghosts, magic and shifts in time and space continue to activate the imaginations of many contemporary authors. Vivian Alcock's *The Haunting of Cassie Palmer,* and the American writer Sylvia Cassedy's *Behind the Attic Wall* (a novel reminiscent of *The Secret Garden,* with a misery-guts and hair-chewer acquiring a better personality by a supernatural means), are among the best of the recent fantasy stock; but there's nothing, to date, to surpass in excellence of construction and imaginative vitality those books on similar themes by Philippa Pearce, Penelope Lively and Alan Garner (see Chapter XIX).

Since 1975, we've been inundated with fiction tackling the tricky business of growing up, biology, psychology and all. (Not to mention the great spate of juvenile "romances" aimed apparently at future addicts of Mills and Boon.) The American Judy Blume is one of the pioneers of this sub-genre, and the plain-spokenness of her early 1970s offering, *Are You There, God? It's Me, Margaret* has influenced many similar stories on both sides of the Atlantic. Some of the most highly-regarded of the "growing-up" books consider the effects of social rejection on the grounds of sex, race or some other supposedly lowering condition. Notable studies of racist issues include Mildred Taylor's *Roll of Thunder, Hear My Cry* and *Let The Circle Be Unbroken*; and *Comfort Herself* by Geraldine Kaye, which has a half-English, half-Ghanaian heroine plentifully endowed with charm and gumption. These, like other similarly successful novels, work well because they never skimp on story-telling in the interests of conveying a social message. Recent developments in feminist and anti-racist fiction for children demand a detailed study which is beyond the scope of this postscript. An excellent outline for such a study is provided in *Ms Muffett Fights Back,* a non-sexist booklist by Rosemary Stones, who, incidentally has compiled what is possibly the first-ever collection of short stories "for young feminists" published at the end of 1985 under the title of *More To Life Than Mr Right.* Contributors include Fay Weldon, Michèle Roberts, Stella Ibekwe and Ravi Randhawa, and the wit and vigour of the stories suggest some interesting new possibilities for the future of girls' fiction.

MARY CADOGAN
PATRICIA CRAIG
1985

SELECT BIBLIOGRAPHY

BOOKS

Adley D. J., Lloyd Ruth & Norman *The American Heritage Song Book*, New York

Brittain Vera,*Lady Into Woman*, Andrew Dakers, London, 1953
     Testament Of Youth, Gollancz, London, 1933

Buckler Helen & Ors. *Wohelo. The Story Of Camp Fire Girls*, 1910-1960, Camp Fire Girls Inc., New York, 1961

Calder Angus,*The People's War*, Cape, London, 1969

Doyle Brian (ed.),*The Who's Who Of Children's Literature*, Hugh Evelyn, London, 1968

Fayne Eric (ed.),*Collectors' Digest*, Crookham, Hants

Gatty Charles N., *The Bloomer Girls*, Femina Books, London, 1966

Green Roger L., *Tellers Of Tales*, Kaye & Ward, London, 1947

Groves Ernest R.,*The American Woman*, Emmerson Books Inc., New York, 1942

Kerr Rose,*The Story Of The Girl Guides*, Girl Guides' Association, London, 1932

Lazell David,*Flora Klickmann And Her Flower Patch*, Bristol, 1974

Lofts W. O. G. &*Old Boys' Books: A Complete Catalogue*, London, 1969

Lutyens Lady Emily, *A Blessed Girl*, Hart-Davis, London, 1953

Muggeridge Malcolm, *The Thirties*, Hamish Hamilton, London, 1940

Newson John,*The Education Of Girls*, Faber, London, 1953

Priestley J. B., *The Edwardians*, Heinemann, London, 1970

Read Donald, *Edwardian England*, Historical Association, London, 1972

Roe F. Gordon, *The Victorian Child*, Phoenix House, London, 1959

Smith Constance Babington, *Amy Johnson*, Collins, London, 1967

Spender Stephen, *Citizens In War – And After*, Harrap, London, 1945

Stuart Dorothy M., *The Girl Through The Ages*, Harrap, London, 1933

Sutherland Gillian, *Elementary Education In The Nineteenth Century*, Historical Association, London, 1971

Thomas Katherine, *Women In Nazi Germany*, Gollancz, London, 1944

Trevelyan G. M., *Illustrated English Social History*, vol.4., Longmans, London, 1949

Woolf Virginia, *Three Guineas*, Hogarth Press, London, 1938

ARTICLES

Muir Lynette, "Fifty Years Of The Hamlet Club", *The Junior Bookshelf*, February 1966

Tatham C. S., "Yesterday's Schoolgirls", *The Junior Bookshelf*, December 1969

WORKS DISCUSSED IN TEXT

(The dates given for American titles are, wherever possible, those when first published in Britain, except for original magazine serializations.)

Chapter I

BOOKS

Eliot George
> *Adam Bede,* Blackwood, London 1859

Ewing Mrs
> *The Story Of A Short Life*, SPCK, London, 1885

Sherwood Mrs
> *The Fairchild Family*, London, 1818

Sinclair Catherine
> *Holiday House*, London, 1839

Walton Mrs Octavius F.
> *A Peep Behind The Scenes*, Religious Tract Society, London, 1877 (paperback, Lutterworth Press, London, 1972)

Yonge Charlotte M.
> *The Daisy Chain*, London, 1856
> *The Little Duke*, originally serialized in *The Monthly Packet*, 1851; reprinted Dent, Dutton, London, 1963

STORIES

Ewing Mrs
> "A Great Emergency", serialized in *Aunt Judy's Magazine*, 1874; reprinted in *A Great Emergency And A Very Ill-Tempered Family* Gollancz, London, 1967

Yonge Charlotte M.
> "A Patchwork Fever", originally published in *Langley*

Adventures, 1883; reprinted in *Village Children*, Gollancz, London, 1967

PERIODICALS

Aunt Judy's Magazine, Mrs Margaret Gatty (ed.), Bell & Daddy, London, issues in 1867 and 1874

Girl's Realm Magazine (The), Hutchinson, London, 1899

Monthly Packet (The), Charlotte M. Yonge (ed.) John & Chas. Mozley, London, issues in 1852, 1860-1861

Chapter II

BOOKS

<u>Alcott Louisa May</u>

  Good Wives, London, 1869

  Jo's Boys, Sampson Low, London, 1886

  Little Men, Sampson Low, 1871

  Little Women, originally serialized in *Merry's Museum*, 1867; first published as a book, 1868

<u>Coolidge Susan</u>

  Clover, London 1888

  In The High Valley, London, 1891

  What Katy Did, Ward Lock & Tyler, London, 1873

  What Katy Did At School, Ward Lock & Tyler, London, 1874

  What Katy Did Next, Ward Lock, London, 1887

<u>Finley Martha</u>

  Elsie Dinsmore, London, 1867

  Elsie's Widowhood, Routledge & Sons, London,1889

<u>Stowe Harriet Beecher</u>

  Uncle Tom's Cabin, originally serialized in *The National Era*, 1851-1852; first published as a book, 1868

PERIODICALS

St. Nicholas, Mary Mapes Dodge (ed.) Century Co., New York, issues in 1886-1887, 1901-1902

Chapter III

BOOKS

Carroll Lewis

> *Alice's Adventures In Wonderland*, Macmillan, London, 1865

Green Evelyn Everett

> *A Difficult Daughter*, Pilgrim Press, London, 1930

Marchant Bessie

> *A Girl Munition Worker*, Blackie, London, 1916
>
> *A Princess of Servia*, Blackie, London, 1912
>
> *The Half Moon Girl, or The Rajah's Daughter*, Partridge, London, 1898

Meade L. T.

> *A Sweet Girl Graduate*, Cassell, London, 1886
>
> *A World Of Girls*, Cassell, 1886

Molesworth Mrs

> *Greyling Towers*, Chambers, London, 1898
>
> *Imogen, or Only Eighteen*, Chambers, London, 1892
>
> *My New Home*, Macmillan, London, 1894; reprint Gollancz, London, 1968
>
> *The Carved Lions*, London, 1895; reprint Dent, Dutton, London, 1964

Sewell Anna

> *Black Beauty*, London, 1877

STORIES

Green Evelyn Everett

> "A Pair Of Pickles", serialized in *Little Folks*, 1891

Meade L. T.

> "Four On An Island", serialized in *Little Folks*, 1891

PERIODICALS

Little Folks, Cassell, London, issues in 1890-1891

Chapter IV

BOOKS

<u>Burnett Frances Hodgson</u>

 A Little Princess, Warne, London, 1905

 Little Lord Fauntleroy, originally serialized in *St Nicholas*,
 1885-1886; first published as a book, Warne, London, 1886

 Sara Crewe, or What Happened At Miss Minchin's,
 originally serialized in *St. Nicholas*, 1887; first published
 as a book, Warne, London, 1888

 That Lass O' Lowrie's, Warne, London, 1876

 The Secret Garden, Heinemann, London, 1911

<u>Gaskell Mrs</u>

 Mary Barton, Chapman & Hall, London, 1848

 North and South, originally serialized in *Household
 Words*, 1854-1855; first published as a book, Chapman &
 Hall, London, 1855

STORIES

<u>Burnett Frances Hodgson</u>

 "Racketty Packetty House", Barne, London, 1907;
 reprinted in *Victoria-Bess & Others*, Gollancz, London,
 1968

PERIODICALS

Girl's Realm Magazine (The), Hutchinson, London, issues in
1898-1899

Chapter V

BOOKS

<u>Brittain Vera</u>

 Testament Of Youth, Gollancz, London, 1933

<u>Nesbit E.</u>

 My Schooldays, originally serialized in the *Girl's Own Paper*,
 1896-1897; reprinted as *Long Ago When I Was Young*, Ronald
 Whiting & Wheating, London, 1966

The Story Of The Amulet, T. Fisher Unwin, London, 1906
The Story Of The Treasure Seekers, T. Fisher Unwin, London, 1899

Vaizey Mrs George de Horne
More About Pixie, Religious Tract Society, London, 1903
Pixie O'Shaughnessy, Religious Tract Society, London, 1900
The Independence Of Claire, originally serialized in the *Girl's Own Paper*, 1915; first published as a book, Religious Tract Society, London, 1915
The Love Affairs Of Pixie, Religious Tract Society, London, 1914
The Salt Of Life, Mills & Boon, London, 1915

Wells H. G.
Ann Veronica, T. Fisher Unwin, London, 1909

PERIODICALS

Boy's Own Paper (The) Religious Tract Society, London, issues from 1879-1900

Girl's Own Paper (The) Religious Tract Society, London, issues from 1880-1916

Girl's Realm Magazine (The) Bousefield, London, issues from 1902-1905; and Cassell, London, issues from 1914-1915

Chapter VI

BOOKS

Montgomery L. M.
Anne Of Green Gables, Pitman, London, 1908
Anne Of Windy Willows, Harrap, London, 1936

Porter Eleanor H.
Pollyanna, Pitman, London, 1913
Pollyanna Grows Up, Pitman, London, 1915

Porter Gene Stratton
A Girl Of The Limberlost, Doubleday, Page & Co., New York, 1909

Webster Jean
Daddy-Long-Legs, Hodder & Stoughton, London, 1912
Wiggin Kate Douglas
Rebecca Of Sunnybrook Farm, Gay & Bird, London, 1903

Chapter VII

BOOKS
Brazil Angela
A Fourth Form Friendship, Blackie, London, 1912
A Patriotic Schoolgirl, Blackie, London, 1918
A Popular Schoolgirl, Blackie, London, 1920
A Terrible Tomboy, Milford, London, 1906
For The School Colours, Blackie, London, 1919
My Own Schooldays, Blackie, London, 1927
The Fortunes Of Philippa, Blackie, London, 1906
The Luckiest Girl In The School, Blackie, London, 1916
The School By The Sea, Blackie, London, 1914
The Third Class At Miss Kaye's, Blackie, London, 1908
The Youngest Girl In The Fifth, Blackie, London, 1914

Chapter VIII

PERIODICALS
Girls' Favourite (The), Amalgamated Press, London, issues from 1922-1923
Girls' Friend (The), Amalgamated Press, London, issues from 1907-1920
Girls' Home (The),Amalgamated Press, London, issues from 1910-1915
Girls' Reader (The), Amalgamated Press, London, issues from 1908-1915
Girls'Weekly (The), D.C. Thomson, London, issues from 1912-1922
Marvel (The), Amalgamated Press, London, issue of 1901
Peg's Paper, Newnes & Pearson, London, issues from 1919-1940

Chapter IX

BOOKS

Brent-Dyer Elinor

>_Judy The Guide_, Nelson, London 1928
>
>_The Princess Of The Chalet School_, Chambers, London, 1927

Christian Catherine

>_The Big Test_, Girl Guides' Association, London, 1947
>
>_The Kingfishers See It Through_, Blackie, London
>
>_The Marigolds Make Good_, Blackie, London, 1937
>
>_The Seventh Magpie_, Blackie, London

Chaundler Christine

>_Bunty Among The Blackbirds_, Nisbet, London, 1925

Darch Winifred

>_Poppies And Prefects_, OUP, London, 1923

Hann Mrs A. C. Osborn

>_Peg's Patrol_, Religious Tract Society, London, 1924

Kerr Rose

>_The Story Of The Girl Guides_, Girl Guides' Association, London, 1932

Moore Dorothea

>_Brenda Of Beech House_, Collins, London, 1927
>
>_Judy Patrol Leader_, Collins, London, 1930
>
>_Terry The Girl-Guide_, Nisbet, London, 1912

Powell Robert Baden

>_Scouting For Boys_, Pearson, London, 1908

Talbot Ethel

>_Patricia Prefect_, Nelson, London, 1925
>
>_Peggy's Last Term_, Nelson, London, 1920

Wynne May

>_The Camping Of The Marigolds_, Marshall Morgan & Scott, London

STORIES

Talbot Ethel

>"Luck", from _British Girls' Annual_, Cassell, London, 1919

Yates Evelyn

"The Girl Scouts", serialized in the *Girls' Reader*,
Amalgamated Press, London, 1909

PERIODICALS

Gem, The, Amalgamated Press, London, issue of 1909
Girl's Own Paper (The), Lutterworth Press, London, issue of 1940
Little Folks, Cassell, London, issues of 1919

Chapter X

BOOKS

Brazil Angela

For The Sake Of The School, Blackie, London, 1915

Devries Julianne

Camp Fire Girls At Holly House, New York, 1933

Oxenham Elsie

Girls Of The Hamlet Club, Collins, London, 1914
Jen Of The Abbey School, Collins, London, 1927
The New Abbey Girls, Collins, London, 1923
Queen Of The Abbey Girls, Collins, London, 1926
Robins In The Abbey, Collins, London, 1947
The Abbey Girls, Collins, London, 1920
The Abbey Girls Again, Collins, London, 1924
The Abbey Girls At Home, Collins, London, 1928
The Abbey Girls Go Back To School, Collins, London, 1922
The Abbey Girls On Trial, Collins, London, 1931
The Abbey Girls Win Through, Collins, London, 1928
Two Queens At The Abbey, Collins, London, 1959

Rietz Harriet

Mary Lee, The Campfire Girl, New York, 1917

Stewart Jane L.

Camp Fire Girls At The Sea Shore, New York, 1914

Chapter XI

BOOKS

Brent-Dyer Elinor

Lavender Laughs In The Chalet School, Chambers, London, 1943
Prefects At The Chalet School, Chambers, London, 1970
Rivals Of The Chalet School, Chambers, London, 1929
The Chalet School Goes To It, Chambers, London, 1941
The Head Girl Of The Chalet School, Chambers, London, 1928
The School At The Chalet, Chambers, London, 1925
Three Go To The Chalet School, Chambers, London, 1949

Bruce Dorita Fairlie

Captain Of Springdale, OUP, London, 1932
Dimsie Among The Prefects, OUP, London, 1923
Dimsie Goes Back, OUP, London, 1927
Dimsie Grows Up, OUP, London, 1924
Dimsie Intervenes, OUP, London, 1937
Dimsie Moves Up, OUP, London, 1921
Dimsie Moves Up Again, OUP, London, 1922
Nancy At St Bride's, OUP, London, 1933
Nancy Calls The Tune, OUP, London, 1944
Prefects At Springdale, OUP, London, 1936
That Boarding-School Girl, OUP, London, 1928
The Best House In The School, OUP, London, 1930
The Senior Prefect, OUP, London, 1920

Chaundler Christine

The Chivalrous Fifth, Nelson, London, 1928

Darch Winifred

Heather At The High School, OUP, London, 1924

Elder Josephine

Evelyn Finds Herself, OUP, London, 1929

Harris Mary K.

Jessica On Her Own, Faber, London, 1966
Penny's Way, Faber, London, 1963
The Bus Girls, Faber, London, 1965

Chapter XII

BOOKS

<u>Crompton Richmal</u>

Just William, Newnes, London, 1922

More William, Newnes, London, 1922

Still William, Newnes, London, 1925

William And The Brains Trust, Newnes, London, 1945

William And The Moon Rocket, Newnes, London, 1954

William Does His Bit, Newnes, London, 1941

William The Bad, Newnes, London, 1930

William The Bold, Newnes, London, 1950

William The Detective, Newnes, London, 1935

William The Fourth, Newnes, London, 1924

William The Gangster, Newnes, London, 1934

William The Good, Newnes, London, 1928

William The Outlaw, Newnes, London, 1927

William The Pirate, Newnes, London, 1932

William's Treasure Trove, Newnes, London, 1962

<u>Price Evadne</u>

Enter Jane, Newnes, London, 1932

Jane At War, Robert Hale, London, 1947

Jane The Fourth, Robert Hale, London, 1937

Jane The Patient, Robert Hale, London, 1940

Jane The Unlucky, Robert Hale, London, 1939

Just Jane, John Hamilton, London, 1928

Meet Jane, Marriott, London, 1930

Chapter XIII

BOOKS

<u>Hamilton Charles</u>

Bessie Bunter Of Cliff House School, Cassell, London, 1949

PERIODICALS

Magnet (The), Amalgamated Press, London, issues from 1908-1909

School Friend (The), Amalgamated Press, London, issues from 1919-1929

Schoolgirl (The), Amalgamated Press, London, issues from
1929-1940
Schoolgirls' Own (The), Amalgamated Press, London, issues of 1921
and 1927

Chapter XIV

PERIODICALS

Magnet (The), Amalgamated Press, London, issues of 1928
School Friend, Amalgamated Press, London, issues of 1950
School Friend (The), Amalgamated Press, London, issues of 1919
Schoolgirls' Own (The), Amalgamated Press, London, issues from
1921-1936

Chapter XV

BOOKS

Johns Captain W. E.

Worrals Carries On, Lutterworth, London, 1942
Worrals In The Islands, Hodder & Stoughton, London, 1945
Worrals In The Wastelands, Lutterworth, London, 1949
Worrals In The Wilds, Hodder & Stoughton, London, 1947
Worrals Of The WAAF, Lutterworth, London, 1941

PERIODICALS

Girl's Own Paper (The), Lutterworth, London, issues from 1930-1945
Heiress, Lutterworth, London, issues from 1948-1956

Chapter XVI

BOOKS

Barne Kitty

She Shall Have Music, Dent, London, 1942

Boylston Helen Dore

Carol Goes On The Stage, Bodley Head, London, 1943
Sue Barton – Student Nurse, Bodley Head, London, 1939

Brown Pamela

  The Swish Of The Curtain, Nelson, London, 1941

  Golden Pavements, Nelson, London, 1947

  Maddy Alone, Nelson, London, 1945

Keene Carolyn

  The Hidden Staircase, Harold Hill & Sons, Newcastle, 1954

  The Secret Of Shadow Ranch, Harold Hill & Sons, Newcastle, 1954

Streatfeild Noel

  A Vicarage Family, Collins, London, 1963

  Away From the Vicarage, Collins, London, 1965

  Ballet Shoes, Dent, London, 1936

  Gemma, Armada Books, London, 1966

  Gemma Alone, Armada Books, London, 1968

  Gemma And Sisters, Armada Books, London, 1967

  Goodbye Gemma, Armada Books, London, 1969

  Party Frock, Collins, London, 1946

  Tennis Shoes, Dent, London, 1937

  The Children Of Primrose Lane, Collins, London, 1941

  The Circus Is Coming, Dent, London, 1938

  The House In Cornwall, Collins, London, 1940

  The Painted Garden, Collins, London, 1949

  White Boots, Collins, London, 1951

Sutton Margaret

  The Ghost Parade, Grosset & Dunlap, New York, 1933

  The Vanishing Shadow, Grosset & Dunlap, New York, 1932

  The Voice In The Suitcase, Grosset & Dunlap, New York, 1935

  The Yellow Phantom, Grosset & Dunlap, New York, 1933

Vipont Elfreda

  The Lark In The Morn, OUP, London, 1948

  The Lark On The Wing, OUP, London, 1950

Chapter XVII

PERIODICALS

Bunty, D.C. Thomson, Dundee, issues of 1970

Girls' Crystal (The), Amalgamated Press, London, issues from
    1935-1953

School Friend, Amalgamated Press, London, issues from 1950-1956

School Friend (The), Amalgamated Press, London, issues from
    1919-1929

Schoolgirl (The), Amalgamated Press, London, issues of 1939

Schoolgirls' Own (The), Amalgamated Press, London, issues of 1930

Schoolgirls' Own Library, Amalgamated Press, London, issues
    from 1960-1963

Schoolgirls' Weekly (The), Amalgamated Press, London, issues of
    1922 and 1933-1939

Chapter XVIII

BOOKS

Atkinson M. E.

    Crusoe Island, Bodley Head, London, 1941

    Mystery Manor, Bodley Head, London, 1937

    Problem Party, Bodley Head, London, 1945

Blyton Enid

    Five Go To Mystery Moor, Hodder & Stoughton, London, 1954

    Five On A Treasure Island, Hodder & Stoughton, London,
    1942

    Six Bad Boys, Lutterworth, London, 1951

    Six Cousins At Mistletoe Farm, Evans, London, 1948

    The Adventurous Four, Newnes, London, 1941

    The Island Of Adventure, Macmillan, London, 1944

    The Mystery Of Banshee Towers, Methuen, London, 1961

    The Mystery Of Tally Ho Cottage, Methuen, London, 1954

    The Mystery Of The Missing Prince, Methuen, London, 1953

    The River Of Adventure, Macmillan, London, 1955

    The Secret Seven, Brockhampton Press, London, 1949

Pullein-Thompson Christine

    I Carried The Horn, Collins, London, 1951

Pullein-Thompson Diana

    I Wanted A Pony, Collins, London, 1946

Ransome Arthur
> *Swallows And Amazons*, Cape, London, 1930
> *The Picts And The Martyrs*, Cape, London, 1943
> *We Didn't Mean To Go To Sea*, Cape, London, 1937
> *Winter Holiday*, Cape, London, 1935

Saville Malcolm
> *Mystery At Witchend*, Newnes, London, 1943
> *Seven White Gates*, Newnes, London, 1944
> *The Sign Of The Alpine Rose*, Lutterworth, London, 1951

Treadgold Mary
> *We Couldn't Leave Dinah*, Cape, London, 1941

Chapter XIX

BOOKS

Aiken Joan
> *Black Hearts In Battersea*, Cape, London, 1965
> *Midnight Is A Place*, Cape, London, 1974
> *Night Birds On Nantucket*, Cape, London, 1966
> *The Cuckoo Tree*, Cape, London, 1971
> *The Wolves Of Willoughby Chase*, Cape, London, 1962

Avery Gillian
> *The Elephant War*, Collins, London, 1960
> *The Greatest Gresham*, Collins, London, 1962
> *The Warden's Niece*, Collins, London, 1957

Bawden Nina
> *Carrie's War*, Gollancz, London, 1973
> *The Peppermint Pig*, Gollancz, London, 1975

Beachcroft Nina
> *Cold Christmas*, Heinemann, London, 1974

Boston L. M.
> *The Children Of Green Knowe*, Faber, London, 1954

Farmer Penelope
> *Charlotte Sometimes*, Chatto, London, 1969

Gardam Jane
> *A Long Way From Verona*, Hamish Hamilton, London, 1970

Garner Alan

    Red Shift, Collins, London, 1973

    The Moon Of Gomrath, Collins, London, 1963

    The Owl Service, Collins, London, 1967

    The Weirdstone Of Brisingamen, Collins, London, 1960

Gordon John

 The Giant Under The Snow, Hutchinson, London, 1968

Lively Penelope

    Going Back, Heinemann, London, 1975

    The House In Norham Gardens, Heinemann, London, 1974

Mayne William

    A Grass Rope, OUP, London, 1957

    Earthfasts, Hamish Hamilton, London, 1965

Storr Catherine

    The Chinese Egg, Faber, London, 1975

    Thursday, Faber, London, 1971

Townsend John Rowe

    Forest Of The Night, OUP, London, 1974

Uttley Alison

    A Traveller In Time, Faber, London, 1939

Index

457

Mary and Patricia in the 1970s.

Mary Cadogan is a well-known writer, critic and broadcaster. Her books include *Frank Richards: The Chap Behind The Chums*, *Richmal Crompton: The Woman Behind Just William*, *Chin Up, Chest Out, Jemima!*, *And Then Their Hearts Stood Still* and *Women With Wings*.

Mary and Patricia today.

Patricia Craig is a well-known critic, anthologist and biographer. Her works include *The Penguin Book of British Comic Stories*, *The Oxford Books of Modern Women's Stories*, *English Detective Stories* and *Schooldays*. She is a regular contributor to *The Times Literary Supplement* and *The Independent*.

Girls Gone By Publishers

Titles in print and forthcoming titles in 2003/2004

Books by Elinor Brent-Dyer
Chalet School series
Chalet School in the Oberland (In print)
Highland Twins at the Chalet School (In print)
Summer Term at the Chalet School (February 2004)

Chalet School Connectors
Monica Turns Up Trumps (In print)

La Rochelle Series
Janie of La Rochelle (In print)
Janie Steps In (In print)

Lorna Series
Lorna at Wynyards (December 2003)

New 'fill-in' Chalet School books completely faithful to the style of
Elinor Brent-Dyer
The Chalet School and Robin by Caroline German (In print)

Books by and about Elsie Jeanette Oxenham
Abbey Connector
Margery Meets the Roses (In print)

Biography of Elsie Jeanette Oxenham
The World of Elsie Jeanette Oxenham and Her Books by Monica
Godfrey (In print)

Books by Gwendoline Courtney
A Coronet for Cathie (In print)
At School with the Stanhopes (January 2004)
464

Books by Dorita Fairlie Bruce
Nancy and St Bride's Series
The Girls of St Bride's (In print)
Nancy at St Bride's (In print)
That Boarding School Girl (In print)
The New Girl and Nancy (In print)

Books by Lorna Hill
Marjorie and Patience Series
Marjorie & Co (In print)
Stolen Holiday (November 2003)

Sadlers Wells Series
Back-Stage (January 2004)

Books by Antonia Forest
Marlows Series
Falconer's Lure (In print)
Run Away Home (In print)
The Marlows and the Traitor (December 2003)

Books by Susan Coolidge
Clover (February 2004)

Pony Book
Pony Thieves by Julia Cotter (In print)

All titles in print may be purchased directly from Girls Gone By Publishers, and we also sell book tokens for our own titles.

For details send an SAE to Ann Mackie-Hunter or Clarissa Cridland at 4 Rock Terrace, Coleford, Somerset BA3 5NF, UK or e-mail ggbp@rockterrace.demon.co.uk or check out our website http://www.rockterrace.demon.co.uk/GGBP

We plan to reprint further titles in 2004 by the above and other authors. Details of these will be announced on our website and in author appreciation society magazines and journals.